W9-BRH-915

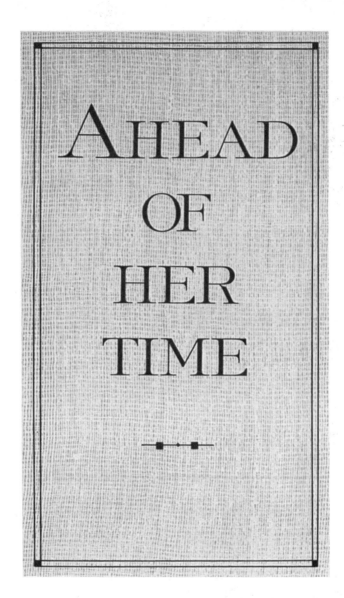

AHEAD
OF
HER
TIME

*Dorothy Sterling is the author of numerous children's
and young adult books as well as the following titles:*

Tender Warriors (with Donald Gross)
*We Are Your Sisters: Black Women in
the Nineteenth Century*

She is also the editor of the following titles:
*I Have Seen War: Twenty-Five Stories from
World War II*
*Speak Out in Thunder Tones: Letters and Other
Writings by Black Northerners, 1787–1865*
*The Trouble They Seen: Black People Tell the Story of
Reconstruction*

W. W. NORTON & COMPANY

NEW YORK   LONDON

AHEAD

OF

HER

TIME

ABBY KELLEY AND THE

POLITICS OF ANTISLAVERY

DOROTHY STERLING

First published as a Norton paperback 1994

Printed in the United States of America.

The text of this book is composed in Granjon,
with the display set in French Light.
Composition by PennSet, Inc.
Manufacturing by Haddon Craftsmen, Inc.
Book design by Guenet Abraham.

Library of Congress Cataloging-in-Publication Data

Sterling, Dorothy, 1913–
Ahead of her time : Abby Kelley and the politics of
antislavery / by Dorothy Sterling.
p.   cm.
1. Kelley, Abby. 2. Abolitionists—United States—
Biography.
3. Civil rights workers—United States—Biography.
I. Title.
E449.K29S74   1991
323'.092—dc20
[B]   91-7435

ISBN 0-393-31131-7

W. W. Norton & Company, Inc.
500 Fifth Avenue, New York, N.Y. 10110
W. W. Norton & Company Ltd.
10 Coptic Street, London WC1A 1PU

2 3 4 5 6 7 8 9 0

In memory of my husband,
Philip Sterling (1907–1989)
and my sister,
Alice Lake (1916–1990)

For Dave Garre

With much
affection

Dorothy Sterling

CONTENTS

Photographs appear following pages 116 and 276.

Here is a woman who has traveled all over the North, laboring for [the slave and] woman's cause. She bore the burden and heat of the day. She was an outcast from society. Other women hated her; men insulted her. Every vulgar editor threw a stone at her, which he picked up from the mire of the street. Many a minister laid sorry stripes on her, with the Epistolary whip of Hebrew Paul. The noble woman bore it with no complaint; only now and then, in private, the great heart of Abby Kelley would fill her eyes with tears at the thought of this injustice; but she never allowed her tears to blind her eyes, or quench the light which was shedding its radiance down her steep and rugged path.

—The Reverend Theodore Parker,
December 23, 1855
(from the *Liberator*, January 4, 1856)

INTRODUCTION

In April 1865, a week before his assassination, Abraham Lincoln said that he had been only an instrument in the freeing of the slaves. The credit for emancipation belonged to the army and to "the logic and moral power of Garrison and the anti-slavery of the people of the country."[1] Had Lincoln known the abolitionists more intimately, he might also have given credit to Abby Kelley, their dynamic leader.

Slavery was "the greatest misery, the greatest wrong, the greatest curse to white and black alike that America has ever known."[2] But antislavery sentiments did not spring up overnight. They were cultivated over a thirty-year period by a dedicated band of men and women who believed in the twin principles of immediate emancipation and equal rights for black people. William Lloyd Garrison's fiery editorials in his weekly the *Liberator* and Wendell Phillips's superb speeches alerted northerners to slavery's evils and the conflict between the institution and the nation's democratic ideals. But while the two men wrote and spoke in New England, it remained for Abby Kelley and a hardy group of lecturing agents to carry their message to the new towns along the Erie Canal, to the rich farm counties of Pennsylvania, and over the Alleghenies to Ohio and Michigan.

Abby Kelley began her crusade in 1838, a decade before the first woman's rights convention in Seneca Falls. A pretty woman—some called her beautiful—she began public speaking at a time when press and clergy decreed silence and submission for women. Denounced as "Jezebel" and "infidel," forced to duck showers of stones and rotten eggs, she braved the wrath of misogynists to bring her message to farmers, shopkeepers, millworkers, housewives across the North. Demurely dressed in Quaker gray, she held audiences spellbound with tales of slave children taken from their mothers, women whipped and forced into concubinage. She lectured for two and three hours at a time, then returned the next day and the next, until she had convinced her listeners to make themselves responsible for bringing about change. Until they had purchased antislavery books, subscribed to antislavery newspapers, dug deep in their pockets to support the cause. Until they had organized local antislavery societies to continue the work after she left the neighborhood.

Abby Kelley probably logged more miles in farm wagons, stagecoaches, and trains, spent more hours on the platform than any other antislavery speaker. Yet her greatest contribution was as an organizer. From the hinterlands she sent word back to the abolitionist brethren in Boston, proposing new tactics to capture popular imagination, advising of pamphlets that needed to be written, planning campaigns for the movement's star speakers. In show business parlance, she knew what would play in Peoria, and she prodded Garrison, Phillips, and the others until they put her programs into action.

While Garrison set the moral tone of the movement in the *Liberator*, Abby Kelley built up a network of regional newspapers. She was largely responsible for the existence of the *National Anti-Slavery Standard* in New York and a founder of Ohio's *Anti-Slavery Bugle*. She recruited their editors, kept close watch over their ideological purity, and assumed responsibility for raising the funds to support them. Out of her Quaker background came an understanding of the importance of money in the struggle. She was always first to make the collection speech at meetings, tugging at people's heartstrings until she had loosed their purse strings and setting an example of self-sacrifice by working without pay and even mortgaging her home when money was needed.

A radical member of the most radical wing of the antislavery movement, she believed that the nature of American society had to be changed in order to abolish slavery and root out people's belief in white supremacy. In the factional fights which divided the antislavery forces, she called for "Revolution Not Reform," attacked the U.S. Constitution as a proslavery document, and demanded that the North dissolve its unholy compact with the Slave Power. Although she detested politicians because they followed rather than led public opinion, she was political to her fingertips, poring over newspapers and congressional reports in order to bolster her emotional appeals with facts and figures.

Equally as significant as her antislavery message was her impact on women. When she took the floor at hitherto all-male conventions and addressed "promiscuous audiences" of both sexes, she made women aware of their capabilities. Her courage, commitment, and personal warmth brought out hundreds of self-proclaimed "Abby Kelleyites." She constantly searched for potential leaders, beckoning them to join her on the platform. Lucy Stone, Susan B. Anthony, and a score of lesser-known women received their training under her before going on to work for woman's rights. "Abby Kelley earned for us all the right of free speech," said Lucy Stone. "The movement for equal rights of women began directly and emphatically with her."[3]

James Russell Lowell described Abby as "a simple Quaker maid."[4] She was anything but simple. A loyal friend and dangerous adversary, she was sharp-tongued and intense, tough and implacable—and charming, loving, and sentimental. After a four-year courtship she married Stephen S. Foster, who was even more radical than she in his willingness to suffer martyrdom for the cause. Although they did not always agree on antislavery tactics, their marriage was long, happy, and unusually egalitarian. She dearly loved her only daughter, Alla, yet weaned her early so that she could return to the struggle, becoming "quite sick"[5] when she had to leave her in another's care. The Fosters' farm in Worcester, Massachusetts, was both a station on the Underground Railroad and a refuge for family, friends, and visiting reformers.

At the end of the Civil War she recognized that emancipation brought about by force of arms would not eradicate the racist beliefs of the nation. Without land and the ballot, the freedpeople of the South would soon be at the mercy of their former masters. While William Lloyd Garrison and other old associates rested on their laurels, she entered mainstream politics for the only time in her life. Working with the Radical Republicans in Congress, she helped secure the passage of the Fifteenth Amendment to the Constitution, thereby giving black men the vote—and earning for herself the enmity of her friends Susan B. Anthony and Elizabeth Cady Stanton, who opposed the amendment because it did not enfranchise women.

Tired and ill in her final decades, she nevertheless strove to radicalize the members of the Massachusetts Suffrage Association. In 1874 the Fosters bore dramatic witness to women's wrongs by refusing to pay taxes on their jointly owned farm until Abby was permitted to vote. Their cows were seized, their house and barns sold at public auction. The protest received sympathetic attention in the press but ultimately fizzled because no one else would follow their example.

Why has this heroic woman escaped the attention of biographers despite her many-faceted life?* In part the answer lies with Abby Kelley herself, who, with a Quaker distaste for personal publicity, shunned interviews, never kept a diary, rarely sat for a photograph. Not until her seventy-fifth year did she attempt a memoir, breaking off after she had written about her first two years on the platform. This brief sketch and her daughter's reminiscences, written four years after Abby's death, remain the only contemporary accounts. Her life and its impact on her society have been pieced together from six or seven hundred contemporary letters and from the weekly reports on her activities in the *Liberator*, the *Standard*, the *Bugle*, and the *Woman's Journal*.

In part, also, the neglect of Abby Kelley may be traced to the bias of male historians. Her contemporaries knew her worth. "How can we ever value you enough?" Wendell Phillips asked, while William Lloyd Garrison called her "most persevering, most self-sacrificing, most energetic, most meritorious" and "the moral Joan of Arc of the world."[6] But as historians told, revised, and retold the history of the antislavery movement, its male leaders became the central figures and Kelley's role was virtually ignored or confused with that of her husband.†

---

* The sole exceptions: Margaret Hope Bacon's young people's biography *I Speak for My Slave Sister*, published in 1984, and Jane H. Pease's doctoral dissertation, "The Freshness of Fanaticism: Abby Kelley Foster: An Essay in Reform," completed in 1969.

† In *The Liberator: William Lloyd Garrison*, John L. Thomas ascribes Abby Kelley's views to Stephen Foster at a time when they publicly differed. In *Wendell Phillips, Liberty's Hero*, published in 1986, James Brewer Stewart puts a quotation from Abby Kelley into Stephen Foster's mouth. Thomas, Stewart, James McPherson, and others write of "the Fosters" although wife's and husband's views often did not coincide.

The women who in her lifetime were fulsome in acknowledging their debt to Abby Kelley also failed to record it for posterity. The first volumes of the *History of Woman Suffrage* were written when Anthony and Stanton were still smarting over Abby's support of the Fifteenth Amendment and her ties to the Lucy Stone wing of the movement. Although they paid lip service to her pioneer role, they gave scant attention to her organizing work and failed to report on her tax protest of the 1870s. Thus today there are no birthday celebrations for foremother Abby Kelley, no commemorative stamps in her honor, no sentimental pilgrimages to the home of the woman whom contemporaries revered as "the moral heroine of the age."[7]

As I complete this book, I cannot refrain from adding a personal note. Initially I was attracted to Abby Kelley as a woman of commitment who dared break with tradition to fight for a better world. During eight years of research and writing I have found not only a heroic figure—"a moral Joan of Arc"—but an intensely human one. Writing her biography has brought back memories of my youth. Coming of age in the 1930's, when the nation's social structure was out of kilter, I, too, joined in a struggle to build a new society. We used words like "the cause," "the movement," "the comrades." We sat through endless meetings, worked with tireless devotion—and sectarian scorn for those who differed with us, however narrowly. As I read of the emotional gatherings in the big tent in Ohio, the Faneuil Hall meetings, the Christmas fairs, and the Fourth of July picnics, I was carried back to rallies in Madison Square Garden and May Day parades down Fifth Avenue when with "a raw feeling of goodness," as one contemporary phrased it, we sang "Solidarity Forever" and "We Shall Not Be Moved," just as Abby's comrades, a century earlier, had sung "I'm Glad I Am an Abolitionist." Even in my personal life I empathized with Abby because I, too, was a working mother whose friends criticized my "desertion" of my children. I shared her pain at leaving her daughter and cheered on her efforts to provide love and guidance at a distance.

Today, in a different time, "humanity-mongering" is out of fashion, but I foresee the day when another generation will appreciate the joy of working together to improve the world and "sweet, devoted, eloquent, heart-on-fire Abby Kelley"—as Wendell Phillips characterized her[8]—will find her place in the pantheon of American heroes.

ACKNOWLEDGMENTS

During the eight years that I have worked on this book, I have incurred debts to scores of librarians and archivists. The bulk of the Abby Kelley Foster Papers are located at the American Antiquarian Society, where I would especially like to thank Nancy Burkett, Georgia Barnhill, Dianne Pugh, Joyce Ann Tracy, and Sidney E. Berger, and at the Worcester Historical Museum, where Mark Savolis and Norma Feingold generously assisted me. (I have a mental picture of Norma Feingold precariously balanced on the museum's stairs, in order to take a snapshot of the Abby Kelley portrait that appears on the cover.)

Sampling the riches of the Antislavery Collection at the Boston Public Library has always been made pleasant by the kindness of Roberta Zonghi and her staff. I am also grateful to Eva Moseley, curator of manuscripts at the Schlesinger Library on the History of Women; Rodney Dennis, curator of manuscripts at the Houghton Library, Harvard University; Susan L. Boone, curator of the Sophia Smith Collection, Smith College Library; Linda Seidman, Archives and Manuscripts, University of Massachusetts; Roland Baumann, archivist, Oberlin College Archives; Nancy Dean of the Cornell University Library; Carolyn A. Davis, George Arents Research Library, Syracuse University; Rosalind Wiggins, archivist for the New England Yearly Meeting of Friends, and her colleagues at the Rhode Island Historical Society, where the Friends' papers are housed. I have written so often to Karl Kabelac of the University of Rochester Library and to Phil Lapsansky of the Library Company of Philadelphia that we are on first-name terms, and I consider them my friends. Thanks should also go to librarians at the Rare Books and Manuscript Library, Columbia University; the New-York Historical Society; Schomburg Center for Research in Black

Culture; Ohio Historical Society; Manuscript Division of the Library of Congress; William L. Clements Library, University of Michigan; Quaker Collection, Haverford College Library; Kent State University Library; Massachusetts Historical Society; Douglass Library, Rutgers University.

As always, I am deeply indebted to the Wellfleet Public Library, particularly to its director, Elaine McIlroy, and to Claire Beswick, in charge of interlibrary loans. I could not have completed this book without the books and microfilm that she borrowed from institutions across the country. And the microfilm and dissertations that she was unable to obtain, my children, Peter Sterling and Anne F. Sterling, borrowed from their university libraries. Professor Jacqueline Jones of Wellesley College and my good friend Rosemarie Redlich Scherman also lent me hard-to-find material.

Ann Gordon and Patricia Holland, editors of the papers of Elizabeth Cady Stanton and Susan B. Anthony, were extraordinarily generous, not only sending me copies of relevant letters from Stanton and Anthony but introducing me to other researchers in the field. Through them I have corresponded with Judy Wellman of SUNY, Oswego, who is completing a book on the Seneca Falls woman's rights convention and who identified several of Abby Kelley's acquaintances in upstate New York, and Elizabeth C. Stevens, who is completing a dissertation on Elizabeth Buffum Chace. Elizabeth Stevens and I have exchanged information so frequently that we, too, have become friends. She was good enough to lend me her precious 1914 biography of Chace so that I could have some of the illustrations copied.

Dorothy Porter Wesley, curator emeritus of the Moorland-Spingarn Research Center, has been supplying me with information and encouragement for more than three decades. Her knowledge of black and women's history is unsurpassed; her generosity in sharing it sets an example for all researchers. Margaret Hope Bacon, biographer of Lucretia Mott as well as Abby Kelley, suggested avenues of research and sent copies of Mott letters that I might not have known of otherwise. Dr. Elizabeth Kirk of Brown University spent precious hours identifying the Shakespeare quotations that decorated the walls of an 1882 Suffrage Subscription Festival.

When I first met Dr. Jean Yellin of Pace University some twenty years ago, we discovered a mutual love for the antislavery women and have been pooling information ever since. She was particularly helpful in pointing out Elizabeth Margaret Chandler's "Mental Metempsychosis" as background for a puzzling Abby Kelley letter and in identifying the people in the daguerreotype of an antislavery meeting that appears opposite page 117. My acquaintance by correspondence with Richard J. Wolfe, curator of rare books and manuscripts, Boston Medical Library, also goes back many years. I am particularly grateful for his photocopies from nineteenth-century medical texts that helped me define the illnesses of Abby Kelley and her family and identify her physicians. Dr. Stanley Robbins of Harvard Medical School, Dr. Nelson Fausto of Brown University Medical School, and my daughter, Anne, also of Brown, shed additional light on Kelley-Foster health problems.

Frank E. Fuller, historian of the Moses Brown School, Providence, Rhode Island, which Abby Kelley attended in 1826, was unusually generous in lending me old books, catalogs, and pictures of the school and answering innumerable queries. Dr. Sidney Kaplan, University of Massachusetts, introduced me to the papers of Dr. Erasmus Hudson and located a picture of Hudson for me. Ellen C. DuBois, of SUNY Buffalo, sent me a wonderful letter from Lucy Stone to Abby Kelley, and Lorraine Jackson painstakingly copied the reports of the 1851 Woman's Rights Convention from the *New York Tribune* and *Herald*. Frank Clarkson, who lived in the Kelley-Foster farmhouse in Worcester as a boy, shared his recollections and gave me an early photograph of the farm. Carolyn B. Casper, my college classmate, deciphered some Lucy Stone letters that were impossible to read on microfilm. I enjoyed comparing notes on many Frederick Douglass-Abby Kelley interchanges with William S. McFeely of the University of Georgia and Wellfleet, Massachusetts, when he was completing his biography *Frederick Douglass*. Rhoda Jenkins of Greenwich, Connecticut, generously sent me copies of pictures of her great-grandmother Elizabeth Cady Stanton, and Jean Stearns of Wellfleet, Massachusetts, helped locate references to the 1787 Constitutional Convention. For all these kindnesses, many thanks.

Linda E. McCausland of Orleans, Massachusetts, did a loving job of copying old photographs and illustrations from nineteenth-century publications. Joan Willis and Ellen Anthony of Wellfleet, Massachusetts, strug-

9

gled with my execrable handwriting until they had turned out neatly organized Notes and bibliography.

For forty years Philip Sterling read the manuscripts of every book I wrote, giving them the benefit of his thoughtful appraisal and skilled editing. He read part of the Abby Kelley biography—I smile when I come across some of his incisive turns of phrase—but he did not live to finish the job. After his death old friends came forward to fill the gap. The book has benefited from the thoughtful reading it received from Milton Meltzer, Richard Stiller, Paula Vogel, Hilda and Herbert Lass, as well as from my friend and editor, James L. Mairs.

Writers often say that their lives are lonely. Mine has been lonely this past year, but as I read over these acknowledgments, I realize how much sustenance as well as information I have received from historians, librarians, and fellow writers who never hesitated to take time from their own work to send me friendly and encouraging as well as informative letters. Going to the post office for the mail is the pleasantest chore of my day. To this network of correspondents I want to express again my gratitude.

NOTE TO READERS

In order to avoid constant repetition, the American Anti-Slavery Society is frequently referred to as the American Society, the New England Anti-Slavery Society as the New England Society, and the Massachusetts Anti-Slavery Society as the Massachusetts Society. The annual meetings of these organizations formed the framework of the antislavery calendar. The American Society held its anniversary meeting in early May in New York, followed by the New England Society's anniversary in Boston some weeks later. The Massachusetts Society gathered for its annual convention in Boston in January and held quarterly meetings in other towns of the commonwealth throughout the year. Other starred dates on the antislavery calendar were July 4 and August 1, the latter commemorating the emancipation of the slaves of the West Indies. These were festive occasions when the abolitionists met in rural settings for a day of speeches, songs, and general camaraderie.

In keeping with Quaker custom, which was widely adopted by the abolitionists, I often use the first names of Abby Kelley and her friends. Only William Lloyd Garrison was customarily addressed as "Mr. Garrison"; his wife called him Lloyd. I have retained "Abby Kelley" even after she became Abby Kelley Foster because people continued to think of her by that name. Long after her marriage her admirers referred to themselves as Abby Kelleyites; as late as the 1860s detractors still inveighed against Abby Kelleyism.

In quoting from letters and speeches, I have excerpted freely, seldom using ellipses to indicate omissions. I have retained occasional misspellings in the letters but have silently corrected punctuation. In no case, however, have I altered the writers' meaning. Scholars who wish to read the full texts of the letters and newspaper accounts will find the sources listed on pages 390–410. Abbreviations used in the footnotes and a selected bibliography are also in this section.

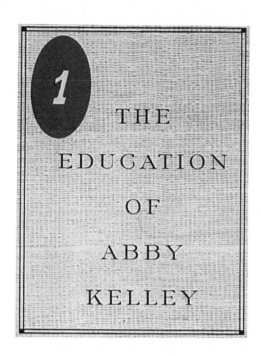

1

THE EDUCATION OF ABBY KELLEY

A burly red-faced man strode down the aisle of the crowded schoolroom, swinging a club. "Where's the damned nigger bitch that's going to lecture here tonight?" Women screamed; candles flickered, then flew in every direction. "Where is she? Tell me where she is!" the man shouted.

The comely young woman in Quaker dress who was standing in front of the room watched him approach. Smash! The intruder's club shattered the oil lamp on the front desk, plunging the room into darkness. In the confusion that followed, friendly hands took hold of the speaker and hustled her out through a side door.

"Nigger bitch" was only one of the epithets leveled at Abby Kelley, white, when, in 1839, she left a teaching job to lecture against slavery. Ministers preached against her, calling her "a very bad woman," a "Jezebel" sent by Satan to entice and destroy. Politicians dubbed her a "man woman"; newspapers labeled her "infidel" or "Communitist." During two decades of public speaking she dodged rotten eggs, rum bottles, and the contents of outhouses. Still, she continued on her way, cheerful and determined, until the guns of Fort Sumter spoke with a louder voice than her own.[1]

Abby Kelley was born in the little village of Pelham, in western Massachusetts, on January 15, 1811. She was the seventh daughter of Wing Kelley, a farmer whose ancestors had emigrated from Ireland a generation earlier. Kelley may well have wished for a son to help him plow his hilly acres, but he named his new daughter Abigail, meaning "father's joy," and never indicated anything but pleasure in her company. A convivial man, he was popular in Pelham, serving a term on the School Committee and twice being elected to the Board of Selectmen. In the 1840s, when most of her contemporaries scorned the Irish immigrants who were crowding into North American cities to escape the potato famine back home, Abby spoke admiringly of the "Irish heart," as exemplified by her genial, even-tempered father.

Her mother was Wing Kelley's second wife. A youthful indiscretion had led to Kelley's hasty marriage in 1792 and the birth of a daughter, Nancy, six months later, a not uncommon occurrence in eighteenth-century Massachusetts. A second daughter, Lydia, followed in 1794. Then their mother died, and Kelley, after some years as a widower, married Diana Daniels.* Her forebears had come from England early in the eighteenth century, settling in and around Uxbridge, a village south of Worcester that housed a substantial community of Friends. A birthright Quaker, Diana was born in Uxbridge in 1774, one of the six children of Ruth and David Daniels. She married Wing Kelley in 1799.[2]

In a memoir written after Abby's death, her daughter ascribed her cheerfulness, simplicity, and lack of self-consciousness to her father's "Celtic

---

* Diana Daniels Kelley's name is variously spelled Diana, Dianna, Diane, and even Diame.

blood" and her "dogged persistence, unyielding will where a principle was at stake, [and] her severe judgment of all who failed to reach her lofty standards of morality" to her English ancestors. Diana Kelley, her grand-daughter said, was "the strictest of Orthodox Friends." One has the feeling that she never would have been so indiscreet as to have a six months baby. Hers were born almost every other year: Joanna (named after Wing's first wife) in 1802; Ruth in 1804; Olive in 1805; Diana in 1808. She had scarcely weaned Abby when she became pregnant again. The Kelleys' only son, Albert, was born in 1813, and their youngest daughter, Margaretta Lucy (always called Lucy), in 1819, when Diana Kelley was forty-five.

In the spring of 1811 the Kelleys moved from Pelham to Worcester, forty miles to the east. The seat of Worcester County, Worcester was a farming community with a population of twenty-five hundred. Surrounded by hills, bisected by the Blackstone River, which flowed south to Narragansett Bay, the village had a prosperous air, a traveler reported, with "wellbuilt, frequently handsome houses. Few towns in New England exhibit so uniform an appearance of neatness and taste, or contain so great a proportion of good buildings."[3]

For six thousand dollars, a substantial sum in 1811, Wing Kelley purchased a hundred-acre farm from one of Diana's kinsmen. Located close to the center of Worcester, its cleared fields and pastures were surrounded by woods and bordered by a brook and pond. Unlike her sisters, Abby was not confined to the farm kitchen and domestic chores. Busy, efficient Diana Kelley, who never had fewer than ten mouths to feed, ten bodies to keep clothed and warm, may have lacked the patience to direct the clumsy fingers of a toddler when she had six older daughters to call on. Besides, Abby was thought to be delicate as a youngster, and both parents encouraged her to remain outdoors as much as possible.

Long before she knew how to sew and cook, she followed her father from barn to fields to woodlot. She learned to feed the chickens, to milk the cows, to ride horseback, and to drive the farm wagon. She climbed trees, scrambled over stiles and fences, explored the brook and pond with a physical freedom that few girls of her age enjoyed.

Still, there were psychological restraints. Her sisters and cousins called her "tomboy" and "hoyden" and demanded to know why she didn't share the housework or at least play with dolls like a proper young lady. When the pond froze in winter, the neighborhood boys brought out their skates; the girls stood along the shore, watching them glide across the ice, performing figure eights and pushing a puck around. Sometimes a boy would hold out his stick and offer to tow a girl behind him. Abby thought this humiliating and went off to play by herself. The boys coasted down the snow-covered hills on homemade sleds; Abby found some barrel staves and did her own coasting.[4]

A New England farm during and after the War of 1812 was scarcely a land of milk and honey. Salt pork and bean porridge were the staple diet, with salted cod for Saturday dinner; bread was a mixture of cornmeal and rye flour ground at the local gristmill and baked in the hearth oven. Clothing was homespun, using wool from the farmer's sheep and linen from his flax crop. Housewives made sheets, towels, quilts, stuffed mattresses with corncobs and pillows with goose feathers. Only salt, tea, coffee, and shoes were purchased or bartered. When money was scarce, as it often was, wild blackberry or raspberry leaves were dried for tea; parched rye and ground chestnuts were a sorry coffee substitute.

As her older sisters married, Abby spent more time assisting her mother. She lugged pails of water for the weekly wash and spread the clean clothes on bushes to dry; clotheslines had not yet come into use. She learned to mold candles and boil soap, to knit socks, hem aprons, churn butter.[5]

In addition to teaching housekeeping skills, Diana Kelley took firm charge of her children's immortal souls. The Bible was read at breakfast, and Quaker principles were carefully expounded. Abby learned "plain talk," saying "thee" and "thou," referring to the days of the week and the months of the year by number rather than by their "heathen" names, and addressing people of all ages by first names, to avoid such titles as Mr. and Mrs.

Diana also insisted on Quaker dress, which shunned new fashions and banned bright colors and such adornments as ribbons and bows. Her household of girls probably accepted these restrictions uncomplainingly. "It seems wondrous queer, when Nature made red apples, peaches and so forth— the grass green and a blue sky" that Friends cling to gray and drab, an acquaintance of Abby's commented. Yet "I like simplicity. I never felt the least disposition to wear gay colors or trimming, or ornamental work."

Besides, another contemporary pointed out, not only were the plain bonnets and white kerchiefs becoming, but they stood for something. "We wore clothing of somber colors made in a peculiar fashion, and believed we were a chosen people."[6]

More important than the outer trappings of Quakerism was Diana Kelley's insistence that her children follow the leadings of "the Spirit." While most Protestants imbibed the gloomy doctrines of Calvinism, which stressed human depravity and required the intercession of Christ and His ministers in order to be saved, Quaker children learned that the "inner light" was the key to salvation. Growing up at the same time as Abby, Elizabeth Cady Stanton was taught that she was a child of the devil and suffered from nightmares in which he came to claim her. "To me, he was a personal, ever-present reality, crouching in the dark corner of the nursery." Young Abby, on the other hand, pictured God as a benevolent elderly Friend who sat on a big chair in the Kelleys' garret. She later internalized Him as divine power, a Good who guided her if she struggled to understand His message. Less frightening than Elizabeth Stanton's devil, her "inner light" placed the responsibility for good behavior squarely on her own shoulders, a responsibility that she never shirked. Many decades later she criticized people "for putting out their thinking as they do their washing, to be done by others. Every individual should feel that he, and he alone, is responsible for his own thought and action." Her mother would have nodded approval.[7]

Diana's teachings were reinforced by attendance at Friends' meetings on First days when the congregation sat in silence, sometimes for an hour, until a man or woman was moved to speak. There was no Quaker meetinghouse in Worcester until 1837, but when weather and farm chores permitted, the Kelleys crowded into their farm wagon for the long drive to Uxbridge. There Abby, doubtless in hand-me-down gray dress and bonnet, sat alongside her mother and sisters on a long wooden bench while Albert and her father sat on the men's side of the aisle. In front were raised benches—"the high seats"—where "weighty Friends" faced the congregation. Quakers scorned a paid clergy—"hireling ministers" they called them—but Friends who consistently "felt a call to speak" were acknowledged as ministers and authorized to address meetings other than their own. Some of these visiting Friends were women, for Quakers did not accept the restrictions that other religions placed on that sex. "May not the spirit of Christ speak in the Female as well as in the Male?" George Fox, the society's founder, had asked more than a century earlier.

Once a month the meeting for worship was followed by a business meeting. Then the children watched, fascinated, as with a creaking noise shutters descended from the ceiling, dividing the room in two so that men and women could meet separately. At their business meetings the women received reports on "clearings" for marriage, requests for transfers to other communities, and permissions to travel. Erring members, who had "married out of meeting" or in some other way broken discipline, were discussed, and committees appointed to reason with them; if the miscreant failed to mend her ways, she might be disowned. The women kept their own records, chose representatives to the quarterly and yearly meetings, and collected money for the needy. Not until she was grown did Abby realize that despite their seeming autonomy, the women's decisions could not be put into effect until the men's meeting had approved them.[8]

When Abby was eleven, the Kelleys moved again, this time to an outlying district of Worcester, in a hilly section known as Tatnuck. Like most yeoman farmers, Wing Kelley was land-rich and cash-poor. In 1822 he sold his 100-acre farm for six thousand dollars, the same sum he had paid for it, and spent fifty-five hundred dollars for a farm of 167 acres with a sawmill that he hoped would provide income. Worcester, and indeed all New England, were experiencing something of a boom in the 1820s, as Americans struggled to catch up with the science and technology of Europe that British colonial rule had kept from them. All along the Atlantic seaboard inventors were tinkering with steam engines and machine tools, engineers were designing canals, and merchants were investing in factories for the manufacture of wool and cotton cloth. Keeping step with this entrepreneurial spirit, New England farmers constructed mills along the riverbanks: gristmills, fulling mills, or carding mills, where the whole family worked during spare hours to produce cotton and wool hand-cards. But Wing Kelley failed to share in the new American dream. The sawmill required too much labor for a man in his fifties and a boy of ten. In 1828 he was obliged to sell 30 acres of pastureland to meet his debts.[9]

Meanwhile, Abby—she dropped the "gail" around this time—was tending to her own business, which was to learn everything she could at the district school. Tatnuck's school was a single room, twenty-five feet square with one teacher for children of all ages. In these cramped quarters they chanted their ABCs, did sums aloud, and copied rules of grammar on their slates. Later, according to Abby's daughter, she attended "the best private school for girls in Worcester." If this was so, and not a bit of understandable filial boasting, the best was none too good. Judged by the poorly written letters of her older sisters, the education Worcester offered girls in the 1820s would be the equivalent of fifth- or sixth-grade schooling today.

The senior Kelleys were doubtless as literate as the average New Englander—that is, they could read a weekly paper, do simple sums, and sign their names—but they do not seem to have set much store by books, save for the Bible. Abby's older sisters all were married, and except for one or two who had gone to Ohio they were raising families on New England farms just as their parents had done. By 1826, however, there were beginning to be options for girls who did not want to follow in their mothers' footsteps. They could work as mill hands in the new factories in Lowell and Waltham if only long enough to save money for trousseaus, or they could become teachers. Women had always taught young children in dames' schools and during the summer term in grammar schools when men were needed for farm work. But as the population increased and more and more men took factory jobs, school boards began to hire women in substantial numbers, finding not only that they were as effective as men but that they worked for far less money.

For Abby the choice was obvious. Few Quaker girls entered the mills. She would become a teacher. Therefore, she needed further schooling. Worcester had no high school for girls, and Wing Kelley could not afford to send her to a private female seminary. However, the New England Friends Yearly Meeting had established a boarding school in Providence, Rhode Island, where their children—girls as well as boys—could receive "a guarded education free from the contaminating influence of the vain fashionable world." Tuition ranged from sixty to eighty dollars a year. The monthly meetings gave a limited number of scholarships, but the Kelleys' attendance at the Uxbridge meeting was so irregular that Abby was not offered one. Instead she borrowed the tuition money from an older sister, promising to repay it as soon as possible.[10]

Getting ready to go away was a simple matter, for the school sent a list of the clothing required: three frocks "of grave dark colors," four white neck handkerchiefs, one plain silk or cotton bonnet, two worsted "upper petticoats" and two flannel petticoats, three aprons, three nightcaps, and so forth. Any clothing that was not sufficiently plain or that required much washing would be stored during the student's stay or altered at her expense, the school superintendent warned.

One morning in 1826 the stagecoach driver hoisted Abby's horsehide trunk to the top of the Providence coach while she climbed inside. Her fellow passengers saw a sturdy apple-cheeked farm girl, above average in height, with a pert upturned nose and smiling blue eyes. She had already begun to pin up her chestnut hair, looping it over her ears and coiling it at the back of her head in the fashion that all save truly fashionable women adopted.*

Since custom frowned on young ladies traveling alone, Abby probably made the journey in the company of Sarah and Pliny Earle, family friends from nearby Leicester. Sarah taught at the boarding school while her brother Pliny was entering as a new pupil.† The forty-mile trip to Providence was an uncomfortable day's ride. Wedged into the lumbering coach, Abby could glimpse the well-cultivated farms and neat villages of Worcester County and the newly built factories in the Blackstone River valley. For the first time in American history the plumes of smoke streaking across the New England sky indicated prosperity—and sometimes boom and bust—rather than a disastrous forest fire.[11]

The New England Friends Boarding School, on a high hill overlooking

---

* Susan B. Anthony, Lucy Stone, Helen Garrison, and Dorothea Dix adopted the same severe hairstyle. Elizabeth Cady Stanton and Maria Weston Chapman preferred curls.

† Sarah Earle later founded the Mulberry Grove Boarding School in Leicester. Pliny Earle became a physician who pioneered in the care of the mentally ill and was superintendent of the State Lunatic Hospital, Northampton, Massachusetts.

the city and Narragansett Bay and less than a mile from Brown University, was a handsome red-brick building, its unadorned facade in striking contrast with the Greek Revival residences on nearby Benefit Street, where Providence's wealthy merchants lived. A five-story Middle House for faculty and meeting rooms was flanked by an east wing for the girls' dormitory and classrooms and a west wing for the boys. More than two hundred feet in length, it was larger than any public building Abby had ever seen.

The interior of the building was both spacious and austere. The meeting rooms were large square rooms heated by fireplaces and stoves, but there was no paint or paper on the walls, no carpets on the floors, no easy chairs, pictures, or other decoration. The high-ceilinged dining room was furnished with long bare tables and backless stools, one table for the girls, another for the boys. The white china was heavy and plain, the knives and forks of iron, but serving bowls were heaped high with such filling fare as pork and beans, while pitchers of milk and molasses and large tin bread pans were set out as well.

In the classrooms, separate for girls and boys, pupils sat two to a desk, writing on slates or painstakingly practicing orthography with quill pens that always seemed to need sharpening. During evening study hours each student shared a tin whale oil lamp with her neighbor. In the second-floor dormitories the girls slept two to a bed. Washing—in cold water—was done in the basement, where tin basins lined low shelves. Twice a week water was heated in great iron kettles, and everyone took turns using the two bathtubs. A pump with a rusty cast-iron dipper stood in the backyard; so did the outhouses.

Behind the building the playground was divided down the middle by a high board fence. On one side the girls played shuttlecock and battledore or skipped rope; on the other the boys played shinny and tossed a ball around. They were not supposed to speak except during meetings for worship on First and Fifth days, but the wooden fence had knots that easily became knotholes, permitting whispered conversations and the passing back and forth of notes. Like students everywhere, they groused about the food, complained that the oil lamps smoked and smelled and that the outhouses were drafty and dirty. For Abby, the discomforts of boarding school were probably not very different from those of the Kelley farmhouse.

The Quaker work ethic was as rigorous as the Puritans'. The school ran by bells, which awakened the students before sunrise, summoning them to classes and meals. Schoolwork occupied six hours a day, with supervised study in the evening; during the long days of summer classes were held before breakfast as well. "If we did not become profound scholars, it was not for lack of sufficient time to study," recalled Elizabeth Buffum Chace, a schoolmate who became a lifelong friend of Abby's. "It was a good school. The learning was thorough and solid." She added: "For gymnastics the girls had the sweeping, the chamber work, the bringing of wood from the cellar and making the fires, with the additional variation of making the boys' beds on busy days; and this last, in our narrow circle of amusements, was considered a privilege."[12]

The school stood on forty-three wooded acres that had been donated by Moses Brown, one of the four wealthy Brown brothers of Providence. An early convert to Quakerism, Brown had dedicated his life to business and philanthropy. His most successful venture had been the establishment with Samuel Slater of the first water-powered cotton mill in the United States, the prototype for factories through the Northeast. A founder of the Rhode Island Peace Society and the state's foremost abolitionist, he was also an agricultural reformer and amateur scientist who kept his own weather charts and used a microscope. Doubtless it was he who installed a telescope in the cupola atop the Middle House so that students could follow the movements of the planets and who encouraged the teaching of "natural philosophy," the collection and classification of plants, animals, and minerals.

Brown was the embodiment of Quaker virtue. He had followed his conscience, courageously defying public opinion. He had also made a lot of money. The very qualities that Friends' religion stressed—plain living, honesty, prudence, order—had led to material success. When "the world's people" discovered that Friends kept their word—"their yea was yea and their nay was nay"—they overlooked their peculiar ways and flocked to do business with them. By the beginning of the nineteenth century the once-despised dissidents had become respected merchants and bankers.

The Yearly Meeting Boarding School and its counterparts in New York and Pennsylvania were the Harvard and Yale of a generation of Quaker boys who would enter their fathers' mills or countinghouses or become doctors and lawyers. Because Friends, uniquely at the time, believed in coeducation, their daughters received similar training.[13] Thus Abby learned to write a firm, clear hand, as legible when she was seventy-five as it had been in her youth. She was drilled in spelling, grammar, and rhetoric, was taught algebra, botany, and astronomy. She also studied accounting and bookkeeping, basic for a boy destined to clerk in a countinghouse but surely unusual for a girl in the 1820s.

Abby read the British classics of the seventeenth and eighteenth centuries, those, that is, that were considered suitable: Milton's *Paradise Lost*, Pope's *Essay on Man*, Cowper's *Task*, and such once-popular works as James Thomson's *Seasons* and Edward Young's *Night Thoughts*. Not only read but memorized stanza after stanza, declaiming them before the class while a teacher corrected expression and pronunciation. These poems and the Bible, required daily reading, gave her a store of quotations which she drew on all her life.

Because the school committee wanted its pupils to stand apart from American society and, if occasion required, bear witness against it, Abby learned of Mary Dyer, who, when banned from the Massachusetts Bay Colony in 1660, challenged the "bloody laws" and was hanged on Boston Common, a martyr to the cause of religious liberty. She read of Friends' testimony against war, which had rendered them unpopular during the Revolution, and took pride in the fact that they had been the first religious group in America to free their slaves.

But the omissions from the curriculum were significant. No "dead languages"—or any living ones save English—were taught. No modern poets, no novels, no plays, no music or fine art. Abby failed to read Keats, Shelley, Byron, or the novels of Scott and Jane Austen that were absorbing her contemporaries. She could quote Thomas Cowper's "I would not have a slave to till my ground/ To carry me, to fan me while I sleep," and "Fleecy locks and black complexion/ Cannot forfeit nature's claim;/ Skins may differ, but affection/Dwells in white and black the same," but she was middle-aged before she read a Shakespeare play. The Quaker merchants

23

to be did not need flights of fancy or imagination; if their female schoolmates were also matter-of-fact and unromantic,* so much the better.[14]

Not every student accepted the narrow curriculum and rigid discipline. Girls took walks out of bounds in order to watch the boys skating on the pond; boys were caught smoking in the cow pasture. One girl had to stand on the platform before school for singing "a very dubious song" called "Auld Lang Syne," and a boy was summoned to the superintendent's office after he was heard reciting Shakespeare. The same superintendent offered daily opportunities for merriment. Like George Fox and William Penn, he wore his broad-brimmed hat indoors as well as out. When he lifted his saucer to drink his breakfast tea, students watched breathlessly. Would the hatbrim clear the upraised saucer or dip into it? If Friends had not frowned on betting, many a wager would have been won or lost.[15]

Although Abby was friendly and outgoing, she was something of a loner at boarding school. Most of the pupils belonged to prominent New England families—the Earles, the Buffums, the Chaces, the Husseys. Their parents served on the School Committee and visited the school so frequently that it was known as the Quaker Hotel. Sarah and Pliny Earle had as many aunts, uncles, and cousins in the Providence area as in Leicester. Prudence Crandall, another classmate of Abby's who became notorious in 1833 when she accepted a black pupil in her Connecticut school, came from prosperous Rhode Island Quakers; so did Elizabeth Buffum Chace and her sisters. There were no other Kelleys in the Yearly Meeting Boarding School during Abby's stay there and few daughters of impecunious farmers.[16]

One of the oldest pupils and one of the few paying her own way, Abby was determined to absorb all the information that was offered. Sometimes she worked so hard on her lessons that "the perspiration stood out on [my] face, as though from hard physical exertion," she later told her daughter. Although not a brilliant scholar, she earned a high rank in her class and

---

* Lucretia Mott, who attended a Friends' boarding school two decades before Kelley, was similarly devoid of artistic sensibilities. Touring the Scottish highlands with a group of women in 1840, she noted in her diary, "Beautiful hills—girls tell me when to admire." (Tolles, ed.)

a recommendation from the faculty that enabled her to obtain a teaching position when she left.

The school, which ran for twelve months a year, had no prescribed course of study leading to graduation. Abby attended in 1826 and again in 1829, spending the intervening years at home teaching in order to repay her sister and accumulate money for tuition. By the time she returned to Worcester late in 1829 she possessed as good an education as any woman in New England, save for the few like Margaret Fuller who were tutored at home. She had also absorbed the Quakers' way of looking at the world, including their willingness to defy convention in support of unpopular causes and their pragmatic, down-to-earth philosophy, which bordered on anti-intellectualism. Long after she broke with the Society of Friends, she still retained her "Quakerish ways."[17]

2

A WIDER WORLD

Abby Kelley was nineteen when she returned to her parents' Worcester farm. Writing sixty years later, her daughter described this period as a carefree one in which Abby took an interest in dress, "did not disdain" parties and balls, and had a string of beaux who were attracted by "her delicate, graceful figure and beautiful dancing." Although no correspondence has survived from these years, her portrait of Abby as social butterfly seems overly romanticized. Certainly she was an attractive young woman whose exuberant vitality won her friends, both male and female. But she was hardly carefree. In addition to teaching winter and summer in an overcrowded, underequipped school, she assumed heavy responsibilities at home. Determined that her brother and younger sister receive an education equal to her own, she paid for a year at the Friends boarding school for Albert and two for Lucy.

As the oldest single daughter she was also the mainstay, emotionally and financially, of her parents. A marginal farmer at best, Wing Kelley was being driven to the wall by the rising prices and shortage of farm labor that accompanied industrialism. Too old to start over again in the West, as many New England farmers were doing, he was increasingly dependent on loans from his daughter. Deeply troubled because it seemed as if her parents' " 'barrel of meal' might waste and 'cruse of oil' fail," Abby encouraged Wing to sell the Tatnuck property. When he received $5,750 for the farm and sawmill, he was able to pay most of his debts and, for $4,000, purchase a farm, in Millbury, six miles away.[1]

Situated on the west bank of the Blackstone River, Millbury was a postcard-pretty village of two thousand with textile mills and tool factories along the river and Georgian houses and gardens in town. After the completion of the Blackstone Canal in 1828, horse-drawn canalboats made daily round trips to Providence; soon there would be a railroad to Worcester and Boston. The village could also boast of being the birthplace of the lyceum, the new adult education movement that was bringing prominent lecturers to small towns across the North.

Abby helped her parents move to their comfortable and pleasant home in Millbury in March 1835 and began teaching in a local school. Now that her father was reasonably debt-free and sister Lucy in her final year at boarding school, she could begin to think of her own future. When she heard through the Quaker grapevine that Friends in Lynn were looking for a teacher, she applied for the job. Early in the spring of 1836, shortly after her twenty-fifth birthday, she set out for Lynn. The trip by train and stagecoach took less than four hours, but it propelled her into a new world.[2]

Lynn lay on the Atlantic coast between Boston and Salem, but an accident of geography had given it a different character from its neighbors'. Marshy shores and a shallow harbor had ruled out whaling vessels or clipper ships that sailed the seven seas. Lynn had no shipbuilding industry, no merchant princes with fine Federal mansions like those on Essex Street in Salem or on Boston's Beacon Hill, no great wealth or aristocracy. The extensive salt marshes that spread westward to rocky hills also discouraged farming, so that the town had grown slowly; it was not until the beginning of the nineteenth century that it had found its place as a shoemaking center.

Unlike the new power mills at Lowell and Waltham, shoemaking was still a handicraft industry requiring little capital. When Abby walked from Central Square, where the Boston stage stopped, to her boardinghouse on Broad Street, a block away, she might have immediately noticed the squat wooden buildings, scarcely larger than outhouses, in the back or side yards of almost every home. These were the ten-footers, ten-foot-square structures in which shoemakers, sitting with lapstones resting on their leather aprons, cut and shaped shoes. The partially finished shoes were then turned over to binders, mostly women, who worked at home stitching uppers to inner and outer soles. The finished shoes then went to central shops to be packed and shipped to wholesalers. With a growing demand for shoes from the South and West, the town was thriving when Abby arrived.

Because almost all the people in Lynn worked with their hands or had done so at some time in their lives, residents prided themselves on their democratic society and openness to progressive ideas. When Salem and Boston were still strongholds of Puritanism, Quakers had found a haven in Lynn and had prospered mightily. Although in 1836 they represented only a tenth of the population, they owned the largest shoe manufactures and were prominent in business and civic affairs. Lynn's liberal newspaper was controlled by the "thees and thous"; so were its bank and the almost completed railway line to Boston.[3]

In Lynn Abby lived in a Quaker enclave, scarcely meeting anyone from outside the society. She boarded with Isaiah Chase, a Quaker shoemaker, his wife, Eunice, and their twenty-nine-year-old daughter, Aroline. The Chase home was directly across the street from the Friends' meetinghouse and burial ground; the school, a substantial structure, stood behind the meetinghouse, only a five-minute walk from the Chases'.

As the principal teacher Abby taught the older girls and boys, some thirty of them, while Anna Breed Smith, whom she had known at boarding school, taught the younger children. Abby's pupils paid a shilling a week for tuition, Anna's twelve and a half cents, fees that nearly covered expenses. Although teachers' salaries were not recorded, Abby probably earned around two hundred dollars a year.

Abby and Anna were serious-minded teachers, interested in their pupils and in new educational theories. The committee of Friends that supervised the school reported "good order and improvement much to our satisfaction" and "deportment of scholars commendable." During the short days of winter the two teachers sometimes remained in the schoolroom until after sunset, correcting papers and planning the next day's lessons. When the last themes had been read and marks duly noted, they joined a circle of lively young women who gathered in each other's parlors to exchange ideas. Anna and Aroline wrote poetry; Lydia Keene, another member of the group, was also a teacher and the daughter of Avis Keene, a noted Quaker preacher. All were single, all in their twenties, and except for Abby, all lived at home with their families.

What did they talk about? "Not about pretty babies nor new caps and gowns, "Anna wryly noted. "Our principal subjects were Phrenology, Physiology, J. G. Whittier and his poetry." The generation that came of age in the 1830s believed that a new era was dawning. Their parents had traveled on foot and horseback. Now steam power carried them swiftly to their destinations and powered all manner of machines. The new industrialism brought with it an impetus for change. All institutions—the church, the state, the family, property—were called into question. The young women in the Chases' parlor discussed peace and temperance, abolition, and Sylvester Graham's new diet. If it was wrong to take a life in self-defense, had the American Revolution been justified? Should one pledge to abstain from whiskey while continuing to serve wine at table, or go the teetotal way? Should one give up cotton clothing and forswear sugar because they were products made by slaves?[4]

Abby and her friends were caught up in the health movement advocated by Sylvester Graham. A decade earlier housewives had hailed the commercially baked bread available in stores as one of the boons of the Industrial Revolution. Now Graham warned that the bakers' bread made from finely milled white flour with its thin crust and soft interior was ruinous to health. He counseled a return to whole wheat bread baked at home and also urged his followers to renounce coffee and tea, whiskey, and tobacco and to eat meat sparingly. If converts would also rise early, take cold-water baths, and exercise regularly, Graham promised both healthy bodies and inner serenity.*

No small part of Graham's philosophic goal was to dampen sexuality. Meat, coffee, even spices caused excessive sexual excitement, he said; a vegetable diet encouraged abstention or at least moderation. His preachment against sexuality was based on a then widely accepted theory of the conservation of energy; if energy were dissipated in sexual pursuits, there would be that much less for "civilizing endeavors." In lectures to young men he warned against masturbation and counseled chastity. To married couples he advised moderation: intercourse no more than once a month, a rule not to be violated even on a honeymoon. Overindulgence in sex, he warned, could bring on nervous exhaustion, dyspepsia, rheumatism, uterine disease, and a host of other ailments. When his separate lectures to women were attacked as indelicate, Mary S. Gove, a Lynn Quaker, began to lecture on anatomy and physiology, throwing in warnings against tightly laced corsets along with a strong dose of Grahamism. Anna Breed Smith told Abby that Gove's lectures were "both edifying and interesting," adding that "I have never seen so intelligent looking a company of women" as those in her audience.

Abby was quickly convinced of the value of Graham's program. On her first Thanksgiving in Lynn she and Anna took a long ride in the country instead of eating a dinner "fit only for the stomach of an ostrich." In a lifelong commitment she gave up coffee and tea, rarely ate meat or spicy foods, and took daily cold baths. Except during dire medical emergencies, she did not consult doctors, preferring to prescribe for herself and family from the pharmacopoeia of health reform. Nor was there anything eccentric

---

* In the 1830s thousands of people attended Graham's lectures, read his books and *Journal of Health and Longevity*, and stayed at Graham boardinghouses, where no meat and no "pepper, mustard, grease, vinegar and other garbage" was served. Graham tables were instituted at such liberal colleges as Oberlin, and stores began to sell packaged graham flour and granula, an early version of the graham cracker. After Graham's death his program was spread by other reformers, notably the proponents of phrenology and water cures. In the hands of John Harvey Kellogg, who operated a water cure establishment in Battle Creek, Michigan, granula became granola, a breakfast cereal that later was named cornflakes. (Nissenbaum; LIB, June 16, 1837.)

about her behavior. Most of the women she knew, including such future activists as Lucy Stone and Susan B. Anthony, adopted the Graham diet.[5] Her attitude toward Graham's argument for sexual restraint is harder to document. It is a safe guess, however, that sex-and-the-single-girl meant something different then from today. Abby and her Lynn friends believed not only that women should be chaste but that they were by nature more spiritual and less carnal than men. As single women who were beginning to joke about being old maids,* it was reassuring to be told that a life of chastity would free them for higher things. Probably it was in Lynn that Abby came to believe that there were worse fates than not marrying. Although spinsters were stereotyped comic figures—plain, prudish, sour— she defended the right of women, including herself, to remain single. Even when she later agreed to marry, she liked to speak of her "old maid ways."[6]

Graham's teachings also eased the way for Abby and her circle to have friendships with men. The men they associated with across the aisle in the meetinghouse on First days, at lectures in the Young Men's Anti-Slavery Reading Room, and in each other's homes were equally convinced of the need for sexual restraint. Quaker John Greenleaf Whittier, whose poetry appeared regularly in the *Liberator*, often rode over from his farm in Amesbury. At twenty-nine he was tall, slender, with an olive complexion, black hair, and flashing almond-shaped eyes. Although he was attractive to women, particularly to lady poets,† down-to-earth Abby never succumbed to his charms, or he to hers. "Abby is a good girl—a little too enthusiastic—but honest and conscientious," he confided to his sister.[7]

Abby did have at least one suitor in Lynn, a "celibataire" (bachelor) Anna called him, who sent her bouquets of flowers. However, most of her

---

* The large number of unmarried women in Abby Kelley's circle in Lynn reflected the unequal ratio of men to women in the Northeast. With men leaving farms for city jobs or taking up land in the West, there were some twenty thousand more women than men in New England in 1850. A corresponding decline in the birthrate may also have reflected the teachings of Sylvester Graham and his successors. (Chambers-Schiller, *Liberty, A Better Husband*; Degler.)

† In *Quaker Militant*, Albert Mordell portrays Whittier as a ladies' man who courted women, particularly poets, until marriage threatened, then ran away. Mordell believes that Whittier was a virgin.

male friends were married men like James N. Buffum, who had gone to boarding school with her, and William Bassett, a member of her School Committee. Although William was eight years her senior and at different times city clerk of Lynn, bank cashier, and president of the Essex County Anti-Slavery Society, he depended on Abby as a sounding board and sought her opinion on matters both spiritual and secular.[8] Her relationship with him was the first in a string of friendships with men that were based on shared aspirations and were never disturbed, as far as can be ascertained, by sexual politics.

Buffum and Bassett were Lynn's leading abolitionists. Through them Abby made her first contact with the organized antislavery movement. Although Friends had squared their consciences by freeing their slaves—"making things honest" they called it—few worked to end the institution. Sharing the prejudices of fellow northerners who did not believe that free blacks could live alongside whites in the United States, Quakers generally supported the American Colonization Society, which proposed that slaves be freed gradually and deported to Liberia, an American-backed colony on Africa's west coast.

Without thinking about the problem deeply, Abby had accepted these views until, while she was still in Worcester, William Lloyd Garrison had come to town to lecture. Garrison was the editor of the *Liberator*, a new weekly dedicated to the immediate abolition of slavery and equal opportunities for black people. A benign-looking man, balding at twenty-seven and looking at the world through wire-rimmed spectacles, Garrison was a fiery speaker who denounced slavery as a sin, called slaveholders "man-stealers," and declared that the Colonization Society was motivated by racism.[9] Listening to him speak in Worcester's Town Hall, Abby had been deeply stirred. But in 1832 Worcester, where the main event of the week was the Saturday farmers' market, there were few with whom she could discuss these new ideas. By the time she arrived in Lynn four years later, the struggle for immediate emancipation had thousands of adherents.

The American Anti-Slavery Society had been founded in 1833 and dedicated to the proposition that the slaves "ought instantly to be set free" and accorded "the same privileges as persons of a white complexion." Advising slaves to reject the use of "carnal weapons" to gain their freedom, the abolitionists believed that moral suasion would bring about a change in public opinion. They determined to organize antislavery societies in every city and town in the North, to send out lecturers, to circulate antislavery publications, and "to enlist the pulpit and the press in the cause of the suffering and the dumb." Once northerners were convinced of the sin of slavery, they would bring pressure on the South and force slaveowners to free their human property. It was an ambitious program, and the abolitionists would need all the allies they could find. Therefore, on the last day of their founding convention, they "respectfully and earnestly invited the ladies of the land" to form their own antislavery societies as auxiliaries to the male organizations.[10]

In 1836 there were almost a thousand state and local societies, including scores founded by women. From Portland, Maine, to Ashtabula, Ohio, members of Female Anti-Slavery societies were raising money at sewing bees and fairs, listening to abolitionist lecturers (all male, of course), and reading and circulating abolitionist publications. At a time when the cult of True Womanhood was in its ascendancy, the female abolitionists were criticized for stepping out of their sphere—the home—to participate in a national debate. In letter after letter to the *Liberator* they defended themselves, explaining that by taking up the cause of the powerless, they were behaving as True Women (always capitalized) should.[11] "Let us listen not to the suggestion that [antislavery] is a subject with which women should have nothing to do, because it has a political aspect," a Lynn woman declared. "Its highest and most distinctive aspect is a moral and benevolent one, and in this sphere it is not denied that woman may operate with propriety and efficiency. It is woman's woes that call most loudly for our efforts to free them from degradation and outrage in every form."

Abby had been in Lynn only a few weeks when she joined its Female Anti-Slavery Society and was promptly elected corresponding secretary. Her fellow members were almost all Quakers. Aroline Chase and Lydia Keene served on the Board of Managers; Anna Breed Smith was a member, along with seventeen-year-old Lydia Estes, a cousin of Aroline's who later won fame as the inventor of Lydia E. Pinkham's Vegetable Compound.[12] As corresponding secretary Abby kept in touch with other female societies and reported back on their activities. The women were still uncertain, feeling their way; the letters that traveled between Boston, New York, Philadelphia, and the small towns of New England were self-deprecatory and very wordy. One letter from the Philadelphia society reported that members were making "fancy articles on which short mottoes or sentiments on the subject of slavery are inscribed—but have as yet produced little in that way . . . being few in number & feeble in resources." A newly organized Connecticut society looked to "our elder and more experienced Sisters for advice," hoping that "we shall prove prompt and efficient laborers according to our strength and ability."[13]

When Abby joined the society, the Lynn women were sewing "fancy articles"—nightcaps, pincushions, aprons, and traveling pockets (gingham bags functioning as pocketbooks), each embroidered with an antislavery motto.* Some of the articles were sold in Lynn; most went to Boston for an annual fair that provided major financial support for the movement. When additional money came in from dues and gifts, Abby forwarded contributions from Lynn to the American Anti-Slavery Society, the Massachusetts Society, and the Samaritan Asylum for Indigent Colored Children in Boston.[14]

In the summer of 1836 the Boston women proposed that the female societies enlarge their activities by petitioning Congress to end slavery in the District of Columbia. (Because the District was federal territory, Congress had the power to abolish slavery there; constitutionally it could not interfere with the institution in the southern states.) Aware that they were treading close to the edge of woman's sphere, the Bostonians pointed out that "as wives and mothers, as sisters and daughters, we are bound to urge men to cease to do evil. We are bound to exercise the only right we ourselves enjoy—the right to petition." Lynn's Female Society promptly voted to follow their advice, and Abby and Aroline were elected to a committee to distribute the petitions and collect signatures.[15]

---

* Mottoes included "Am I Not a Woman and a Sister?," "Oh sisters! sad indeed's the thought /That in our land poor slaves are bought," "Under the sable skin you will find/The richer Jewels of the mind." (PAS Papers.)

Circulating petitions was disagreeable work. With pen and inkhorn in hand and "armed with affectionate but unconquerable determination," the women walked from door to door, approaching strangers as well as friends. For diffident young ladies engaged in their first public venture, it was daunting to hear, "My darter says that you want the niggers and whites to marry together," or, "I hope you get a nigger husband." Some women were willing to sign as long as it did not cost money; others refused because their husbands said, "Women are meddling with that that's none of their business." Occasionally a man met them at the door and bade them "begone and never bring such a thing to the house again," concluding, "It's none of your business, gals, and you'd better go right straight home."[16]

Despite the rebuffs, Abby threw herself into the work enthusiastically. Collecting signatures to petitions, she reminded the Lynn women, was effective propaganda because it brought them in contact with all groups in the community: "with the pro-slavery, the indifferent, with those who are as much as ourselves opposed to slavery, but-but-but . . . so that many who would not otherwise think at all about it are induced to give it a little place in their minds, and some are brought to embrace Abolitionist principles." Although there is no record of the number of signatures collected by the Lynn society in 1836, the following year she mailed four separate petitions to Boston, each with close to fifteen hundred names; almost half of the women in Lynn had signed one or more petitions.[17]

The Female Anti-Slavery Society met monthly at members' homes; on other days the women gathered to sew "fancy articles" or to attend lectures at the Young Men's Anti-Slavery Society Reading Room. Teaching school, circulating petitions, going to lectures, selling subscriptions to antislavery publications kept Abby busy until a fortnight before Christmas the even tenor of her days was interrupted by an urgent message from Millbury: Father very ill. She hurried home, reaching his bedside in time to see his face light up in greeting and then to watch his life ebb away. Wing Kelley died on December 17, 1836, and Abby was profoundly shaken.

Dazedly she made arrangements for the funeral, taking over for her mother, who suddenly seemed old and frail. Fortunately Wing Kelley had died solvent, his largest debt being the money he had borrowed from Abby, which he had kept count of to the penny—$227.69 plus interest of $17.75—

and a smaller sum, $68, from Albert. When these debts were paid, the farm would be free and clear and Diana Kelley would be able to live out her days in comfort.[18]

After making sure that her mother was settled with seventeen-year-old Lucy for company, Abby returned to Lynn a changed person. The death of her father, whose loving presence had meant more than she had realized, left her questioning the purpose of her own existence. "It seems like a troubled and tear-watered dream," she wrote her sister Olive. "Father's death taught me the necessity of looking beyond earthly things for support."

For more than a year she suffered "an anguish of soul," an identity crisis that her contemporaries recognized as conversion. A familiar rite of passage for young people in those days, conversion usually signified the end of adolescence and the assumption of adult responsibilities. Youthful introspection and self-doubt gave way to faith. One opened up one's heart to God, applied for membership in a church, and submitted to the will of God's ministers.

For Abby at twenty-six the crisis came late and was prolonged. When she asked the convert's familiar question "What shall I do to be saved?" she found the answer lay not in submission but in commitment. During a year of introspection, a year in which she traveled outside New England, encountering new people and fresh ideas, she struggled to ascertain her priorities. To love God, she concluded, did not mean worshiping "graven images or imaginary beings. To love Him is to love his attributes, mercy, justice, truth, and to sacrifice every selfish consideration to the advancement of them." By year's end she felt sure that "mercy, justice, truth" encompassed all manner of good causes: antislavery, peace, and the claims of women to equality.[19]

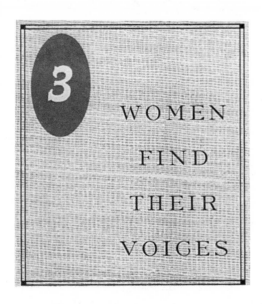

3

WOMEN
FIND
THEIR
VOICES

In the months following her father's death Abby joined forces with William Bassett to convince older Friends to open Lynn's meetinghouse to abolitionist speakers even though the Yearly Meeting had decided to bar them. When William Lloyd Garrison lectured in the meetinghouse on Broad Street, he praised Lynn as a progressive town, and a friend of Abby's congratulated her on "the laudable and glorious victory" that had been won. Garrison was followed by Henry B. Stanton, one of the Band of Seventy agents appointed by the American Anti-Slavery Society in a new stepped-up propaganda effort. The Seventy—their number chosen to symbolize the seventy disciples Christ appointed to spread his word—were young men who after weeks of intensive indoctrination in New York were fanning out across the North to spread the message of antislavery. They had barely commenced when the panic of 1837, one of the worst depressions in U.S. history, threatened to cut short their work. When its chief financial backers were forced to retrench, the society lacked money to pay the agents' skimpy salaries or traveling expenses.[1]

Abby immediately assumed the task of fund raising. Continually exhorting the women to double their contributions, she sent two hundred dollars to the treasurer of the Massachusetts Anti-Slavery Society from the Lynn Female Society. But by spring money was harder and harder to come by. Many of Lynn's shoe manufacturers had closed their shops; unemployed cordwainers were scratching out bare subsistences on the clam flats and in backyard potato patches. The members of the Female Society, most of them the wives and daughters of shoemakers, had little spare cash to contribute. Some met in the evenings and bound shoes to earn extra money for the cause. But with depression prices of three cents for binding a woman's kid buskin shoe, it took a long time to earn a hundred dollars, or even ten. Most of the money contributed by Lynn's Female Society in 1837 came from Abby Kelley's pocket. The money from her father's estate was paid into the antislavery treasury as soon as she received it. Later she sold some of her most expensive clothes and contributed the proceeds.[2]

Still her inner voice insisted that she do more—more—more. The Band of Seventy reached thousands of people while she could bring her urgent message to only a handful of women. Nor was she alone in wishing for wider fields in which to work. A year earlier members of the Philadelphia Female Anti-Slavery Society, most of them Quakers accustomed to meeting with men, had proposed that women abolitionists send delegates to the annual convention of the American Anti-Slavery Society. Would the men admit them? Elizur Wright, Jr., secretary of the American Society, gallantly, if ambiguously, assured the Philadelphians that they "would doubtless be received with the courtesy and high respect which it is the glory of the *Christian* religion to pay to the *better half* of human nature." However, the response from the New England women had been generally negative. Mary Clark of the Concord, New Hampshire, Female Society spoke for many when she wrote: "Our more experienced *brethren* who are accustomed to speak in such assemblies [could] more justly represent us than we could represent ourselves." In Boston, where the proposal lost by a close vote, Maria Weston Chapman, the corresponding secretary, suggested instead that leading members of the female societies form an executive committee "to devise plans for the advancement of this cause. Great good might result from the collision of such minds as those of A. E. Grimké, Lucretia Mott, Mary Parker, Mary Clark of Concord, the Balls, the Westons, the Childs & others." After an exchange of letters the women decided on a bold step. They would call a national convention of antislavery women to meet in New York City in May 1837.[3]

With Lynn less than an hour from Boston—from Burrill's Hill one could see the golden dome of the State House—Abby knew many of the "minds" on Chapman's list. Mary Parker,* proprietor of a boardinghouse on Hayward Place where visiting abolitionists stayed, was the dignified president of the Boston Female Society. Martha and Lucy Ball, daughters of a West Indian immigrant and a Boston woman, were described by a contemporary as "slightly colored." They ran a school for "young ladies of color" and served respectively as recording secretary and treasurer of the Boston Female Society. Lydia Maria Child† had been the most popular woman writer in the North until she wrote *An Appeal in Favor of That Class of Americans Called Africans*, the first book to call for immediate emancipation. The *Appeal* brought numbers of converts to the cause and swift reprisals to its author. Sales of her books dropped precipitously; subscriptions to her magazine *Juvenile Miscellany* were canceled, and literary critics who had once sung her praises now attacked her for entering the male world of politics.

Thirty-one-year-old Maria Weston Chapman, a regal beauty with a razor-sharp mind, was the spark plug of the Boston Society. Educated in England, she had returned to Boston to become principal of the Young Ladies High School before marrying Henry Grafton Chapman, a wealthy merchant. The oldest of the six Weston sisters and the only one who was

---

* New Hampshire-born Mary Parker was not a sister of Theodore Parker, as some historians have written.

† When a young woman, Child dropped the name Lydia, adopting Maria instead. She signed herself L. Maria Child or Maria.

married, she could always call on Anne or Caroline or Deborah to take charge of her children or her correspondence while she ran the antislavery fair and wrote editorials for the *Liberator*. Witty, talkative Anne Warren Weston was less imposing than her older sister, and Abby found her more approachable. She was soon addressing letters to Maria as "My dear friend" and to Anne as "My very dear friend."

Except for Mary Clark of New Hampshire, the other "minds" were Philadelphians. Lucretia Mott, a generation older than Abby, was a well-known Quaker preacher and independent thinker,[4] but the woman Abby was most attracted to that winter was Angelina Grimké. A member of a prominent slaveowning family in Charleston, South Carolina, Angelina and her older sister, Sarah, had rejected slavery and lives as southern belles for a meaningful existence in the North. They found peace of mind temporarily in the Society of Friends until Angelina discovered that antislavery was her true vocation. Her letters to the *Liberator* describing slavery at first hand were followed by a pamphlet, *Appeal to the Christian Women of the South*. Few southern women read the appeal—copies were publicly burned in Charleston—but antislavery leaders recognized that a southern witness of her impeccable lineage could be a valuable asset. In the fall of 1836 she and Sarah had been invited to New York to join the crash course in abolitionism being given to the Band of Seventy by Theodore Weld. An antislavery leader and charismatic public speaker whose voice had been damaged by overuse, Weld drilled the agents on the history, philosophy, and profitability of slavery, the biblical arguments for and against the institution, and also introduced them to black speakers, who gave "truly affecting" accounts of the effect of prejudice on their lives. After three weeks of twelve-hour days, the male agents—"the brethren" Angelina called them—left to speak in New England and the mid-Atlantic states. The Grimkés remained in New York to hold parlor meetings for women under the auspices of the Ladies' New York City Anti-Slavery Society.

Angelina surprised everyone including herself by a talent for oratory— a musical, carrying voice and pleasing manner. Although Sarah tended to fall into the singsong speaking style favored by many Quaker ministers, her ideas were logically and forcefully expressed. "The deeply interesting information they had to communicate, and the earnest and powerful appeals with which their hearts seemed almost bursting were calculated to rivet the attention and absorb the sympathy of every Auditor," Abby Ann Cox, an officer of the Ladies' Society, reported.

So many women wanted to hear them that parlors proved too small. The Reverend Henry G. Ludlow, their host during their New York stay, offered them a lecture room in his church. Angelina spent hours in tearful questioning before accepting. Had not St. Paul said, "Let your women keep silence in the churches: for it is not permitted unto them to speak"? Ludlow opened each meeting with a prayer, then ostentatiously left the room so that it would be clear that the gatherings were only for women.

For the next two months the Grimkés lectured weekly, at first in the sessions room of Ludlow's Spring Street Church and then, as their audiences continued to grow, in the church itself. Occasionally a curious man slipped into a rear pew; once one refused to leave when Ludlow informed him that the meeting was exclusively for ladies. "Somehow I did not feel his presence at all embarrassing and went on just as tho' he was not there," Angelina said.

It does not seem newsworthy today—two sedate women speaking to an audience of women in a New York church. Eight years earlier Frances ("Fanny") Wright of Great Britain had lectured in the city, but since she had espoused woman's rights, birth control, and divorce as well as abolition, she had been stigmatized as a "free lover" and ignored by respectable reformers. Indeed, some of the brethren had objected to the Grimkés' public gatherings for fear that they might be called Fanny Wright meetings. The abolitionist women, however, had no such misgivings.[5]

Still searching for ways to widen her field of activities, Abby was one of dozens of women who wrote to Angelina that spring. In an adulatory letter to her "Esteemed Friend and Beloved Sister" she invited her to speak in Lynn or, if this proved impossible, to send an encouraging letter to the Female Society indicating her opinion of "the approaching convention of Ladies in N.Y. and whether it is desirable that many should attend."

A flowery final paragraph indicated that Abby was still in the throes of her conversion: "Many in Massachusetts who have never known thee in person supplicate the throne of grace in thy behalf that thou may be upheld, strengthened and preserved, in the straight path thou art now pursuing, till thou shalt be finally brought to a state of perfectness in the glories of heaven."

Angelina replied that although she and Sarah would be unable to visit Lynn immediately, they were planning a lecture tour in Massachusetts in June. Meanwhile, she urged the Lynn Society to send delegates to the convention. "We ought to have the councils of the wisest women in our female associations," she wrote. "Responsibilities will rest on us as an American Convention which have never belonged to any individual Society & if we do not meet them as Women & as Christians, it would be far better for us never to have assembled. Let all the willing hearted come."[6]

Any doubt that Abby might have had about going to New York was dissipated by Angelina's letter. At the April meeting of the Lynn Female Society, which she chaired, she was one of seven women appointed as delegates to the forthcoming convention. On May 8 they joined other New England delegates in Providence for the overnight steamboat trip to New York. Steamboats had no individual staterooms in 1837 or for many years thereafter. Abby and the others slept in the ladies' cabin, a large room with two tiers of berths. Aside from some queasiness as the boat plowed through the choppy waters of Long Island Sound, the most noteworthy aspect of Abby's first steamboat trip was the presence in the ladies' cabin of a black woman, a convention delegate from Rhode Island.

As a rule steamboat companies barred blacks from the ladies' and gentlemen's cabins, obliging them to spend the night on deck with little shelter from wind and salt spray. On this occasion the white women welcomed their black sister as proof that they were on the threshold of a precedent-breaking adventure. A New Hampshire woman wrote: "I was happy, in the early stages of this journey to have our feelings tested with regard to that bitter prejudice against colored which we have indiscriminately indulged, and to find it giving place to better feelings. Our colored companion slept near my side—she rode with us in the carriage—sat with us at the table of the public boarding-house—walked in company with us."[7]

Carpetbag in hand, Abby disembarked at the Battery early the next morning and strode across the cobblestoned streets of America's largest city. Three hundred thousand people, thirty times the population of Lynn, lived in the metropolis; more than a thousand ships from a hundred foreign ports dropped anchor there that year. The harbor was breathtaking—a forest of masts and sails and smokestacks dwarfing anything she had seen before. Yet along lower Broadway, where the spire of Trinity Church and the cupola of City Hall dominated the skyline, the city lacked the charm—and cleanliness—of Boston. A disastrous fire eighteen months earlier had wiped out a whole neighborhood of colonial structures. Rebuilding was proceeding rapidly, but Abby could still see charred, crumbling walls and debris-littered streets, where tribes of pigs rooted for their daily sustenance, and bustling carters and barrowmen made walking difficult. Farther north along the broad thoroughfare were hotels, theaters, shops, and the five-story mansions of the wealthy.

Probably Abby took little notice of the architecture or of the elegant ladies with their bright parasols who strolled by, intent on a morning's shopping. It was Anniversary Week, the week set aside each May when philanthropic organizations from all over the North—the American Physiological Society, American Bible Society, American Temperance Society, American Tract Society, and American Anti-Slavery Society—held their annual conventions in the city. Some well-to-do reformers put up at the new Astor House. Abby and the other women chose a downtown temperance hotel, where prices were modest and only free produce—food not grown by slave labor—was served.

Tired and travel-stained though they were, Abby and her companions hastened from their lodgings to the Tabernacle, a church on lower Broadway, where at 10:00 A.M. the American Anti-Slavery Society's annual meeting began. The largest house of worship in the city, the Broadway Tabernacle could accommodate four thousand people. On this occasion every seat was filled, and the women, present only as spectators, strained to hear President Arthur Tappan's welcoming remarks and the reading of the annual report by Secretary Elizur Wright. When the session adjourned at three, they hurriedly adjusted shawls and bonnet strings before traveling uptown to their own meeting.[8]

The Anti-Slavery Convention of American Women convened at 4:00

P.M. on Tuesday, May 9, 1837, in the Third Free Church* at the corner of Houston and Thompson streets, in the district now known as Greenwich Village. Some two hundred delegates from nine northern states assembled "in fear and trembling" for the first public political meeting of women in the United States.

Every woman present was conscious that she was violating a powerful taboo. "To attend a Female Convention!" a New England delegate wrote. "Once I should have blushed at the thought, and exclaimed, prophecy it not in the streets of America that her daughters will ever thus pass through the circumference of their accustomed sphere." Aware that they would encounter reproaches for their daring, the women were also afraid of looking foolish. Perhaps, as they had been told all their lives, they really were not competent enough to organize a public meeting. Yet when Theodore Weld, who had remained the Grimkés' mentor, offered to assist them, they turned him down, deciding to bar men from all of the sessions.

To avoid having the convention become all talk and no action, the officers of the big-city female societies had been conferring with the Grimkés by mail for weeks beforehand. The Philadelphians and some of the Bostonians had come to New York a day early. Meeting with the New York women, they had outlined an agenda and chosen a tentative slate of officers.

Abby was seated in a high-backed pew when a tiny woman—she was only five feet tall—mounted to the pulpit and called the convention to order. Lucretia Mott's bright eyes and firm chin conveyed intelligence and assurance, and her clear, sweet voice carried to the farthest reaches of the church as she read the proposed list of officers. For president, Mary S. Parker. For vice-presidents, Sarah Grimké, Lucretia Mott, Lydia Maria Child, Ann C. Smith of Peterboro, New York, wife of Gerrit Smith, an important financial backer of the American Society, Abby Ann Cox, and— here heads may have turned or elbows jabbed a neighbor—Grace Bustill Douglass, a black matron who was a founding member of the Philadelphia

---

* "Free Church" because the pews were not auctioned off to wealthy members but were open to all. (Wyatt-Brown.)

Female Society. The secretaries who were to draw up the membership roll and painstakingly take down the convention minutes (shorthand was still several years in the future) were Anne W. Weston, Angelina Grimké, and Mary Grew and Sarah Pugh of Philadelphia.

After the slate of officers was unanimously accepted, Mary Parker took the chair, and the convention set about organizing itself. Should participation be limited to delegates with credentials from their societies or should everyone present be invited to take part? It was quickly decided that all who agreed with the convention's goal—to abolish slavery in the United States—be enrolled as members. As the secretaries walked along the aisles, taking down names, Abby had an opportunity to look around. She nodded to acquaintances from boarding school days, sisters of Elizabeth Buffum Chace, and stared with frank interest at Angelina Grimké, a small, spare woman with a long face and large, expressive eyes. Most of the audience were in their twenties and thirties. Twenty-four-year-old Mary Grew and Anne Weston, twenty-five, who were approaching with quill pens and inkpots in hand, were among the youngest present; Angelina Grimké was thirty-two, and motherly-looking Maria Child, thirty-five. The oldest women in the church were Lucretia Mott and Sarah Grimké, aged forty-four and forty-five respectively, and graying Grace Douglass, who was fifty-two. As a whole it was an unfashionable assemblage with Quaker drab predominating and fewer furs and feathers than might have been expected in New York. They could have been any church group meeting to support missionary work in the Sandwich Islands except for one thing: One out of every ten women was black.[9]

For Abby and the other white delegates, sitting alongside black women was a novel experience. There were few black families in Lynn, and fewer still in Worcester; indeed, blacks made up only 2 percent of the population of the North. Excluded from schools, denied any but menial jobs, segregated in ghettos with names like Nigger Hill, New Guinea, or Little Africa, they lived separate and notably unequal lives. Not until the advent of the Garrisonian antislavery movement had there been any serious attempt to bring the races together. Garrisonians realized that prejudice against black people was one of the pillars upholding slavery. As long as whites perceived blacks as an inferior species with limited mental capacity and limitless appetites—

45

and there were scientists who supported this stereotype*—slaveholders could hold them in bondage in the South and freeholders segregate them in the North with clear consciences.

Black men had participated in the founding of the American Anti-Slavery Society; a few became officers and spoke at the annual conventions. But token black faces on the platform had not led to interracial friendships. Many whites were afraid of being accused of "amalgamationism," the code word for intermarriage. This was particularly true in New York, where abolitionist leaders were largely evangelical ministers who confined black worshipers to the upper galleries of their churches†—"nigger heaven"— and looked on the fight against slavery as a white endeavor.[10]

When the Grimkés began their lectures, they were shocked to find that the members of the Ladies' New York Society followed in the footsteps of their husbands and fathers. "No colored sister has ever been on the Board & they have hardly any colored members," Angelina told a friend in Philadelphia. To prevent this "wicked prejudice" from being reflected in the women's convention, they had alerted the integrated New England and Philadelphia societies to the importance of sending black delegates and had personally invited black women's groups in New York to attend. The Colored Ladies Literary Society and the Rising Daughters of Abyssinia had turned out in full force, along with members of other church and social circles, to produce the North's first broadly integrated gathering. There might have been a larger attendance had the convention been better publicized. Fearful of arousing antagonism in a city where abolitionism was unpopular and women speakers anathema, the Grimkés' advisers had counseled against sending advance announcements to the press. Not even the *Colored American*, the city's black weekly, had been notified. "This was

---

* Louis Agassiz, noted Harvard zoologist, taught that blacks were a separate species, separately created. (Sterling, *We Are Your Sisters*.)

† Charles Finney, an evangelist, opposed "racial mixing" in his church and protested when black and white choirs shared the same platform at a meeting of the American Anti-Slavery Society. (Wyatt-Brown.)

brother Garrison's advice," Angelina said afterward, "but I do not think it was good."[11]

Schoolteachers, ministers' daughters, seamstresses, members of the small black elite of the city,* the black women kept a low profile at this first public meeting with their white sisters. They served on committees but took the floor only when resolutions touching on prejudice were under discussion. Their testimony against "the dreadful effects of the scheme of expatriation" proposed by the Colonization Society was "most touching and emphatic," a white woman said. The black New Yorkers also won friends by acting as hosts to the out-of-town delegates, serving lemonade during an evening sale of "fancy articles" and bringing lunch on the convention's third day when there was no time for a recess. "We should have been famished had not our thoughtful colored friends brought us baskets of refreshments," said Sarah Pugh. "They are a race worth saving." If the Ladies' New York Society disagreed with this sentiment, its comments were not recorded.[12]

The convention's main goals were to collect a million signatures on petitions calling on Congress to abolish slavery in the District of Columbia and in Florida, then a federal territory, and to publish half a dozen pamphlets addressed to the women of the North and Great Britain, and so forth. The leaders of the big-city antislavery societies took charge of the petition campaign, but Abby volunteered to secure Lynn's participation. She also served on the committee preparing the "Appeal to the Women of the *Nominally* Free States." Mornings and evenings, when the convention was not in session, she met with such older hands as Angelina Grimké, Lucretia Mott, Maria Child, and Grace Douglass to write a stirring seventy-

---

* Probably few recognized Maria W. Stewart, a member of the Colored Ladies Literary Society, who had been the first American woman to lecture in public, anticipating the Grimkés by five years. Other black members of the convention included Sarah M. Douglass, Grace Douglass's daughter, an outstanding educator and leader in black and antislavery circles in Philadelphia, and Julia Williams, a teacher from Boston, who later married the Reverend Henry Highland Garnet, a noted black spokesman. (Sterling, *We Are Your Sisters; Turning the World Upside Down*.)

page pamphlet whose theme was expressed by a poem from Sarah Forten, a black Philadelphian:

> *We are thy sisters. God has truly said,*
> *That of one blood the nations he has made.*
> *O, Christian woman! in a Christian land,*
> *Canst thou unblushing read this great command?*
> *Suffer the wrongs which wring our inmost heart,*
> *To draw one throb of pity on thy part!*
> *Our skins may differ, but from thee we claim*
> *A sister's privilege and a sister's name.*

During the three days of the convention speakers condemned the "death-like apathy" of the churches on the subject of slavery, appealed to women to refrain from using slave produce, and proposed concrete action to dissipate prejudice. Angelina Grimké and Maria Child urged women to "act out the principles of Christian equality" by associating with black people "as though the color of the skin was of no more consequence than that of the hair, or the eyes" and suggested that abolitionists "encourage our oppressed brothers and sisters in their different trades by employing them whenever opportunities offer for so doing" and that "as long as our churches are disgraced with side-seats and corners set apart for them, we will, as much as possible, take our seats with them."

On the second afternoon delegates sat bolt upright in their pews when Angelina Grimké proposed an even bolder break with tradition:

> *Resolved,* That as certain rights and duties are common to all moral beings, the time has come for woman to move in that sphere which Providence has assigned her, and no longer remain satisfied in the circumscribed limits with which corrupt custom and a perverted application of Scripture have encircled her; therefore that it is the duty of woman, and the province of woman, to plead the cause of the oppressed in our land, and to do all that she can by her voice, and her pen, and her purse,

and the influence of her example, to overthrow the horrible system of American Slavery.

In the context of the time the resolution was a declaration of independence for women, an assault on the concept of True Womanhood that insisted on silence and submission. "An animated and interesting debate respecting the rights and duties of women" followed, the secretaries reported. The resolution was finally adopted, although not unanimously. Twelve women, almost all of them from New York, asked that the minutes record their disapproval.

Another difference of opinion surfaced on the final morning of the convention, when participants were asked how they preferred to have their names appear in the printed proceedings. Should each name be prefixed by "Mrs." or "Miss" or should the appellation indicating marital status be omitted? More than four-fifths of the women chose to have their names published without a prefix; again, of those who insisted on being labeled "Mrs." or "Miss," a large majority were New Yorkers.

Abby sat in unaccustomed silence during most of the discussions, content to listen and to learn and only occasionally offering a comment. Not until the question of raising money to carry out the convention's work came up did she venture to take the floor. In the spirit that had led her to sustain the treasury of Lynn's Female Society, she proposed "that we consider it an imperious duty to make retrenchments from our own personal expenses, that we may be better able to contribute." Then, lest her audience should fail to understand, she amplified the resolution by remarks on "the duty of retrenchment, especially in dress, to enable women to contribute more liberally to the antislavery cause." It was a minor point among weightier ones, but she caught the attention of the audience. A seventeen-year-old delegate from Philadelphia was always to remember "how my heart burned within me for joy to hear [your] earnest almost solemn words. At that Womens Convention thou gave signs of great promise."[13]

When the convention adjourned after deciding to meet again in Philadelphia in 1838, the women walked back to their lodgings feeling proud of their achievements. "The sittings of the convention were conducted with dignity and talent which was truly gratifying," one wrote. "There was a depth of intellect—a warmth of feeling—a unity of spirit—and an energy of soul most beautifully combined." "Tell Mr. Weld," Anne Weston gleefully counseled Angelina, "that when the women got together they found they had *minds* of their own, and could transact business *without* his directions."

Despite favorable comments from the *Liberator* and from friends overseas, where Harriet Martineau, the British sociologist, called the convention "a great event in history," the New York papers poked fun at "the Amazonian farce." "Yes, most unbelieving reader," the *Commercial Advertiser* editorialized, "it is a fact of most ludicrous solemnity, that 'our female brethren' have been lifting up their voices. The spinster has thrown aside her distaff—the blooming beauty her guitar—the matron her darning needle—the sweet novelist her crow-quill; the young mother has left her baby to nestle alone in the cradle—and the kitchen maid her pots and frying pans—to discuss the weighty matters of state—to decide upon intricate questions of international policy."

For several more paragraphs the editorial continued with a put-down of "resolutions spontaneously cut and dried beforehand" and "oratoresses" whose "eloquence breathed sweetly from their sweeter lips" but who had deprived "the world of men of the high privilege of drinking from those rich rivers of rhetoric."[14]

Never mind. Let them ridicule the women. A first momentous step had been taken, and Abby Kelley returned to Lynn brimming over with plans for the future. Although she tried to concentrate on her teaching duties, every post brought fresh reminders of antislavery work to be done. The pamphlets prepared for the convention were ready for distribution; the petition drive was under way, and money was needed to pay printing costs. Abby's first task was to organize the annual meeting of Lynn's Female Anti-Slavery Society, scheduled for the third week in June. Ordinarily this was a routine affair, at which the annual report was read and officers were elected for the coming year, but she planned an ambitious program "to stir us up to good works." Angelina and Sarah Grimké, who were to lecture in Massachusetts that summer, agreed to make Lynn the first stop of their tour. With the sisters as guests of honor, Abby hoped to convince the Lynn women to pledge five hundred dollars to carry on the work of the convention and thus set an example for all the New England women.

Early in the afternoon of June 21, 1837, a carriageload of visitors arrived from Boston. The Grimkés were escorted by the Reverend Amos Phelps, who as general agent of the Massachusetts Anti-Slavery Society was in charge of their lecture schedule, and Henry C. Wright, one of the Band of Seventy who was to report on their tour for the *Liberator*. In response to Abby's plea, Anne Weston and Henrietta Sargent, who had also attended the women's convention, came as representatives of the Boston Female Society.

When Lynn's Female Society met for business at 3:00 P.M., five hundred women—more than ten times the usual attendance—crowded into the Young Men's Anti-Slavery Reading Room. Abby proudly introduced the visitors, shepherding them to the front of the room, then read the society's annual report. Like annual reports the world over, it told of work done and not completed, with hope for greater success in the future. "We may not stop to raise the shout of joy for what has been accomplished nor in the least relax our energies." Pedestrian as the report was for the most part, it enunciated principles that were to guide Abby in the future. When she emphasized the need for individual responsibility—"each has a duty of her own to perform"—and proposed that "as moral warriors" her listeners adopt as their motto "We consider nothing done while anything remains undone," she was not striving for felicitous phrases but rather for a philosophy to live by. No matter how many petitions were circulated, how many members recruited, how much money raised, Abby Kelley was not going to rest until the work was completed—until the slaves were free. Even—for she was optimistic then—if it took ten years.

In her summation she touched on another theme that was to become almost as important to her as abolition. Women must enlist in the "moral conflict against wrong" despite "the contumely and scorn" heaped on them for stepping out of their sphere. Although most of the Lynn women were shy about speaking in public, she urged them to forget themselves in "the absorbing objects" of the work, "thereby overcoming diffidence" that stopped them "from coming forward and communicating [their] thoughts unreservedly."

Members of the society volunteered to circulate the convention's publications and agreed to contribute "their mite to a public sale of useful articles." However, they failed to pledge the five hundred dollars that Abby had hoped for "on account of the low state of funds" in the community. Still, more than thirty women enrolled as new members. It was a good afternoon's work.[15]

That evening Angelina Grimké was scheduled to lecture in Lynn's Methodist Church under the auspices of the Female Society. Men were not expected to attend, but Amos Phelps, Henry Wright, and one or two others who were curious to hear her took inconspicuous seats in the gallery. Seeing them, a woman asked if her husband couldn't come too. Although the answer was negative, other men whose wives had told them of Angelina's eloquence, presented themselves at the door. By the time the meeting began, her audience of a thousand included as many men as women, and Angelina Grimké found herself speaking, in the language of the times, to her first "promiscuous audience." The heavens did not fall—not yet anyway. Instead the men were "spellbound" by her firsthand account of slavery, "impatient of the slightest noise which might cause the loss of a word." The next evening, when she lectured in a smaller church, they came back for more. Six hundred people squeezed into the building; another hundred or so crowded into the vestibule or peered through the windows. "Great openness to hear & ease in speaking," Angelina told a friend.

Once the barrier had been breached, the Grimkés continued to speak to "promiscuous audiences." While Abby remained in Lynn for her school's summer session, they traveled with their entourage to Salem and Newburyport, Andover and Groton, Lowell and Pepperell and on into the western part of the state. Speaking in schoolhouses and barns when churches were denied to them, they reached more than forty thousand people that summer. Few evangelical preachers promising hellfire or salvation had heavier schedules or larger audiences. Many who came out of curiosity— to hear a *woman* speak—stayed to join an antislavery society and subscribe to the *Liberator*.[16]

However, a backlash was not long in making itself felt. The Congregational Church, which had lost its monopoly of moral leadership in recent decades and had been fighting a rearguard action against Methodists, Baptists, and Unitarians, suddenly found itself threatened by an enemy within. Church leaders who had never taken a strong stand against slavery and had resisted demands to sever ties with Protestant denominations in the South now saw thousands of their members converted to radical antislavery by two women who were lecturing in bold defiance of the doctrines of St. Paul. Women were the backbone of the church, making up the bulk of the congregation on Sundays, depositing their pennies in mite boxes to support missionaries, sewing clothing for needy theological students. There was a real and present danger that they might desert church circles for antislavery work. Already the Lynn Female Society had resolved at its annual meeting "That while we hold two millions and a half of our countrymen in slavery, and shut them out from the light of the Gospel, it is inconsistent for us to lend our aid to any foreign mission."

When the General Association of Congregational Ministers met in North Brookfield in late July, it issued a Pastoral Letter to be read in every orthodox pulpit in the state. After reasserting the authority of the clergy—"Your minister is ordained of God to be your preacher"—the letter turned to "the dangers which at present seem to threaten the female character. . . . We appreciate the unostentatious prayers of woman in advancing the cause of religion. But when she assumes the place of man as a public reformer, she yields the power which God has given her for her protection, and her character becomes unnatural. If the vine, whose strength and beauty is to lean upon the trellis-work, thinks to assume the independence of the elm, it will not only cease to bear fruit, but fall in shame and dishonor into the dust."

As a final slap at the Grimkés, who frequently told of female slaves who were at the mercy of the "brutal lust" of their masters, the letter deplored the "intimate acquaintance and promiscuous conversation of females with regard to things which ought not to be named; by which that modesty and delicacy which constitutes the true influence of women in society is consumed and the way opened for degeneracy and ruin."

Undoubtedly some True Women heeded the ministers' warning, but for many the backlash generated a backlash of its own. Nineteen-year-old Lucy Stone who was sitting with a cousin in the gallery of the church where the letter was first read recalled that her cousin's "side was black and blue with the indignant nudges of my elbow at each aggravating sentence; and I told her afterwards that, if I ever had anything to say in public, I should say it, and all the more because of that Pastoral Letter." While Abby Kelley used the controversy to spur on the Lynn women to even greater efforts in collecting signatures to petitions, Maria Chapman responded to the "Clerical Bull" with rollicking verses titled "The Times That Try Men's Souls":

> Confusion has seized us, and all things go wrong,
> The women have leaped from "their spheres,"
> And, instead of fixed stars, shoot as comets along,
> And are setting the world by the ears!
> In courses erratic they're wheeling through space,
> In brainless confusion and meaningless chase.
>
> They've taken a notion to speak for themselves,
> And are wielding the tongue and the pen;
> They've mounted the rostrum; the termagant elves,
> and—oh horrid!—are talking to men!
> With faces unblanched in our presence they come
> To harangue us, they say, in behalf of the dumb.
>
> Our grandmothers' learning consisted of yore
> In spreading their generous boards;
> In twisting the distaff, or mopping the floor,
> And obeying the will of their lords.
> Now, misses may reason, and think, and debate,
> Till unquestioned submission is quite out of date.[17]

The controversy intensified when the True Women found a spokeswoman in Catharine Beecher, daughter of Lyman Beecher, the noted evangelical preacher, and sister of the not-yet-noted Harriet Beecher Stowe. Addressing *An Essay on Slavery and Abolition with Reference to the Duty of American Females* to Angelina Grimké, she declared that women should not enter the public arena but should use their superior moral sensibilities within the domestic circle. Angelina replied in a series of open letters that were published in the *Liberator* and reprinted as a pamphlet. Defending women abolitionists, she deplored "the anti-Christian doctrine of masculine and feminine virtues" that depicted man as warrior while woman was "to be admired for her personal charms and caressed and humored like a spoiled child. . . . I recognize no rights but *human* rights—I know nothing of men's rights and women's rights, for in Christ Jesus there is neither male nor female," she concluded.

Then Sarah Grimké, a better writer than she was a speaker, joined the fray with fifteen "Letters on the Province of Women," which appeared in the *New England Spectator* and were published as a book, *Letters on the Equality of the Sexes, and the Condition of Woman*, the first significant exposition of woman's rights to appear in the United States. Comparing that "extraordinary document" the Pastoral Letter to Cotton Mather on witchcraft, she insisted on women's equality in every field and declared: "Whatever is morally right for a man to do, is morally right for a woman."

From her desk in the Friends' schoolroom Abby followed the Grimkés' progress through the state, cheering their every word in the polemical battle. Not all male abolitionists were as enthusiastic. Amos Phelps, who in a sense had started it all by taking a seat in Lynn's Methodist Church, now begged the sisters to state that they preferred speaking exclusively to women. They politely rejected his request but were "wrathy" when they received critical letters from John Greenleaf Whittier and Theodore Weld. Whittier chided them for asserting the rights of women at the expense of the slave while Weld, although insisting on his own belief in woman's equality, said that their discussions were "producing alienation in our ranks and introducing confusion. What is done for the *slave must be done now, now, now* whereas woman's rights are not a life and death business *now or never*."[18]

When Abby's school closed for a few weeks in September, she went to Millbury to see her mother and to meet the Grimkés, then lecturing in central Massachusetts. Although the stay at home brought back poignant memories of her father, it was brightened by the presence of three of her sisters: Lucy, still teaching in the village, and Diana and Lydia, who were visiting with their children. Around the breakfast table there was a chance to catch up with family news. Sister Nancy was ill; Sister Ruth and her husband had gone to the West, and it was "a sad disappointment" when Sister Olive, Abby's favorite, failed to arrive as expected.

After Diana and Lydia had left, Abby joined the Grimkés in Worcester, where they attended the quarterly meeting of the Massachusetts Anti-Slavery Society. The meeting in Brinley Hall was an exceptionally large one with a sizable delegation of women. Although they had come only as auditors, the *Liberator* reported that they listened "with tireless vigilance, lest some compromise of principle should be made. They will not be terrified by ecclesiastical anathemas, nor corrupted by clerical appeals." There was unconscious irony in this encomium, because some of the women were beginning to chafe at their silent role. During the debate Angelina several times shook her head in disagreement and murmured to Abby and Sarah. Abby urged her to speak, but Angelina, mindful of the criticism she had been receiving, shook her head. "The brethren will not like it," she said.

Abby, who had almost a schoolgirl crush on Angelina, questioned her idol's judgment for the first time. She questioned it again four months later, when they sat together at the society's annual meeting in Boston. In keeping with the abolitionists' policy of a free platform, a slaveholder had been permitted to offer a defense of slavery. During the debate that followed, Angelina whispered, "He has not been fully answered," and then, despairingly, "Oh! I wish I could speak." Abby begged her to take the floor, but she refused, repeating, "The brethren will not like it." This time Abby challenged her. "Is it better to listen to the brethren or to the divine voice in our own souls?" she asked. Angelina remained silent, but Abby still remembered the incident a half century later.[19]

Following the Worcester meeting, Abby invited the Grimkés to visit in Millbury. Proud to welcome them to her home and eager to show them hospitality, she almost overwhelmed the older women. At the end of three months of public appearances they wanted nothing so much as rest and quiet. Instead Abby and her mother planned a series of receptions and meetings. After their first evening at the Kelleys, when friends and neighbors arrived to greet them, Sarah came down with a cold, and Angelina privately noted, "We saw a room full of company. It was a wearisome time to my spirit."

56

The following night, when Sarah was scheduled to lecture in a meetinghouse in Millbury, it was raining so hard that Angelina insisted on going in her place. Abby drove her in the family chaise, an open two-wheeled vehicle whose hood gave scant protection from the storm. All along the way they passed groups of men braving the weather in order to hear Angelina Grimké. Once, as they drove up a steep hill, their horse lost its footing in the mud. Angelina was sure that the chaise would turn over, but Abby, calling on all her farm girl skills, pulled back sharply on the reins and kept it upright. Despite the downpour five hundred villagers turned out. "The Lord strengthened me & I spoke with ease for 1-3/4 hours," Angelina reported. By the time she lectured in Millbury on a second rainy night, she, too, had a cold, which laid her up for a fortnight.[20]

After bidding good-bye to the Kelleys, the Grimkés continued their tour for another month before returning to Boston for a much-needed rest. Abby went back to Lynn, full of new vigor. More and more she was beginning to think and speak for herself. William Lloyd Garrison had been under attack all summer for diluting the fight against slavery with extraneous issues, at first for his support of women lecturers and his condemnation of the Pastoral Letter, then for giving space in the *Liberator* to the writings of John Humphrey Noyes. A former divinity student who now espoused the doctrine of perfectionism—the quest for perfect holiness—Noyes had renounced his allegiance to the government of the United States because it was "trampling on its own Constitution; with one hand whipping a Negro, and with the other dashing an Indian to the ground." Declaring that he could no longer participate as citizen or voter in his country's "ungodly deeds," he asked in a letter to the *Liberator*, "Is it not time for Abolitionists to abandon a government whose President has declared war on them" and instead work for "Universal Emancipation from Sin?"*

Read today, Noyes's words may sound like fundamentalist preaching,

---

* Noyes went on to found utopian communities in Vermont and, later, in Oneida, New York. When he advocated not only communal living but communal marriage, most abolitionists parted company with him.

but in the context of a more religious period, when large numbers of people believed that the Second Coming of Christ would soon usher in the millennium, his writings were radical perhaps but not ridiculous. To Abby, his criticism of the United States seemed entirely justified. Andrew Jackson who had been president for most of her adult life was not only a slaveowner who bitterly opposed the abolitionists but a leader in a war of extirpation against the Indians. His successor, Martin Van Buren, although a northerner, did not promise to be much of an improvement. As a Quaker and a woman who lacked a vote anyway, she was not frightened by the thought of renouncing civil government. Even before her Millbury vacation she had convinced the Lynn Female Society to pass a resolution supporting Garrison's conduct of the *Liberator* and pledging fifty dollars to the paper. After Garrison published Noyes's letter, she wrote him again, expressing the hope that "the time is now *fully* come when thou will take a decided stand for *all truths*, under the conviction that the whole are necessary to the permanent establishment of any *single one*. I believe that the *Liberator* will not be rejected by many of its present subscribers should it *lay the axe at the root of the tree*, as expressed by [Noyes]. I make this statement not thinking it will have the least influence on thy mind in determining thy future course, but because I thought thou would like to know to what degree of the moral thermometer our sentiments had risen." The letter was signed "Thine for the *whole truth*, Abby Kelley."[21]

Her moral thermometer rose a few more degrees the following month, when Elijah Lovejoy, an abolitionist newspaper editor, was murdered by a proslavery mob in Alton, Illinois. His assassination angered thousands in the North who had never sided with the abolitionists but who saw his death as an assault on freedom of the press and their own civil liberties. Boston authorities granted the use of Faneuil Hall, the famed "cradle of liberty," for a protest meeting at which leading citizens mourned the martyred editor. Twenty-six-year-old Wendell Phillips, who was to become Abby's close friend, made his first major address at the meeting, launching his career as the abolitionists' eloquent spokesman.

Phillips defended Lovejoy's use of arms in his own defense, but Abby sharply disagreed. Although she saw to it that Lynn's Female Society raised twenty-five dollars for the editor's widow, she found it "shocking" that he had died with a gun in his hand. "He had better have died as did our Savior, saying 'Father forgive them, they know not what they do,' " she said.

"The subject of Peace has of late claimed much of my attention," she confided to Maria Chapman a month later. "Is Slavery the greatest sin of this nation? Is not something more required of us than what we are doing?" As corresponding secretary of the Lynn Female Peace Society she had been taking part in numerous discussions on the subject. Should one fight in a war for liberation? In a defensive war? In view of the commandment "Thou shalt not kill," was capital punishment justified? After William Ladd, the avuncular president of the American Peace Society, spoke in Lynn, he wrote to Abby to say that it was as wrong for the American patriots to take up arms in 1776 as it would be for slaves to fight for their freedom.

Abby's year of self-examination was drawing to a close. Although she was not yet sure what her future held, she was a different person than she had been a year earlier. As the anniversary of her father's death approached, she sat down to write a long letter to Sister Olive: "It is a snowy evening and I feel very much in a sober mood. . . . I pace the same old track, which is become so smooth that there is neither rise nor fall. My variety is made up in watching the progress of moral enterprises—Grahamism and Abolition and Peace—and these three questions are sufficient to take up all spare time. 'Tis great joy to see the world grow better in any thing. Indeed I think endeavors to improve mankind is the only object worth living for."[22]

4
THE CALL

The Grimkés ended their New England tour on a note of triumph with Angelina speaking before the state legislature—the first U.S. woman to address a political body—and both sisters lecturing at the Odeon, Boston's largest hall. After they had returned to Philadelphia, Abby received a note from Angelina and Theodore Weld announcing their engagement and asking her "presence & sympathy and prayers" at their wedding, to be held on the eve of the antislavery women's convention in Philadelphia.

Reactions to the impending marriage were illuminating. Almost all the men, conservatives who called Angelina "Develina" or "Miss Grimalkin" and abolitionists who admired her, agreed that she was "utterly spoiled" for domestic life. One man said that she could never be anything but "an obtrusive clamorer . . . repelled and repelling"; another had expected her to marry "a great strapping nigger." Abolitionist Lewis Tappan thought Weld was "showing great moral courage" by marrying her while Garrison warned that Weld's religious orthodoxy "would bring her into bondage unless she could succeed in emancipating him." John Greenleaf Whittier, who was Theodore's closest friend, wrote a half-bitter, half-comic poem titled "On Leaving Me and Taking a Wife," which began:

> *Alack and Alas! that a brother of mine,*
> *A bachelor sworn on celibacy's altar,*
> *Should leave me alone at the desolate shrine*
> *And stoop his own neck to the enemy's halter!*

The women were equally surprised but more generous. They rejoiced in Angelina's happiness while expressing concern that the marriage of "a public property" might cut short her work. Anne Weston thought the engagement "a complete triumph over the pastoral brethren who threatened *such* a woman with the withdrawal of man's protection" but confessed to Angelina that "I believed you had thrown yourself entirely beyond the ordinary lot of women and no man would wish to have such a wife."[1]

Abby, whose opinion of the marriage was not recorded, set out for Philadelphia in early May 1838, in the company of four other delegates from the Lynn Female Society. Staying with Mary Pennock, a Quaker member of the Philadelphia Society, she went to Angelina's sister's home on the evening of May 14 to attend the wedding.

Some forty women and men, black as well as white, were gathered in the parlor of the house on Spruce Street when Abby arrived. In addition to such abolitionist notables as William Lloyd Garrison, Henry B. Stanton, and Henry C. Wright, there was a sizable contingent from the Boston and New York female societies while Grace and Sarah Douglass represented the Philadelphia women. Because Angelina was marrying outside the Society of Friends, she would be disowned for breaching discipline; Quakers who witnessed the ceremony were also liable to excommunication. Therefore, Mary Pennock, Lucretia Mott, and other Quaker women had chosen to absent themselves, while Whittier solved the problem by waiting impatiently outside the door until the ceremony was over. Abby Kelley was one of the few Friends who ventured to break discipline and attend. She had begun to question many aspects of the society; this was her first quiet challenge to its restrictions.

Since Pennsylvania law did not require the presence of clergyman or magistrate, the couple had planned the marriage ceremony themselves. Theodore, ordinarily noted for his sloppy dress, was resplendent that evening in a new brown coat, white vest, and cravat when he opened the proceedings by addressing Angelina "in solemn and tender manner." Alluding to the "unrighteous power vested in a husband by the laws of the United States [he] abjured all authority save the influence which love would give to them over each other," Sarah reported. Angelina, wearing a new dress that matched Theodore's coat, responded by promising to love and honor him while carefully omitting the word "obey." After prayers from black and white ministers and a heartfelt outpouring from Sarah, Garrison read the wedding certificate and invited the guests to sign it. Abby was the first woman to step forward to sign the parchment scroll, following Garrison and Stanton; Maria Chapman's signature was the largest and boldest. "A more interesting service it never was my fortune to witness," she told a British friend. "It was an abolitionist wedding."[2]

The convention of antislavery women convened the next morning in Pennsylvania Hall, a large, luxurious building newly erected by a group of reformers and dedicated to the right of free discussion. With a pillared marble facade fronting on Sixth Street, its first floor contained lecture and committee rooms, a free produce store, and an office for the *Pennsylvania Freeman*, a weekly that Whittier was editing. Brilliantly lit by gas, a new innovation, its second-floor "great saloon" contained blue plush chairs for three thousand people, with a blue damask sofa on the platform.

Even before the women assembled for their 10:00 A.M. meeting, there were signs of trouble. The second-largest U.S. city, Philadelphia was only forty miles from the Mason-Dixon line demarcating North and South. It was the first port of call for steamers laden with cotton; its hotels and theaters were filled with southern planters, its medical schools with their sons. Merchants depended on trade with the South; white workingmen, unemployed during the current depression, competed for jobs with the city's large black population. In May 1838 William Penn's City of Brotherly Love was a powder keg waiting to be ignited.

As Abby and her friends walked to the hall they saw posters everywhere calling on "citizens who entertain a proper respect for the right of property and the preservation of the Constitution to interfere, *forcibly if they must* and demand the immediate dispersion of said convention." The threat hardly seemed real when they gathered in a first-floor lecture room to chose officers and take the roll. There were almost three hundred delegates and corresponding members, most from Pennsylvania but with a solid representation from New York and New England. Mary Parker was again chosen president; the vice-presidents included Maria Chapman, Anne Weston, Lucretia Mott, and Sarah Grimké. Three black women, Susan Paul and Martha Ball from Boston and Sarah Douglass, were respectively secretaries and treasurer while a fourth, Hetty Burr of Philadelphia, was on the business committee.

To Abby, who served on the arrangements committee and spoke on several resolutions, the convention seemed tame compared with the year before. Women had established their right to hold conventions. Wasn't it time now to meet and work with men? However, when it was proposed to invite men to a meeting that night, so many delegates objected that a compromise was reached. The women would hold a public meeting, but it would not be officially sponsored by the convention. Although Lucretia Mott hoped that "such false notions of delicacy and propriety would not long obtain," she agreed to be one of the speakers, along with Angelina Grimké Weld and Maria Chapman. Abby quietly resolved that she, too, would speak at the meeting.

By the time the women made their way to the hall after supper, the streets were filled with hundreds of men and boys, who jeered and catcalled as they approached. The sight of blacks and whites walking together brought shouted denunciations of the "amalgamationists." Inside, every seat and every foot of standing room in the "great saloon" were taken, with the women, for the most part, occupying the center section while the men filled the side aisles and galleries.

William Lloyd Garrison opened the meeting with a few words, then introduced Maria Weston Chapman, who was making her first public speech. As she began, a mob burst into the building and ran up the stairs, "yelling and shouting as if the very fiends of the pit had suddenly broken loose," Garrison said. "The audience rose in some confusion and would have been broken up, had it not been for the admirable self-possession of some individuals, particularly the women." Maria continued, bravely attempting to ignore the confusion—Sarah Grimké thought she looked like "an angelic being amid that tempest"—but her words could not be heard beyond the first rows.

Rocks and brickbats crashed against the windows as Angelina followed. A more experienced speaker, she was able to raise her voice above the tumult and to challenge her listeners. "What if the mob should burst in upon us, break up our meeting and commit violence upon our persons?" she asked. "Would this be anything compared to what the slaves endure?"

Then Abby Kelley rose. As she walked to the podium, the roars from outside and the shouts of "Order!" from within grew louder. No matter how panicky she may have felt, she appeared composed when she asked permission to say a few words. True to Quaker tradition, she had not prepared a speech ahead of time. "I have never before addressed a promiscuous assembly," she began. "Nor is it now the maddening rush of those voices nor the crashing of those windows, the indication of a moral earthquake, that calls me before you. No, these pass unheeded by me. But it is the still small voice within which may not be withstood, that bids me open my mouth for the dumb; that bids me plead the cause of God's perishing poor."

A fresh volley of stones struck the windows, punctuating her words as she recalled the story of Lazarus, the beggar, comparing the North with the rich man "clothed in purple and fine linen" and the slaves with Lazarus, ill, hungry, begging "to be fed with the crumbs that fall from our luxurious table. Look! See him there!" she exhorted her listeners. "We have long, very long passed by with averted eyes. Ought we not to raise him up? Is there one in this hall who sees nothing for himself to do?"

Amid the shouts and shattering glass she returned to her seat. Would anyone heed her? Or had she failed in her first attempt to move an audience? She did not have to wait long to find out. After Lucretia Mott closed the meeting with a few earnest words, Theodore Weld elbowed his way through the crowd to find her. A powerful orator himself, he put his hands on her shoulders and urged her to take the field as a lecturer. "Abby," he said in his vehement way, "if you don't, God will smite you!"

Abby had little opportunity to ponder her future, for the present was too threatening. When the women left the hall that night, they ran a gauntlet of taunts and threats. The next morning the crowd was larger and more unruly. Throughout the day's sessions the delegates passed resolutions and planned future work to an obbligato of "swearing and hallooing" from outdoors. Several times their deliberations were interrupted by messages from the Pennsylvania Hall Association. When an association spokesman requested that black women stay away from the evening meeting because their presence exacerbated the mob, Lucretia Mott read the request but thought "that our colored friends ought not to absent themselves" and hoped "that no one would be alarmed by a little *appearance* of danger." Speaking for the New England delegation, Abby Kelley concurred, saying that "not one" would stay away. A black New Yorker, too, thought it would be "selfish and cowardly" to shrink from danger. "Our friends have suffered much for us and shall we fear to suffer a little for ourselves?" she asked.

A second message requested the convention to remain in session without taking a supper break, in the belief that the mob would not attack the building while women were present. Mary Parker laid the request before the meeting. "Will you remain?" she asked. After brief deliberation the answer came: "We will." But a third message soon followed. The mayor had demanded the keys to the hall and was canceling all meetings.

As the delegates gathered their wraps, preparing to leave, Angelina proposed that the white women "protect our colored sisters while going out by taking each one of them by the arm." Two abreast, the women walked through a mob of some three thousand "fierce, vile-looking" men and boys.

After the women had gone, the mayor appeared on the steps of the building. He had been asked to call out the militia to keep order, but he told the crowd, "We never call out the military. You are my police." The mob got the message. After three cheers for His Honor, men carrying axes and wooden beams burst open the doors of the hall. Racing upstairs, they pulled down the window blinds, piled the plush chairs around the platform, adding books and papers for tinder. Then they opened the gas jets to set the auditorium on fire. The State House bell pealed an alarm, but the firemen turned their hoses on the neighboring buildings and let the hall continue to burn. The roof fell in, then the floors, as thousands watching roared their approval.

From the Pennocks' windows Abby could see the flames illuminating the night sky and could hear the cries of the mob, now fifteen thousand strong, as they ran through the streets in search of fresh targets. The next morning she joined the other delegates at the blackened, smoking ruins of Pennsylvania Hall—"the beautiful temple consecrated to Liberty," which was now a "sacrifice to the Demon of Slavery." Barred from nearby Temperance Hall, where they had planned to meet, the women trudged across town, whites again linking arms with blacks, to Sarah Pugh's schoolhouse on Cherry Street.

In this last convention session they pledged themselves anew to carry on the struggle. Abby reminded them to contribute "with unsparing liberality to the treasury of the slave." She also spoke in favor of a strong resolution against prejudice, which called on abolitionists to identify themselves with blacks not only in public places but "by visiting them in their homes and encouraging them to visit us, receiving them as we do our white fellow citizens." Some timid delegates opposed the wording, fearing it would lend credence to the enemy's charge of "amalgamationism," but her speech helped carry the resolution. Weeks later in Lynn she received a letter from Sarah Douglass thanking her "for having stood forth so nobly. It rejoices my very heart to meet with an Abolitionist who has turned her back on prejudice."[3]

Maria Chapman and Anne Weston had missed the final sessions of the convention. Exhausted by the frightening events of the past days, Maria had come down with a fever and Anne and other members of the Boston delegation decided to take her home. They had caught the night train to New York, but by the time they reached Stonington, Connecticut, where they could take a Boston boat, Maria's fever was raging and she was delirious. While the others went on, Anne brought her to a doctor, who, after listening to her incoherent babble, diagnosed brain fever. It was a chilling diagnosis, causing her friends to fear insanity, which her critics said was only to be expected of a woman who had stepped out of her sphere. Henry Chapman hurried to her side while the doctor applied leeches and ordered her heavy auburn hair cropped short. Weeks later Anne was able to report: "Her mind appears to dwell less on exciting events and abstract things. She answers questions and gives the Doctor some notion as to her state." Late in May she was finally well enough to return to Boston.[4]

Knowing nothing of Maria's breakdown at the time, Abby returned to Lynn by a circuitous route, stopping first to visit her sister Olive, whose husband, Newbury Darling, was a prosperous farmer in East Hampton, Connecticut. While staying at the Darlings', she organized her first small antislavery meeting in their village. From there she went to see her mother. To reach Millbury from the Darlings' meant taking a boat up the Connecticut River to Hartford, where she could catch the stagecoach for Worcester. While waiting for the mail stage, which did not leave until 8:00 P.M., she visited the Asylum for the Deaf and Dumb, the first free school for the deaf in the United States and a regular tourist sight for socially minded visitors to Hartford. Abby found it "one of the most interesting places I ever visited" and advised the Darlings to go there on their next trip to Hartford.

Reaching home the following morning, tired from her long journey, she was disturbed to find her hitherto prudent mother "keeping house in *great magnificence*—too great for my ideas of retrenchment," Abby wrote Olive. Albert and Lucy stayed with her occasionally "but not often enough to keep things within the *bounds of moderation*," and other family members who had been scheduled to visit had not arrived. Feeling that it was "entirely improper" for Diana Kelley to continue to live alone, Abby was deeply troubled by the time she returned to Lynn.[5]

Before reopening her school, she traveled to Boston with other Lynn abolitionists for the annual meeting of the New England Anti-Slavery Society. This was the first convention to be held in Marlborough Chapel, a large new hall that, like Pennsylvania Hall, had been built by reformers and dedicated to "the cause of humanity and free discussion." When it was rumored that the chapel would also be attacked by a mob, Boston's mayor promised to call out the constabulary if necessary. Although he was not an abolitionist, he recognized that a fire in the chapel would damage the adjoining Marlborough Hotel and threaten the safety of the whole city.

Although the women were still coming to the male antislavery society meetings as spectators, the leaders of the New England Society had decided to involve them more directly in the work. When the convention opened Oliver Johnson, Garrison's right-hand man, moved "that all *persons* present, whether men or women, who agree with us on the subject of slavery, be invited to become members and participate in the proceedings of the Convention." Because some who might have opposed the resolution had not yet arrived, it passed unanimously, and Abby and sixty-four other New England women enrolled as members.

On the first day of debate no women ventured to take the floor. Unaccustomed to their new status, they were unable to shake off the inhibitions of a lifetime. On the second day Abby could keep still no longer. In the morning session she spoke in favor of two resolutions. Later in the day she was appointed to a three-person committee, along with Oliver Johnson and Alanson St. Clair, to prepare an address to the ecclesiastical bodies of New England that would ask them to bear witness against slavery. Had Maria Chapman been present, the appointment might have gone to her. As it was, Abby Kelley was propelled into the limelight.

The limelight grew uncomfortably warm when a group of ministers, including Amos Phelps, protested against the admission of women. After the convention by a large majority had refused to reconsider Johnson's resolution, the ministers convinced Seth Sprague, the venerable seventy-eight-year-old president of the convention that Abby's appointment had been a blunder. Before calling the meeting to order the next morning, Sprague sought her out and asked her to withdraw from the committee. It was hard to say no to the silver-haired man whom everyone respected. For a moment Abby assented. Then, realizing what her resignation would mean to the cause of women, she sent word to Sprague that she had changed her mind. She would remain on the committee.

Her opponents had only begun to fight. The better part of the day was taken up with parliamentary maneuvers to oust her. First came a motion to reconsider yesterday's vote appointing the committee. When after a spirited discussion it was clear that this motion would fail, it was amended to discharge the committee altogether. If anyone had doubted the purpose of the amendment, Abby made this clear when she gave her maiden speech "in defence of the rights of woman, with much feeling, force and propriety. It was genuine eloquence," an observer said, and "she was loudly applauded by the audience."

When she sat down, her normally red cheeks doubtless flushed to a deeper color, she feared that the motion would pass unless others supported her. Nudging the man next to her, Charles Burleigh, a young lawyer turned abolitionist lecturer, she begged him "in an earnest whisper" to say a few words. Burleigh spoke "boldly and plainly to the point" and was followed by Henry C. Wright, who was also "on the right side." When the question was put, the motion lost. Still, Abby's critics were not satisfied. Twice they challenged the vote, and twice those in favor and those opposed were asked to stand and be counted. At last Seth Sprague announced that the motion to dismiss the committee had lost by a vote of eighty-two to fifty-five.

After Abby and her associates had presented their address to the convention, there was still another round of debate. "Rough-edged words were drawn across tender nerves" as the ministers attempted to bury the address by referring it to the business committee. Replying to them, Garrison was "as usual, direct, forcible, sound & discriminating" while Phillips "made a very neat speech, clear, to the point, short, well expressed & convincing," Burleigh reported.

The convention ended with the right of women to participate reaffirmed by a considerable majority and with an opposing "Protest" signed by seven clergymen, including Amos Phelps, which declared that the admission of women was "injurious to the cause of the slave" because it raised "an irrelevant topic." To many people's surprise, John G. Whittier, who had covered the convention for the *Pennsylvania Freeman*, supported the "Protest," writing that the admission of women had no more to do with antislavery than "a discussion of the merits of animal magnetism or the Mormon Bible."[6]

Nor was Whittier's the last word on the subject. Although the address to the ecclesiastical bodies had been couched in earnest, respectful language, most ministers refused to read it because a woman had helped prepare it.

"Miss Kelley's Memorial," as the address became known, was ignored by the General Association of Massachusetts Congregationalists, the body that had given the world the Pastoral Letter a year earlier, and was rejected by the Rhode Island Congregational Consociation after a minister reminded his listeners that when God wished to describe the ultimate debasement of His people, He had declared, "Children are their oppressors, and WOMEN RULE over them!" Since a woman had helped write the address and women had voted to accept it, it could be said that "Women ruled the convention" from which it came. Approving the action of the consociation, the *Christian Mirror* asked: "What man who loves his wife would feel honored by having her closeted in close consultation with two men, in the preparation of a public document? Or in hearing her raise her voice in the debates of a deliberative assembly? Would it not be as if she were shorn of her honor, her loveliness, her glory?"[7]

For the first time Abby was feeling the wrath of the clergy. Undoubtedly hurt by their intimations of immorality, she was nevertheless consoled by the approval of progressives in many parts of the country. The Philadelphia women who had begun to participate in the work of the Pennsylvania Anti-Slavery Society followed the convention in Boston with special interest. James Mott, who often wrote letters for his busy wife, told Anne Weston that "some of our northern gentlemen abolitionists are as jealous of any interference in rights they considered as belonging to them exclusively, as the southern slaveholder is, in the right of holding his slaves." What was needed, he said, was the recognition of "human rights."

The most supportive letter came from Sarah Grimké, who was living in New Jersey with Angelina and Theodore. She rejoiced, she told Abby, "that strength has been given thee to plead the cause of woman and that thou wast not dismayed at the opposition & hadst counted the cost. What thou hast done will do more toward establishing the rights of woman than a dozen books."

Theodore had heard from a friend, probably Whittier, that Abby had spoken so frequently in the convention as to make herself and her cause ridiculous. "I don't believe this," Angelina wrote Anne Weston, "but should like to hear how often she spoke & what effect was produced on the minds of those with whom thou hast conversed." Reassured by Anne that Abby

70

"had not rendered herself ridiculous," Angelina hoped that Abby would "feel it her duty to come out as a public lecturer" even though she would have "a fiery baptism to pass through."[8]

Indeed, Abby had been giving serious thought to lecturing. For some time she had felt what Friends described as "a divine call" to speak on behalf of the slave. Only opportunity and a lack of confidence in her ability had kept her silent. But when she returned to her teaching duties, Lynn suddenly seemed parochial and schoolwork stale. Her worry about her mother helped bring her to a decision. She would resign as a teacher and, as soon as the School Committee had found a substitute, would go to Millbury. After remaining with her mother at least through the winter of 1838, who could say what she would do?

While waiting for a replacement teacher, Abby attended a Fourth of July celebration in Lynn's Methodist Church. The Fourth, with its parades, fireworks, and patriotic speeches celebrating the Declaration of Independence, was a particularly painful day for black people. In recent years abolitionists had begun to organize countercelebrations in place of the "old rum-soaked, powder-smoked anniversary," to point up the irony of hailing a declaration that all men were created equal while millions remained enslaved. Wendell Phillips had come from Boston as the main speaker on this occasion, giving Abby what was probably her first opportunity to spend time with him. Tall, handsome, wealthy, the son of a former mayor of Boston and a graduate of Harvard College and Law School, Phillips had been the perfect model of a Boston Brahmin until he had fallen in love with Ann Terry Greene, a cousin of the Chapmans and Westons and an enthusiastic member of the Boston Female Anti-Slavery Society. Through Ann, whom he had married a year earlier, he had met the Boston abolitionists and had heeded the *Liberator*'s clarion call. Just Abby's age, he was rapidly becoming not only the movement's most talented orator but a policy maker as well. By the time Abby heard him in Lynn, he had been appointed general agent of the Massachusetts Society, replacing Amos Phelps, who had resigned because of his opposition to the admission of women to antislavery work.[9]

The Friends' School Committee found a teacher for Abby's school in late July, leaving her free to go to Millbury. While she organized the household and took care of her mother, who was ill, she continued to keep in touch with reform activities. Accompanied by her brother, Albert, she traveled to Boston in mid-September to attend a peace convention that promised to be more radical in its goal than the American Peace Society. The convention opened at Marlborough Chapel on September 18, 1838, with upward of 160 people present, a third of them women. Before attendance was taken, Garrison suggested that because mistakes were often made in preparing the membership roll, each individual should write "his or *her* name" on a slip of paper, "thus mooting the vexed 'woman question' at the very outset," he told his wife. "There was a smile on the countenance of many abolition friends while others in the Convention looked grave."

Smiles and frowns became more pronounced when Abby and a Rhode Island woman were appointed to the business committee, and Maria Chapman, now fully recovered from her illness, was named to the rules committee. Then Abby heightened tensions by calling to order the Reverend George Beckwith, leader of a group of moderates, when he spoke out of turn. "Endurance now passed its bounds on the part of the woman-contemners," Garrison reported as Beckwith and many of his followers angrily withdrew from the meeting.

Abby did more listening than talking during the remaining sessions. The convention leaders were attempting to move beyond the pacifism of Quakers and the American Peace Society that condemned all wars to a sweeping condemnation of organized government. Government that used coercive power to wage war, imprison wrongdoers, and uphold the institution of slavery was "a sin against God." From this conclusion it was only a short leap of faith to disassociate oneself from government altogether, thus refusing to vote, hold office, or sue for the redress of grievances.

Abby served on a committee that drew up a Declaration of Sentiments and a constitution for a new organization, the New England Non-Resistance Society. Written largely by Garrison, with rhetorical echoes of the Declaration of Independence, the document stated: "We cannot acknowledge allegiance to any human government. . . . Our country is the world, our countrymen are all mankind. . . . As every human government is upheld by physical strength, we therefore voluntarily exclude ourselves from every legislative and judicial body, and repudiate all human politics."

Rejecting the old code of an eye for an eye, a tooth for a tooth, the declaration said that "physical coercion is not adapted to moral regeneration; there is great security in being gentle, harmless, long-suffering and abundant in mercy; that it is only the meek who shall inherit the earth, for the violent who resort to the sword, shall perish with the sword."

Nevertheless, "While we shall adhere to the doctrines of non-resistance and passive submission to enemies, we purpose to speak and act boldly in the cause of God, to assail iniquity in high places. We shall employ lecturers, circulate tracts, form societies and petition our state and national governments in relation to the subject of Universal Peace. It will be our leading object to devise ways and means for effecting a radical change in the views, feelings and practices of society respecting the sinfulness of war, and the treatment of our enemies."

"Never was a more 'fanatical'* or 'disorganizing' instrument penned by man. It swept the whole surface of society and upturned almost every existing institution," the ebullient Garrison said. Others agreed. Maria Child, who had been unable to attend the convention but who followed the proceedings carefully, thought it "unquestionably the greatest event in the 19th century. Posterity will marvel at the early adoption of such transcendental principles." Ralph Waldo Emerson called the nonresistants "the simplest and purest minds" of his generation while his friend Henry David Thoreau borrowed from their ideas when he wrote his essay "Civil Disobedience" a decade later.

Despite their enthusiasm, nonresistance seemed an ultra doctrine, which was denounced not only by clergymen and politicians but by abolitionists who deplored the idea of not voting. They quickly denominated it "no-governmentism," thus adding another "ism" to the American lexicon. Nor

---

* Eventually the "fanatical" document circumnavigated the globe. In 1893 Count Leo Tolstoy experienced "spiritual joy" when he read of the New England nonresistants and reprinted excerpts from their Declaration of Sentiments in his treatise *The Kingdom of God Is within You*. The *Kingdom* in turn became an important influence on Mohandas Gandhi, whose philosophy later underlay the nonviolent civil rights revolution led by Martin Luther King, Jr., in the United States. (Green.)

73

did all members of Garrison's coterie rubber-stamp the declaration. Wendell Phillips, retaining a belief in original sin and skeptical of man's ability to perfect himself, never became a nonresistant, although he continued to work closely with Garrison in the antislavery cause. Edmund Quincy, another Brahmin whose father had been mayor of Boston and president of Harvard College, was willing to reject a government based on force but believed that some functions—coining money and legalizing contracts, for instance—were indispensable. After Garrison amended the declaration to answer his objections, Quincy joined the society and, with Maria Chapman, edited its bimonthly publication, the *Non-Resistant*. He later resigned his commission as justice of peace, explaining to the governor that he renounced "all allegiance to any government of man's institution."

With her Quaker background Abby had no hesitation about joining the Non-Resistance Society. Nor was she troubled by the charges of "no-governmentism," believing that the nonresistants were working toward the only true government, the government of God. Although the New England Non-Resistance Society was comparatively short-lived—its paper suspended publication in 1842, and its last convention was held in 1849—its philosophy continued to shape her life and political thinking. Even in the turbulent 1850s, when the nation was moving toward armed conflict, she remained a nonresistant, albeit a notably combative one.[10]

In Millbury Abby quickly fell into a routine of keeping house for her mother while attempting to decide about her future. A letter from Sister Joanna expressed "great anxiety" at the idea of Abby's becoming an antislavery lecturer. "She thought I should render myself quite contemptible and should not be able to accomplish any good," Abby wrote Olive. "She thinks too that I have nothing to recommend me to the public. I wish she would read her Bible and see if the great have ever been the special laborers in the Lord's vineyard. Who were the twelve apostles? Poor fishermen." But "I do not expect to do anything in that way for the present," she added. "I need much preparation and, besides, I must stay some time with mother."

Despite Abby's brave words, Joanna's comments had hit home. "I have nothing to start upon, no name, no reputation, no scrip, neither money in my purse," she wrote Theodore Weld in January 1839. "What is the greatest, is the feeling of my own inability for the work. I have not the gift. How can I make bricks without straw? Had I the qualifications of Sarah or Angelina, I could not wait another day." Yet the inner voice commanding her to speak grew daily more insistent. "When I feel the pressure I can do nothing but weep," she told Theodore. "My own family throw every obstacle in my way. They think me under a delusion. I am truly alone, if God be not with me."

She felt an "indescribable repugnance" to discussing her plans with anyone but the Grimké-Welds. The trio were living in a cottage in Fort Lee, New Jersey, across the Hudson River from New York. Weld commuted by ferry to the antislavery office, where he was compiling a documentary study of slavery, later published as *American Slavery as It Is*. At home Angelina and Sarah combed through some twenty thousand southern newspapers, cutting out articles and advertisements for the book. Abby helped, too, by collecting information on slaveowners and ex-slaves who were living in Millbury. Her most memorable interview was with Dolly Harris, a runaway slave now working as a domestic. "When I was separated from my husband I thought it was a dreadful thing," she told Abby, "but when they came and tore my child from me, it would have been easier for me to have died than to endure it." Although she had witnessed severe beatings, she had never been whipped herself. Nevertheless, she said, "We don't want to be slaves [even] if we are treated ever so well." Here were facts to be reported to Theodore and to be stored away as raw material for the future.

Angelina and Sarah were turning down all requests to speak, insisting that they were best serving the cause by proving that "the same woman who can hold an audience in profound attention" could also fill "the appropriate sphere of woman." Abby sometimes feared that they were being "swallowed up & utterly annihilated by Theodore." Nevertheless, she asked them what studies she should pursue if she entered the lecture field.

Angelina replied with an emotional letter that recalled her own feeling of "utter incapacity" and her "childlike confidence in God." As for "intellectual preparation," she thought that "Lecturing is something like School-keeping—a person may begin on a very small stock of knowledge.

The preparation to teach is found in the act of teaching—so it is in lecturing. The teacher is constantly *acquiring* the very knowledge he is imparting to others."

Writing in an execrable script that was barely decipherable, Theodore bluntly contradicted his wife. "God will help those who *help themselves*," he asserted. "Do, pray, make yourself familiar with the whole subject. Start reading today the existing Anti-slavery works, think out trains of argument to take up objections one by one. Do not leave an objection until you have not only fully answered it to your own mind but effectually shut up cavilling mouths. *Think*. Exercise your mind—do it habitually—do it thoroughly. Don't be content to use arguments you hear others use." He was sure "that *your manner of speaking* will be interesting and would I should think make people wish to hear you. I have no doubt that you will do good as a lecturer, *if you will prepare yourself by getting a thorough knowledge of your subject and by strengthening your reasoning powers &c.*" He also offered to send her the most important antislavery publications by way of the Boston antislavery office so that she could obtain them without expense. "Now keep a good heart, dear sister," he concluded. "Don't faint. Wait on the Lord and he will strengthen you."[11]

This was excellent advice. With the same intensity that she had applied to her studies in boarding school, Abby pored over the pamphlets he sent, memorizing facts and figures and training herself to anticipate arguments so that she would be able to think on her feet. She also studied at least one book on public speaking, Hugh Blair's *Lectures on Rhetoric and Belles Lettres*, which recommended plainness and simplicity of style rather than the overblown metaphors and turgid language that characterized contemporary oratory.[12]

She was still doubtful of her ability to carry on the work until during her daily Bible reading with her mother her eye fell on a passage from Corinthians: ". . . not many wise men, not many mighty, not many noble are called: But God hath chosen the foolish things of the world to confound the wise; and God hath chosen the weak things of the world to confound the things which are mighty." As she recalled the incident years later, she closed the Bible and told her mother, "My way is clear. How true it is that all great reforms have been carried forward by despised and weak means. The talent, the learning, the wealth, the church and the state are pledged to the support of slavery. I will go out among the honest-hearted common people, into the highways and byways, and cry, 'Pity the poor slave!' "[13]

Abby's moment of epiphany had come in the middle of a New England winter. She would have to wait until spring before setting out on her mission. Meanwhile, she used some of her corked-up energy to found a Millbury Female Anti-Slavery Society and to respond to the letters from Lynn that seemed to come by every post.

William Bassett's tiny, precise handwriting covered page after page as well as the margins of his paper as he ranged from the free produce movement and revelation versus scriptural authority to the attitude of Lynn Friends who were increasingly critical of his involvement in "the Abolition excitement." He had had his phrenological chart drawn up by Lorenzo Fowler, a leading practitioner of the new "science of the mind," which analyzed people's characters from the bumps on their heads. He applauded Mary Gove's lectures to women on physiology even though Friends took a dim view of her venture. "May she do much good," William commented. "I am more and more convinced of the need for a radical physiological reform." But he was not writing merely to chronicle the news. His letters were peppered with "What dost thou think?" and "I would be glad if thou would inform me how thou stands" while his signature was invariably "Thine for the truth."

The letters from women were more personal, including gossipy reports on marriages and births and regrets that they had so little time to write between teaching duties and obligations at home where most seemed to be caring for ailing mothers. Anna Breed Smith had enjoyed three of Mary Gove's lectures, two on bone structure and a third on the evils of tight corseting. "She is censured, ridiculed and misrepresented, of course, but has a pretty good share of independence," Anna reported. Anna and Aroline had also heard Edmund Quincy speak against slavery and had talked with him afterward at James Buffum's house. "He is not so ready a speaker as I had supposed, but there is an amiability and gentleness about him that makes him very agreeable," Anna wrote. Sophisticated Quincy confided that his greatest sacrifice to reform was to give up wine. "He said when his friends came to visit, it seemed perfectly ridiculous to them and at first to him not to treat them with *wines*."

They had heard, too, from Wendell Phillips and Maria Chapman. "Phillips as usual splendid and eloquent," Lydia Keene reported. "Spoke of our own Abby Kelley with well deserved praise. M. W. Chapman's lecture was well written but in the delivery almost everyone was disappointed."

On one point all her correspondents agreed. They missed Abby. Mary Robbins, who had taken over as corresponding secretary, thought that the Female Society needed her "awaking power." Voluble Anna best captured the leadership role Abby had played in Lynn. "I write," she explained, "because I wish to ask thee questions, that I may hear thy replies and receive instruction from them—because I wish to talk nonsense, that I may hear thy reproof and profit by it—because I wish to excite thy enthusiasm that the icy coldness of my own may be aroused—because I wish to induce thee to give ample evidence of thy singleness of purpose, that my own inefficiency may shrink into utter insignificance—because I wish to provoke thee to anger that a manifestation of thy Peace Principles may cause my own instability to hide its head for very shame."[14]

In Abby's absence, the Lynn women had not been idle that winter. Aroline had written a poem for the *Liberator* praising the peace convention and had also initiated a petition drive "to repeal all laws which make any distinction among its inhabitants, on account of color." Massachusetts statutes forbade marriage between whites and blacks or Indians and denied blacks and Indians the right to serve in the militia. The "petition of Aroline Augusta Chase and 785 ladies of Lynn" was summarily rejected by the legislature. One lawmaker asked "if these ladies desire a law authorizing them to marry blacks" while a second declared, "I don't believe there is a virtuous woman among them."

The press had a field day, taking its lead from the *Boston Post*, which suggested that "Caroline [always misspelled] Augusta Chase and 785 ladies from Lynn have petitioned the legislature for the privilege of marrying black husbands. This is rather a cut at the white Lynn beaux—or perhaps some of these ladies despair of having a white offer and so are willing to try *de colored race*."

Some 150 "white Lynn beaux" followed with a petition asking that Aroline and her fellow signers be given "the exclusive right to marry any Negro, Indian or Hottentot." Still another petition that protested the Lynn petition purported to be from Phillis Hathaway and other "ladies of color." The legislature concluded that the latter was "false and fictitious . . . designed as a scurrilous jest."

"I suppose you have heard of our *heretical* petition," Mary Robbins wrote Abby. "Many of its signers seem troubled by the ridicule. But it strikes me as a nail well hit. There is nothing like *shocking* people's prejudices sometimes. It reveals their extent and power and sometimes works much good."

The protest continued. Maria Child, who was rusticating in Northampton, Massachusetts, where her husband was raising beets in order to produce a "free" substitute for slave-grown sugar, asked the legislature to add her name to the petition of "the honorable women of Lynn," and seventy Boston women drew up their own petition. After a four-year campaign, in which women led the protests, the law against intermarriage was repealed.[15]

Abby remained on the sidelines during this campaign, nursing her mother, still quite ill, and taking care of a small niece, sister Diana Ballou's daughter, who was staying with her grandmother while her parents moved from their Rhode Island farm. Not until early spring was Abby able to go to Boston for a few days to attend the quarterly meeting of the Massachusetts Anti-Slavery Society.

The meeting opened on what was now a familiar note: "all persons" present were invited to take part. For the balance of the day and far into the night a debate raged over the relationship of the Massachusetts Society to the American Anti-Slavery Society. Ostensibly the dispute was about money. The Massachusetts Society had pledged ten thousand dollars as its annual contribution to the parent society—a larger sum than any other state society—but had failed to keep up its payments. The New York-based Executive Committee had dispatched Henry B. Stanton to Massachusetts to raise the money, thereby challenging the sovereignty of the state society.

Money, however, was only part of the problem. The conservative New Yorkers who controlled the national organization had long disapproved of the radical stands taken by Garrison and his supporters. Teaming up with Garrison's critics in Massachusetts, they had started the *Massachusetts Ab-*

olitionist as a competitor to the *Liberator* and had sent Elizur Wright, secretary of the American Society, to Boston to edit it. Stanton and Wright had lined up conservatives to attend the quarterly meeting, hoping to force the Massachusetts Society to withdraw from the national organization. Forewarned, the Garrisonians had come to the meeting determined to be conciliatory. They refused to be trapped into a debate on "no-government, no-voting" and readily agreed that the pledge to the national society must be paid. Silent through most of the sessions, Abby made one attempt to act as peacemaker by promising to contribute $50 herself and $150 from the Millbury Society toward the unfulfilled pledge. "Abby Kelley spoke very well indeed," Anne Weston said.

However, the time for sweet reasonableness had passed. Shortly after the meeting Amos Phelps resigned from the Massachusetts Society to protest its "woman's rights, no-government" position and helped form a rival organization, the Massachusetts Abolition Society. The signs of a split in the abolitionist movement were evident.[16]

After her exile in Millbury all winter, Abby enjoyed the chance to talk with Aroline, William, and other members of the Lynn delegation, as well as with Boston friends. She stayed with Thankful Southwick, a wealthy Quaker matron who, with her daughters, Sarah and Abby, had attended the women's convention in Philadelphia the year before. The morning after the meeting Maria Chapman and Anne Weston came to the Southwicks' to call on Abby. Inevitably the talk turned to the women's convention that was scheduled to meet in Philadelphia in May. Was Abby going?

Abby must have hesitated before replying. The position of women in the movement had changed so rapidly that she questioned the wisdom of separate meetings. Were women not thus segregating themselves and accepting an inferior position? A few weeks earlier she had written to Lucretia Mott to ask her opinion. Troubled by Abby's letter and by one from Maria Child, who wrote that a separate woman's meeting "always seemed to me like half a pair of scissors," Lucretia had been "at a loss how to answer." She agreed that those women who felt able to do so should "mingle in discussions with their brethren." But for the timid and for those not yet convinced that "in Christ Jesus there is neither male nor female," the separate conventions boosted women's confidence in themselves, thus preparing them for future work with men. Besides, she reminded Abby, Quaker women had always held separate women's business meetings as well as their meetings for worship with men. "Will not the ground thou assumes, oblige thee to withdraw from the Society of Friends?" She concluded by urging Abby to come to Philadelphia to discuss the question more fully, "and if it can clearly be shown that the course we are pursuing is inconsistent with the principles we recognize, I shall then be willing to abandon it."

Although Abby looked up to Lucretia, her contemplative winter had taught her to think for herself. So it was that she informed the group in the Southwicks' parlor that she had decided to pass up the women's convention and to go directly to New York in May for the annual meeting of the American Anti-Slavery Society. And after that, Anne Weston told her sister Deborah, "She has a call to lecture which she will obey."[17]

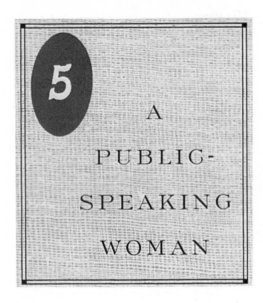

5

A PUBLIC-SPEAKING WOMAN

Leaving Lucy on the farm with her mother, Abby headed for New York in May 1839. On the dock in Providence she joined a group of Massachusetts delegates to the convention, including Anne Weston, the Southwicks, Wendell Phillips, and William Bassett. To save money, they decided to travel on "the $1 boat," but as soon as they crossed the gangplank, they had misgivings. With more than four hundred people aboard, the boat listed to one side and seemed about to tip over. Frightened, they switched to a more substantial steamer when they reached Newport. Rough seas soon sent the women to the ladies' cabin—"a scene of anguish," Anne Weston said—where everyone, including four babies, was seasick. By morning the wind had died down, and Abby and Anne were able to walk on deck and "have a good deal of talk." Disembarking at the Battery, Abby parted from her well-to-do friends, who were staying at the American Hotel, while she went uptown to the home of Rebecca Buffum Spring, a friend from boarding school days.[1]

When the anniversary meeting of the American Anti-Slavery Society convened in the Chatham Street Chapel on May 7, it was the largest convention the society had ever held, and its past year had been its most successful. More than three hundred new societies had been organized, the antislavery weeklies had upwards of twenty-five thousand readers, and there was even a balance in the treasury. Despite the healthy state of the society, the *Christian Mirror* reported that delegates "were on the tenterhooks of anxiety." Differences became apparent with the first business before the convention, the making up of the membership roll. Should "our beloved sisters" be counted, a Friend from upstate New York wanted to know. Certainly not, replied a Massachusetts minister. "The roll should be made up according to former usage. *Men* shall constitute the roll." When Oliver Johnson amended this resolution to substitute "persons" for "men," the battle was on.

All that day, until ten at night, and well into the next day the delegates spoke for and against the amendment. The old chapel with its uncushioned seats, uncarpeted floors and uncurtained windows was not only uncomfortable but an acoustical disaster. Speakers had to shout to make themselves heard above side conversations and the constant coming and going of delegates. Although a large number of women were present, only Abby Kelley and Eliza Barney, a Friend from Nantucket, spoke—"with excellent propriety and to great acceptance," the *Liberator* said. A less friendly paper reported that "not a word" of Mrs. Barney's speech "could be heard at a distance of ten feet" but that Abby "succeeded in making herself heard."

When a vote was called for at last, Gerrit Smith of Peterboro, New York, chosen as chairman because he belonged to neither faction, judged that the side favoring the admission of women had won. After Lewis Tappan, president of the society, questioned Smith's decision, another noisy hour was spent counting ayes and nays, state by state, delegate by delegate, until all agreed that the women's supporters were in the majority, 184 to 141.

However, the struggle was not over. Amos Phelps promptly moved that although women might sit as delegates, they could not speak, act on committees, or fill offices. In support of this motion, he pointed to the society's constitution, which spoke of "he" and "his." In a reply that presaged similar philological discussions more than a century later, Gerrit Smith said that he was not "perplexed" by the use of "his" in the constitution. "The whole human family is included in the generic term *man*. By common usage 'persons' includes women." For the balance of the day Smith carefully used the plural "they" instead of "he."

After Phelps's motion was defeated, Garrison declared: "Women are equally entitled to membership with men. We hail it as an era in the history of human rights. It is settled we trust irrevocably."

But there was no such word as "irrevocably" in his opponents' vocabulary. During the final days of the convention, while Abby Kelley and Eliza Barney served on committees and occasionally took the floor, the New Yorkers and their clerical allies from Massachusetts circulated a petition to protest the admission of women "because it was repugnant to the wishes, the wisdom, or the moral sense of many of the members" and would "bring unnecessary reproach and embarrassment to the cause of the enslaved" as well as be "at variance with the general usage and sentiments of this and all other nations." No, the question was far from settled.[2]

After the tense days on Chatham Street Abby was relieved to board the little ferry that took her across the Hudson for her long-planned visit to the Grimké-Welds. All spring she had been hearing from Maria Chapman and her sisters of the "vile" letters that Angelina had been writing in which she criticized the Garrisonians and refused invitations to lecture. Although Abby found it hard to believe that the women she revered had changed so radically, she was determined to rebuke them for failing to attend the anniversary and for holding themselves aloof from the struggle.

"I found to my own mortification that I had passed judgment before examining the witnesses," she wrote Anne Weston a fortnight later. Angelina, in the third month of a difficult pregnancy, was "truly very feeble." Her "labors in lecturing" and her work on *American Slavery as It Is* the past winter had "entirely prostrated her physical as well as mental energies," and Sarah and Theodore doubted that she would ever fully recover. Under

84

the circumstances Sarah did not think it proper to leave her, so she, too, was homebound.

Abby was deeply moved by the simple, principled way in which the trio lived. Theodore had introduced them to the Graham diet. The tyro housekeepers had learned to bake bread, which, with milk and vegetables from Theodore's garden, supplied their daily needs. When it was Sarah's turn in the kitchen, she went a step further toward austerity by cooking the whole week's meals in a day, thereby saving time for more important work. Abby, who had a strong streak of asceticism in her own nature, approved, finding "a spirit of love pervading all daily work and conversation."

Her admiration for their way of life did not prevent her from criticizing their politics. Theodore was unalterably opposed to nonresistance, believing that its espousal by abolitionists would damage the antislavery cause. Although he condemned the conduct of "Phelps & Co.," he was determined to remain outside abolitionist circles as long as the Garrisonians supported "no-governmentism." And where Theodore led, Angelina and Sarah followed.

Once, after Theodore had been "unsparingly severe" on those "who have adopted the will a wisp delusions of non-resistance," Abby came close to losing her temper. "What use will it be to undertake to reason with you?" she snapped. But he failed to reply. In the end her old affection for them won out. "I think I never passed a week more profitably," she told Anne Weston. "It was a school which called into exercise almost every better principle and feeling of the heart."[3]

Perhaps she had had a lingering hope of persuading Angelina to return to the platform and thus free herself from the necessity of taking up the work. If so, the hope was dead. Now she headed for her sister's home in Connecticut to begin her new life.

For the next nine months Olive and Newbury Darling's farm in East Hampton, in central Connecticut, served as Abby's headquarters while she traveled to nearby towns and villages, seeking audiences for her antislavery message. Connecticut was the most conservative of the New England states. Dominated by the Congregational Church, which had remained the official state religion until 1818, it had scarcely been touched by the Unitarian secession, which had opened Massachusetts to liberal ideas. The small state antislavery society was, in Abby's words, "highly evangelical," and the only abolitionist she knew was George Benson, Garrison's brother-in-law, who farmed in Brooklyn, some thirty miles from East Hampton. There were few, if any, female antislavery societies in the state.

Why then had she chosen Connecticut? In part because of Olive's sympathy and support; in part because she still felt diffident. If she were to make a fool of herself, as Joanna had predicted, she preferred to do it in strange territory rather than in front of friends in Lynn and Boston. And there may have been still another reason. Abby Kelley chose Connecticut precisely because it was difficult terrain. She was looking for a challenge, not an easy path.

The problem at first was to find any path at all. There were no guidelines for her to follow. When the Grimkés toured Massachusetts, local antislavery societies had scheduled meetings for them, Amos Phelps and Henry C. Wright had escorted them from town to town, and prominent people had showered them with hospitality.

In rural East Hampton and the villages nearby the few hardy souls who thought of themselves as abolitionists were lukewarm at best and lacking in organizational experience. "I am in a desolate land and hunger and thirst for sympathy," she wrote Anne Weston.

During her first week at the Darlings' she gave a lecture on prejudice against blacks, a provocative subject in a region where all knew the fate of Prudence Crandall, her boarding schoolmate, who, five years earlier, had been driven from her home after opening a school for "Young Ladies and Little Misses of Color." Abby probably said, as she would often say later, "I rejoice to be identified with the despised people of color. If they are to be despised, so ought their advocates to be." The lecture, she reported, "was well received, notwithstanding its ultra aim which I hoped would raise some feeling."[4]

Then, slowly, "way opened," as the Quakers said. She began to travel to other communities, speaking against slavery in churches if a minister would permit, otherwise in schoolrooms or town halls. She arranged for the meeting places herself, posting announcements of her lectures in public places. In nearly every town some friend could be found to give her lodging and to bring her to the next meeting place. And if no one volunteered, she made her way by stagecoach or on foot.

Her audiences were small, many drawn out of curiosity to see "a public-speaking woman." Sometimes those who had come to mock were won over by her earnestness and sense of urgency. In the Quaker tradition she spoke extemporaneously. None of her early lectures has been preserved, but a speech delivered to the Boston Female Anti-Slavery Society a year later, one of the few to be taken down verbatim, illustrates her approach.

"It is not my vocation to string together brilliant sentences or beautiful words. My mission has been back among the people, among the hills and the hamlets, and I have had no weapon but the gospel truth in its simplicity," she began. This was followed by an appeal to pride of country, a reminder of what the nation had stood for sixty years earlier. The Declaration of Independence was more than a schoolbook text for her listeners. Almost everyone in her audience had parents or grandparents who had taken part in the Revolution, when, "armed in the glorious panoply of liberty," as she phrased it, the new United States had hurled its principles across the Atlantic until "thrones trembled and monarchs blanched with fear."

But now—her voice grew deeper—the United States was "a hissing— a mockery—a reproach" before the rest of the world because this "freeest nation on earth" held one-sixth of its population in chains. "Her sons were free, yes! Free to snatch the babe from the arms of its father or mother— free to drag the husband and wife asunder. The very mention of *liberties* mocked the slave's anguish.

"We sit down and weep over the infants whom famine or superstition consigned to the waters of the Ganges," she reminded her listeners. "But the seventy-five thousand infants in the United States, annually swept down into the waters of darkness and despair—who wept for *them?* We shed tears over the East Indian widows whose religion it was to ascend the funeral pyre, but the widows of the United States—made widows by law— reduced to widowhood by system—and that system sanctioned by our religion—we had no tears for these.

"The mere existence of slavery in any section of our land" endangered everyone's freedom, she declared. "All the great family of mankind are

87

bound up in one bundle. When we aim a blow at our neighbor's rights our own are by the same blow destroyed. Can we look upon the wrongs of millions—can we see their flow of tears and grief and blood, and not feel our hearts drawn out in sympathy?"

With her voice rising and falling, her gestures emphasizing her text, she went on to call for action. "We must dislodge slavery from every place we visit," be "willing to withstand the wild waters of the opposition," and "be ranked with the poor and oppressed."[5] Speaking two or three times in each village, she succeeded in stirring the consciences of small groups of people, only to have them sink back into apathy when she departed. More than lecturing was needed. People must be stimulated to organize societies, circulate petitions, read antislavery newspapers. Although she had opposed separate women's conventions, she now realized that if she were going to build an antislavery movement in Connecticut, she must start with the women.

Mid-July found her in Hartford, the state capital, where a female antislavery society had been formed the year before. The society had disintegrated, but Abby hoped to revive it. Given a note of introduction to a Congregationalist minister reputed to have abolitionist sympathies, she called to solicit his support. The interview began inauspiciously when he refused to shake her hand because she was "a non-resistant and went for woman's rights." Despite his coldness, she held three meetings with Hartford women. However, in the face of clerical opposition, no one would take leadership. "Some do not dare to do anything for fear that they may get rid of their 'sphere,' " she wrote to the *Liberator*. Others say, "We shall not accomplish anything if we organize."

Before leaving the city, she approached another minister who had at first promised to help. He gave lame excuses for his failure to support her, "whiffling from one to another," she said, until he finally told the truth: "I am afraid you will get the fidgets into our women."[6]

Gradually, as her reputation grew, abolitionists in different parts of the state sought her out. One member of the state society thought that her lectures in Meriden "will prove as seed sown in a good soil. Many who would not like to have it known that they were convinced by a woman are thinking intently on the subject and will be ready by and by to avow their faith in the efficacy of freedom."

Her closest Connecticut friend became Erasmus Darwin Hudson, a physician six years her senior, who had given up his medical practice to work as a lecturing agent for the Connecticut Anti-Slavery Society. His critics called him "an ultra, simon pure unadulterated abolitionist," which meant that he and Abby saw eye to eye on most issues. With friends and relatives scattered through the state, he and his wife, Martha, were able to direct Abby to places where she would be welcome. In one letter to the Doctor, as she called him, she wrote appreciatively of the reception she had received from his friends: "They all seemed like our folks. Bro. and Sister Rhoads are just the stamp to make one comfortable. So affectionate. Tell Martha that her sisters don't appear so squeamish as she about women's talking."

Sometimes her path crossed Hudson's, and they traveled together. His diary for 1839–40 contains numerous references to "Sister Abby"; "Called on Sister Abby in Avon. Found she had not been able to accomplish anything. The minister opposed her. She hauled him over the Coals. . . . Hear that Sister A. Kelley's labors in Meriden were productive of much good & instrumental of a revival there. . . . Sister Abby's meeting well attended & a good impression made by her. She went home with us and had a fine visit."

The Hudsons, who lived in Bloomfield, only a short distance from Hartford and East Hampton, helped Abby keep in touch with her family. She and Olive wrote frequently, but postage* was expensive—twelve and a half cents for a letter, with parcels far higher—so Hudson often delivered her letters himself or left them in the post office in Hartford for Newbury to pick up.[7]

Olive and her husband were becoming ardent abolitionists. "N. has got so much excited about those slaves that he is going to start for H[artford] tomorrow morn before light. Don't laugh but he will speak in the court-

---

* Postage could be paid by either sender or recipient. Stamps were not introduced until 1847.

house," she wrote Abby. When they planned a big antislavery meeting, Olive wished that she could get some abolitionist leaders to speak. "If I could get Garrison by taking our old pleasure wagon and going after him he should be here. I want you to invite everybody that will come and open their mouths in behalf of the slave." Then, because she was proud of Abby's standing in abolitionist circles and conscious of her own educational deficiencies, Olive assured Abby that she need not fear that her "poor relations" would disgrace her.

Lucy also wrote long, chatty letters. Mother was "generally pretty well for her" although she had tired herself on a visit to Albert's. Lucy was keeping house "after a fashion" while teaching school and, in her spare time, stitching shoes to earn extra income. A young man whom she liked was now squiring someone else, but, twenty-year-old Lucy emphasized, *"There is as good fish in the sea as ever was caught even if I don't happen to get any of them."* Mary Gove and her family had boarded with the Kelleys recently and had converted Lucy to the Goveite diet, which was similar to Graham's. In fact, Lucy had become so much of a convert that when she broke the diet to eat some doughnuts, she was sick all the next day.

Sister Joanna, who, with her husband, Amos Ballou, was visiting in Millbury, added a postscript. Despite her misgivings about Abby's mission, she, too, was attending abolitionist meetings. In Worcester the week before, she had learned from William Bassett that Friends in Lynn were going to disown Mary Gove because her lectures were "a reproach" to the society. "What could be more absurd," Joanna commented. "If I had some of those Quakers I would sputter a little moral suasion or condemnation."[8]

Reassured that her mother was well taken care of, Abby decided to stay in Connecticut through the fall and winter. When she left Olive's in July, she had carried little more than a change of clothing. The logistics of travel then were infinitely more difficult than they are today. There was no ready-made clothing; even stockings and underwear were homemade. Consequently, with the first chilly days of fall she sent an urgent message to Olive asking for the cloak that she had left behind. Olive not only sent the cloak but packed a quilt and other warm things in a small trunk, which was forwarded to Abby with the help of Dr. Hudson and the antislavery network.

Abby had started out with a purse as light as her wardrobe. In the tradition of Friends, who disapproved of a paid ministry, she refused to accept a salary as a lecturing agent or to ask for contributions at meetings. When she ran out of money, then would be the time to go home. The time never came because someone always came forward to help. Once, when her funds were low, the men and women who had heard her lecture spontaneously put money, including a gold coin, on the desk in front of her when they left. On another occasion, when she had only ten cents in her purse, she received a letter from Francis Jackson, the Boston merchant who was president of the Massachusetts Anti-Slavery Society. It contained five dollars and the wish that she would use it "for any little comfort" on her travels.[9]

While speaking against slavery, Abby also found it necessary to defend her right, as a woman, to speak at all. When Elizur Wright, now a leader of the anti-Garrison forces in Massachusetts, scoffed at women activists, saying that they had no desire to take part in meetings with men but were manipulated by a "clique of woman's rights men," she dashed off an indignant letter to him, with a copy to the *Liberator*.

In the past women had been led by "the great 'clique' of arrogant 'lords of creation' " and had found it difficult to "slip the bridle," she wrote. But nowadays this was changing. Women not only were willing but considered it "of high obligation" to take part in antislavery meetings. They had held back "as our colored friends are now kept back, even by some who professed to be free from prejudice. If you could imagine a colored man's feelings, when kept at bay by his white brother, then you can have some faint conception of a woman's heart, when she awakes to a sense of her true position as a responsible being and sees herself fenced in by the iron prejudice of centuries.

"When at the N[ew] E[ngland] convention a year ago I offered a few words, I had not the most distant expectation of being sustained by the meeting. But I had well counted the costs, and had decided to obey the dictates of my conscience, [even] if all my friends should turn against me." And there were many others who felt as she did. "Be not deceived; this is no freak of the hour." In order to work for the antislavery cause, women were willing to endure "scorn, contempt and ridicule. We are happy that some brethren have extended their sympathy and encouragement. With these and others who are not ashamed of our company, we will continue to labor for the breaking of the yoke." She signed her letter "For the truth at whatever cost."[10]

Her letter was a convincing message to the already convinced, the readers of the *Liberator*. But she must also reach the people of Connecticut. After sending several letters which were ignored to the Reverend E. R. Tyler, editor of the *Connecticut Observer*, a weekly that professed to believe in "free discussion," she called on Tyler during a visit to Hartford and convinced him to publish a series of articles on "The Woman Question." Her first appeared in the *Observer* on February 3, 1840.

Speaking for women who wanted "to leave the world better than they found it," she took as her thesis a statement of Sarah Grimké's: "Whatever ways are right for men to adopt in reforming the world, are right also for women." Buttressing this in one, two, three fashion, she argued that the human mind was the same "whether enveloped in a black or white, a male or female exterior," that women were endowed with the same moral powers as men and thus must employ the same measures to advance their cause. To reduce the objection to women speaking in public to an absurdity, she reported a conversation she had had with an eminent Doctor of Divinity:

"Said I to him, 'If fifty gentlemen and as many ladies were in your parlor, and any question of religion or morals should be under discussion, would it be wrong for the ladies to take part?' 'Certainly not,' said the Dr. 'Well, suppose this company should appoint a chairman and secretary— would it then become wrong for the women to speak?' 'O no,' said the Dr. 'Then, suppose they were to remove from your parlor to a public hall or meeting-house, would it then become sinful for the women to open their lips?' 'No, no,' said the Dr. 'but public opinion is against it.'

"Let us listen to this omnipotent Public Opinion, and hear what it says. Women may talk in congregations, large or small, in parlor, kitchen, hall, if the formalities that are adopted in meetings are laid aside. At the levee where hundreds are assembled, they may pour out their treasures on all ears. But if the name, levee, should be changed to meeting, public feeling would be most grossly outraged.

"Public Opinion says, that, although men may save time and the wear of lungs by speaking to large assemblies when acting in order, yet women must speak to disorderly assemblies, whether large or small. Will Sir Public Opinion show how it becomes sinful to speak in orderly meetings, when it is no sin to speak in disorderly ones?"

Abby concluded by appealing to common sense rather than public opinion as a guide. Unfortunately common sense lost the argument. When she submitted her second article, Tyler refused to publish it. Too many of his readers objected.[11]

When Abby returned to Millbury in March 1840, she wrote to Garrison to sum up her first nine months in the field. Connecticut's "true-hearted abolitionists" were so few and scattered and so glad to have help that they had not yet divided on the "woman question" or begun to battle about "no-governmentism." Only twice in the sixty-five meetings that she had held in the central and western part of the state had ministers claiming to be abolitionists criticized her. Even in conventions of county and state antislavery societies, she had been permitted to speak, with few questions raised about propriety. She had not moved mountains, to be sure, but she thought that a beginning had been made.

Publishing her letter on the first page of the *Liberator*, Garrison commented: "She has exhibited a great deal of moral courage, benevolence and firmness of purpose, in thus attempting to make good the loss of the Grimkés, and to hasten the great American jubilee. If she has not received so much *éclat* as attended the labors of those excellent women, she has nevertheless devoted herself not less unreservedly to the cause of liberty and peace, and labored not less arduously. May she still find it in her heart to remain in the anti-slavery field, which is eminently her 'appropriate sphere.' "[12]

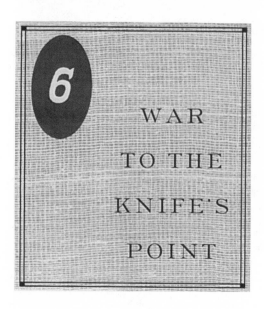

6

WAR
TO THE
KNIFE'S
POINT

A bby's work in Connecticut had kept her away from the battle that was rapidly dividing the abolitionists. After the 1839 anniversary meeting the New York leadership, largely Presbyterian, and its Congregational allies in Massachusetts, stepped up its effort to wrest control of the movement from the Garrisonians. No single issue—not the "confounded woman question," nonresistance, or political action—was the major cause of the division. Rather, there were philosophic as well as personality differences that divided the two groups.

The founders of the American Anti-Slavery Society had believed that by relentless propaganda—through lectures, newspapers, meetings, petitions—they would gradually convince northerners that slavery was wrong.

Once this had been accomplished, all the institutions of the North—the church, the state, the press—would bring pressure on the South to effect a change. Eight years of persistent propaganda had seen the proliferation of antislavery societies, but their members still made up only a small minority of the population. No major religious denomination had gone on record opposing slavery or had broken with its southern affiliate that supported the institution. Regularly refusing to receive antislavery petitions, Congress had passed gag laws silencing the few antislavery men in the House. A Quaker-led boycott of slave goods—the free produce movement—was proving ineffective.

The New York leaders who controlled the Executive Committee of the American Society nevertheless favored continuing the struggle along traditional lines. They believed that American democracy was basically sound, with only minor flaws in need of correction. Once slavery was abolished, there would be little need to tamper with other aspects of American life. Some of their adherents, moreover, men like Elizur Wright, Henry B. Stanton, and James Birney, wanted to shift emphasis by organizing a third party, the Liberty party, whose candidates would be pledged to antislavery.

William Lloyd Garrison and his followers in New England had come to view slavery as not only a moral issue but one that was deeply embedded in the social structure of the nation. All-powerful in the South, its supporters were also influential among northern merchants and in Washington. Slavery had betrayed the ideals of the American Revolution and had corrupted both church and state. Its tyrannical spirit stifled freedom of expression, fostered inequality, and supported war. To root it out required radical methods of agitation and an eventual restructuring of American society.

The conservative New Yorkers and their Congregational allies in Massachusetts—led by Amos Phelps—believed that the Garrisonians, many of whom had left the churches of their youth, were laying themselves open to the charge of heresy. The harsh language with which they attacked churches, their acceptance of women as partners in disregard of biblical authority, and their campaign against segregation in the North were alienating thousands of supporters. Even northerners who believed that slavery was wrong were shocked to see women on the lecture platform and blacks sitting alongside them in churches and trains. To this catalog of differences,

Wright and Stanton pointed out that since many Garrisonians had scruples against voting, they would also withhold their support from the newly organized Liberty party.

The Garrisonians replied that only harsh language and confrontational tactics could effect a radical change in northern public opinion. Not only was it *right* to accept women and blacks as equals, but they were proving to be valuable allies. As for political action, even those who did not subscribe to nonresistance held that politics was the wrong arena in which to fight. Politics was the art of the possible; politicians compromised and made deals in order to survive. The abolitionists must remain in the vanguard, not form coalitions that would inevitably dilute their message. Nevertheless— and here they attempted to be conciliatory—the antislavery platform was broad enough for all viewpoints. People could still unite on the single issue of abolition while disagreeing on other questions.

Following the quarrel in the pages of the *Liberator*, Abby dubbed the conservatives' position as "abolition made easy." Her brief experience in the field had convinced her that only a hard struggle would win people to a cause that threatened their basic assumptions about themselves and their country. From Connecticut she watched as both sides mobilized their forces.[1]

Amos Phelps and his fellow ministers organized day and night to convince local antislavery societies to break with the Massachusetts Anti-Slavery Society and affiliate with their new Massachusetts Abolition Society. When Garrison charged that there was a clerical plot to destroy the *Liberator* and the Massachusetts Anti-Slavery Society, he was not being paranoid. "Don't fail to write to every orthodox clergyman on the Cape to be on hand," one "clerical plotter" advised Phelps. "Have an eye on Bristol Co. If they notify a meeting, send in a good stock of agents to drum up. Don't fail to have Scott in New Bedford & Colver in Fall River beforehand to pick open the eyes of the Methodists and Baptists."

While the ministers concentrated on activating the clergy, Elizur Wright, editor of the *Massachusetts Abolitionist*, and Henry B. Stanton raised political issues in hope of embarrassing the nonvoters among the Garrisonians. With the 1840 presidential election only a few months away, Wright urged Stanton to see that the Liberty party nominated candidates for office. "Unless you do take such a stand, our new organization [in Massachusetts] is a gone case," he warned. "It has been, *inter nos*, shockingly mismanaged. Everything has been made to turn on the woman question."[2]

The Garrisonians were equally energetic. Maria Chapman, who said she had felt "dull and idle" while the "unnatural union" with the conservatives lasted, was exhilarated by the struggle. "War to the knife's point," she scrawled across one memorandum. Writing to her sister Deborah, who was teaching in New Bedford, she forwarded handbills announcing a county antislavery meeting and told her to see that "the resolution about the New York business run thus, Resolved that 'we are surprised and pained at the rash, unkind and unbrotherly course taken by the ex. com. of the Am. Society' and most heartily approve the spirited and judicious course of the Mass." In another message she asked Deborah to obtain a letter that Phelps had written to John Emerson, principal of Deborah's school. If Emerson would not turn it over to Garrison "as a specimen of the letters now in circulation to break up the Mass. Anti-Slavery Society, at least let it *somehow or other get into my hands. I must have it. I must.*"

There were no telephones to tap in those days, but private letters written by the opposition "somehow or other" fell into Garrisonian hands. Maria almost surely received a copy of Phelps's letter to Emerson and sent it to people like Gerrit Smith and Samuel J. May to convince them that "men will sometimes lie." Elizur Wright's letter to Henry Stanton "somehow or other" reached Garrison. He gleefully published it in the *Liberator*, not once but five separate times.[3]

Despite their efforts, the conservatives failed to win many adherents in Massachusetts, where most abolitionists remained loyal to Garrison. They were able to form small splinter groups in Essex and Worcester counties, but their one outstanding success was in the Boston Female Anti-Slavery Society. "The seeds of evil"—Maria Chapman's phrase—had been germinating there since the publication of the Pastoral Letter. In 1839 they began to bear fruit. At a suspiciously large meeting in April the Garrisonians noticed many new faces. Lydia Gould, a black member of the Board of Managers and the daughter of a conservative minister, objected to giving one hundred dollars to the *Liberator*, as was customary, while treasurer Lucy Ball moved that five hundred dollars of the money to be raised at the society's annual fair go to the American Anti-Slavery Society instead of the Massachusetts Society. When Maria tried to amend Lucy's motion by pledging a thousand dollars to the Massachusetts Society, her amendment was defeated. "Mrs. Chapman roared like a *female bull!*" Henry Stanton wrote Elizur Wright. "The debate took a wide range—caps, ribbons, curls & flounces flew at each other most furiously."[4]

If Stanton was amused, Maria was not. She had been aware for some time that Mary S. Parker, the society's longtime president, was under pressure from Amos Phelps, her pastor, to break with the Garrisonians. Lucy and Martha Ball may also have been Phelps's parishioners; at least Maria lumped them with Parker when she wrote of "the wicked Phelps & his harem, the Boston Female 'Spiritual wives.' " Add to them conservatives Lydia Gould and Catharine Sullivan, the society's vice-president, and there were a surprising number of women in positions of leadership who opposed the Garrisonians.

"The *Liberator* folk" did not take this first defeat lying down. Since the proceeds of the society's fair were to go to the American Society, they organized a "fair of individuals" for the benefit of the Massachusetts Society. The "individuals," led by Maria Chapman, had been running successful fairs for years. Most of them were women of means and social standing with friends throughout the state and in England, where abolitionists contributed generously. Their fair brought in eleven hundred dollars; the official fair only seven hundred dollars.

The next contest took place at the annual meeting in October 1839, when the society's officers were to be elected for the coming year. Maria Child, who had been persuaded to lend her not inconsiderable prestige to the gathering, nominated Thankful Southwick for president, pointing out that the society needed an impartial head and that "in all kindness to Miss Parker that was not the case at present." When the election was held, however, Catharine Sullivan announced that Parker had been reelected by seventy-seven to thirty-five. Shouts went up from all over the hall. Some doubted the count; others declared that nonmembers had voted. Before a recount could be considered, a motion for adjournment was made. As if on cue, Lucy Ball opened the door, announcing, "The meeting is adjourned. Ladies, go home." In the confusion that followed, further business could not be transacted; the meeting adjourned to meet again in a fortnight.

When the society reconvened in a spacious hall below Marlborough Chapel, everyone and her sister were there: Mary and Lucy Parker, Martha and Lucy Ball, and, on the other side, Henrietta and Catharine Sargent, Thankful Southwick and her daughters, and all five Westons, including Maria. With twice as many present as at the previous meeting, the vote was taken by roll call. As secretary pro tem Lucy Ball kept the tally. When she announced that 150 women had voted for Parker with 65 opposed, there was an uproar. Caroline Weston insisted that she had heard 138 votes against 82, and Deborah corroborated her figures, while others declared that their names had never been called.

Since the society's constitution required a two-thirds majority, challenges to only a few votes would mean Parker's defeat. Coolly ignoring the objections, Parker proclaimed, "Miss Mary Parker is elected president." After a second roll call she announced that Catharine Sullivan had been reelected vice-president. "I doubt the vote," a member called out.

"Take your seat," Parker ordered. "Then you may doubt it till the day of your death."

When similar high-handed tactics resulted in the election of conservatives to the other offices, she adjourned the meeting.

The Garrisonians had been routed, but not for long. Seventy-eight members of the society signed a statement, published in the *Liberator*, saying that they had voted against Parker. Further, they had gone over Ball's tally sheets and had found seventeen more anti-Parker votes that had not been counted. Despite what seemed overwhelming evidence that she had failed to receive a two-thirds majority, Miss Parker again ruled in her own favor.

At the April 1840 meeting, a year after the "painful and disgusting" wrangle had begun, the conservatives came up with a new tactic: a motion that the Boston Female Society be dissolved. Shocked, the Garrisonians attempted reconciliation. Surely they could find people on whom all could agree, Anne Weston said. One by one, "the ladies of the minority," as Parker called them, argued against breaking up the society. Ignoring their pleas, Parker took a quick poll, then declared, "I pronounce the Boston Female Anti-Slavery Society dissolved."

Although she was eight months pregnant, Maria Chapman was still quick on her feet. "The Boston Female Society is *not* dissolved but will hold a meeting to choose officers on Saturday next at Marlborough Hall," she announced.

Three days later 120 members of the society assembled and, with Maria Child as president pro tem, agreed that the report of dissolution was premature. Without a dissenting vote, they chose a new slate of officers and reaffirmed their loyalty to the Massachusetts Society and William Lloyd Garrison. "We go forward joyfully in the holy work of abolishing slavery," they concluded.[5]

The Garrisonian women continued to work effectively in the Boston Female Anti-Slavery Society until the Civil War. However, there was an ugly aspect to the fight that was never mentioned in Maria Chapman's account, "Right and Wrong in the Boston Female Anti-Slavery Society," or in numerous private letters of the participants. Except for Mary Parker and Catharine Sullivan, the conservative leaders and many of their followers were black.

The radical women prided themselves on having overcome prejudice. They had petitioned for the repeal of the intermarriage law, opposed segregation on steamboats and trains, and had given heartfelt support to the resolutions against prejudice passed at the conventions of antislavery women. Hadn't they, in fact, elected the Balls and Lydia Gould to office to demonstrate their belief in equality? They had, indeed, and surely some of their barely concealed anger at the black women was a feeling that they had proved ungrateful.

Despite their avowed freedom from prejudice, their private letters reveal unconscious, if not overt, racism. The Westons did not hesitate to use the word "nigger" in their correspondence, putting it in quotes to show that they were joking. Maria Chapman betrayed her feelings of superiority when she told a British abolitionist: "The inhabitants of Massachusetts are of pure English descent. New Englanders will always cherish the thought that they share with you a common ancestry, that in their veins and yours flows the 'sangre azul'—the azure Gothic blood." Others belied their color blindness by commenting on the light complexion of Susan Paul or Martha Ball. To prove her own lack of prejudice, Henrietta Sargent went in the opposite direction, telling friends that she planned to have Samuel Snowden, a conspicuously dark-skinned minister, pray at her funeral. "I couldn't help laughing to think how my relatives would act," she said. "They would come into the room pretty sober and then when they saw Father Snowden, they would look all confounded, and I'd look down and laugh."[6]

The Ball sisters, who had been active members of the society from its first days, clearly resented Maria Chapman and her sisters. At the 1839 annual meeting, when Maria piously said that she knew nothing of persons but would vote for principles, Lucy Ball retorted, "Yes, you do know persons, Mrs. Chapman. You think nobody is an abolitionist who does not think as you do. You told us the other evening you did not consider us abolitionists." And at a later meeting, when Caroline Weston said that the officers' conduct could not be tolerated, Martha Ball slyly asked, "That is to say, you will mob us?"[7]

Behind the scenes both radicals and conservatives vied for the support of Boston's black women. In this, the radicals were more successful. Garrison, the first person to link the fight against slavery with support for the free people of color, was universally beloved in black Boston. While black men called meetings in his support, their wives and sisters, women like Lavinia Hilton, Louisa Nell, and Susan Paul, worked with the anti-Parker faction. They were joined not only by Phillis Salem, the Southwicks' servant, but also by such prominent women as Nancy Prince, who was beginning a lecturing career after nine years at the Russian court.

In addition, someone, probably Anne Weston, drew up a list of twenty-six names, labeling it "Women of Colour who handed in their names to Miss [Lydia] Gould previous to the meeting—i.e. the day before" but who were never entered on the membership roll. To be sure that this was not lost on the black community, Anne reminded the society that "one of the most painful features" of the factional fight was that those members "least able to vindicate their own claims" were ignored by the officers in order to further "their own election."[8]

The conservative women organized a short-lived Massachusetts Female Emancipation Society. Seeking support for it, Martha Ball wrote to the Philadelphia Female Society and to Elizabeth Pease, a leader of the British antislavery women. As an outsider she might have known that her appeal would win little sympathy. Responding for the Philadelphians, Lucretia Mott wrote that she approved of Maria Chapman's defense against the "high-handed measures" of her opponents while Pease simply forwarded Ball's letter to her friend William Lloyd Garrison for comment. Ball gave up schoolteaching to work as an agent of the Massachusetts Abolition Society. As late as 1846 she was still an abolitionist, still at war with the Garrisonians.[9]*

Abby Kelley, of course, sympathized with the reconstituted Boston Female Society,[10] but by the spring of 1840 it was clear that the women's fight was only a dress rehearsal for a larger battle, the struggle for control of the American Anti-Slavery Society. Both sides recognized that the anniversary meeting in May would be the final conflict. They called out their troops accordingly.

"We are preparing," Henry Stanton wrote Amos Phelps. "We shall generally go for dissolution, unless we can open the whole field as it used to be. Someone *must* come on here & get out the voters." Phelps responded by redoubling his efforts. "*Every* minister, influential deacon, or active sectarian, for miles and miles round, has been furnished with the N. York side of the case. Private letters *innumerable* have been written in every direction," Maria Child reported from central Massachusetts.[11]

The Garrisonians were equally industrious. While the *Massachusetts Abolitionist* charged that Abby Kelley in Connecticut, Charles Burleigh in Pennsylvania, and Henry Wright in New York were "mustering the clans to the convention," the *Liberator* kept up a weekly drumbeat to expose the "cloven foot" of its enemy. The paper's claim that the New York leadership planned to disband the American Society if it could not control it received startling confirmation in April from James S. Gibbons, the only Garrisonian on the Executive Committee. The committee had given away the *Emancipator*, the official paper of the national society, turning over subscription lists, files, even desks and chairs to the conservative New York City Anti-

---

* Lucy and Martha Ball survived until 1891 and 1894 respectively. During their later decades they lived as whites. (Death Records, Department of Vital Statistics, Boston, Massachusetts.)

Slavery Society. It stated that there were insufficient funds in the treasury to continue the paper, but as Lewis Tappan explained many years later, the true motive was to keep the paper from falling into the hands of the Garrisonians.[12]

This "extraordinary" giveaway spurred the Massachusetts Society to greater efforts to get delegates to New York. John A. Collins, then general agent of the Massachusetts Society, chartered a special train and steamboat that would make the round trip from Boston to New York for only five dollars; in New York lodgings would be provided for fifty cents a day. "A special invitation is given to our colored friends to be fully represented as they will be admitted to equal privilege with others, both in the cars and on board the boat," Collins's announcement concluded.

On May 11 Abby, accompanied by her sister Joanna, went to Providence to meet the Boston travelers. Arriving early, they boarded the *Rhode Island*, "one of the safest and best boats in the country," and stood at the rail as hundreds of delegates from New England swarmed up the gangplank. Edmund Quincy, who was standing with them, thought the scene "most interesting and exciting. Every moment I met with an unexpected friend. About 450 were on board." Abby greeted the large contingent from Lynn as well as the Westons, Southwicks, and other Boston women. She may also have noticed a tall, intense young abolitionist from New Hampshire whose name was Stephen Symonds Foster. She would see him again.

After a glorious sunset the travelers crowded into a cabin for an evening of antislavery speeches and songs. "There never has been such a mass of *ultraism* afloat," Garrison reported. Their feeling that they were bound together by a high and noble purpose compensated for a lack of comfort when they retired. The ladies' cabin was overflowing. The two tiers of berths were filled, every foot of floor space covered with mattresses, and some were obliged to sleep on deck with waterproofs and shawls for covering and carpetbags for pillows.

Arriving in New York at dawn, the weary travelers repaired to their lodgings. The well-to-do, including Quincy, the Westons, and Southwicks went to a downtown hotel. Those who had signed up for the cheap lodgings went to St. John's Hall on Frankfort Street. John Collins had reserved the entire house, but when the proprietor saw the black faces among the

103

delegates, he refused to admit them. With a crowd at their heels shouting epithets and throwing an occasional rock, the New Englanders walked on to Barclay Street to find shelter in the Graham House.

Abby and Joanna hurried to the Fourth Free Church, where the American Anti-Slavery Society convention opened at 10:00 A.M. with a public meeting. During the morning of speeches they looked over the crowd anxiously in an effort to estimate the strength of the rival factions. More than a thousand delegates—double the year before—had crowded into the church. Abby spotted Dr. Hudson and Newbury Darling with others from Connecticut as well as acquaintances from Pennsylvania. There was no doubt that the New England delegation was impressive. Still, there were many New Yorkers present, including some who had never been seen at an antislavery meeting before. Apparently Arthur Tappan, president of the society, had concluded that the Garrisonians had an edge. He absented himself from the meeting, leaving the chair to vice-president Francis Jackson of Massachusetts.

The first test of strength came that afternoon, when Jackson announced his nominations for the business committee, the committee that would set the convention agenda. "William Lloyd Garrison . . . Lewis Tappan . . . Charles Burleigh . . . Amos Phelps." Delegates nodded approvingly. He was conscientiously chosing representatives from both sides. Only when he came to the final name was there a sharp intake of breaths: "Abby Kelley."

"Great sensation prevailed," Edmund Quincy reported. People leaped to their feet to protest. Lewis Tappan and Amos Phelps insisted that women had never been members and that "persons" meant men. Not so, others replied. When the convention seemed disinclined to hear her, Abby stood on a pew to remind the delegates that in Congress the masters spoke while the slaves were denied a voice. "I rise because I am not a slave," she declared.

Ordinarily approval of the chair's nominations was a formality; on this extraordinary occasion each name was taken up separately. "All went swimmingly till it came to A. Kelley," Anne Weston wrote Maria. "Then there was first an immense *yea* and when the contrary was called a perfect *No*." The voice vote was so close that it was retaken, this time with delegates rising. While the tellers walked down the aisles, Charles Denison, a minister from New Jersey, called on all the women to vote against Abby. Amos

Phelps hoped that the ladies would abstain from voting, and a third clergyman sarcastically proposed that since children were persons, they, too, should have a voice. Abby waited tensely for Jackson to announce the final count: "451 opposed to Miss Kelley; 557 in her favor." She had won by a substantial majority.

"Went home in great glee," Edmund Quincy wrote in his diary. "We achieved a glorious victory," Anne Weston told Maria, although she thought that the opposition would call for a reconsideration the next day. "[The Reverend Duncan] Dunbar has said he would bring up 200 old women to outvote us."

However, no old women put in an appearance the next day. Instead Lewis Tappan invited all who opposed Abby Kelley's presence on the business committee to meet in a lecture room of the church. The walkout, clearly orchestrated beforehand, brought almost three hundred men together to form the American and Foreign Anti-Slavery Society. The constitution of the new organization—"new org" in abolitionist slang—forbade women to vote or hold office and refused membership to nonresistants.

The convention of the American Anti-Slavery Society—now the "old org"—went on with its work, although the Garrisonians' joy at having won control was tempered by the discovery that the seceders had stripped the organization of all its assets. In addition to giving away the *Emancipator*, the Executive Committee had turned over the society's other publications, membership lists, and remaining funds to Lewis Tappan and an associate, ostensibly so that they could settle unpaid bills. Even the furniture in the antislavery office on Nassau Street had been cleared out, some of it ending up in Tappan's study.

With no newspaper, no book depository, and no funds, the delegates pledged to raise ten thousand dollars to start a new weekly paper. Lindley Coates, a respected Friend from Pennsylvania, was elected president, and a new Executive Committee, headed by James Gibbons, included not only black Thomas Van Rensselaer but Lucretia Mott, Maria Child, and Maria Chapman.[13]

The long-predicted split in the antislavery movement had taken place, and Abby Kelley was widely blamed for causing it. John Greenleaf Whittier, who had been too ill to attend the convention, told his sister: "Our friend Abby was the leader in the affair—the bombshell that *exploded* the society." Writing to Benjamin Jones, a Philadelphia Friend, he compared Abby with such predatory females of history as Eve, Delilah, and Helen of Troy. "I am getting rather off from woman's rights," he said. "This last exploit of my good friend Abby in blowing up the Amer. A. Slavery Society is too much for me. Abolition women, Benjamin. Think of the conduct of Mrs. Adam—how Delilah shaved Sampson—how Helen got up the Trojan War—and last but not least this affair of Abby's and the society."

The press, too, turned on her. One paper denounced her "effrontery in asserting the right of her sex to an equal place with men"; another titillated its readers with an account of "a blooming young lady" who had been closeted in a committee room with ten men. In the week following the convention, a new phrase was coined—"Abby Kelleyism"—which a minister defined as "an unlovely and unteachable sport."[14]

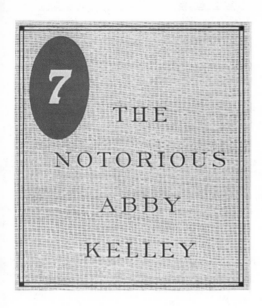

THE
NOTORIOUS
ABBY
KELLEY

Thrust into the limelight almost involuntarily, Abby was unprepared for the waves of misogyny that threatened to engulf her. Leaving New York in the company of Dr. Hudson and Charles Burleigh, she went to New Haven for the annual convention of the Connecticut Anti-Slavery Society. The society, so small and ineffectual a year earlier, was now a staging area in the struggle between new and old organizationists.

When the meeting convened in Saunders Hall, its first business was a resolution to exclude women. After half a dozen men spoke in its favor, Abby rose to reply. "Sit down," ordered the chairman, Henry G. Ludlow. Ludlow was the minister who had been host to the Grimkés three years earlier and had turned over his pulpit to Angelina for her first public speeches. Obviously regretting his action, he now curtly told Abby to keep quiet. To his chagrin, the meeting voted to hear her.

She criticized male supremacy, calling it "the lust for domination," which denied women "their inalienable heaven-derived right" to take part in the struggle for emancipation. Burleigh reported that hers was "one of the best speeches made during the day: brief, clear and to the point, proving by unanswerable argument that the proposed change was hostile to the anti-slavery enterprise." When she finished, Ludlow was "in a state of excitement," and his reply "contrasted strikingly with the calm dignity and lucid reasoning of Abby Kelley."

"No woman will speak or vote where I am moderator," the clergyman declared. "It is enough for women to rule at home. It is woman's business to take care of the children in the nursery; she has no business to come into this meeting and by speaking and voting lord it over men. Where woman's enticing eloquence is heard, men are incapable of right and efficient action. She beguiles and blinds men by her smiles and her bland winning voice."

Becoming more and more agitated, he warned that "the magic influence of Miss Kelley's voice and beauty" had convinced the meeting to hear her. "Men have not strength to resist woman's appeal. This meeting would not have voted to let Miss Kelley speak, but for their gallantry. But I will resist all such appeals. I will not sit in a meeting where women are allowed to speak and vote." Seizing his hat, he stalked down the aisle and out of the hall.

A vice-president took the chair, and the meeting turned to other business. But not for long, for Ludlow returned to elaborate his opposition to "the rule of women": "We will not sail under the Garrison flag. No. Never! Never! NEVER! I will not sit in a meeting where the sorcery of a woman's tongue is thrown around my heart. I will not submit to PETTICOAT GOVERNMENT. No woman shall ever lord it over me. *I am Major-Domo in my own house*."

Few thought his outburst ludicrous, nor did anyone attempt to respond until Abby stood up. "Take your seat, madam," the chairman peremptorily ordered.

"I am bound by duty to God and man to speak, and the constitution of this society gives me the right," she insisted.

Her protest was fruitless. Ludlow's diatribe had convinced the majority of delegates that Miss Kelley must "learn some decency and modesty, and not presume to speak and vote for men." For the balance of the two-day meeting, when women attempted to express an opinion, they were told, "Put down your hand!" or, "Your vote will not be counted." Once Abby managed to get the floor to remind the delegates that John Quincy Adams, whom they all admired, had been silenced by a congressional gag rule. "Like Adams, we refuse to submit to an unconstitutional rule," she said. However, she was ignored. The convention not only denied membership to women but voted to disaffiliate from the American Anti-Slavery Society because women served on its committees and were allowed to speak and vote.

The psychosexual undertones of Ludlow's speeches went unnoticed in New Haven in 1840. His audience recognized that his highly charged warning was based on the third chapter of Genesis. Hadn't woman, in the person of Eve, beguiled man "by her smiles and winning voice" until he ate the forbidden fruit? Thus it followed that Eve's descendants were forever condemned to be ruled over by men. This fundamentalist argument against the equality of women was widely accepted then, by women as well as men. Although Abby did not believe in a literal interpretation of the Bible, as progressive a woman as Sarah Douglass, her black friend from Philadelphia, agreed that woman's subordinate role was divinely ordained. "God has not repealed what he said to [Eve] when she took the forbidden fruit," Sarah wrote in 1841. "Humiliating as it is, I am willing God's word should stand."

Unshaken by her defeat, Abby gave a lecture in Saunders Hall after the convention had adjourned. With foes as well as friends in attendance, she was in top form, Charles Burleigh wrote. "There was sound argument—there was melting pathos—there was loftiness of thought and felicity of language—and binding all together was the deep earnestness which told how fully the speaker's soul was enlisted in her work." Even the *New Haven Register* reported: "Miss Abby Kelley made a powerful defence of the right of her sex to the pantaloons. The gray mare proved the better horse."[1]

Leaving New Haven with Burleigh and Henry C. Wright, then agent of the Non-Resistance Society, Abby headed for Boston for the annual meeting of the New England Anti-Slavery Society. The trio broke their trip at George Benson's farm in Brooklyn, Connecticut, where Abby had a weekend to relax. Perhaps she was more keyed up than she admitted to herself, for she wrote to the Darlings to say, "Play is necessary sometimes, after hard work, to refresh the spirit"; the genial Henry understood this "to perfection." There was, however, no danger of all play and no work, for even during the brief stopover she held an antislavery meeting. George Garrison, William's sailor brother, who was working on the Benson farm while struggling against alcoholism and who took a dim view of women in general, reported that Abby had "stentorian lungs which would put some of our Naval Boatswains to the blush."[2]

In contrast with New Haven, the Boston meeting opened with a resolution for a free platform, which would permit all persons to speak and vote. A third of the participants were women, Anne Weston serving as a secretary and Thankful Southwick as a member of the business committee. Abby, however, was the only woman to take the floor, speaking several times with increasing confidence. She proposed "rigid economy and self denial" so that delegates could increase their contributions to the American Society and its new newspaper, the *National Anti-Slavery Standard*. She attacked prejudice against color and even invaded that most masculine of arenas by speaking on national politics. Not that she supported Martin Van Buren or William Henry Harrison, the Democratic and Whig candidates for president. On the contrary, she opposed both, declaring that the United States' toleration of slavery made it a "despotism," so that its political parties "had no claim to the appellation democratic, republican, whig or conservative."

When the convention ended, she went to Lynn for a visit. Aroline and the Bassetts welcomed her, but "some of the old bigots looked away," she wrote the Darlings. "As my heart goes forth involuntarily to all my old friends, I could not refrain from shaking them heartily by the hand, whenever I could get hold of them, and sympathy is so strong that even their frozen countenances put on a warmer aspect." Apparently her friendliness won out, for two weeks later the Lynn Female Anti-Slavery Society formally hailed Abby Kelley's "devotedness and self sacrifice in the name of crushed humanity" and commended her "to the friends of human freedom for the perishing bondsman's sake."[3]

After a short stay in Millbury, where she worried about her mother's persistent cough, she took a stagecoach to Connecticut "to the seat of war." George Benson thought that the new organizers' victory in New Haven had been for the best, "for now they will sit quietly down feeling secure, and we can go on and get things straight." With a sharper political insight Abby disagreed. "They have the power in their hands and will see to it that it is not left unemployed. Nevertheless I am in no wise disheartened. On the contrary I feel more zeal and faith than ever," she wrote Dr. Hudson. Then, in her only acknowledgment that she was the focus of enemy attack, she added, "Tell Martha that I care so little of what the world says, that I am intending to go forward in good earnest, whether they hang me or not. The Lord is on our side and let us not fear what man can do."[4]

When she joined Hudson in mid-June, the shape of their work was clear. The new organization was dispatching teams of ministers from New York and Massachusetts to capture every outpost of abolition in the state. Like a "truth squad" in a twentieth-century political campaign, Abby, Hudson, and a handful of supporters followed them from convention to convention and endeavored to outtalk them. In Middletown their resolutions were tabled; in Willimantic "political wolves in abolition clothing" voted against admitting women delegates; in Wethersfield they met outdoors because no minister would lend them a church.

The issue was not always the woman question, but the right of people to be lukewarm abolitionists. The Garrisonians demanded that clergymen break with their colleagues in the South and refuse to associate with slaveowners who came North in the summer. "New organizers" had kind words for both clergy and laity—"trying to hug abolition to death," Abby said—while at the same time denouncing "old org" for its intolerance.

All this was going on against the backdrop of the presidential election campaign in which the Whigs were selling William Henry Harrison as a man of the people, born in a log cabin and content with a barrel of hard cider, while Van Buren was depicted as the candidate of privilege who toasted his supporters in champagne. Log cabins were everywhere—cabins on wheels that were hauled down Main Streets in parades, cabins in village squares, surrounded by free-flowing cider barrels for all comers. Struggling to straighten out "the antislavery harness of Connecticut which is in such a tangle"—Abby's metaphor—while most of her countrymen were succumbing to the Whigs' winning combination of demagoguery and hard cider, was a difficult task. When "new org" continued victorious in the county and city antislavery societies, Abby parted from Hudson to work in rural areas. Traveling and lecturing by day, she used her evenings to write letters and catch up with the newspapers.[5]

The big news in the antislavery world in the summer of 1840 was not the Harrison-Van Buren campaign but the World's Anti-Slavery Convention in London. The American Society and the female societies of Philadelphia and Boston had elected women as well as men delegates, but the British and Foreign Anti-Slavery Society, host of the convention, refused to seat them. Thus, while Abby was embattled in Connecticut, Lucretia Mott, Ann Phillips, Abby Southwick, and others were contending for their rights in London. In the absence of Garrison, who had not yet arrived at the convention, Wendell Phillips became spokesman for the women, with his wife advising him on tactics. "Maintain the floor—no matter what they do," Ann directed at the beginning of the debate and at a tense moment warned, "Wendell, don't shilly-shally!" Wendell spoke forcefully on behalf of the women; but his motion to seat them was overwhelmingly defeated, and they were relegated to a curtained-off gallery in the rear of the hall. Bred to politeness, Phillips then assured the assemblage that the women would "sit with as much interest behind the bar, as in the convention. All we asked was an expression of opinion, and, having obtained it, we shall now act with the utmost cordiality."

Loud cheers from the floor greeted his statement. Only the women in the gallery were silent. Ann Phillips's reaction was not recorded, but Elizabeth Cady Stanton, Henry Stanton's bride of a month, later recalled her dismay. "Could Wendell Phillips have so far mistaken [the women's] real feelings as to have told a Convention of men who had just trampled on

112

their most sacred rights that 'they would no doubt sit with as much interest behind the bar, as in the Convention?' " Although her husband was a "new org" delegate, his expenses paid from the plundered American Society treasury, Elizabeth became friendly with Lucretia Mott and other "old org" delegates and dated her belief in woman's equality to the World's Convention.

Did Henry Stanton vote to seat the women at the convention? His wife and Wendell Phillips said that he did, but his "new org" colleague James Birney stoutly denied this.

No more was said on the subject until Garrison arrived five days later. To protest the women's exclusion, he joined them in the gallery and refused to take part in the convention.

After reading the *Liberator* account of the women's banishment, Abby wrote Garrison to thank him for his stand and to criticize not only Wendell but Lucretia Mott, who, she thought, should have insisted on speaking despite the opposition. In the abolitionists' close-knit community, it was only to be expected that Garrison would show Abby's letter to Lucretia, and reasonable for her to respond by writing to Maria Chapman: "Abby Kelley asks W. L. G. if L. Mott has sacrificed principle at the altar of Peace. Now I don't know how far she will consider me as having done so. I have sometimes shrunk from a defence of our rights, when others have gone forward & stood in the breach—& I am very willing to crown such with laurels that I may not deserve. I was glad that Wendell Phillips & Ann were not so easily put by & that he came forward & manfully plead for the right. I shall ever love Ann for her earnest appeals to her husband to stand firm in that hour of trial—and him for doing so. Tell Abby Kelley if I am not much bold myself I respect those most who are. I never failed in our several tea-parties, soirees, &c to avail myself of every offer made for utterance for our cause—& then I shrunk not from the whole truth as those who heard can testify."

Abby, who was learning confrontation politics in the rough-and-tumble of Connecticut antislavery meetings, was in no mood to be impressed by tea party conversions. Yet as the summer wore on and Lucretia addressed public meetings in Dublin and Glasgow, it was clear that her quiet but firm manner was influencing British public opinion. The two women's exchange through intermediaries was only one of many times that they would disagree on tactics although working for the same goal.[6] While the American delegates were spreading goodwill in the British Isles, Abby was having one bruising encounter after another in Connecticut. Traveling through the northwestern part of the state, she arrived in Norfolk on a muggy July day and went to the home of Dr. Benjamin Welch, known as an abolitionist sympathizer. The doctor was out, but his wife, Sarah, invited her to stay—not to do so would have been a breach of hospitality—although it was clear that she was not pleased with her visitor. At teatime Alice Welch Cowles, the doctor's sister, came to meet Abby. Alice and her husband, Henry, had moved to Ohio, where Henry taught ecclesiastical history at Oberlin College and Alice headed the Female Department and was a member of the Women's Board of Managers.

Admiring Oberlin as an antislavery stronghold—it was the first college in the country to admit both black and women students—Abby greeted Alice warmly, only to find that although she opposed slavery, she disapproved of women lecturers. Nor did she think that anything could be accomplished in Norfolk because "the neighborhood was much agitated." Abby was being compared with freethinking Fanny Wright, "called a *man woman*, one who had done more to injure the abolition cause than any one else," Alice wrote her husband. "On many points, I sympathized with Miss K. She is devoted to the slave, to the whole human family. She is very intelligent, her conversation elevated, and excellent in every respect, except when she reproved those with whom she was conversing."

When brother Benjamin, "in a kind and proper manner," expressed his objections to women speakers, Abby rose from her seat, her face flaming, and, "in the strongest terms, denounced that spirit which should fetter any of the human family." Despite Abby's breach of taste in arguing with her host, Alice continued to admire her, finding her "ladylike, simple & unaffected, nothing masculine about her, except that she walks on to the ground which men have occupied alone."

That night and the following morning, a Sunday, a series of prominent townsmen dropped by to make clear to Abby that her presence was unwelcome. When one man shook his fist in her face and warned that if she attempted to speak, "it will be at your peril," Abby replied with "insulting language," adding, "Then I shall shake the dust [of Norfolk] off my feet as a testimony against you."

On his departure, Sarah Welch, who had barely concealed her distaste for her guest, informed her that as long as she had behaved like a lady, she had been welcome. But now she must go.

Mustering her dignity, Abby swept upstairs to pack her few belongings. In the room next to hers she saw one of the doctor's medical students. Could she find a public or private conveyance to take her to Canaan, the next town? she asked. "Not on Sunday," he replied.

"Is there a hotel in the town?"

"They will not receive you," he said. "They believe you to be a bad woman; the vilest woman of New York could, I presume, be received as soon as you."

Poor Abby. "Words cannot describe the spiritual anguish of that long day and night," she recalled. "A rap at my door announced dinner, another supper, and then breakfast, [but] I could not eat in that house."

The next morning Alice Cowles came to her rescue. Arriving in her father's wagon, she drove Abby to the home of Quaker farmers in Canaan. When the elderly couple welcomed her without question, Abby felt physical relief, as if a heavy burden had fallen from her shoulders. "I wanted to kiss those dear old people," she later wrote. "I went into the orchard and ran about like a colt let loose. I climbed the trees and sang with the birds. I hopped, skipped, and danced. Such ecstasy comes but rarely." At dinnertime she ate hungrily. "A farmer's boiled pot had never had such flavor." And although it was the busiest season of the year for Canaan's farmers, she held three antislavery meetings before departing.[7]

Refreshed by her Canaan stay, she was soon back on the lecture circuit. "Bro. and Sister Rhoads," Hudson's in-laws, drove her around in a borrowed carriage on "an exploring expedition in search of free land," but communities hospitable to her message were scarce. The limestone hills of northwestern Connecticut had once been a source of iron. During the Revolution, Connecticut's mines and forges had supplied the American army and navy with cannon and anchors. Although richer mines in the West had since captured most of the market, men still worked in local forges and charcoal kilns. The ironworkers and charcoal burners were even more unsympathetic to abolitionism than the farmers in other parts of the state. "Rhoads is a nail driven in a sure place," Abby wrote Hudson, "but the little handful who have taken up this cross think they have fiery trials all about them and are almost ready to give back. I encourage them to faithfulness, telling them the fire will have no power upon them if they have on the true shield."

A shield would not have been amiss when she held a meeting in Salisbury, headquarters of the iron industry. She was speaking in a schoolhouse when a rum bottle hurled from the doorway struck the desk in front of her, splintering into fragments. Then came a fusillade of stones and clubs through the windows, until the meeting broke up in confusion. While she lectured at the town hall a day later, a militia company surrounded the building, rang church bells, tooted horns, and banged tin pans, rendering her lecture inaudible. "They seemed to think it quite a joke to see a woman speaking," she said. When one of her backers remonstrated with the crowd, he was told, "The boys might as well have their sport."

From Salisbury she traveled to the village of Cornwall Bridge, so called because it was reached by a covered bridge spanning the Housatonic River. She had announced that she would speak in the schoolhouse at early candlelight. She was standing at the teacher's desk, waiting for people to settle in their seats, when a drunken man strode down the aisle, swinging a club and shouting, "Where's the damned nigger bitch that's going to lecture here?" Down came his club, left and right, overturning candles and smashing the oil lamp in front of Abby. With the room plunged in darkness, the audience fled, "amid the sounds of the falling club, the screams of the wounded, and the horrible oaths of the drunken wretch," she wrote.

Having grown accustomed, if not yet hardened, to hostile action, Abby went ahead with her plan to hold a meeting in the Methodist church the following day. At the appointed hour a score of abolitionists seated themselves in the front pews while she mounted to the pulpit. Before she could begin, her assailant of the night before, a charcoal manufacturer with a reputation as a drunk and bully, marched down the aisle, shouldering a rifle. "The first person who speaks for the nigger shall have the full charge

The earliest known portrait of Abby Kelley, a lithograph drawn from a daguerrotype in 1846 by Robert Douglass, black artist and brother of Kelley's friend, Sarah Douglass (*American Antiquarian Society*)

Maria Weston Chapman, described as "beautiful as the day, tall in her person and noble in her carriage," was the dominant figure in the Boston Female Anti-Slavery Society as well as a powerful force in the Massachusetts and American Anti-Slavery Societies. (*Boston Public Library*)

Lucretia Mott, who worked with Chapman, L. Maria Child, and the Grimkés to organize the first Anti-Slavery Convention of American Women, held in New York in 1837.

L. Maria Child

Angelina and Sarah Grimké, above left and right, lectured against slavery to audiences of women in 1837. Their meetings were held in the Spring Street Church, left, in New York City. (*Library of Congress*)

Ann Smith of Peterboro, New York attended the first convention of antislavery women. (*Madison County Historical Society*)

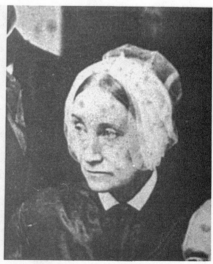

Sarah Pugh, left, and Mary Grew, right, lifelong members of the Philadelphia Female Anti-Slavery Society were also present at the first convention of antislavery women.

Wendell Phillips was Abby Kelley's closest friend among the leaders of the antislavery movement. (*National Portrait Gallery, Smithsonian Institute*)

The silhouette of Ann Greene Phillips, made in 1841, is the only known likeness of Phillips's wife.

William Lloyd Garrison, editor of *The Liberator*, who Abby Kelley first heard speak against slavery in 1832.

Theodore Weld, pioneer abolitionist and husband of Angelina Grimké, encouraged Abby Kelley to speak in public. (*Library Company of Philadelphia*)

John Greenleaf Whittier, the antislavery poet, disapproved of Abby Kelley's role in the 1840 split in the American Anti-Slavery Society. (*Boston Public Library*)

Destruction of Pennsylvania Hall by a proslavery mob during the second convention of antislavery women in 1838. (*Historical Society of Pennsylvania*)

Frederick Douglass made his first extended antislavery tour with Abby Kelley in Rhode Island in 1841. They continued to lecture together in New York State and Massachusetts through the 1840s, until Douglass broke with the Garrisonians. The two were reconciled after the Civil War. (*J. B. Lieb Photo Co.*)

Dr. Erasmus Darwin Hudson, above left
(*University of Massachusetts Archives*),
Charles Burleigh, above right (*Boston
Public Library*), and Parker Pillsbury, left,
were Abby Kelley's lecturing companions
during her early years on the antislavery
circuit.

Although Gerrit Smith and Kelley were on opposing sides in the factional disputes dividing the antislavery movement, they nevertheless exchanged ideas and sometimes worked together amicably. (*Boston Public Library*)

Oliver Johnson, an early associate of Garrison's, went to Ohio to edit *The Anti-Slavery Bugle* after Abby Kelley raised the money for his salary.

Amy Post, left (*Post Family Papers, University of Rochester Library*), and Paulina Wright Davis, below, offered Abby Kelley friendship when she came to New York State as an abolitionist organizer. Davis, a beautiful woman in her youth, was a pioneer lecturer on physiology and a leader in the woman's rights movement. Post was active in all progressive causes in Rochester until her death at the age of 85.

Alice Welch Cowles, left, headed the Female Department at Oberlin College, the first college in the nation to admit female and black students. Cowles lent a reluctant but helping hand to Kelley during her first difficult months as an antislavery lecturer. (*Oberlin College Archives*)

Elizabeth Buffum Chace, antislavery and woman's rights activist, was a friend of Kelley's from boarding school days. This portrait was painted circa 1856.

Helen Benson Garrison, wife of William Lloyd Garrison, at the age of 42. Too burdened by the care of their home and large family to play a public role in the antislavery struggle, she was host to many reformers, including Abby Kelley. (*Library Company of Philadelphia*)

Wherever Abby Kelley went she urged women to participate in the antislavery movement. Her best-known recruits were Lucy Stone, left, who became an antislavery agent in 1848 after graduation from Oberlin, and Susan B. Anthony, above, who took charge of teams of antislavery lecturers in New York State in the 1850s before assuming leadership in the struggle for women's rights. The portrait of Anthony shows her at 25, shortly after she put aside Quaker gray for more worldly dress. (*Susan B. Anthony Papers, University of Rochester Library*)

A daguerrotype of an antislavery meeting in New York State, circa 1850. The bonneted woman at the desk is probably Abby Kelley, with Frederick Douglass seated at her right and Gerrit Smith standing between them. The black women wearing plaid shawls may have been Emily and Mary Edmondson, recently freed slaves who later attended Oberlin College. (*J. Paul Getty Museum*)

of this gun," he shouted. When other armed men with the smutty faces of charcoal burners filled the balcony and blocked the doorway, the abolitionists decided on discretion. One of Abby's backers announced that the meeting was adjourned to his home—"and I give full warning that if any attempt be made to crush freedom of speech there, blood will flow. You all know the character of *my* shotgun," he concluded. Although this was hardly the kind of support that a nonresistant would choose, Abby addressed the twice-postponed meeting and went on her way the next day "with faith for the future."[8]

After a meeting of the Litchfield County Anti-Slavery Society, where she had been permitted to observe but not participate, she was invited to lecture in Washington, a village south of Cornwall Bridge. Sponsored by the superintendent of the Sabbath School and the sheriff, she gave four lectures there to increasingly large and interested audiences. Moved by her account of the slaves' plight, a group of women sought her out to ask how they could help. Although she was obliged to leave to fulfill speaking engagements elsewhere, she promised to return in a fortnight.

Back in Washington in early September she met with "a respectable assembly of females." For the first time she seemed to be making progress in Connecticut. That Sunday she accompanied her hosts, the Sabbath School superintendent and his wife, to church services. The Congregational minister, Gordon Hayes, had been out of town during her previous visit. At the conclusion of his sermon he announced that he had been asked to read a notice of a meeting in which a woman would address a mixed audience. Not only had St. Paul declared it "a sin and a shame for women to teach men," but the woman in question, he informed his parishioners, was a nonresistant who advocated doctrines "which would open our prisons, prevent the collection of taxes and give unrestrained sway to lawless violence."

As if that were not enough, he then read a warning from Revelation: "I have a few things against thee, because thou sufferest that woman Jezebel, which calleth herself a prophetess, to teach and to seduce my servants to commit fornication." Now a Jezebel had come to Washington "with brazen face" and "fascinations exceeding those of her Scriptural prototype," he said. Although she made high pretensions to philanthropy and Christianity, she was "a servant of Satan in the garb of an angel of light," and her aim was "to entice and destroy this church."

Abby sat in stunned silence as Hayes, calling her by name, cited as proof of her "vile character" that she traveled "by night and by day, always with men and never with women." He concluded by asking the congregation to decide whether she should be permitted to speak in their church. It took only a few minutes to pass a resolution disapproving of "the introduction of female lecturers."

As people filed out of the church, Abby and her hosts stood in the doorway. "There were many women present who had thanked God that He had sent me among them and several of whom had kindly and hospitably entertained me," she said. "But all passed me as if I had been a block."

What should she do about the lecture scheduled for that evening? She went ahead with it, although her audience was "small indeed," and her address "short and heavy with grief." No Washington women save the two who had originally invited her to the village were present.

A sympathetic observer reported the incident to the *Liberator*, concluding, "The slanders by which her character was assailed had no other effect than to increase her faith and animate her zeal." He could scarcely have been further from the truth. That night she went to her room but not to sleep. "In agony of prayer and tears, my cry was that of the prophet: 'O, that mine head were waters, and mine eyes a fountain of tears, that I might weep day and night for the slain of the daughter of my people!' " she said. Although she later wrote that her anguish was not personal, but rather because she was prevented from speaking for the slaves, Hayes's accusation of immorality cut deep. To be called Jezebel, a whore who painted her face in order to entice men, was the worst insult that could be leveled at her.

Nothing in the Grimkés' experience had prepared her for this attack. The plain, staid sisters, southern ladies to the core, had never been accused of immorality. Their critics had mocked them as stereotypical old maids who could not attract a man. Pretty, youthful Abby, with her full figure and farm girl high coloring, aroused male fantasies as well as fears. The Grimkés had also had the advantage of traveling together while Abby went alone. For a young woman to travel without a companion or chaperone was to invite all manner of harassment, both verbal and physical. Painfully aware of this breach of propriety, Abby tried to persuade women to accompany her, with small success. Time after time in the next years, a woman would agree to go, then send last-minute regrets. "I was disappointed on returning home to find company from the country which prevented my accompanying you," one explained. "Husband wishes me to say that he regretted very much that I could not accompany you, but circumstances were such that it could not be so. His best wishes for your complete success," another wrote.

Abby soon schooled herself to ignore personal attacks, but forty-five years later she still recalled the day she was called Jezebel and was rejected by the good people of Washington. Her friend Elizabeth Buffum Chace remembered "the trembling of her voice, the quiver of her lips and the tears in her eyes as she related the insults, the unkindness and the cruel scandals that were heaped upon her."[9]

Still, she persevered. As she told the Hudsons, she had recently gone to a phrenologist to have her "bumps" read. He had found an unusually large bump of "concentrativeness," "which I suppose gives me the desire to see work *well done up* before leaving." In one village, she recounted, she had called on Deacon Mowbray, a supposed ally, "and was almost frozen by the first glance, but as it was now evening I concluded to accept (because I knew not how to do better) their reluctant invitation to stay the night. Held two meetings at this place, two at the brick schoolhouse and one on Barrow's Hill, besides attending a discussion on slavery before the Lyceum of Hope Valley. The women, I think, will form a society as soon as the weather and traveling will permit. They would have done so while I was there, had it not been so muddy."

Occasionally she interrupted her work to spend a week with the Darlings; at Thanksgiving she visited the Ballous' farm in Rhode Island. When the country roads were impassable in late fall, she left Connecticut, where, the *Liberator* said, the attacks of "a pro-slavery priesthood have been almost demoniacal," and returned to Massachusetts.[10]

At home, as she took care of her mother and caught up with her washing and mending, she kept busy. In one three-week period she took part in conventions in Worcester, Springfield, and Methuen and was the featured speaker at the annual meeting of the Boston Female Anti-Slavery Society.

Convention chairmen were now seeking her out, inviting her to prepare resolutions "on any subject you choose," and she was a regular fixture on business committees, although usually the only woman. The "brethren" had changed in the three years since Angelina Grimké had feared to displease them, and so had Abby Kelley. Edmund Quincy, a sophisticated gentleman farmer and a man better known for his caustic wit than for flowery tributes, was bowled over when he met her that winter. "Abby is one of the most charming women of my acquaintance," he wrote Caroline Weston. "Her experiences of the last year or so, in bringing her in contact with men & enemies has been of great service to her both in mind & manner. It is not the pleasantest way of seeing the world but I am not sure that it is not the best for the character."

Abby was reminded of her new status in the movement when she stood on the platform of the Melodeon, a popular concert and lecture hall, and looked down on the expectant faces of the Boston Female Anti-Slavery Society. So many of the women had been active abolitionists while she was "in the ABC of the cause," she told them. Yet now she was coming from the front lines with a message to deliver. Speaking extemporaneously, she called for action rather than discussion and for sacrifice as well as sympathy. Her listeners responded with a tribute, doubtless written by Maria Chapman, which contrasted Abby's labors with theirs. "While we have sat by our firesides, or discharged the lighter obligations for the cause which use has made easy and agreeable, she has labored amid obloquy and persecution—in inclement season, and with bodily fatigue, unsustained by the funds of any society. Calling no man master, she is sure of her reward: the gratification of the few—the malignant scorn of many—the blessings of coming generations."

Both the *Liberator* and *National Anti-Slavery Standard* published her speech on their front pages, commending it to their readers. "This extraordinary young woman," the *Standard* said, "unites a power of intellect that is exceedingly rare and an eloquence that nothing but flint can withstand."[11]

Abby was far from vain, but praise was pleasant after a season of attacks and rebuffs. Perhaps that was why she gave in to Maria's importunities and agreed to work for the Female Society's Christmas Fair. She had never approved of fairs. Living plainly, with a Quaker distaste for "furbelows and frippery," she felt it wrong to encourage people to buy unnecessary "fancy articles."

The Boston fairs had originated in 1834, when Maria Child and a few friends held a modest bazaar in the Anti-Slavery Office on Washington Street, raising two hundred dollars for the cause. The next year Maria Chapman had arrived on the scene, a queenly stranger so different from the other women that at first, Child said, "We thought her a spy, or maybe she was a slaveholder." From then on Chapman had taken charge. In place of Child's homely aprons and artificial flowers, she had solicited expensive antiques and works of art from English and French acquaintances and put on so splendid a display that even Boston's high society folk came to buy the elegant goods that they could not find elsewhere. The Female Society's fair now brought thousands of dollars to the antislavery treasury and was a starred event on the holiday social calendar.

Abby could not help admiring Maria's generalship as, weeks beforehand, she put all hands to work. Back in Millbury Abby was unable to attend the preliminary Work and Conversation Meetings, where members of the fair committee addressed circulars, opened boxes and barrels from abroad, and priced articles for sale. However, letters from Maria regularly enjoined her to talk to Worcester County farmers "and get them to pledge to send in vegetables and produce, *anything* eatable and things that *you* would not count eatable."

The week before Christmas she joined the Boston women to decorate the walls of Marlborough Hall with evergreen boughs and antislavery slogans and to arrange the merchandise on display tables. More than forty Massachusetts towns had contributed, Nantucket sending shells and coral from the Sandwich Islands, Lynn, shoes and morocco work, Salem, work-baskets and woodenware, while English sympathizers had shipped fine china tea and breakfast sets. Maria and David Child, still in Northampton, sent beet sugar candy and a box of butter; Amelia Opie contributed copies of her novels, and Dr. William Ellery Channing his sermons. Grahamism advocates who opposed extravagance, Maria Chapman pointed out, could purchase useful articles—soap, candles, seeds, antislavery tracts—while the more worldly indulged their taste for quilted bonnets, jewelry, and bead-work. And if some did not care to buy, they could listen to lectures on physiology and enjoy the good company. "However our heads may differ, our hearts are one," she summed up.

In charge of the Worcester-Millbury table, Abby busily bagged onions and potatoes while greeting friends from all over the state. The climax of the festivities was a "soiree" on Christmas Eve, when for a dollar a couple, guests attended an "elegant" supper, followed by speeches and singing. The women boasted that no servants were hired for this affair; they did the work themselves with substantial assistance from a team of black caterers who contributed their services. Thus "all distinctions of color and class were forgotten."

The 1840 Christmas Fair netted over two thousand dollars, more than ever before. Impressed, Abby buried her objections and planned to organize a fair in Millbury in the near future.

The only somber moment of the festive week came when it was time to say good-bye to the Chapmans, who were sailing to Haiti on December 28. Henry had been ill all fall with "a weakness" in his lungs, and his doctor had prescribed a winter in a warm climate. Since abolitionists could not go to the South without risking their lives, the couple were heading for the black-ruled island in the Caribbean, entrusting their seven-month-old baby,* two older children, and their multifold antislavery activities to the Weston sisters.[12]

Spending the winter with her mother gave Abby the opportunity to think through a question close to both their hearts: whether she should break with the Society of Friends. Many members of the reform community were "coming out" of orthodox churches because the religious establishment had failed to denounce slavery. The Society of Friends, once in the vanguard of the antislavery movement, was scarcely progressive now. Abolitionist lecturers were barred from meetinghouses, and Friends who joined "the world's people" in the antislavery and nonresistance movements were

* Little Gertrude Chapman died while her parents were in Haiti.

frowned on. "Thee must keep in the quiet till the Lord opens a way," elders counseled.

For several years William Bassett had been telling Abby of his differences with the Lynn Friends. In 1840, after an open letter in which he criticized the society for its negative attitude toward abolition and for permitting segregated "Negro pews" in meetinghouses, he was finally disowned. Abby shared his concerns but had hesitated to hurt her mother or the Friends she had known since childhood. Recently she had quietly ignored some of the prohibitions of Quakerism. "Plain language" and the rigid dress code, which paid more attention to the tilt of a bonnet than to a slave's immortal soul, were, she believed, mere empty forms "made to stand in the place of vital religion." Still, "the fundamental principles of the society [had] taken deep root in my heart," she said, and she was reluctant to make a final break. After a painful period of deliberation she felt she could no longer keep silent about the Quakers' "departures from the high ground of truth." In March 1841 she wrote sorrowfully to the Uxbridge Monthly Meeting, saying "I hereby disown all connection of fellowship with the Society of Friends, feeling it a duty to 'come out and be separate.'"

Ordinarily such a letter would have been read at a Meeting for Discipline and then referred to a committee for action. But the Uxbridge Friends, some of them active abolitionists,* kept the matter quiet, perhaps hoping that Abby could be induced to change her mind. After waiting six months for their response, she broke the silence by sending a copy of her letter to the *Liberator*. Shortly afterward the Uxbridge Meeting formally disowned Abby Kelley.

The separation meant some broadening of her interests. She read at least one novel—*Tristram Shandy* by Laurence Sterne—that year, but her belief in the inner voice remained unchanged. Nor was she ever able to put aside Quaker ways of thinking and behavior.

---

* Lydia Capron, who, with her husband, Effingham Capron, was associated with Abby Kelley in antislavery work throughout the antebellum years, was the Uxbridge Friend appointed to notify her of her disownment.

Abby's letter to the *Liberator* was only one of a great number of church withdrawal letters that were published in the antislavery press in the 1840s. Although most were written by "come-outers" disassociating themselves from orthodox churches, other Quakers broke with their society. Abby Hopper Gibbons, wife of James Gibbons, disowned the New York Society of Friends in 1842; Elizabeth Buffum Chace came out of the Rhode Island Society the following year.[13]

Throughout the winter of 1840–41 the letter box in the Anti-Slavery Office in Boston was crammed with requests to have Abby speak. "There never was a time when a lecture was so much needed and it is the opinion of all the old friends that a woman will do more than a man," a Massachusetts woman wrote. "I want Abby Kelley. We must have her," a man from New York State insisted. "I love Abby Kelley. My heart responds to every word she utters," an elderly Pennsylvanian told William Lloyd Garrison. A Massachusetts legislator asked Abby for her autograph, and a Philadelphia admirer celebrated her in verse, which the *Liberator* printed:

> *Miss Kelley of Lynn,*
> *Some esteem it a sin*
> *And a shame that thou darest to speak;*
> *Quite forgetting that mind*
> *Is to sex unconfined.*
> *That in Christ is nor Gentile nor Greek,*
> *Abby K!*
> *That in Christ is nor Gentile nor Greek!*[14]

Tempting as it must have been to accept invitations that promised hospitality rather than hostility, Abby had unfinished business in Connecticut. With the first lengthening days of spring she traveled with William Lloyd Garrison to Willimantic for an antislavery convention organized by Erasmus Hudson and George Benson. Appearing "with uncovered head and unblushing face," an opposition paper said, Abby debated Ichabod Codding, general agent of the Connecticut Anti-Slavery Society, who had come to do battle with the Garrisonians. Although her friends thought she had bested him, a resolution approving her work in Connecticut was defeated by a large majority.

After visiting the Darlings, she set out alone to tackle towns and villages in the eastern part of the state. "From Lebanon to Willimantic, I held four meetings and the Ladies' society one afternoon," she reported to the Hudsons. "Went to Chaplin and gave two lectures, as strong as truth and stern as justice. Have another meeting this afternoon and then go on to Franklin."

She spent two weeks in Norwich, a shipbuilding town on the Thames River, a day's sail from New London and Long Island Sound. When she arrived, all churches barred her from their premises, and the selectmen refused her the use of the town hall. Only after a citizens' committee, which included the mayor, protested this violation of her civil rights was she permitted to hold meetings in the town building. Because of its location, Norwich was a stop on the Underground Railroad with a considerable population of ex-slaves. They greeted Abby warmly, and she "was proud to be identified with them," she wrote to the *Standard*. "When it was said by some that they would as lief be seen walking the streets with a 'nigger' as with myself, I thanked the God of the poor that I was accounted worthy of such honor."[15]

Although she still refrained from taking up collections to defray her own expenses, she now concluded each meeting by selling subscriptions to the *Liberator* and the *National Anti-Slavery Standard*. The *Standard*, which had replaced the *Emancipator* as the organ of the American Anti-Slavery Society, was published in New York and thus was geographically close to the people of Connecticut. Abby regularly mailed in announcements and reports of her meetings, along with an occasional open letter to an opponent. Started hastily in May 1840, the paper lacked a permanent editor and was compelled "like a Yankee schoolma'am, to 'board around,'" Oliver Johnson said. This practice sometimes made for inaccurate reporting and a wobbly viewpoint. Reading it carefully each week, Abby was often critical. "The last number contains a crowner," she told Hudson. "Do write to headquarters forthwith. The Ex. Comm. must protest."

Recognizing the importance of the *Standard* as an organizing tool, Abby went to the Executive Committee to propose the appointment of Maria Child as editor. The Childs, whose finances were at a low ebb, agreed to take on the assignment. David would be assistant editor, spending most of his time with his beet sugar experiment in Massachusetts, while Maria moved to New York to work on the paper full-time. Before accepting, however, Maria insisted that she did not want to edit a sectarian sheet filled with "fight and controversy" but would "aim more at reaching the people." She planned to broaden the paper's audience by including literary notes and "popular explanations of subjects much talked of and little understood," such as transcendentalism or homeopathy. Abby, who played a leading role in the negotiations, assured her, "You are just the editor we want. We need oil upon the waves. We have made too much of fighting; there is now an opening for something better."

Maria Child moved to New York in May 1841 and immediately discovered that she had taken on a thankless task. The paper's finances were precarious; some weeks there was barely enough to pay the printer, to say nothing of the editor. Even more disagreeable was the discovery that she had not one but scores of bosses. The *Liberator* was Garrison's personal publication, but she was accountable to the Executive Committee of the American Society—and to every one of her readers. "One complained that I don't put in editorial enough! Another that I write about subjects not strictly anti-slavery; another that I neglect non-resistance and woman's rights, another that I don't quote more from Garrison."

Her most persistent critic during her first year in New York was Abby Kelley. "The *Standard* gives good satisfaction *in the main*," Abby would begin diplomatically before going on to ask Maria to praise a friend or castigate an enemy who needed dressing down. Forty-year-old Maria Child was an experienced journalist with a reputation for accuracy and literary style. Abby Kelley at thirty was a partisan who not only saw the *Standard* as a weapon in the struggle but lacked Maria's sensitivity to language. She tended to use flamboyant or trite phrases that, while not out of place on the platform, were jarring to Maria.

When Abby or an associate sent in a meeting report, Maria, determined to avoid what she described as "hyena soup with brimstone seasoning," blue-penciled the most caustic comments, then braced herself for complaints. "I have run my pen pretty freely through one of Abby Kelley's letters, and destroyed one of Hudson's," she confided to a friend a month after taking on the editorial job.

Homesick for her husband, living in cramped quarters with the family of James and Abby Gibbons, struggling to make the *Standard* "a first-rate paper," Maria longed for encouragement and was pained by the continual criticism. Hurt because Abby disapproved of her "conciliatory tone," she was "grievously tried" by the younger woman's extreme positions, which she feared would "drive away all the tender-spirited and judicious from our ranks."

Abby, who was going through her own trial by fire, never realized how sensitive Maria was and how disagreeable she found her work. Unaccustomed to sparing herself, she saw little reason to temper her language in either her reports to the *Standard* or her private letters to its editor. After David Child took over the editorial chair, she was equally frank with him and even more critical.

Despite her disagreements with the Childs, Abby remained the *Standard*'s chief booster. She sold subscriptions at all her meetings and insisted that the paper receive adequate support from the American Society. At the anniversary meeting in May 1841, when the committee on finance proposed a six-thousand-dollar budget for all of the society's work, she spoke "almost indignantly." The budget was increased to fifteen thousand dollars, and she pledged to raise one thousand dollars. James Gibbons, the *Standard*'s business manager, had already mortgaged his household furniture to pay printing and paper bills. When he heard Abby's pledge, he borrowed an additional five hundred dollars to keep the paper afloat until her money came in.[16]

After the anniversary meeting Abby traveled to Hartford with the Hudsons and George Benson for the annual meeting of the Connecticut Anti-Slavery Society. This year "new org" was firmly entrenched, and there was no need for Henry Ludlow's emotional diatribes. As soon as "the notorious Abby Kelley" attempted to speak, the chair ruled her out of order and was sustained by a three to one vote.

Perhaps it was time to leave Connecticut. After the Hartford convention had adjourned, Abby and her companions separated. Dr. Hudson was going to Ohio as an agent of the American Society; George Benson, who had sold his farm, was heading for upstate New York to look for a new place to settle. Abby, for her part, had decided to go to Concord, New Hampshire, to attend the annual meeting of the New Hampshire Anti-Slavery Society.[17]

8

A NEW HAMPSHIRE FANATIC

I f someone had asked Abby Kelley why she went to New Hampshire in June 1841, she would undoubtedly have said that she had long admired the leaders of the state antislavery society who had put "new organizers" to rout and were known throughout the region for their militant stand on every issue. Nathaniel Peabody Rogers, a middle-aged lawyer who had forsaken his practice to edit the influential *Herald of Freedom*, had traveled to the World's Anti-Slavery Convention with his good friend William Lloyd Garrison the year before. In his absence the weekly had been edited by Parker Pillsbury, a youthful farmer turned minister who had come out of the church to preach freedom for the slave. Pillsbury—"a tough oak stick of a man" Ralph Waldo Emerson called him—worked closely with another come-outer, Stephen S. Foster. Although a virtual newcomer to the movement, Foster was acquiring a reputation for his uncompromising assaults on apologists for slavery. At a meeting in Boston the past spring he had supported a resolution that called the clergy "a brotherhood of thieves." Even Garrison, who often used harsh language, thought the phrase too strong and had insisted on deleting it. When the identical resolution, including the offensive phrase, passed with scant debate in New Hampshire, the *Liberator*'s account of the meeting was headed DOINGS OF THE NEW HAMPSHIRE "FANATICS."[1]

Stephen Symonds Foster was born in Canterbury, New Hampshire, on November 17, 1809, the ninth child in a family of twelve. His parents, Sarah and Asa Foster, were descended from English colonists who had settled in Massachusetts Bay Colony in the 1630s. As a youth Asa Foster had fought in the American Revolution, acquiring the honorary title of colonel. Convinced in later years that war was wrong, he refused to accept the land bounty awarded to revolutionary war veterans, even though his farm, several hundred acres on a hill overlooking the Merrimack River, barely enabled him to support his family. A member of Canterbury's Congregational Church, he was also treasurer of the local antislavery society.

After receiving a common school education, Stephen had been apprenticed to a carpenter. At age twenty-two, however, he heeded the call of the church for missionaries to go west "to the great valley of the Mississippi." To prepare himself for the ministry, he went to Dartmouth College in western New Hampshire, where his brother Asa had been graduated a dozen years earlier. One of a growing number of farmers' sons who were leaving impoverished farms to become members of a rural intelligentsia, Stephen took a classical course, which included, in addition to Greek and Latin, four years of rhetoric, with emphasis on public speaking. A serious student who supported himself by teaching during summers, he was graduated third in his class.

In the spring of his senior year he ran into trouble when a local clockmaker had him arrested for a debt of $12.14. Thrown into state prison,* he was appalled to find that debtors were housed with thieves and murderers in dank, dirty cells that were swarming with vermin. Before friends bailed him out a fortnight later, he had written a letter of protest to a local paper—"such a letter as few but he could write," Pillsbury said. His letter aroused so much indignation that the jails were cleaned up, and two years later the legislature abolished imprisonment for debt.

After his graduation in 1838 Foster went to the Union Theological Seminary in New York. A convinced abolitionist by then—in his junior year he had invited Angelina Grimké to address Dartmouth's Young Men's Anti-Slavery Society—he had a brush with seminary authorities when he attempted to hold an antislavery meeting. The faculty forbade the meeting but offered Stephen a scholarship if he would call off his abolitionist proselytizing. He rejected the bargain, saying he "could not be bought to hold his peace." Finally disillusioned with the church, he returned to New England in the spring of 1839 to become a lecturing agent for the New Hampshire Anti-Slavery Society.

Tall, spare, with rugged features and a farmer's roughened hands, Stephen Foster was a commanding figure on the platform. He was a master of invective, whose eyes flashed fire, and whose deep voice had a compelling, almost magnetic quality. Listening to him, people were reminded of the Old Testament prophets, full of wrath and righteousness. In private, however, his blue eyes, half concealed behind rimless spectacles, were gentle, and his manner warm and friendly. "He was the sunshine of any circle, enjoying wit and every kind of intellectual life," Wendell Phillips later said. "But he never trifled. You felt he had a great work to do, and 'could not come down' to your worldly level."[2]

Abby, who had the same unswerving commitment, was much taken with

___

* Pillsbury and other contemporaries had a more romantic explanation for Foster's jailing. They said that he had been imprisoned for refusing to perform militia duty. However, a letter in Foster's alumni file from Charles H. Griswold, March 5, 1889, reports that he was imprisoned for debt.

the "pepper and ginger" of Stephen's rhetoric when she heard him for the first time in Concord. Stephen, who had observed her from afar at earlier conventions, was immediately captivated when they met and he saw close up a "vigorous, animated bounding creature, full of life and vivacity." The stage seemed to be set for romance, but theirs was no simple girl-meets-boy story. At thirty and thirty-one respectively Abby and Stephen were dedicated to the abolition of slavery and determined to avoid entanglements along the way. Abby was so sure that she had renounced all thoughts of love and marriage that she concealed her personal interest in Stephen even from herself, revealing it only by the way she managed to mention him in letters to others and by her championship of the "wild and fanatical" New Hampshire abolitionists.

When, after a three-week speaking tour in New Hampshire, she returned to Massachusetts, she sent a closely written four-page letter to Nathaniel Rogers, ostensibly to commend the state "where there is more agitation than in any other place I am acquainted with." In the letter, which surely was intended for Stephen's eyes, she defended his denunciatory style. Although not referring to him by name, she asserted that "God will hold us responsible if we do not warn those who are guilty of the 'concentrated sum of all villainies,' by softly calling them 'a brotherhood of thieves.' American slavery was not contemplated when our language was framed and it has not changed or enlarged to describe this unutterable system." Since the "criminality" of supporters of slavery could not be adequately described in words, she proposed that "we resort to the expedient of barbarous nations, and express ourselves by significant signs, eloquent gesticulations and lines of light that shadow forth the soul in every muscle of the face."

Obviously stimulated by her New Hampshire stay, she included in her letter a remarkable paragraph that went far toward explaining the wellsprings of her growing oratorical power.

"When I come to sit down in the cool of the day, alone with none but God to hold communion with, and in the exercise of love to him, become myself the slave—when at such a moment I feel the fetters wearing away the flesh and grating on my bare ankle bone, when I feel the naked cords of my neck shrinking away from the rough edge of the iron collar, when my flesh quivers beneath the lash, till, in anguish, I feel portions of it cut from my back; or when I see my aged and feeble mother driven away and scourged, and then the brutish and drunken overseer lay his ferocious grasp upon the person of my sister and drag her to his den of pollutions—ah! when I see the fires of liberty going out in her bosom and the light of intellect gradually giving place to the blank of idiocy, and she becoming a mere plantation brute. . . . [W]hen I witness all the unutterable abominations that spring from slavery, myself reduced to slavery by, if you please, a sanctified Doctor of Divinity, who not satisfied with picking my pockets of all my hardearned wealth, not content with small villainy, goes on to pick away from me, one after another, bone by bone, and then filches my flesh away, and robs me of my heart's blood and lays his iron grasp on my immortal soul—when I see you and others standing by to witness it, what do I hear from your lips? You call the perpetrator and his accomplices a 'brotherhood of thieves.' "

Melodramatic as this language sounds today, Abby was describing an experience shared by sensitive women of her time who identified with their sisters in bondage. Angelina Grimké had said that she felt scarred by the whip when she saw a slave woman being taken to the workhouse for punishment. A decade earlier Elizabeth Chandler, a Quaker poet and abolitionist, had written an essay, titled "Mental Metempsychosis," in which she urged white women to put their souls into the bodies of slaves in order to understand their pain. Abby was following Chandler's advice. By a kind of self-hypnosis, she had *become* the slave. She could feel the fetters cutting into her ankles, the iron collar around her neck. She witnessed the degradation of her mother and sister. Small wonder that she found no language strong enough to characterize the oppressors or that reliving the experience in front of audiences, she could move them to tears by her "melting eloquence."[3]

After fulfilling speaking engagements in western Massachusetts, Abby spent the balance of the summer in Millbury with her mother and sister Lucy. Despite her travels, there was always a part of her that longed for home—"home, sweet home" she frequently called it, using the phrase just then coming into the language from the title of John Howard Payne's popular song.* To sleep in her own bed, to be able to arrange her clothes in her wardrobe, to enjoy the plain meals that her mother prepared—these were simple pleasures that she savored while they lasted.

Her main assignment that summer was to prepare for the quarterly meeting of the Massachusetts Anti-Slavery Society in August. The society held its annual meeting in Boston each January, but the quarterly meetings were scheduled for different parts of the state. This would be the first time the abolitionists convened in Millbury. Two hundred people from out of town were expected, and Abby was anxious to have everything run smoothly. As chief of logistics for the occasion she had to arrange for a suitable meeting place and find lodgings for the visiting delegates. She was eager to show hospitality to people like Henrietta Sargent, who had often put her up in Boston, and to have her mother meet the prominent abolitionists. The Kelley farmhouse was too small to house everyone, so she persuaded neighbors to take in the overflow. She and Lucy, who was secretary of the Millbury Female Anti-Slavery Society, were also organizing a fair to be held at the time of the meeting. The high point of the fair was to be a "collation" honoring "friends from abroad"—Maria and Henry Chapman, recently returned from Haiti; Ann and Wendell Phillips back from their European honeymoon; and John A. Collins, general agent of the Massachusetts Society, who had been on a fund-raising tour of Great Britain.

Afraid that not enough people would come, Abby sent an urgent appeal to Maria a week before the meeting: "Your presence here is ardently desired. We want to make Millbury an anti-slavery stronghold. We want you to come from Boston and take it by storm—your sisters and Mary Chapman, the Southwicks—E. Quincy. I trust Ann Phillips will not fail to come. We will give her a comfortable home and she need not attend any meeting. Even some of our pro-slavery houses are open to welcome company. . . .

---

* "Home, Sweet Home" was first heard in John Howard Payne's opera *Clari* in London in 1823.

Did you know how much is on my shoulders you would wonder I have stopped to say so much."

On the morning the meeting was to begin, Abby—"the presiding genius of the place" Quincy called her—was at the depot, waiting for the Boston train. At the last minute both Maria Chapman and Ann Phillips sent regrets. Henry had had a recurrence of "bleeding from the lungs," and Ann, on her way to becoming a chronic invalid,* was too ill to make the trip. But Boston was represented by William Lloyd Garrison and Wendell Phillips, Henrietta Sargent, Anne and Caroline Weston, with Edmund Quincy as their escort. Abby probably brought Henrietta home with her, but she was so eager to make everyone comfortable that she quartered the Westons and Quincy with Asa Waters, the wealthiest man in Millbury, who manufactured guns for the U.S. government. While admiring Waters's spacious house, greenhouses, and well-tended gardens, Quincy, who was still a leader of the Non-Resistance Society, noted in his diary that the family received them kindly "though they were plainly not of A[nti] S[lavery] Faith."

Abby's hostessing duties did not end with supplying lodgings. On the meeting's second day the delegates walked a mile to the Kelley farm for a midday dinner. That evening she and Lucy welcomed them to the collation at Academy Hall, where the fair was held and where there was "an elegant sufficiency" of food, followed by speeches and song.

Although Abby spoke at the collation and at sessions of the meeting, she also did considerable listening. A highpoint of the two-day gathering was the "eloquent and thrilling remarks of a fugitive slave." A tall bronze-skinned young man with a mane of brushed-back hair, he held the audience

---

* Although she continued to take a lively interest in antislavery affairs, Ann Phillips was confined to her room in the Phillips house on Essex Street almost continuously from 1841 until her death in 1885. Edmund Quincy thought she had "one of those mysterious complaints in which organic disease is mixed up with a good deal that is imaginary." Irving Bartlett, a Phillips biographer, speculates that she suffered from the effects of rheumatic fever or acute rheumatism. (Bartlett, New Light.)

enthralled as he told of his life in bondage. Scarcely three years out of slavery, he had given his maiden speech on Nantucket a week earlier and had so impressed his listeners that John Collins had immediately signed him on as an agent of the Massachusetts Society. His name, the *Liberator* reported, was Frederick Douglass.*

Abby had invited the New Hampshire "fanatics" to attend the meeting, but only Stephen Foster and Parker Pillsbury had come. Stephen lived up to his state's reputation by presenting several innovative resolutions. When the delegates discussed topics for petitions, he proposed a petition to impeach President of the United States John Tyler because he owned slaves. He advocated this "with great warmth and devotion," but his colleagues rejected it. During a debate on the abolitionists' role in ending segregation in trains, steamboats, and churches, he insisted that whites take their seats in the "Jim Crow cars" and "Negro pews" along with "their oppressed colored citizens." Although this tactic would soon be adopted, his listeners were not ready for it that day. After Garrison and Quincy spoke against his resolution, it was tabled; a substitute resolution to petition the legislature to outlaw the Jim Crow cars passed instead. Reporting the meeting for the *Standard*, Henrietta Sargent thought that Stephen and his supporters "ought if they would be consistent send their children to the African schools, or, perhaps, ought to assume yokes and fetters and be consigned to southern task masters. The noted warriors from the Granite State became very much excited on the subject and called Garrison and his associates 'recreants to the cause.' " Although she thought that "the mimic war was quite novel and amusing," it is doubtful that Abby agreed. She did not join in the discussion, but after the meeting had adjourned and she had driven the last guests to the depot, she asked Stephen to remain and lecture in Millbury.[4]

The village had borne the presence of so many abolitionists with equa-

---

* The *Liberator* account of the Nantucket meeting said that "———— Douglass of New Bedford had spoken." His first name was not recorded until reports of the Millbury meeting appeared in the *Liberator* on August 27 and September 10, 1841.

nimity. Curious to see such well-known figures as Garrison and Phillips, residents had turned out good-humoredly for the meeting and fair. While interest was still high, Abby and a handful of local abolitionists judged it a favorable time for further discussion, particularly on the significant role of the church in supporting slavery. "As S. S. Foster, by speaking in stronger terms of condemnation of a man-stealing, woman-whipping, adulterous and murderous church, than any other, had become particularly odious, he was solicited to remain a few days to do the work," she wrote Garrison.

Abby and her friends had underestimated Millbury's proslavery sentiments. While Stephen spoke on four successive days, opening with a "thrilling and expressive discourse"—Abby's description—his listeners grew increasingly angry. One man threatened him with a pistol; another declared that his object was to destroy the church. Asa Waters, Quincy's host, whose guns, Abby was told, "go to murder the poor Seminoles," proved to be Stephen's chief opponent. He asserted that the abolitionists' object was "the destruction of the sabbath, church and ministry. They are in one word infidels, and of the Fanny Wright school," who wished to abolish the institution of marriage. Stephen's final meeting was brought to an abrupt close when the "mobocracy hissed and shouted and stamped and uttered demoniac laughter," wrote Abby.

In this, their first collaboration, Abby and Stephen had tested the theory that you catch more flies with vinegar than with honey. What had they accomplished? "I have much hope of my own loved Millbury; for with all its faults, I love it still," she told Garrison. While timid friends said that the cause had been put back fifty years, she believed that the controversy had awakened people from apathy. "From this day henceforward Millbury is an anti-slavery town," she concluded.[5]

No doubt Stephen stayed at the Kelley farmhouse while he was barnstorming Millbury, but there is no record of his conversations with Abby or of Diane Kelley's opinion of her outspoken visitor. He was still at the Kelleys' when Parker Pillsbury wrote to say that they must enlarge their reputations as "dangerous men. Devise some plan by which we may improve on the operations of the past. If we scourged the pro-slavery church and clergy last year with whips, let us this year chastise them with scorpions!"

Two weeks later, on a quiet Sabbath in September 1841, Stephen Foster entered the old North Church, the first Congregational church in Concord, New Hampshire. Taking a seat with others of the congregation, he waited until the minister was about to begin his sermon. Then he rose to announce in a mild, friendly voice that as a man and a Christian he wished to speak against slavery. The astonished minister ordered him to sit down. When he continued to speak, three stalwart parishioners dragged him down the aisle and pushed him outdoors.

Sunday after Sunday he repeated the tactic, always choosing a church that had barred antislavery meetings. As soon as the opening prayer was concluded, he solemnly rose to say a few words in behalf of his two million countrymen who were enslaved. Sometimes a minister let him speak or parishioners demanded to hear him. More often he barely had chance to say a word before strong hands seized him. Then, as any convinced non-resistant would do, he went limp, obliging his opponents to carry him from the building. Arrested—the New Hampshire legislature hastily passed a law forbidding the interruption of church services—he acted as his own lawyer and used the courtroom as a platform. Convicted, he went to jail instead of paying a fine.

Four months after he had begun his career as "a steeple-house troubler," he told the readers of *Herald of Freedom* that he had been ejected from churches twenty-four times. Twice "my countrymen have thrown me with great violence from the second story of their buildings. Once they gave me an evangelical kick in the side which left me for weeks an invalid. Times out of memory have they hunted me with brick-bats and bad eggs. Four times have [prisons] opened their dismal cells for my reception."

From the moment that he commenced to speak to the final disposition of his case in court, he was teaching, preaching, winning converts—and making enemies. His was the kind of direct nonviolent action that was applauded in the twentieth century, after Mohandas Gandhi and Martin Luther King, Jr., had introduced their theories of satyagraha and "creative tension." In 1841 his supporters, who sometimes seemed to consist only of Pillsbury and Rogers, defended him by comparing him with Jesus when He entered the temple in Jerusalem or with the seventeenth-century Quakers who also disrupted church services.

Abby, who admired Stephen's "speak-ins" although she did not attempt to emulate them, was dismayed to find that most abolitionists were disapproving. Both Garrison and Phillips thought his methods were coercive and doubted their wisdom. When she proposed that Foster be sent to lecture in Connecticut, she was surprised to learn that even Charles Burleigh had vetoed him. Burleigh, who cultivated a Christ-like appearance with shoulder-length ringlets and a beard almost covering his waistcoat, hardly seemed the person to defend convention. "Has the slave to see his professed friends walking in velvet slippers and singing lullaby to his oppressors, while his real friends sit by and fold up their hands apathetically?" she asked George Benson. "Well Charles is doing what seems to him right. I shall, however, endeavor to convince him that he is not entirely destitute of that bigotry which he condemns so severely in others. *His* manner will do much for a certain class, at certain times, but another class need Foster's preaching. I deeply regret the spirit of intolerance that condemns all, except they use our particular weapons."

If Connecticut would not employ Stephen, perhaps Massachusetts would. No, wrote Ellis Loring, a member of the society's Board of Managers. "I honor the New Hampshire men for their courage & disinterestedness, but petitions for the impeachment of the Presdt of the U.S. for being a slaveholder, do not inspire me with great confidence in their good sense & discernment. Unfit agents do more harm than good and to find the right man is no easy matter."[6]

Abby was in Rhode Island when she received Loring's letter. The state antislavery society had asked her assistance in an unusual campaign. Rhode Island was still operating under a 1663 charter that restricted suffrage to men who owned at least $134 in land and to their eldest sons; seats in the legislature were apportioned so that the seacoast cities had greater representation than the new inland towns. More than any other New England state, Rhode Island had changed from a mercantile to an industrial economy in recent decades. Immigrants, most of them Catholics from Ireland and French Canada, had streamed into the state to work in the mills of the Blackstone Valley. In 1840 almost 60 percent of Rhode Island's male population was denied the right to vote. Appeals to the legislature for a new democratic charter were inevitably vetoed by the landowner majority.

However, a militant Rhode Island Suffrage Association had recently been organized. Its founders planned to hold a People's Constitutional Convention in October 1841, to be followed by a vote on the constitution two months later. The convention and constitution would have no legal standing, but the propaganda value of a large turnout of voters would, it was hoped, convince the legislature to move toward a broader suffrage.

The abolitionists enthusiastically backed the Suffrage party and its leading spokesman, Thomas Dorr, a portly Harvard-educated lawyer, until, at a meeting in Providence in September, the men who were fighting for suffrage for themselves voted to exclude blacks. When the People's Constitutional Convention met the following month, delegates, over the opposition of Dorr and his abolitionist backers, ratified a "whites only" suffrage clause.

Abby had been on the scene before the convention and had struggled to convince the Suffrage party that it was wrong to fight for their own rights while denying them to blacks. Not all abolitionists agreed with her. Some who had been working for many years for a broader suffrage found it hard to come out against it. "Let us get a *part*, if we can't obtain the *whole*," they told her. The majority, however, recognized that the "whites only" suffrage clause was a step backward in the fight against slavery and a desertion of Rhode Island's small but vocal black community.

During the months leading up to the vote on the People's Constitution, the Suffrage party waged a massive propaganda campaign, blanketing the state with speakers, parades, and leaflets to urge a vote for "equal rights." Less vocal for the most part, the landowners issued appeals to nativism, warning that foreigners and the pope at Rome would take over Rhode Island if the millworkers voted. Making the campaign a three-way struggle, Abby had the difficult task of convincing people to vote against a broader suffrage unless it included the entire male population. After starting her work in the coastal communities, whose wealth had come from the African slave trade and whose citizens had little interest in the rights of black people, she called for reinforcements from outside the state. By the time the Rhode Island Anti-Slavery Society held its annual convention in November, she had three stalwart co-workers: Frederick Douglass, Parker Pillsbury, and Stephen Foster.

At the antislavery convention plans were made to hold meetings in every town and village before the election, now set for late December. Almost a thousand dollars were raised, some in ten- and fifteen-dollar contributions, others from individuals like a washerwoman who gave a silver dollar "to help *blow out* the word 'white' from the constitution." The *New Age*, organ of the Suffrage party, warned against these outside agitators whose real object was to destroy church and state "and convert people to transcendentalism!!!" (The exclamation points were Abby's when she reported the article to the *Standard*.)

The campaign was nastier than anything Abby had encountered before. In Connecticut, as she had battled "new org," the issues had sometimes seemed abstract to her listeners. Now she was asking people, against their own self-interest, to postpone their chance for suffrage for the sake of an unpopular minority. When Stephen offered a resolution declaring "that the white suffrage constitution is more odious and hateful to the true principles of liberty than the old charter," machinists and millworkers disagreed, often violently. Although Abby and her team did their best to explain "the democracy of anti-slavery and the identity of its interests with those of the laboring classes," they were accused of being in the pay of the landed aristocracy.

In East Greenwich all halls and churches were closed to them. In Scituate their meeting was brought to an abrupt halt despite the plea of the "fascinating Abby Kelley" that they be permitted to continue. In Woonsocket Falls angry men drowned out the speakers with shouts against "nigger voting." In Providence a "boisterous and malignant crowd" pelted the speakers with snowballs and stones, and Abby returned to her lodgings "accompanied by the howls and snow-balls of the suffrage party." In Newport a mob of nearly a thousand broke up the abolitionists' meeting and followed them home, "rending the heavens by their fiendish shouts, and pelting with decayed apples, eggs, etc."

With her usual optimism Abby told the readers of the *Standard* that the violence had served to awaken the state to the antislavery question. "Few can see a crowd following a defenceless woman through the streets, hurling missiles at her, and shouting, without inquiring 'why?'" Nor was she as vulnerable to rejection as she had been a year earlier. "Such scenes a few days after their occurrence are to me like a troubled dream," she wrote. "They leave no clear impression, from the fact, I suppose, that I cannot persuade myself the people are really so wicked."

The Rhode Island campaign provided a unique experience for all the abolitionist speakers. Young Frederick Douglass, who had been an anti-slavery agent for only three months, had much to learn from Abby, the most experienced of the group, about the practical business of entering a strange town and organizing meaningful meetings. He listened, he later wrote, to the "splendid vehemence" of Parker Pillsbury and to Stephen Foster's "terrible denunciations." Although he sometimes found Stephen "extravagant and needlessly offensive," he was convinced that "no white man ever made the black man's cause more completely his own." But it was Abby "who was perhaps the most successful of any of us," he wrote. "Her youth and simple Quaker beauty, combined with her wonderful earnestness, her large knowledge and great logical power bore down all opposition, wherever she spoke, though she was pelted with foul eggs and no less foul words from the noisy mobs which attended us."

Abby left no account of her impressions of Douglass, but in some ways she gained the most from their collaboration. Until then she had been working *for* black people and lecturing against prejudice in the abstract. Now she was working *with* a black man on a daily basis and experiencing the prejudice against him at first hand. A year earlier she had traveled briefly with James L. Smith, another ex-slave, who had lectured in Connecticut with Dr. Hudson. She had seen the doctor's "distressed-looking carriage horse" after proslavery vandals had cropped its ears and shaved its mane and tail to express their anger at Smith's presence. But she did not feel the full impact of northern racism until she heard Rhode Island mobs shouting, "Nigger!" Nor could a dozen platitudinous resolutions against prejudice prepare her for the cold December day when Frederick was peremptorily ordered to the Jim Crow car on a train and his companions followed. When they shared the rough seats, covered with snow drifting in from a broken door, and breathed the foul, tobacco-laden air, they were truly "remember[ing] them that are in bonds as bound with them."

At their meetings this "fugitive prodigy," as one abolitionist called him, was a revelation. Abby had been telling audiences that blacks were the equal of whites. In Frederick they saw a man who was more than equal. Speaking of prejudice at the convention in Providence, he described his own experience in New Bedford, where no one would hire him at his trade of caulker, then went on to relate a poignant story about a colored girl who had gotten religion at a revival meeting. After she sipped from the communion cup, the white woman next to her "who had been baptised in the same water and put her trust in the same beloved Savior rose in disdain and walked out of the church." Following this with a humorous anecdote—in itself a departure from abolitionist practice—he concluded by asking, "Whence comes this prejudice? People will not allow that we have a head to think and a heart to feel and a soul to aspire. You degrade us and then ask why we are degraded—you shut our mouths and then ask why we don't speak—you close your colleges and schools against us and then ask why we don't know more."

Although Frederick started out speaking less aggressively than his companions, he moved closer to their "tomahawk" style of advocacy as the campaign continued. By late November he was defending a resolution that said that the churches were "combinations of thieves, adulterers and pirates and should be treated as brothels and banditti by all who would exculpate themselves from the guilt of slaveholding."

Abby and her crew remained in Rhode Island until after the vote for the People's Constitution was held. Although their appeals to white voters made little headway, their work helped unite and energize the black community. At abolitionist meetings, particularly in Providence, the state capital, where blacks had some strength, they agitated for better schools and wider job opportunities. When the Suffrage party convened in January 1842 to count the vote, Abby and Frederick led a delegation to the meeting to plead once again that the word "white" be dropped from the proposed constitution. The plea was ignored, and the People's Constitution was approved by an overwhelming vote of 13,944 to 52.

The Suffrage party hoped that the election would demonstrate the widespread sentiment for broader suffrage. When the landowners, by now organized into a Law and Order party, refused to make concessions, the Suffrage leaders scheduled another unofficial election at which they chose Thomas Dorr as governor. In May 1842 Dorr, escorted by armed militia companies, entered Providence and moved to seize state buildings. After an attempt to capture the arsenal failed, the legal governor, who had the backing of President Tyler and the promise of federal troops if necessary, put down the rebellion and posted a thousand-dollar reward for Dorr's capture.*

During these tense days the Law and Order party, grateful for all allies, were glad to accept the support of Providence blacks who joined the Home Guard in return for a promise that they would be permitted to vote. When a new more democratic constitution was finally ratified in the fall of 1842, the word "white" was omitted from the suffrage clause. "I think that our labors in Rhode Island during this Dorr excitement did more to abolitionize the state than any previous or subsequent work," Frederick Douglass later wrote.† A member of the Law and Order party was more cynical. "They would rather have the Negroes vote than the damned Irish," he told a friend.[7]

Abby and her associates had left Rhode Island before the final months of the Dorr Rebellion. Back in Millbury after enduring "the brutal jeer and the murderous threat," she rejoiced to hear "the bland voices of mother and sisters" instead of "the discordant shouts and yells of the mob," she said. The Rhode Island campaign had been a hard one, but home brought a different problem. Her mother, ill for some time, was growing steadily weaker. Abby spent anxious days at her bedside, leaving only when a sister came to relieve her.

Late in January 1842 she was able to go to Boston for four days to attend the annual meeting of the Massachusetts Anti-Slavery Society. At the busi-

---

* Dorr was arrested in 1843, convicted of treason, and sentenced to life imprisonment. He was pardoned in 1845. (Gettleman.)

† Until recently, historians have characterized the Dorr movement as a struggle for broader democracy. In *The Age of Jackson*, Arthur Schlesinger, Jr., devoted seven pages to the movement without mentioning the "whites only" clause or the role of blacks and abolitionists in the campaign. The enfranchisement of Rhode Island's blacks in 1842 was a considerable victory because blacks were not then permitted to vote in Connecticut, Pennsylvania, New Jersey, or Ohio and had only limited suffrage in New York.

ness sessions Anne Weston thought she was needlessly severe when she called the clergy "thieves, robbers, adulterers, pirates and murderers." Others must have agreed, for Abby's resolution was tabled. Five thousand people attended the society's public meeting, which was held for the first time in the hall of the house of representatives in the State House. After Wendell Phillips and Frederick Douglass had spoken, the audience called for Abby Kelley, "longing to glut their vulgar curiosity in seeing a beautiful woman speaking," Nathaniel Rogers reported. No doubt she spoke well, but her words were ignored by the Boston newspapers, whose columns were filled instead with descriptions of her appearance. The *Bay State Democrat*'s smitten reporter wrote that "A lady next appeared in the Speaker's chair, with a rich but plain Quaker dress, her dark hair smoothed placidly down on her fair cheek which glowed with the carnation's own deep hue, with beautifully curved lip, and full melting eye, and open brow of alabaster—the celebrated Abby Kelley—who with her sweetly melodious yet trumpet tones, poured forth her woman's soul in depicting the wrongs of the colored man. It was a touching piece of eloquence. That angel voice would call us back to bow at the shrine of her beauty and gentleness. No wonder that the abolitionists produce a sensation in the community, when such sweet enchantresses, with their magic wand of poetic enthusiasm, are suffered to play at will among the finest sensibilities of the soul." Few authors of romantic novels could have been more fulsome.[8]

Abby found time during the convention to take dinner with Maria and Henry Chapman, who were getting ready for another winter in Haiti, but she hurried home as soon as the sessions concluded, thereby missing a chance to meet Charles Dickens, who had just arrived in Boston at the start of an American tour. The Chapmans, Wendell Phillips, and Anne Weston all called at the Tremont House to meet the celebrated author. Anne found Mrs. Dickens "a pleasant nice looking woman about as ladylike looking as Mrs. Garrison." Dickens was "a decidedly small man, not much larger than Quincy," who dressed in bad taste and whose manner was not "high bred." "Be that as it may, he was very warm in the shake of my hand & we all sat down," she wrote Deborah. She managed to say a few words against slavery before "other ladies and lots of children" interrupted.

Perhaps her words had some influence, for Dickens's *American Notes* contained a strong antislavery chapter.* She was probably put out, however, by his comments on Boston women, whom he thought "unquestionably very beautiful" but not too bright. "Blue ladies [bluestockings] there are in Boston but like philosophers of that colour and sex in most other latitudes, they rather desire to be thought superior than to be so."[9]

Abby remained at her mother's bedside until on February 14, 1842, Diana Kelley died at the age of sixty-seven. Almost all her children attended the funeral, but it was Abby, the take-charge daughter, who was left to settle the estate and dispose of her mother's possessions. She was doubly bereaved because according to the terms of her father's will, the farm was to be sold and the proceeds divided among all his heirs. Lucy, the other single daughter, was engaged to marry in June. Only Abby would be homeless.[10]

During the winter and spring, when she was not conferring with lawyers and land agents or sorting out her parents' possessions, she lectured in nearby Massachusetts towns, working to raise the last two hundred dollars of her thousand-dollar pledge for the *Standard*. She was frequently accompanied by John M. Fiske, a lawyer from Brookfield who had broken with his family and church to become president of the Worcester County South Anti-Slavery Society. "I prophesy a match between Abby & John M. Fiske," Anne Weston, ever on the lookout for a romance, wrote Deborah.

Abby respected Fiske, but when she went to Brookfield to lecture, she was more interested in twenty-three-year-old Lucy Stone. A schoolteacher who was saving her money to go to Oberlin College, Lucy had followed Abby's career since the first time her name had appeared in the *Liberator*. Secretly she hoped to emulate her. Whenever Abby spoke in the neighborhood, Lucy came to hear her. Searching for women who could be brought into the work, Abby invited Lucy to sit in the pulpit with her. Lucy held back, suddenly grown timid. Her hair was "all blown about" from her three-mile ride from home, she said. Besides, although she knew

---

* The antislavery chapter in *American Notes* was largely based on Weld's *American Slavery as It Is*.

it to be irrational, she felt that the pulpit was too sacred a place for her to enter. "Oh, Lucy Stone," Abby teased. "You are not *half* emancipated!"[11]

Early in May Abby traveled to New York for the anniversary meeting of the American Society. Along with delegates from Boston and Philadelphia, she stayed with Abby and James Gibbons and their four children. During anniversary week every room in their small house was crowded, and beds were made up on the floor for the out-of-towners. This year they included Anne, Deborah, and Caroline Weston with their inevitable companion Edmund Quincy, Charles Burleigh, John A. Collins, and Sarah Pugh from Philadelphia.

At breakfast and during midday dinners "there was wisdom and wit—serious discourse and playful jest most beautifully blended," Sarah Pugh reported in a letter to a friend. Abby Gibbons was eager to talk about the Quakers, who had recently disowned her father and husband because of their abolitionist activities; she was preparing her own letter of resignation. Anne Weston, who enjoyed stirring up controversy, remarked that in abolitionists' estimation "blackness was next to goodness, followed by odiousness," and another speaker wished "for the faculty of Henry C. Wright and S. Foster of heating words seven times hotter than they are wont to be heated."

Serious Abby Kelley came in for her share of teasing. Everyone had noticed her support of resolutions calling the church a "brotherhood of thieves" and "the bulwark of slavery." At breakfast, when she mentioned going to a meeting in "Deacon Somebody's carriage," James Gibbons quickly penciled a resolution: "Whereas Abby Kelley by her own confession rode in a Deacon's carriage, said Deacon being a member of the Bulwark, Therefore, Resolved that she has not come out and separated herself from the American church and is 'striking hands' with living body snatchers and 'cat-o-nine tail devils.'"

At the convention Abby served on the business committee and on a special committee of forty that she had proposed. ("Committee of forty—forty thieves?" one of her tablemates asked. "Yes, we have been picking pockets," was the reply.) The society had limped along for the past two years, slowly extricating itself from the debts its predecessors had left. Before the split half a dozen men had been employed in the Anti-Slavery Office in New York, with twenty or more agents in the field. Currently the society had no full-time employee in the city and only six traveling agents. Gibbons, who as chairman of the Executive Committee bore the brunt of the society's problems, favored keeping it small and solvent. But Abby, pointing out that eight northern states had no antislavery societies, urged the national society to regain its former position. Her point of view prevailed. When the committee of forty reported back to the convention, it was agreed to employ a general agent in New York, to dispatch twenty agents to organize local societies in all the free states, and to raise fifty thousand dollars, more than three times the budget of the previous year. Abby pledged to be responsible for five thousand dollars.

Because her committee work occupied most evenings during the week, Abby had scarcely seen Stephen Foster. He had taken the floor only twice at the meeting, once to amend a resolution that said, "We cannot but regret" John Quincy Adams's failure to take a stronger antislavery stand—Stephen wanted to substitute "condemn" for "regret"—and the second time to move that the society return a gift of ten pounds sterling because it had come from a brewer. Both his motions were voted down.

After the convention they probably traveled by boat to Boston together. A crowd of rowdies turned up at the pier to see them off. With shouts of "White niggers" and "Take that to your black wife, damn you," they pelted the departing abolitionists with eggs and oranges. Quincy thought the oranges an improvement over brickbats. "Next year we shall be pelted with bouquets," Anne Weston said.[12]

At the New England Society's annual meeting, which was held in Boston the week of May 24, Stephen moved into the spotlight for a day, after he had attempted to speak at the Evangelical Congregational Anti-Slavery Convention at Marlborough Chapel and been hauled off to jail. While he languished in his "dungeon" in Leverett Street, Abby was one of several speakers who attacked the Congregationalists for "bigoted sectarianism and hostility to free discussion." When he was set free the next day, he was greeted at the antislavery meeting with great applause. "Our faithful Foster distinguished himself and won the love and admiration of the beloved abolitionists," Nathaniel Rogers reported.[13]

Weary after the weeks of conventions, Abby returned to Millbury for the last time. On June 8 Lucy married Samuel W. West and left with him for his home in East Hampton, Connecticut, where he was a neighbor of the Darlings. Abby remained in Millbury for another few weeks, completing the disposition of her parents' property. Then, with her "home, sweet home" lost to her forever, she returned to New York to begin a lecture tour in the state.[14]

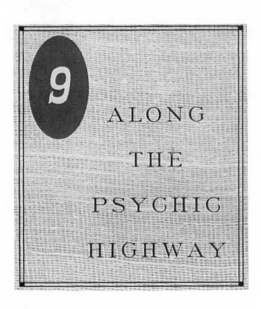

9

ALONG
THE
PSYCHIC
HIGHWAY

New York, the largest of the North Atlantic states, had been a sparsely settled wilderness of forest, lake, and mountain until the construction of the Erie Canal. After 1825, when the much ridiculed "big ditch" was completed and the waters of the Great Lakes mingled with those of the Atlantic Ocean, the population bordering the canal doubled, tripled, quadrupled, as emigrants from New England and Pennsylvania poured into the state.

In a decade isolated settlements of log huts had been transformed into villages, villages became towns, and towns, cities. Albany, Utica, Syracuse, Rochester, Buffalo sprang up along the banks of the canal, becoming terminals for trade between the western frontier and New York City, now the nation's leading port. Smaller rivers were connected to the Erie by tributary canals, and the settlements along their shores prospered accordingly. Mills were built to grind the farmers' grain; sheep shearings were converted into woolen cloth, and oak trees felled to clear the land kept sawmills busy.

Most of the people Abby met in New York in 1842 and 1843 resembled those she had grown up with: yeoman farmers and their wives who were beginning to leave agriculture to become millers or small-scale merchants. While this new emerging middle class might lack the culture of Boston— there was, after all, only one "hub of the universe"—they tended to be less hidebound than New Englanders. Many had been touched, in one fashion or another, by the wave of religious revivals that swept western New York in the 1820s and 1830s. Carl Carmer, a regional historian, has dubbed the route along the Erie Canal a "psychic highway," which was traversed by founders of new religious sects (Shakers, Mormons, Adventists), by Utopian socialists and Millerites, mesmerists, hydropathists, spiritualists, and the like. Freed from the bonds of Calvinism, these converts had a moral fervor that left them receptive to temperance crusaders, to the conscience-tugging abolitionists, and even to the claims of women seeking their rights.

Laboring men and women, largely foreign-born, also lived along the psychic highway, although they were not always in accord with their neighbors. Brought in to build the canal, they had remained to run its boats and loading docks. The "canawlers" tended to be hard drinkers and tobacco chewers who shrugged off the temperance campaigns, opposed the blue laws that shut down all travel and recreation on Sundays, and had scant interest in antislavery talk. Although a stone crashing through a window had greeted Abby during her first lecture in New York, she had far less conflict with working people there than she had had in Rhode Island. Not until she reached Rochester did she comment on the crowds in the railroad station who swarmed around her "as thick as bees. Jostling and crowding and trying to get [their] hand in your pocket," they exemplified her idea of Babel.[1]

Abby's goal in New York was to rebuild the state antislavery societies that had been active in the 1830s but had disintegrated after the 1840 split. After a quick survey of the field she planned a whirlwind three-month campaign of small-town conventions, to be climaxed by "mammoth" ones in Rochester, Syracuse, and Utica, where the "big guns" of the movement would speak. John A. Collins, who had moved to New York to become general agent of the American Society, stood ready to assist her. "What number of towns ought to come within the call for the conventions?" he asked after she had been in the state for a fortnight. "How many ought to be held a week and how many speakers ought to attend them? Do get the thing arranged in your own mind so that all I shall have to do will be to prepare the calls."

Abby and Frederick Douglass were to be present at all the conventions while half a dozen other agents, including Dr. Hudson, were to join them from time to time. "Dear friends," John Collins wrote in his call for action, which was printed in the *Standard* and *Liberator*, "When an agent proposes to visit your town, let no pains be spared to get him a good house to speak in, and a large audience to listen to his address. Let me entreat you to excite the abolitionists to rally at these gatherings. When the weather is favorable, it would be well to have the conventions in a grove."

In courthouses, town halls, and picnic groves in good weather, Abby and Frederick held two conventions a week, each lasting two or three days. It was a punishing schedule, but they were rewarded by enthusiastic audiences almost everywhere. Even the newspapers, although regretting that "a lady with such advantages of person and talent should not have found a more appropriate sphere of action," admired Abby's oratory. Some also agreed with her message.

A correspondent for the *Albany Tocsin of Liberty* was "astonished to behold a plain, simple girl, plain in her dress, simple in her manner, no affectation, no noisy declamation, standing before an audience, and in strains of simple eloquence, and in language as chaste and pure as I ever heard, depict that American abomination, slavery, in all its horrors." The *Seneca Observer* described "a fair young woman, with a form and features of just proportions, rising up before a large auditory with as much nonchalant self-possession as the best practised professor of law or divinity. Then the truths she uttered—what were they? Nothing less than a sermon from that great democratic text, to wit—'that all men are born free and equal.' She soon made you feel that she was the true priestess of equal rights."

There were detractors, of course, who accused her of "Fanny Wrightism." " 'Tis enough to know that she accompanies a pack of men about the country", one declared. Ministers, who almost to a man refused to allow the conventions to be held in their churches, singled out Abby as a special target. "Abby is doing more to promote the cause than any ten men and the 'Reverend Clergy' are opposed to her labors," a fellow agent wrote. "It was amusing, although painful, to see three of these sermon-brokers a few Sabba-days since, refuse to read from their pulpits a notice for [her] lecture, although they all read one for myself at the same time. So much for sex-governed caste."

"I have now been hastily over a large part of Western New York," Abby wrote to the *Liberator* after two months on the road. "I think myself safe in saying, no part of the field in which it has fallen to my lot to labor will better pay the culture. Such frankness, such readiness to receive the truth and to follow it is rarely found. When half the labor shall have been bestowed here that has been in Massachusetts, abolition will carry all before it."[2]

In November Frederick returned to Boston to work for the release of George Latimer, a runaway slave who had been arrested. After Frederick's departure Abby visited Rochester, Syracuse, and Utica to lay the groundwork for the "Great State Conventions." In Utica she spoke for five successive nights in the courthouse. Presenting her first lecture in the form of a "judicial investigation," she aimed a barrage of accusations against the state and the church as perpetrators of "falsehood, theft, robbery, concubinage and murder." On subsequent evenings she invited listeners who disagreed to take the floor, replying to their arguments afterward. Perhaps because the harvest was in and farm families had leisure, perhaps as a tribute to her showmanship, the courthouse was increasingly crowded—"a perfect jam" at her third lecture, "crowded to suffocation" for her fourth. When a man, attempting to prove that slavery was a normal constituent of society, thought he could stump her by asking, "When did slavery commence? How long has it existed?" she coolly replied, "About as long as murder," and the house "with one acclaim burst into loud applause."

The *Utica Daily Times* disliked Abby's politics but praised her "impressive oratory, very correct and polished language, evident sincerity, set off by a graceful delivery, admirable gesticulation and expression of emotions on quite a fair, comely face." In its account of one lecture the paper applauded her for having done her homework: "When she took up the subject of the relations which the United States held to [slavery] in a moral, political, statistical, and commercial view, she displayed much varied and minute information in regard to the political history of the country, and its commercial and manufacturing interests. Her argumentative powers were of no mean order. We have in by-gone days listened to John Randolph [and] Henry Clay. We are not alone in saying that in *her line* and in *her way*, no public speaker we have ever heard could have held his audience in fixed attention to an equal degree of absorption."

While planning the conventions with local abolitionists, Abby wrote to Boston to line up speakers. Garrison, Collins, and Charles Remond from Salem, who had been the movement's leading black orator until Douglass's arrival on the scene, had promised to come, but she also wanted Wendell Phillips. "You cannot possibly appreciate the importance of your presence at this juncture," she wrote. " 'There is a tide' in our affairs—God's affairs rather—and will you not take advantage of it to lead Western and Central N.Y. on to the fortunes of liberty?" Carried away by her fondness for farming metaphors, she continued: "The agents of the American Society have done much for the past few months to plough in the seeds of truth, and now with a warm gust of sunlight, such as you can throw, with Garrison's showers and Remond's bland breezes, we may expect a harvest as will make even the floods of apathy clap their hands for joy."[3]

Tied to home by Ann's illness as well as by the exigencies of the campaign to free George Latimer, Wendell managed to resist Abby's extravagant plea. William Lloyd Garrison was the main speaker at a crowded three-day convention in Rochester, where, as Abby had anticipated, delegates organized a Western New York Anti-Slavery Society and a women's committee was appointed to encourage antislavery sewing circles and fairs. Afterward friends drove Garrison and Kelley, "on a very blustering and severe day," to nearby villages, where they lectured on slavery in meetinghouses and talked informally at night on "phrenology, mesmerism, anti-slavery, non-resistance &c," Garrison wrote his wife, Helen. A thoroughgoing hypochondriac himself, he added his concern that "Abby

Kelley is tasking her lungs too severely and ought to be more careful for the future."[4]

After Rochester their reception in Syracuse was disappointing. Unable to obtain a church to meet in, they convened in a small hall owned by the Library Association. Although placards had been posted about town announcing that Garrison, Remond, and Kelley would speak, only eleven people turned out for the afternoon session, but the speakers' "scorching remarks and 'ultra' resolutions"—Garrison's description—brought out a much more numerous crowd that evening. The real excitement came the next day, when Stephen Foster arrived.

Since last seeing Abby, Stephen had lived through tumultuous times. He had been thrown out of the Friends' meetinghouse in Lynn, jailed again in Boston, and almost lynched in Portland, Maine, where hundreds of men had interrupted his lecture and rushed to the rostrum, shouting, "Murder the damned abolitionist!" They had beaten him over the head, bloodied his nose, and shredded his coat until he was rescued by members of the Female Anti-Slavery Society, who had managed to lock arms with him and drag him from the hall.

Attending the second day of the Syracuse convention, Stephen seemed unintimidated by recent difficulties. He listened to the discussion for only a short time before moving that delegates pledge to separate themselves from any church or political party that was not in favor of immediate emancipation. That his listeners regarded this proposal as too radical and accordingly tabled it had no chastening effect. He opened the evening session by reading from Matthew. After quietly intoning, "Woe unto you, scribes and Pharisees, hypocrites!" and "Ye serpents, ye generation of vipers," he then declared that leaders of the Methodist Episcopal Church were worse than brothel keepers in New York because they held thousands of slave concubines.

"A terrible yell" from the back of the hall interrupted him. Hisses, curses, and the breaking of windows and seats followed. "My parents are Methodists. I'll be damned if I hear 'em abused," one man called out, while others shouted, "Damn the niggers," and, "Hustle 'em out." The last was a signal for an attack on the speakers. By the time the sheriff arrived to quell the disorder, they had been shepherded to the door by prominent citizens. The only damage suffered was to Garrison's coat, which had been splattered with a foul-smelling egg. He counted himself lucky, he wrote Helen, for the crowd had prepared tar and feathers, "to give us a coat without any cost to ourselves."

The following morning officers of the Library Association refused to permit the abolitionists to use the hall unless they agreed to pay for damages. Garrison favored adjourning, but Abby, indignant that "liberty of speech was stricken down in Syracuse," proposed that they meet outdoors in the public square. In the end they were permitted to use the hall during the day, when potential troublemakers would be at work, but not at night. Stephen had a chance to support his "terrible charges" against the Methodists by explaining that prostitutes worked in brothels voluntarily while slave women owned by southern clergymen had no liberty to resist their advances.

"Foster obtained a very respectful hearing and produced an impression decidedly in his favor," Garrison wrote Helen. "The whole town is in a ferment. Every tongue is in motion. If an earthquake occurred, it would not have excited more consternation. We have no doubt that the result will be good for our cause." Nevertheless, he expressed concern for the next convention, to be held in Utica. "As bro. Foster will be there, I presume we shall have a repetition of the scenes in Syracuse, as he is remarkably successful in raising the spirit of mobocracy wherever he goes. It is useless to reason with him, with any hope of altering his course, as he is firmly persuaded that he is pursuing the very best course."[5]

The Utica convention was so fully reported in the press that it is possible to follow the interplay of forces and to see the roles assumed by each speaker. Stephen was the extremist, infuriating his listeners with extravagant charges, which he later patiently and plausibly supported. Abby was almost equally outrageous, but her charm and rapport with audiences made her statements seem less offensive. Garrison, ordinarily no mean polemicist, played the unaccustomed role of "good guy," backing up his younger colleagues but implicitly apologizing for their excesses. The policy of free discussion that was customary at abolitionist meetings meant that critics as well as sympathizers could take the floor. In Utica the hall was crowded with ministers and businessmen, including Horatio Seymour, mayor of the city who later became New York's governor. Everyone who wanted to speak was given a chance. In their answers to what were often simplistic charges, the abolitionists had an opportunity to educate the audience in the ABCs of antislavery.

Stephen opened the general debate with a resolution calling the U.S. government "a wicked and nefarious conspiracy against the liberty of more than two million of our countrymen." Northerners who supported the government were "the basest of slaves, the vilest of hypocrites and the most execrable of man-stealers, inasmuch as they voluntarily consent to be the watch-dogs of the plantation."

Abby followed with a speech attacking the churches for their complicity with slavery and criticizing the Bible Society, which sent missionaries to the Great Wall of China but refused to send Bibles to slaves in the South. When one minister declared that Stephen was insane and others complained of the pair's hard language, she asked, "Pray tell me, who are offended?" She had no desire to secure the approval of slaveholders, "but to speak as though my mother—my sister were now before me on the auction block."

Requesting a patient hearing, Garrison pointed out that although there was a universal cry for reform from the religious and political world, "the first device of the devil" was to condemn reformers as "a few fanatics seeking notoriety" and to declare, "Your principles are good but your spirit is bad." And if reformers showed signs of being successful, then their opponents could always call out the mob.

Several times during the meetings there were demonstrations from the floor. Torpedoes—firework devices that exploded when they struck a hard surface—were thrown, and shouts often drowned out the speakers. When the "mobocratic spirit" threatened to take over, Mayor Seymour, although not an abolitionist, defended their right to speak and threatened to prosecute those responsible for the disturbance.

That the mood of the opposition in Utica never approached the lynch spirit of Syracuse was due in part to the fortuitous arrival of a party of runaway slaves who had just reached the city from the South. Escorted down the aisle, one fugitive stepped to the rostrum to tell of their escape.

"Is there safety for these men in Utica?" the chairman asked. He was answered by "a deep-welling 'Aye'!" For that moment at least, everyone in the hall was an abolitionist.

Before the meeting adjourned, Abby rose again to point out that "the progress of freedom will be in proportion to the fidelity of its friends and their liberality in pecuniary contributions." Agents ought to be crisscrossing the North, "kindling up the fires of liberty," but the treasury of the American Society was empty. "Who is prepared to consecrate himself, his all, to the cause of human freedom?" she asked. Other business came to a halt as men and women walked up the aisle to turn in pledges and donations and to subscribe to the *Standard* and *Liberator*.

At each convention she also displayed antislavery publications. Since her arrival in New York she had sold more than a thousand copies of a forty-eight-page *Anti-Slavery Almanac*,* compiled by Maria Child. "It is antislavery light," she grandly explained. "Like the little foxes of Solomon that destroyed the vines, the book will eat out the fibres of slavery. Let it go into every American family."

Another good seller was the *Anti-Slavery Pic-Nic*, a collection of songs put together by John Collins. Songs had only recently been introduced at antislavery meetings. Abby probably felt some Quakerish discomfort when she first heard Garrison's poem "I am an Abolitionist / I glory in the name," sung to the tune of "Auld Lang Syne," or "Our grateful hearts with freedom burn,/ Hurrah, hurrah, hurrah." But she quickly recognized the value of the "liberty songs" in arousing emotions and contributing to a feeling of unity.

At the conclusion of the convention Utica's abolitionists organized a Central New York Anti-Slavery Society, which affiliated with the Western New York and American Anti-Slavery societies. Abby's tireless work of the past months had paid off.[6]

In contrast with the hostility she had encountered elsewhere, Abby found

---

* The almanac contained weather forecasts and meteorological statistics as well as antislavery wisdom.

ungrudging hospitality wherever she went in New York. In Albany, her first stop, she had boarded with Abigail and Lydia Mott, maiden sisters who were members of a large Quaker family* originally from Long Island and now deployed along the psychic highway as far west as Battle Creek, Michigan. Supporting themselves by shirtmaking, the sisters opened the spare bedrooms of their little house on Maiden Lane to fugitive slaves on their way to Canada, to itinerant abolitionists, and to woman's rights activists who came to the state capital to lobby. Several years older than Abby, they fussed over her, plying her with good food and advice while admiring "the burning truths" she poured out "like melted lead" upon the "Albanians."

"I was amused the other evening as I was by the door with a couple of fugitives who had been confined closely all day," Abigail wrote after Abby's visit. "I wished them to take some exercise before they slept and was giving them directions which way to walk. A company of lads passed and spoke out in one voice—'there is Abby Kelley's race.' So you see you are not forgotten here." Reading over her sister's shoulder, Lydia added a postscript: "*Caution.* As you are traveling about with Fred Douglass, I advise you to be careful who hears your regrets that you are not a colored woman."

Lydia's advice implied no racism. The sisters demonstrated their color blindness when Frederick Douglass went to Great Britain in 1845, leaving his wife with four young children. The Motts assumed the upbringing of his eldest, six-year-old Rosetta, until his return to the States almost two years later.[7]

In Utica Abby lived with Paulina and Francis Wright. Thirty-year-old Paulina, a striking blonde with blue eyes and a fine figure, was brainy as well as beautiful. Orphaned at an early age and brought up in a strict Presbyterian household, she had planned to become a missionary to the Sandwich Islands until she met and married Francis Wright, a well-to-do merchant. Before Abby's arrival on the scene she had already interested herself in woman's rights and had been one of a handful of women who petitioned the legislature on behalf of a married women's property law.

---

* Abigail and Lydia Mott were distantly related to James Mott, Lucretia's husband. (Cornell.)

Save for this aberration, she and Francis had been respectable members of the community and pillars of their church—until Abby Kelley became their guest.

After hearing her explain the complicity of the church in sustaining slavery, they wrote a *"grand* letter of excommunication" to their minister; the church fathers retaliated by accusing them of "Moral Loaferism." Throwing themselves into antislavery work, they made arrangements for all of Abby's meetings in and around Utica and served on the executive committee of the Central New York Society as soon as it was organized.

Recognizing Paulina's leadership qualities, Abby began grooming her for the lecture platform. When Paulina accompanied her to meetings, she encouraged her to take the floor. At one convention she thought Paulina spoke "most delightfully although it was too short"; at others, Paulina acted as chairman. But Francis, who, Paulina said, "does not see his way as clear as I think I do," soon put his foot down. Presiding at meetings and serving on committees were fine, but he did not want his wife to speak in public. After "some unhappy hours," Paulina regretfully decided not to "lecture on antislavery or woman's rights so long as my husband feels as he does about it. I could joyfully bear all the trials and reproach that would follow but it is my duty to seek the *happiness* of my *husband*."

Despite her acquiescence to Francis's wishes, Paulina's "reputation in a worldly point of view" was destroyed after she traveled to a meeting with Abby and black Charles Remond. "There is scarcely a woman in the city who will speak to me. They are really making a worse fuss about that than anything else," she wrote Abby. One former friend had called to see if she "had changed into a monster of frightful mien"; others refrained from calling. "I do sometimes feel the want of female sympathy, but I don't think I shall fret about those poor toads," she concluded. "I trust in the Lord and am ready to do my duty as fast as I can see what it is."

If Abby revolutionized the Wrights' lives, they changed hers, too. Making their home her headquarters during much of her New York stay, she enlisted Paulina as sister, confidant, and best friend. "She is indeed a rare spirit," she wrote Stephen. "You know not how delightful it is to be so highly favored in my journeyings and wearisome labors. It takes away half the trials, or, rather, the trials are not half so severe." Paulina, in turn, delighted in teasing single-minded Abby, hoping to enlarge her "bump of fun."

Stephen stayed with the Wrights during and after the Utica convention, and the four young people became fast friends. Less solemn than their guests, the Wrights introduced Abby and Stephen to current parlor games. Animal magnetism, or mesmerism, was all the rage that year in reform circles. Its practitioners used a combination of hypnotism and hocus-pocus to read minds and to "cure" illnesses. Paulina, who could put herself into a "magnetic sleep," enjoyed showing off her skill. The two couples sat around a table holding hands while she solemnly "made passes" at them. Finding that the "magnetic witching" eased tensions, Abby took a turn at it, too. After Stephen went back to New England, she tried "magnetizing" in order to transfer her thoughts to him. She half believed that it worked.

Along with many of their contemporaries, they also gave credence to phrenology, another "science of the mind." Phrenology's recognition that the brain was a bodily organ capable of development through education and attention to physiological laws was another blow at Calvinism and predestination. Its adherents looked on phrenology as a method of understanding and improving themselves in somewhat the same way as later generations turned to psychotherapy.

Orson S. Fowler, the most popular American phrenologist, published not only "how-to" books on phrenology but also marriage manuals and books on diet and health. Abby was away when he lectured in Utica in December 1842, but Paulina and Stephen attended his lecture and had their heads "read" afterward. "He did not give me much of a character, only for being a good whole-souled friend," Paulina said, but Stephen's analysis was so astute that Francis sent it to the *Liberator*, where it appeared months later.

"Your leading quality is action, both mental and physical," Fowler had written. "You feel intensely . . . can perform an astonishing amount of mental labor without fatigue. You enjoy and suffer much. . . . You have a remarkable faculty of operating on the mind and *feelings* of others. Are full of bold, striking remarks and thoughts. Love the good opinions of men and are cut to the heart by the reproofs of friends. . . . Are firm as a rock always driving at some important object, but can never be discouraged by difficulties. You require self-confidence, and should cultivate self-assurance. . . . You are a very social man, fond of society, especially female society— yet love women as a friend more than for animal love. . . . You care little for money, are all for doing good and reforming mankind. You have great moral courage . . . are a REAL RADICAL. . . ."

Thin-skinned Stephen was embarrassed by its publication, but "It will do you no harm," Abby assured him. "I am afraid you have not got above what the world says about you."

While he was in Utica, Stephen and Abby spent a "never to be forgotten mesmeric evening" in the Wrights' parlor and at last admitted their love for each other. They agreed to marry, but Abby steadfastly refused to set a wedding date or even let their engagement be known. Paulina and Francis were the only ones in on the secret, and their home was the only place where the pair could meet "as we wish to meet. In other places we must be only friendly," Abby insisted. The secret tied her even closer to Paulina, who shared their confidences and read much of their correspondence after Stephen left.[8]

The letters Abby and Stephen exchanged in the initial stage of their courtship hardly qualified as love letters. Writing to "My dear friend," later "My very dear friend," Abby interspersed accounts of antislavery work with concern for Stephen's poor health. "Do you intend to commit suicide?" she scolded when he reported overtaxing himself. "I have a strong incli- nation to write to your mother and entreat her to keep you at home." "Are you careful about your diet?" she asked in another letter. "I hope you are as firm as myself who have set down my determination not to eat any pastry or cake other than 'Simon pure' Graham." After she recommended "food entirely in its natural state," Stephen, who eschewed half measures, announced that henceforth he would eat only raw food. Regretting her advice, Abby replied, "I certainly will be cautious how I challenge you again."

As the winter progressed, Stephen's health worsened. In a play for sym- pathy he told Abby that he felt like "an old man," his "energies exhausted" and "once dauntless spirit broken." Abby refused to be impressed by his despairing tone. "You are not wont to look on the bright side," she wrote. " 'Tis your somber thoughts, I fear, that make your body sick." And when he described the fine nursing care he was receiving from New Hampshire neighbors, she ignored the implied reproach. "Since you tell me that Mrs. Tappan and her daughters are such excellent housekeepers and nurses I am quite at ease and hope you will put yourself in their care again. I have had so little experience in either kind of business I fear almost to risk my reputation as an accomplished woman in engaging in [nursing]."

Despite her unsentimental response to Stephen's reports of his ailments, she made it plain that she missed him and longed for better ways to communicate. "I have not the temperament for writing. I would much rather talk on a subject." After covering a large sheet of paper, she found that it contained "but few of the many things I wish to place upon it." When Stephen pointed out that she wrote as she spoke—two words to his one—and therefore should write "twice as often and twice as much," she agreed and envied him his "great condensing power."

Occasionally she engaged in "castle-building," dreaming of the day when they would have a home of their own. After boarding with a German family in Herkimer County, all of whom sang and played musical instruments, she discovered, somewhat to her surprise, that music was "refining, soothing and elevating," adding, "very much to the pleasures of domestic life." "I want to hear music and hope you do," she wrote. "Shall we not take lessons together when we have time?" But her "moral organization" quickly took over as she realized that she could not "sit down to a banquet of domestic sweets while the only music I can hear is the wail of the southern wife and the groan of her heartbroken husband."[9]

Had Stephen been her only correspondent, Abby might not have disliked letter writing. But he was one of dozens of people with claims on her attention. Mornings before beginning the day's work, evenings before retiring, she dashed off a note scheduling next week's meetings, outlined a spring campaign, reported her activities to the *Standard*. She arranged rendezvous with Frederick Douglass and Erasmus Hudson and tried to bolster the flagging spirits of others who were growing tired of the fray. James Gibbons, who felt that he alone was supporting the *Standard* and the American Society, needed frequent hand-holding, and a letter from her old friend Aroline Chase required a sympathetic response.

Aroline reported that some Lynn friends had become apathetic; others had deserted the struggle to go to *dancing parties*." "Abby, I pray don't go into extremes of any kind," she added. Although pleased that the legislature had repealed the law forbidding intermarriage—"the only thing I can put my finger on as having done in the Anti-slavery cause"—she did not know how much longer she could continue. "You say I must not give up until fifty. I am thirty now [and] I feel as though I stood alone."

In addition, Abby had to reconcile conflicting advice from the New York abolitionists. One wanted her to hold meetings in his town on Sundays "as we could get the best turnout of people at that time." Another thought it prudent "in a community where nine tenths of the people recognize the divine institution of the Sabbath" to refrain from Sunday lectures. She also had to reassure the latter that neither William Lloyd Garrison nor "the Garrison school" was opposed to Christianity despite the criticism of churches. "From my particular acquaintance with [Garrison] I have evidence that his walk is with God and that Christ has been to him a Savior indeed. I would that you knew him. You would feel, I think, to sit at his feet and learn from his deep experience," she wrote.[10]

As she ventured farther west along the psychic highway, Abby found other congenial souls. In the village of Waterloo in the Finger Lakes district, she stayed with Margaret and George Pryor, an elderly Quaker couple. Abby had met Margaret five years earlier at the first convention of anti-slavery women; George, a hardy sexagenarian, now took charge of scheduling Abby's county conventions, and both were founders of the new Western New York Society. Longing for family ties, Abby adopted the Pryors as "Aunt Margaret" and "Uncle George" and made their farm another of her homes from home. In Waterloo she also visited Mary Ann and Thomas McClintock, recent emigrants from Philadelphia who had belonged to the reform circle around Lucretia and James Mott. Thomas kept a drugstore on Waterloo's Main Street; his daughter Elizabeth clerked in the store and ran a school in a room above it.

In Rochester Abby lodged with Amy and Isaac Post in their comfortable home on Sophia Street. Quakers, and cousins of Lydia and Abigail Mott, they had come originally from Long Island. Isaac had initially opened a butcher shop in Rochester but was now a successful pharmacist. They, too, were founders of the Western New York Society. Forty-year-old Amy was a bundle of energy and enthusiasm who seemed to have been waiting for Abby Kelley to come along and channel it. Shortly after hearing Abby at her first Rochester convention, Amy and her extensive circle of sisters, sisters-in-law, daughters, cousins and close friends formed an antislavery sewing society that met weekly to prepare articles for fairs and to raise money to bring antislavery lecturers to the city. Before long they were part of a network of similar societies in nearby towns and villages and were exchanging fair merchandise with Paulina Wright in Utica and Maria Chapman in Boston.

Before long, too, the Society of Friends warned Amy that she was "fast getting out of the quiet" and appointed a committee to counsel her on "her attitude [in] working with the 'world's people.' " Unmoved, she anticipated further charges, she wrote Abby, because she had taken notes for a Friends' meeting on writing paper that depicted a kneeling chained slave. "I have but little doubt but that imploring immage will disturb their quiet, at least I hope it will." Disowned by the Quakers in 1845, the Posts joined the McClintocks and Pryors in organizing a Yearly Meeting of Congregational Friends (later Progressive Friends), a society that retained some Quaker doctrines and practices but worked toward larger goals.[11]

Although Amy Post would become a pioneer in every ultra reform in her part of the world, she felt unsure of herself and looked to Abby, many years her junior, for help. "We had hoped that we should have had some of thy company and assistance this winter to learn us and give us a fresh start," she wrote in December 1843. "We earnestly hope thou will not fail to be here at our annual meeting. We fear there will be no one here capable of conducting a meeting or of making it interesting."

Nor was Amy Post the only activist woman who lacked self-confidence. When young Elizabeth McClintock served on the Rochester Fair committee, she asked Abby, "whose tongue, pen & wit are all so ready," to write an open letter calling for the cooperation of all New York women. We need your assistance, she explained, "not in plying thy needle, but in that most difficult of all work—brainwork."

The requests might have flattered a different kind of person, but Abby, whose ego needed little bolstering, was sometimes exasperated by the women's self-effacement. There was no longer any question of their right to membership in antislavery societies. Through their work on committees and their role as fund raisers, they were providing significant support to the movement. But in the five years since the Grimkés' retirement, not one woman had come forward to join her on the platform.

She still needed a companion on her travels, someone to take over the bookkeeping chores at meetings and to protect her from the harassment she encountered when she rode alone on stagecoaches and trains. For several months, she had prevailed on Laura Boyle, a middle-aged matron, to act as her chaperone. Laura's "suggestions and sympathy were invaluable," but she proved to be a weak reed to lean on. Reserved and diffident, she had "always been cherished like a delicate plant and therefore is illy qualified to bear up against the rude blasts like some of us," Abby wrote Maria Chapman. After the Boyles had moved to Massachusetts to join the North-ampton Association, a new utopian community, Abby enlisted Margaret Pryor whenever she could be spared from home. Aunt Margaret traveled with her, conscientiously taking down the names of new subscribers to the *Standard* and endeavoring to see that her charge had hot water and a clean bed at the end of a long day. But even fifty-eight-year-old Aunt Margaret with her Quaker bonnet and her "honest almost angel face" was not enough to shield Abby from what she called the "forked tongue of slander." As they went from town to town, the pair were vilified as a "traveling seraglio."

When Abby learned that Elizabeth Neall, a Philadelphia Quaker, was spending the winter with her cousins the McClintocks, she immediately sought her out. Elizabeth had impeccable abolitionist credentials. Her grandfather had been president of the nation's first antislavery society; her father, of the Pennsylvania Hall Association. As a girl of seventeen she had attended the first convention of antislavery women and in 1840 had ac-companied Lucretia Mott to London for the World's Anti-Slavery Con-vention. With no family responsibilities and no ideological scruples to overcome, she seemed the perfect recruit. But Abby had not reckoned with the effect that daily doses of the cult of True Womanhood had on her psyche. When she proposed that Lizzie travel and lecture with her, Lizzie thought that she was joking.

"Thee is not acquainted with me or thee would not speak so seriously about this matter. My qualifications are not such as would justify me in throwing myself into the midst of battle," Lizzie responded. "I have not the gift of speech and certainly not the gift of seeing clearly through a knotty argument. It aint in my nature."

Patient as she had been with Laura Boyle, Abby was severe with Lizzie, who ought to know better. In a letter to the McClintocks she complained that Lizzie was sitting out the winter in Waterloo, "sucking her thumbs," while she, Abby, was being "cut into mince meat"—implying, Lizzie retorted, "that either I ought to be cut into mince meat too, or else should hinder the same from happening to thee. . . . I have no excuse of other duties to urge in my defense. I am free to do as I please and I do please, before I go forth into the world as the champion of enslaved humanity to make myself more worthy the name of Abolitionist, Woman & Christian. Thou must not, dear Abby, be so hard on me."

Hard on herself, Abby found it difficult to excuse others, especially someone like Lizzie, who was a birthright member of the antislavery family. Disappointed, she continued to press Aunt Margaret into service when she was available and occasionally to call on Jeannette Brown, a youthful admirer from Little Falls who wished that all abolitionists "would be more like you and S. S. Foster." Some lecturers Jeannette had met "wore gold rings, drank tea and smoked cigars."[12]

As the only representative of the American Society in western New York during the winter and spring of 1843, Abby set her own pace. She had taken a lesson from the temperance crusaders, who worked over a country district, holding nightly meetings until virtually everyone was converted and distilleries and rumshops closed down. The first temperance societies had warred only against whiskey and rum, but by 1840 a new Washington Temperance Society, organized by reformed drunkards, opposed all fermented beverages—beer, wine, and cider—as well. At emotion-charged meetings ex-alcoholics told stories of their downfalls and conversions until audiences were ready for the teetotal pledge, a promise to abstain from all alcoholic beverages for the remainder of their lives.

Borrowing from their technique, Abby spoke night after night with mounting intensity until she had worked up her listeners to a fever pitch. She started with the Declaration of Independence, then went on to relate "heart-sickening and astounding" facts about slave life. "With an elocution more rapid and declamatory," one observer said, she arraigned slavery "and all its lukewarm opposers, its nominal enemies, and its blind, interested friends." Finally she involved her audience directly. "It was not sufficient that a Christian did not hold his brother in bondage," she said. "They must also enlist as self-devoted missionaries in the holy cause of human rights." The climax came when she read her own "Tee Total Pledge"—essentially the pledge that Stephen had proposed at the Syracuse convention—which called on people to withdraw from all churches and political parties that failed to demand immediate emancipation.

To add to the drama of her meetings, she lined up support from local people ahead of time. In one central New York town where an antislavery lecturer had been mobbed the year before, fifty young men marched into her meeting with a banner that read ABOLITION OUR MOTTO, LIBERTY AND EQUALITY OUR AIM. Before the evening was over, dozens had signed the Tee Total Pledge, and a much larger number was "heartily engaged for the cause."

The pledge, she wrote to the *Standard*, "has been the greatest aid of any measure I have ever adopted, in producing agitation. Those who have got but one foot out of the mire of slavery extend their hand to us, and we grasp it in good faith, saying 'Friend, come up a little higher.' It throws corrupt politicians and sectarians into most delightful spasms."[13] It was also causing spasms among some loyal abolitionists, notably the editor of the *Standard*.

"Abby Kelley is eaten up with zeal to have every abolitionist pledge himself to belong to no religious association, or show sympathy with, or aid in the support of any association that is not publicly in co-operation with the anti-slavery Society," Maria Child wrote a friend. "She says that the *Standard* should take this ground, and maintain it against the world. It seems to me utterly *sectarian* in its character. To push everybody off the anti-slavery platform who will not leave their religious associations seems to me narrow and proscriptive. I resist their effort to co-erce the free will of individuals."

At the anniversary meeting of the American Society in May 1843 the Tee Total Anti-Slavery Pledge was adopted as an effective propaganda weapon but was not made obligatory. It was then that Maria Child resigned the editorship of the *Standard* and withdrew from all organized antislavery work for more than a decade. "I will work in my own way according to the light that is in me," she wrote Ellis Loring. She remained alienated from the movement until the mid-fifties, when the outrages of the Fugitive Slave Law and the fighting in Kansas drew her back into the struggle. Although she and Abby were often on the same side of a question, they never again became close friends.[14]

In addition to a large delegation from upstate New York, including the Wrights, McClintocks, and Elizabeth Neal, a sizable number of people had come to the meeting from Ohio and Indiana. They had made the long trip on horseback or in wagons, bringing their own provisions—graham bread and apples. The Hutchinsons, a family of musicians who were to become a fixture at abolitionist gatherings, enlivened the sessions with their songs despite the disapproval of some Friends. "We have enough of interest in rational appeals at our A. S. Convention without descending to mere excitement to carry on the work," Lucretia Mott thought.

At the conclusion of "an extraordinary speech" by Frederick Douglass Abby Kelley joined him on the platform. Greeted with warm applause, she reminded the assemblage that Frederick, now free, could speak for himself but that "his mother and sisters were still in the hands of the outragers. It was therefore fit that she, a woman, should stand by his side and bear her testimony in favor of the cause which, under God, would make them free."

A reporter for the *New York Express*, admiring Abby's "clear blue eyes, delicate complexion, fair hair and lady-like hand," found that after "she had uttered two sentences, all sense of the difference between the sexes so far as the propriety of a female speaking in public was concerned, entirely vanished. Her argument was clever, her remarks to the point, her illustrations happy, and her address was impressive and powerful." Disagreeing, the *Washington Globe* grumpily advised Abby to "go spin; attend to your household; get married, if you can; administer to the happiness of the domestic circle; and mind your own business."

Abby served on the business committee with Stephen, whom she had not seen in five months. Writing to him beforehand, she had promised that in New York "we can take a walk occasionally in that forest of people, where, above all other places, *two* can be alone." She had also warned that he must behave "as any good orderly old bachelor should, keeping blank as well as mum as you value my high opinion of your circumspection."

After the anniversary sessions ended, they traveled to Hartford with Frederick Douglass for the annual meeting of the Connecticut Anti-Slavery Society. Barred from all public buildings in the city, the abolitionists met on the sidewalk in front of a church. When Stephen gave "one of his usual cutting speeches," a mob howled him down with shouts of "Hustle him out!," "Where's Abby?," and "Where's the nigger?" Although the trio escaped unharmed, a friend in New York State heard rumors that Abby had been killed.[15]

Parting from her companions, Abby went to the Darlings' farm for her first vacation in a year. With sisters Diana and Ruth visiting and Lucy living nearby, she had a chance to catch up on family news. Joanna and her husband, Amos Ballou, had joined the Hopedale Community in Milford, Massachusetts, a Christian socialist community founded by Amos's cousin Adin Ballou. Diana and her husband, Olney, Amos's brother, planned to move there soon.

Lucy—little sister Lucy—was expecting a baby the following month. After Abby's return to New York Lucy wrote to announce the birth of eight-pound Harriet Lucy and to report on her "sickness," which had lasted two days and had worn out her husband as well as herself. He had stayed with her throughout her labor, "but at the last if it had not been for the bed-post I hardly think he could have supported his own person," she wrote.

After the other visitors departed, Abby found East Hampton delightfully secluded. In a playful, almost poetic letter, she told Stephen that while he was "in the smoke of battle," plying his "bludgeon, broadsword or battleaxe," she was playing "dummy, too stupid even to roll in the grass with the children or caper with the dog." No stagecoach or train intruded on her solitude. Only the "quiet-jogging" mail wagon came twice a week, bringing news of the outside world. "Empires may rise and fall before the fact reaches the rocks and winding rills of East Hampton," she said. The neighbors, "who almost start at the sight of so ungodly a being as myself," seldom visited, "not daring to come so near such a monster. There are a few, *very few* fanatics for whom the pastor puts up most devout prayers. One of them is my Sister Darling."

The vacation was just what Abby had needed. "I was not aware to what an extent my physical and mental strength was exhausted until I came to throw off all care and responsibility," she concluded. "The bow string was not broken but needed waxing and twisting and after three weeks I think it may be as elastic as ever. You cannot conceive what a new creature I have become. Now I feel almost a giantess."[16]

ANTISLAVERY
POLITICS

From her first to her last day in New York, Abby's chief opponents were the leaders of the Liberty party. Founded by "new organizers" just before the split in the American Anti-Slavery Society, the party had nominated James Birney as its presidential candidate in 1840, with the only plank in its platform the abolition of slavery. Although the Liberty men later broadened their program to point to the increasing political and economic strength of the Slave Power and its disastrous effect on northern free labor, they remained basically committed to a one-idea party. Even those Garrisonians who opposed voting criticized the party on practical grounds, insisting that until a significant portion of the electorate could be abolitionized, Liberty men were throwing away their votes. More could be accomplished by supporting the handful of antislavery Whigs or Democrats and thus forcing concessions, however minimal, from the major political parties. Above all, the Garrisonians were committed to antislavery as a moral movement whose goal was to transform public opinion. By entering the political arena, Liberty men would inevitably sacrifice principles for expediency.

Despite these disagreements over tactics, one might suppose that two organizations with a similar goal would be able to work together. However, the bitter feelings aroused by the 1840 split could not be forgiven or forgotten. Each group still called the other apostate and spent an inordinate amount of energy saying so.

When Abby spoke of being "cut into mince meat," she had been referring to attacks on her in the Liberty press that depicted her as "half witch and half devil." Liberty men were still accusing the Garrisonians of "no churchism, no governmentism, no biblism, no sabbathism, no marriageism, and every other ism." Abby retaliated with all the weapons in her arsenal, even calling the party "dirty"—an adjective she was later obliged to retract—and reminding her audiences of the treachery of the "new organizers" who had stripped the American Society of its assets and had stolen the *Emancipator*.

She quickly discovered that most New Yorkers were not interested in a rehash of old battles. People were flocking to her banner "in multitudes," eager to build the Central and Western New York Anti-Slavery societies. At the same time they saw nothing wrong in going to the polls on election day to vote for Liberty party candidates. "The fires kindled by me are used by third partyites," she wrote Maria Chapman. They are "visiting my coops and hawking up my chickens."

After months of trading epithets with the Liberty leadership, Abby began to wonder if the Garrisonians did not need a new position on political action. As a nonresistant she was opposed to voting under any circumstance, but she had discovered that "men *will* go to the ballot box" and there would be many elections before "the final jubilee." "The third party abolitionists of this state—the people not the leaders—are as sound as our old organizationists," she told Maria. "They hear so little on the question [of voting] through our organs that they have no idea there can be any political effort except third partywise."[1]

Her newly discovered tolerance did not prevent her from replying saltily to Gerrit Smith, a founder of the Liberty party and its chief financial backer. A maverick who tried to avoid sectarianism, Smith invited Abby to spend two months lecturing in Madison County, where he lived, because there was "no person whose lecturing would be so advantageous to the anti-slavery cause." He sweetened the request with an offer of a salary of a hundred dollars and an invitation to make his home her own during her stay.

Abby angrily rejected the offer. "You do not realize what you ask at my hands," she replied. "It is nothing less than to identify myself with the Liberty party, that party which is in deadly hostility to those whom I believe to be the slave's best friends." Reminding him of the "heartless gibes" and "slanderous letters" in the Liberty newspapers, she wrote: "Is it possible that you can ask *me* to cooperate with those who have been so traitorous to the slave's cause, who would trample me in the dust because I am a woman? My brother, I do not think it was in your heart to bribe me,* but when I look over your proposition in the light of the anti-slavery history for the last four or five years I am constrained to think you must have a most contemptuous opinion of my character." Concluding the letter with affectionate regards to Smith's wife and daughter, she signed herself "Yours with all plainness of speech for the slave's sake."

Forty-six-year-old Gerrit Smith, the wealthiest man in the abolitionist movement, was not accustomed to having his invitations rejected. Most acquaintances and many who hoped to scrape up an acquaintance with him wore a path to his mansion in Peterboro, looking for handouts. Perhaps Abby's independence intrigued him, for he sent a brief chiding reply, and

---

* Since antislavery agents were paid no more than two hundred dollars a year, Abby could easily have construed Smith's offer of one hundred dollars for two months' lecturing as a bribe.

she—who had once said, "My heart cannot retain anger any more than the flint can fire"—answered in conciliatory fashion. Through most of the summer of 1843 the two carried on a "pen and ink conversation," as Abby tried to wean Smith from his "new org" associates and to show him his responsibility for their slanders against her and the American Society.

As their letters grew increasingly friendly, she conceded that "a person may be doing something to abolish slavery even though he is sustaining it through the ballot box and the communion cup." For his part, Smith reported that he had broken with the Presbyterian Church because of its support of slavery and was heartily in favor of her Tee Total Pledge. In the end neither succeeded in changing the other's views, although Abby and Stephen spent a few pleasant days with the Smiths in Peterboro that fall.[2]

Aware of Abby's conflicted feelings about Smith and his associates, Maria Chapman sometimes feared that she was being taken into their camp. Since Henry Chapman's death a year earlier, Maria had become increasingly active in antislavery affairs. Almost since its inception the New England abolitionist movement had been controlled by what friend and foe alike called the Boston clique, an informal group that, Edmund Quincy said, "wobbles round a centre somewhere between 25 Cornhill and the South End"—that is, between the Anti-Slavery Office and Maria Chapman's home on Summer Street. There was nothing covert about the group. They were simply close friends and neighbors, sharing a common goal: Garrison, the ideological leader; Phillips, the clique's most eloquent spokesman; Francis Jackson, president of the Massachusetts Anti-Slavery Society; the Weston sisters; and Quincy, who traveled to town almost every day from his Dedham farm to join the "magic circle." Except for Garrison, who came from a poor Methodist family and had worked as a shoemaker's apprentice in his youth, they all were well-to-do patricians, members of the Boston Brahmin aristocracy, whose values they were now challenging.

In the early days of the movement Maria had played a conventional hostess role, offering hospitality to clique leaders and to out-of-town visitors during conventions. After women were increasingly accepted as partners in reform, she became, by informal consent, the clique's chief executive officer.* During the summer and fall of 1843, when Garrison was recuperating from an illness at the Northampton Association,† a community that George Benson had cofounded, she and Quincy edited the *Liberator*.

After the 1840 split the clique's domain had expanded. New York had remained headquarters of the American Society until 1843, when, with almost all of the members of the Executive Committee residents of Massachusetts, it was formally decided to move record books and committee meetings to Boston. Soon the decisions of the Executive Committee of the American Anti-Slavery Society and those of the Board of Managers of the Massachusetts Anti-Slavery Society were indistinguishable. Policy for both organizations was more and more often made in Maria Chapman's drawing room.[3]

In her capacity as guardian of the Garrisonian gospel Maria encouraged Abby to write frequently. "You might perhaps, nay doubtless modify our plans for the better, if you could give the time & take the trouble," she said. Abby scarcely needed the invitation, for she turned regularly to Maria in times of crisis. "I write this morning in desperation," one letter began. "You may think me impatient, obstinate, perverse, but I must still insist that you come to the rescue." She was objecting to the appointment of David L. Child as editor of the *Standard*. Child was not only a loyal Whig (one of the few in the abolitionist leadership who was affiliated with a political party) but an ineffectual man "with a killing influence on everything he touches. The Central and Western Societies will do a wonderful work next year if they can have a good paper. If they cannot have one in the *Standard* one will be started out there and they will 'go on their own

---

* Although clique members accepted Chapman and Kelley as partners in reform, they were not as accepting of their own wives. Helen Garrison, chained to the nursery by five young children, seldom attended meetings and never accompanied her husband when he traveled. Lucilla Quincy remained in Dedham when Edmund visited Chapman and rarely appeared at abolitionist functions. Only Wendell Phillips valued Ann's sharp insight into antislavery affairs and regularly consulted her.

† The Northampton Association of Education and Industry was established in Northampton, Massachusetts, in 1842 and disbanded four years later.

hook.' Divisions and disunion will be the order of the day, and imbecility of course."

"To avert such a catastrophe," Abby wanted Maria to take charge of the paper "if only for a little time." Accustomed to sacrificing her own personal desires for the cause, she failed to realize that no plea, however urgent, would move Maria to leave Boston for the gritty work of editing a weekly paper in New York. Besides, David Child had been a founder of the New England Anti-Slavery Society and an early associate of the Boston clique.

"I have had hours of conversation with him," Maria replied to Abby. "I rely with the most unhesitating confidence on his honesty, uprightness, noble mindedness & devoted love of the cause." Thereupon she wrote to Child, over Garrison's signature, and invited him to become editor of the *Standard*.

Abby accepted the inevitable and turned to other problems. In June 1843 the Massachusetts Society had decided on an ambitious program of "100 Conventions." Starting in New England, teams of lecturers were to fan out across New York State and go on to Ohio and Michigan. Abby thought the program usurped the prerogatives of the American and New York societies, thereby lending credence to Liberty party charges that Boston called the tune for all affiliates. "Does it not in effect annul the American Society? Does it not look like arrogance on the part of Boston?" she asked Maria. "New Organization will now say 'See, we have always told you that the American Society was nothing but Garrison and his clique.' " In addition, she thought the program was ill conceived. Conventions were more expensive than individual lectures and less effective. "I venture the assertion that my last five months in central N.Y. accomplished ten times the amount of antislavery fruit, than the preceding five in convention labor did."[4]

Once again Abby's protest failed to move Maria. Acquiescing as a good soldier should, she made arrangements for the lecturing teams when they arrived in New York, only to find herself at odds with John A. Collins, who was in charge of the project. A man of great ability who had carried out successful campaigns in the past, Collins no longer saw antislavery as the main work. He had become a disciple of Charles Fourier and Robert Owen and now believed that the reform of reforms was "communitarianism." Once people organized communities in which private property was abolished, all other reforms would fall into place. He was spending much of his time in New York looking for land for the community he hoped to establish.

Abby's conflict with Collins came to a head at a convention in Syracuse when he criticized antislavery as a limited reform and invited the audience to attend a "no-property" meeting the next day. Accompanied by Frederick Douglass and Charles Remond, Abby went to Collins's meeting and publicly rebuked him for betraying the antislavery cause.

Maria was inundated with letters from the aggrieved parties. Frederick threatened to resign if Collins continued as general agent. Collins had a right to his opinions, Abby wrote, "but has the Boston board a right to employ such a man?" Collins wrote Maria that he forgave Douglass, who, as a former slave, could be expected to object to any cause save his own, but he blamed Abby for whipping Frederick and Charles "into a frenzied state." "She hates the property question as the slaveholder hates anti-slavery. She is intolerant beyond degree," he said.

Abby was not unsympathetic to the communities that were springing up everywhere. She had thought fleetingly of going to Brook Farm when it was organized in 1841, had approved of Hopedale when she visited there, and had asked the Hudsons for a report on the Northampton Association "as I shall want to rest the soles of my feet, and, more especially, the crown of my head pretty soon." Basically, though, as she told Stephen, "My *judgment* is with them but my *feelings* are against them. I am a natural exclusive. My instincts revolt at the thought of *mixing up*." However, her complaint against John Collins had little to do with communitarianism. He was using his position as an abolitionist agent to divert attention from the movement.

From her desk on Summer Street Maria Chapman rendered judgment. John Collins had been a member of her coterie since 1837, when he had helped uncover the "clerical plot" against Garrison. He still had her "sympathy and esteem," she wrote Abby, although she, too, wished he would not call "property" meetings. Gentle as she was with Abby, she was severe with Frederick. Reprimanding him for rebelling against his superior, she warned that if his insubordination continued, his pay would be stopped.

When Douglass wrote his autobiography a half century later, he had warm memories of his antislavery comrades but still recalled Maria Chapman's letter as "a strange and distressing revelation."*[5]

The dispute over Collins became moot when he purchased a three-hundred-acre farm in upstate New York and resigned as general agent to organize the Skaneateles Community.†[6] Maria urged Abby to take over his job, but she refused, a decision that at least one abolitionist applauded because he had a "horror of the Gyneocracy which would be constituted by having Miss Kelley in the field and Mrs. Chapman in the council."

As the 100 Conventioners moved on to Ohio, Abby remained in New York, again turning her attention to the Liberty party, whose "vile papers" continued to attack the Garrisonians. When a Liberty party convention was scheduled to meet in Buffalo at the end of August to nominate candidates for the 1844 presidential election, she made up her mind to meet the enemy and refute its allegations face-to-face. Accompanied by Stephen Foster, who had come to New York a fortnight earlier, she traveled to Buffalo. Despite opposition from Henry B. Stanton, she was popular with the delegates, who greeted her appearance "with three rounds of applause" and permitted her to take the floor to expound the principles of the American Anti-Slavery Society. Although the Liberty men did not retract the slanders that had appeared in their press, they "indignantly rejected" a resolution condemning nonvoters and passed others of which she approved. On the whole she concluded that "the mass of the party acted a most manly and noble part," standing "on as good ground" as could be expected at a political convention.

What seemed to her a modest triumph had a different aspect in Boston, where Maria, reporting the convention in the *Liberator* apologized for Abby's presence and stated unequivocally that she was not "in fellowship

---

* Only weeks after Chapman's rebuke of Douglass, she wrote a patronizing editorial in the *Liberator*, criticizing the Reverend Henry Highland Garnet, a black leader who had called on the slaves to revolt. Her comment that Garnet had "received bad counsel" was resented by him at the time and is still cited by historians as an example of the condescension that white abolitionists expressed toward their black colleagues. (LIB, Sept. 22, Dec. 3, 1843; Quarles, *Black Abolitionists.*)

† The community failed three years later because, said Collins, "Human nature is too low, too selfish and too ignorant for such exalted principles." (Cross.)

with the Liberty party." Before Maria had a chance to write an admonitory letter, she received one from Abby announcing that she was coming to Boston, not to defend herself but to demand an explanation for an editorial in the *Standard*.

Under the heading "Where We Stand," David Child had espoused a "stay-inner" position, recommending that abolitionists remain in their churches and political parties and work there to win converts. He had attacked Abby's Tee Total Pledge and defended his own support of the Whigs. Reading "this atrocious article," Abby had expected Child to be dismissed from the *Standard* immediately. Instead Maria had reprinted the editorial in the *Liberator* without comment.[7]

Abby had caught cold during her Buffalo stay after a visit to Niagara Falls, where she had been soaked by the spray. Wrapped in her thick green shawl, she took a night train to Waterloo, alternately chilled and feverish. From her sickbed at the Pryors', she wrote long, indignant letters to both Chapman and Garrison. "The 'come-outer' ground is the genius of our enterprise—No communion with any thing that sustains slavery," she wrote. "Either the American Society and the Mass. Society must stand on the 'come-outer' ground or I must, as an individual, detach myself from them."

Still ill, she made the trip to New England by easy stages, stopping with Paulina in Utica and with the Motts in Albany. In Boston she stayed with the Southwicks. Anne Weston reported her "looking well as to beauty though delicate as to health," and Maria used all her wit and charm to convince Abby that the American Society had room for both "come-outers" and "stay-inners" and that she would have to put up with Child until the next annual meeting since no one else could be found to edit the *Standard*. Garrison, who was still at the Northampton Association, sent her "a short but good letter" agreeing that Child's editorial was "defective" and regretting that "D. L. C. does not more keenly apprehend the philosophy of the anti-slavery reform" but cautioning her "not to be hurried into any act that might gratify our enemies."

All the members of the Boston clique put themselves out to show her hospitality. Over tea at Summer Street Edmund Quincy and Maria engaged Abby in a discussion on "the metaphysics of the cause" in an effort to wean her from her heretical sympathy for the Liberty party. Dr. Henry Bowditch, a member of the Massachusetts Society's Board of Managers, took her for a Sunday drive; Maria invited her to "a sumptuous dinner"—roast chicken and peach pudding—at her in-laws' home and drove her in a carryall to Wendell and Ann Phillips's summer place at the seashore. At a meeting of the Massachusetts Board of Managers convened for her benefit, everyone had "a good full talk," and Anne Weston thought that Abby was "assuaged about Child and convinced that it was her duty to attack the Liberty party."[8]

Abby returned to New York in better health and spirits than when she had left but by no means repentant. "My very soul loathes [Child's] truckling towards the Whig party," she wrote Maria from Utica. "Had we only such a paper as you would have given us we should be able to crush the foe right speedily. That I have been used by Liberty party for the destruction of moral influences is not evident to my own eyes. Perhaps it was bad policy to attend the Buffalo Convention but I am not yet satisfied that it was," she concluded. "Had I not gone there I should not have the satisfaction of knowing that the Party men are informed of the principles and measures of the American Society. They will have an opportunity of choosing with their eyes open. Some will be saved that otherwise would not."[9]

Meanwhile, she had gone to Seneca Falls, a village four miles from Waterloo, where she had worked intensively during the summer. Located on the Seneca River with a waterfall providing power for textile and flour mills, and linked to the Erie Canal by a smaller canal, the village had long been a stopover on the psychic highway. Religious zealots had been followed by temperance reformers until by the time of Abby's arrival Seneca Falls was a "cold-water" village whose newspaper, the *Water Bucket*, linked temperance and abolition as twin aspects of the struggle for freedom from sin.

Abby had spent most of August "shaking up" Seneca Falls and returned there in September to support an antislavery fair. Although there had been no abolitionist society in the village when she arrived, she had judged the people ready for "a grand awakening" and had proceeded accordingly. Barred from the churches, she held daily outdoor meetings in an orchard belonging to Ansel Bascom, one of the village progressives. After the town was "stirred to the foundations," Liberty men put in an appearance and began to attack her.

Ansel Bascom's daughter recalled a characteristic slander. "Abby Kelley always [wore] a snowy kerchief crossed upon her breast. In the excitement of speaking, that kerchief became disarranged. Knowing this intuitively, as a woman always does know of any disorder in her dress, she put up one hand and, going on with her impassioned address, readjusted the disordered folds of the kerchief. It was all done in a womanly and modest way, but not long afterwards, the local papers commenting on her speech remarked that 'Abby Kelley's dress became immodestly disarranged, and instead of retiring she stood before that throng and brought it into order, not in the least disconcerted by an exposure that would have made a modest woman sink into the ground.' "

Keeping silent in face of the attack, Abby asked for outside help. The Reverend Samuel J. May,* an old friend of Garrison's who was now the respected pastor of a Syracuse church, came to lecture, followed by Stephen Foster. "The place is now lashed into a perfect fury," she reported to Maria. "I got up a storm and Foster increased it to a tempest." Seneca Falls, she thought, had become "a stronghold for the cause."

While there is no quantitative way to measure the effect of Abby's campaign, her impact on Seneca Falls can be inferred from an unusual document, the record of an ecclesiastical trial of a young village matron who was charged, among other misdeeds, with absenting herself from church to attend Abby Kelley's meetings. As was her practice, Abby had made a special effort to involve the women. She had organized a sewing society to work on the antislavery fair, but the women had been too timid to participate in other ways. Except for Rhoda Bement. A woman in her thirties whose husband had owned a carriage factory which had failed after the 1837 depression, Rhoda agreed to sit on the platform during Abby's "revivals" and had volunteered to ask her minister to announce the meetings from his pulpit.

---

* Samuel Joseph May (1797–1871), a founder of the New England Anti-Slavery Society, is sometimes confused with his younger cousin Samuel May, Jr., who was for many years general agent of the Massachusetts Anti-Slavery Society.

Rhoda belonged to the Presbyterian Church, the oldest and most conservative in the village. Its minister, Horace P. Bogue, could hardly have been expected to look with favor on Abby, who denounced him as a supporter of the Colonization Society, saying with characteristic hyperbole that Bogue would see her "burned at the stake" if he had the power. Nevertheless, on two successive Sundays Rhoda Bement had written out notices of Abby's meetings and had left them in a conspicuous place on Bogue's desk. After he failed to read either notice, she stopped him in the vestibule of the church as he was leaving. "I asked him how it could be he did not see the notice when it lay before him," she later testified. "Said he, I see a paper but did not read it until after I dismissed the congregation. I asked him if it wasn't his practice to open papers to see if it was anything which ought to be read? In answer, he says, Mrs. Bement, I think your course a very improper one. I think you very unchristian, very impolite and very much out of your place to pounce upon me in this manner."

That afternoon a number of Bogue's parishioners, including Rhoda Bement, skipped a scheduled church service and went to Bascom's orchard to hear Abby Kelley. The next day a committee of church elders called on Rhoda "to labor with her." When she proved unrepentant, Bogue prepared formal charges. During the course of a trial that stretched over four months, the charges escalated to include not only "unladylike" behavior and "disorderly & unchristian conduct" but "attending in a conspicuous manner the exhibitions made by Abby Kelley."

"Exhibitions made by Abby Kelley!" Rhoda Bement responded with asperity. "Is it right, is it honest so to misname a gospel lecture on the duty of Christians & the condition of God's poor? Who could ever *dream* or imagine from the record what was meant by this charge."

As Bement based her own defense on a defense of Abby Kelley's teachings, witness after witness, almost all from the elite of the village, testified that Abby's lectures had been "moral & religious in character," calculated to teach "our duty to God and to our fellow creatures." Tailoring her message to an unsophisticated audience, Abby had exercised a restraint that would have surprised Maria and David Child. Even when she introduced the Tee Total Pledge, she had not pressed her listeners to sign it, recommending rather that they stay in their church "if they thought they could do more good by remaining." No witness found it improper for "a female to call a promiscuous meeting," and many reported that although they had come to her lecture "opposed to abolitionist agitation," Abby had converted them.

"Did the Lecture change your views on the subject of American slavery?" the prosecutor asked Colonel Thomas Van Alstyne, a Seneca Falls businessman and one of Bogue's leading parishioners.

"It did," he replied. "Previous to that time I supposed the Bible upheld American slavery."

"Did [Miss Kelley] connect the churches at the North with those at the South, and say that they at the North were more guilty than at the South?"

"I did not so understand her. She said they were all connected & all equally guilty."

"Was there an uproar and considerable disturbance?" the prosecutor continued.

"There was considerable talking & Miss Kelley requested they would be as still as possible for it was the Sabbath."

"Did that talking arise from some dissenting to what Miss Kelley had said?"

"No Sir, it appeared to be discussions about the Lecture, comparing it with the scriptures, etc."

"Did individuals take exception to what Miss Kelley had said, it not agreeing with the Bible?"

"I did not hear them," Van Alstyne concluded.

Conducting a spirited defense, Bement elicited the same kind of reply from others.

"Was that the first Abolition Lecture you ever attended?" she asked Cornelia Perry, a fellow church member.

"It was."

"Were your views on American slavery changed by attendance on that Lecture?"

"They were."

"What had been your views?"

"I never thought much about it. Our ministers had never told us anything about it & I had supposed there was no very great sin in it."

"Do you think you have received light from attending that Lecture?"
"I think I did receive light."
"Where did the light come from?"
"I think from above," Perry replied.

Despite the testimony, few were surprised when Rhoda Bement was found guilty on all charges and was suspended from the Presbyterian Church "until she give evidence of repentance." When repentance was not forthcoming, she was excommunicated, and she and her husband joined the Wesleyan Methodists, the only religious group in Seneca Falls that took a stand against slavery.

The aftermath of the trial was a brief witch-hunt as a church committee endeavored to "labor" with others who had attended Abby Kelley's lectures. Even her host in the village was reprimanded for harboring Abby; he defended himself by saying that she had behaved "quite respectably," committing no "indecorum that would have justified turning [her] out."

The excitement gradually subsided. Ansel Bascom begged Abby to come back. "I doubt whether you can do as much good in any other part of America just now as within the bounds of this Presbytery," he wrote. But there were demands for her elsewhere, and she never returned.[10]

Over the next years, as residents of Seneca Falls kept up an interest in antislavery affairs, Henry B. Stanton decided that the village was a likely place from which to launch a political career. In 1847 he moved his family there from Boston. Tied to home by three lively boys, Elizabeth Cady Stanton had not pursued her interest in woman's rights, although she had continued to correspond with Lucretia Mott. In 1848, when she learned that Lucretia was visiting in the neighborhood, she drove to nearby Waterloo to see her. Over tea with a group of abolitionist women, including Mary Ann McClintock, Elizabeth poured out her discontent with her life as a housewife. Her companions agreed that a meeting to discuss equal rights for women was needed. Before parting for the night, they wrote a notice for the *Seneca County Courier* announcing that a convention to discuss "the social, civil and religious condition and rights of women" would be held at Seneca Falls on July 19 and 20.

So it happened that on a warm July day in 1848 Rhoda Bement and her husband walked to the Wesleyan Methodist Chapel to attend the world's first woman's rights convention. Elizabeth Stanton, Lucretia Mott, and Frederick Douglass* spoke convincingly, and members of the audience came forward to sign a Declaration of Sentiments that asserted that "all men and women are created equal." Abby Kelley was in Massachusetts that day, but Rhoda Bement must have thought of her as she listened to the proceedings.[11]

Abby had left western New York in the winter of 1844 in response to Maria Chapman's urgent "Come-Come-Come" to the annual meeting of the Massachusetts Society. "This is the meeting that 'gives the pitch' as they used to say in the old singing schools. It utters the key note," Maria explained.

The keynote of the meeting, held in Faneuil Hall in late January, was an attack on the United States Constitution. A hallowed document, reverently invoked by Fourth of July orators, the Constitution was scarcely understood by ordinary citizens. The debates of the Constitutional Convention had been conducted in secret, the delegates entering into a gentlemen's agreement not to reveal what was said until fifty years later. Only after the Constitution's Golden Jubilee in 1837, followed in 1840 by the publication of James Madison's *Notes of Debates in the Federal Convention of 1787*, had it become possible to assess the intent of the Founding Fathers.

In the North people had believed that the framers of the Constitution intended to contain and eventually abolish slavery. But Madison's *Notes*, an almost verbatim record of the debates, revealed a series of shoddy compromises. "We the People" was never meant to include blacks—or Indians or women. "In order to form a more perfect Union," delegates had sacrificed principle for commercial interest. In article after article—postponement of the ban on the African slave trade, the three-fifths slave representation clause,† the federal government's responsibility for capturing runaway slaves and suppressing slave rebellions—delegates from the north-

---

* Although a number of men were present, Henry B. Stanton was conspicuous by his absence.

† Each slave was counted as three-fifths of a person when determining the number of representatives a state was entitled to.

ern states had capitulated to the South. John Rutledge of South Carolina had captured the mood of the convention when he said, "Interest alone is the governing principle. Religion and humanity have nothing to do with [the slavery] question. If the Northern states consult their interest, they will not oppose the increase of slaves, which will increase the commodities of which they will become the carrier."

Examining the document in the light of Madison's *Notes*, Garrison had concluded that the Constitution was a proslavery document, "a guilty and fatal compromise by which slavery had been nourished, protected and enlarged to the impoverishment and disgrace of the nation,"* Attacking the Constitution in the 1840s was like attacking motherhood or God. But Garrison went further by declaring that the union between North and South should be dissolved. Since slavery was dependent on the economic and military might of the North, dissolution would lead to its abolition. This startling conclusion was not immediately accepted by his associates, but Garrison had persisted, even adopting a new slogan for the *Liberator*: "The Compact which exists between the North and South is a 'Covenant with Death and an Agreement with Hell' and should be immediately annulled.†

Both Abby Kelley and Wendell Phillips appreciated the moral correctness and the tactical possibilities of disunion and had defended it at the American Society's anniversary in 1843. Disunion was the final step in come-outer-ism—to come out from everything that supported slavery, "from governments, from constitutions, from statute laws, from all political machinery."

---

* By the time of the bicentennial of the Constitution in 1987, Supreme Court Justice Thurgood Marshall was one of several authorities to point out that the Constitution had indeed been a proslavery document until it was amended after the Civil War. Archivists at the Library of Congress and National Archives unearthed letters by framers of the Constitution that further confirmed the Garrisonian position. Among their discoveries were letters from Benjamin Franklin, president of the Pennsylvania Society for the Abolition of Slavery, in which he wrote that he had not presented the society's statements to the Constitutional Convention because he "thought it advisable to let them lie over for the present." (Marshall; *New York Times*, May 21, July 4, 1987.)

† Failing to recognize that the quotation was a paraphrase of Isaiah 28:15, editors complained of Garrison's "harsh and vituperative language." (O. Johnson.)

Further, it offered northern states a way to abolish slavery unilaterally. If they withdrew from the Union, they would peacefully bring about a collapse of the slave system.

Stephen Foster had at first disagreed with the idea of disunion, but at the Faneuil Hall meeting in 1844, he read a lengthy protest against the Constitution and the Union. He started with the by then familiar litany of constitutional wrongs. "The Constitution prohibits us from giving succor to fugitive slaves, requires us to aid in furnishing a military force" to put down slave rebellions, "grants to the slaveholding States a property representation in Congress," thus enhancing their political power. Continuing, he listed other grievances: the legalization of the slave trade in the nation's capital, where northern tax money supported prisons that held slaves awaiting sale; the South's suppression of freedom of speech and press and interference with the mails; unlawful arrest of black northerners; and harassment of free-state congressmen. For these good and sufficient reasons, Stephen concluded, "We now publicly abjure our allegiance to the Constitution of the United States and the Union."

Foster's protest was followed by a resolution from Garrison which said that it was "the duty of all the friends of impartial liberty to withdraw their allegiance from the national compact, and by a moral and peaceful revolution to effect its overthrow." With many participants still frightened by this extreme position, the society voted to publish Foster's protest and the accompanying resolution, but not to act on them.

The debate continued throughout the year. Madison's *Notes* were published serially in the *Liberator*. Wendell Phillips closed his law office because he would not take the oath to support the Constitution, which state and federal courts required. Francis Jackson resigned as a justice of peace, explaining in a letter to the governor written on the Fourth of July that he, too, could not swear to uphold the Constitution.[12]

Abby readily accepted the challenge of bringing the new Garrisonian line to the public. When Phillips as general agent of the Massachusetts Society invited her to take part in a new series of 100 Conventions in New England, she asked only to be given a free hand in deciding where to work. "I want to be left at liberty to remain *a week or one day* and not be compelled to go where there is no 'opening,' " she said.

188

In the two years since her mother's death she had been living out of a well-worn carpetbag. Now she made her headquarters with sisters Joanna and Diana in Hopedale, only a few miles from the old Kelley farm. Hopedale was taking shape as a community of Christian nonresistants who shared the work and slender profits of the enterprise. Amos Ballou was intendant (superintendent) of agriculture and animals. Men tilled the fields under his direction or worked in the mill they had built on the banks of the river flowing through the property; the women kept house and took care of the children. With members pledged to withdraw from all worldly government and to support temperance and antislavery, Abby found the moral atmosphere of the community congenial but was less pleased with living conditions. Housing was still in short supply, so that six or seven families shared a single dwelling, with resultant disputes and misunderstandings.[13]

Although her first lectures were given in the neighborhood of Hopedale, she immediately set out to find a woman traveling companion. Shortly before leaving New York, she had become friendly with thirty-year-old Jane Elizabeth Hitchcock of Oneida, who had shown a talent for public speaking. However, Jane Elizabeth's older brother would not consent to her joining Abby. He was involved in establishing a community and needed her assistance, he said. Abby suspected that his real reason for keeping his sister in New York was that he did not want her to associate with "such an anti-communitist as myself." Jane Elizabeth, no "communitist" either, promised to join Abby later. Meanwhile, Abby turned to Abby Southwick, who, like Elizabeth Neall, came from an abolitionist family and had been attending antislavery meetings since she was a young girl. Although her father gave his permission, she backed out, confessing that she dreaded "cold houses, cold chambers" and lacked the "moral courage" to undertake the work.

Frustrated, Abby asked Stephen if his sister Caroline would go with her—"for I must have some one"—then took back the request less it "confirm suspicions" of their still-secret relationship. Her own sisters were tied down by their families. She had pressed Diana into service for two weeks, but that was as long as she could be spared. Abby Price of Hopedale seemed a possibility. She later became a public speaker, warning that Hopedale could never be a truly equal society until women cut down on housekeeping chores and assumed what might be called "mannish" work. But in 1844 Mrs. Price was burdened by a large number of children, including an unusually cranky baby. Although she accompanied Abby to nearby meetings, she could not go far from home.

Abby's urgent need for a companion was influenced by the fact that when she lectured in Worcester County, she was inevitably teamed with John M. Fiske, whose name was still linked with hers by those inveterate matchmakers the Weston sisters. Many months earlier Abby had written John to dispel any thoughts he might have of marriage, but it was embarrassing to spend long hours with him as he drove her to meetings in his sleigh. No one could have been more correct in his demeanor or more considerate of her welfare, but John could not conceal a gloomy countenance. "I regret, very deeply, that this field was assigned to me," Abby wrote Stephen. "He is a truly estimable man and I would he were happy."[14]

Traveling farther north in Massachusetts and venturing into Vermont, Abby went with Erasmus Hudson and Sydney H. Gay, a youthful lawyer on the fringes of the Boston clique who had recently become an abolitionist agent. Sometimes they were joined by Frederick and Anna Douglass, who were now living in Lynn, where Anna bound shoes to augment her husband's precarious income. Abby was in charge of the lecturers, renting the halls in which they spoke, paying their salaries—she still took no money for herself—keeping track of subscriptions and contributions, and scrupulously recording credits and debits in letters to Wendell Phillips. A report in April showed that during a two-month period her team had taken in $292.73 and spent $206.16, leaving a balance of $86.57, which she forwarded to the treasurer of the Massachusetts Society.

The main theme of the 100 Conventions was the proslavery character of the Constitution and the call for disunion. The forthcoming presidential election with its parades and flag-waving made the lecturers' task difficult. Patriotic audiences were in no mood to hear the Constitution disparaged, and disunion was a hard concept to accept. Even though the major party candidates, Henry Clay and James K. Polk, were slaveholders, few New Englanders were prepared to stay away from the polls in order to back disunion. To compound Abby's problems, Henry B. Stanton and other

Liberty men were also stumping the state, drumming up support for James G. Birney, their presidential candidate. They stoutly defended the Constitution as antislavery and pointedly replied to the speeches of "the woman from Millbury," as Stanton called her. Usually confident on the rostrum, Abby felt at a disadvantage when answering her opponents' legal arguments. "I do wish you would come," she wrote Wendell Phillips from Vermont. "I want you to take up the Constitutional question." "Although I can arouse people," she wrote in a second letter, "I don't know much and so can't tell them much. I want those who can to use the ears I give them."

Wendell joined her occasionally on the lecture circuit and also utilized his legal training and knowledge of history to write a lengthy pamphlet, *The Constitution, a Pro-Slavery Document*, which quoted from the Madison papers to show how "with deliberate purpose our fathers bartered honesty for gain and became partners with tyrants that they might profit from their tyranny." He wrote it, he told a friend, to "keep Abby Kelley from teasing me—she wanted something to sell after her lectures and I had to provide it."

Because Abby encountered so many people in different regions, she knew far better than the Boston leaders which "keynote" was readily accepted and which sounded sour. One of her greatest contributions to the movement was the reports on public reactions that she regularly conveyed to Wendell and Maria. Some months after the publication of *The Constitution, a Pro-Slavery Document* she saw a need to expand on the Garrisonian position on disunion. Wendell responded with *Can an Abolitionist Vote or Hold Office Under the United States Constitution?*, a witty summary of the arguments for "No Union with slaveholders." "I hope you'll think my poor non voting pages worth selling," he wrote Abby. "I will take it kindly if you will write me which part is weakest so that in another edition I may amend."

As the teams of lecturers progressed through New England, they occasionally met and compared notes. Writing for the *Liberator*, Sydney Gay described their friendly rivalry. "Each of us declared that 'our series' had passed over the worst roads, been through the hardest rains, slept with more people in the same bed, encountered the worst mobs and were, on the whole, the sickest of the whole business; or on the other hand had seen the most beautiful scenery, had the pleasantest weather, held the most enthusiastic meetings, and had done by far the most good."[15]

Gay's sprightly report served to remind Abby that the anniversary meeting of the American Society was only a month away and David Child's term as editor of the *Standard* was due to expire. The Boston clique now agreed that he must be replaced, even Maria Chapman describing him as "a fine magnanimous being, full of good feeling and mistakes." Writing to Wendell, Abby proposed that Erasmus Hudson and Sydney Gay become coeditors of the paper, with Chapman and Quincy lending them assistance from Boston. "The Dr. [is] a bundle of facts always seizing on every new 'hook' on which to hang an excitement," she said, and Sydney is "a fine writer if a little wanting in vigor." Gay accepted the position on condition that he be made sole New York editor. He admired Dr. Hudson, he told Abby, but "our literary tastes differ too entirely to make us fit associates."

The May 23, 1844, issue of the *Standard* carried a lengthy valedictory from David Child. Filled with resentment against Abby Kelley, it blamed her extreme come-outerism for his differences with the American Society. The following week, the paper's masthead listed as editors Sydney Gay,* Maria Chapman, and Edmund Quincy.[16]

At the 1844 anniversary, where Abby Kelley, Stephen Foster, and Paulina Wright served on the business committee, a majority of the delegates voted in favor of Wendell Phillips's resolution "That secession from the present U.S. government is the duty of every abolitionist." Although there were protests from such old-time Garrisonians as James Gibbons and Ellis Loring, the American Society was now officially on record in favor of disunion. "Henceforth, therefore, until slavery be abolished, the watchword, the rallying cry, the motto on the banner of the American Anti-Slavery Society shall be 'NO UNION WITH SLAVEHOLDERS!'" the *Liberator* reported.

---

* Gay served as editor of the *Standard* for thirteen years, resigning to become an editor of the *New York Tribune*.

Abby, who closed the meeting with a "very powerful speech," Garrison said,[17] had decided to spend the summer in New Hampshire. The series of 100 Conventions had concluded, and for the first time in many months she was on her own, free to appoint meetings where she thought they were needed and to remain in one place until it was thoroughly abolitionized. After Jane Elizabeth Hitchcock joined her in late July, they traveled in jolting wagons through the southern part of the state, lecturing in mill villages along the Merrimack River as well as in prosperous farming centers like Keene and Concord. Abby was troubled by an inflamed throat, an ailment endemic to lecturers in premicrophone days, which she "cured" by fasting and "taking a sweat." On occasions when hoarseness kept her from speaking, Jane Elizabeth substituted for her, delivering "an eloquent and indignant rebuke" to the enemies of abolition. "You can understand how delighted I was to receive Jane," Abby wrote Stephen. "I now shall not be obliged to go a begging for a companion."

Abby's and Stephen's paths crossed rarely that summer, although she was in his home state. She had turned down an invitation to visit his parents' farm in Canterbury—"I should feel awkward there before a declaration"—and refused his suggestion of a vacation in the White Mountains. Nevertheless, Joanna, her most censorious sister, warned that people were gossiping about "Abby & Foster" and advised her to conduct herself "more properly in the future" so that her "character may in a measure be retrieved."

However, there was little likelihood that Abby's reputation could be salvaged as she preached the dangerous doctrine of disunion to Whigs and Democrats, who were rallying around the standards of their presidential candidates. In Portsmouth, New Hampshire, where the chief industry was building ships for the U.S. Navy, she lectured daily for a week in the Temple, a temperance hall. Attracted by the novelty of "an intelligent female lecturer who possesses some powers of oratory, no small share of sarcastic wit, and occasionally a little impudence," people filled the Temple night after night. Abby convinced them that the North had become subservient to the South in politics and business, but when she "urged trampling of the Constitution under foot," she lost their sympathy, the *Portsmouth Journal* reported. Although the *Journal* had halfhearted praise for "this modern Amazon," another newspaper declared that she was "unsexing herself [as] she swung her hands, stamped her feet, struck her breast. She stood in the middle of that great assembly and boldly met the gaze of the boldest" while a thousand people listened "to her crudities or gloated at the public exhibition of her form. She talked fluently, superficially, impertinently and seditiously."[18]

Few Liberty men were campaigning in New Hampshire that summer, but although Abby did not have to contend with "new organization," she faced a new enemy: "no organization." For some time Nathaniel P. Rogers had been supporting an anti-institution position that bordered on anarchism. At meetings he objected to the preparation of an agenda or the election of officers and insisted that anyone could speak on any topic at any time. To express his belief in a "spontaneous press," he suspended publication of the *Herald of Freedom* for a few weeks, defending this action by saying that the paper belonged to him, not to the New Hampshire Society.

Abby, who had known nothing of the situation when she came to the state, found that she could not count on the *Herald* to announce or report her meetings. Further, she was caught in a crossfire with Rogers and other "no organizationists" on one side and the more conventional members of the New Hampshire Society on the other. "Bro. Rogers gives no word of cheer, blows no bugle rallying-cry for the efforts now being put forth," she wrote Garrison at the end of the summer. "This affair is most trying and soul-sickening. Can you not bring him to his senses? Your influence over him is greater than that of any other."

Garrison, feeling sympathy for Rogers's extreme individualism and reluctant to hurt an old friend, remonstrated gently, to no avail. Aroused after reading an "ugly" attack on Abby in the *Herald of Freedom*, Maria Chapman was less patient. "We are used down this way to having people talk wittily against spiritual bondage but know from sad experience of the tribe of Transcendentalists that such talk is painfully consistent with proslavery," she confided to Abby. "I have a sincere friendship for Rogers but I am used to plucking out offending eyes."

Nothing was done about the New Hampshire situation until Abby and Jane Elizabeth, in Boston for a meeting of the New England Non-Resistance Society, called on Garrison to give him a full report. Recognizing the threat that "no organization" could pose if it spread to other antislavery societies, the Boston clique at last was thoroughly alarmed. Late in November Garrison, Phillips, Quincy, and Anne Weston accompanied Abby to Concord for a meeting of the New Hampshire Anti-Slavery Society. Appointed to an investigative committee, the Bostonians concluded that the *Herald of Freedom* belonged to the society but that Nathaniel Rogers should continue as its editor. When he refused, Parker Pillsbury took on the assignment. Recounting the controversy, Garrison regretfully concluded that on the subject of "no organization," Rogers had "really lost his wits and become a raving monomaniac."[19]

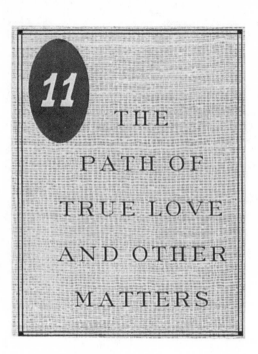

11

THE PATH OF TRUE LOVE AND OTHER MATTERS

W hen winter snows blanketed New Hampshire's granite hills, Abby and Jane Elizabeth headed south. All fall Edward M. Davis,* the leading Garrisonian in Pennsylvania, had been pleading with Maria Chapman for help. His state's abolitionists were mostly liberal Quakers who had broken away from the orthodox Friends two decades earlier. Less contentious than their Boston colleagues, they deplored the factional fighting in

---

* Best known to history as Lucretia Mott's son-in-law, Davis was a successful merchant and substantial contributor to the antislavery and woman's rights movements. (Sterling, *Lucretia Mott*.)

the movement and never fully shared their aversion to a third party. Even James Miller McKim, secretary of the antislavery society, and Charles Burleigh, currently editor of the *Pennsylvania Freeman*, had doubts about the proslavery character of the Constitution and the call for disunion, while Thomas Earle, one of the society's lecturing agents, openly supported the Liberty party. A strenuous campaign was needed to sell the American Society's "new frontier" to the Pennsylvanians, Davis wrote Chapman. "We must have Abby Kelley as soon as possible."[1]

After bidding good-bye to Stephen in Boston and stopping in Hopedale to see her sisters and pack a winter wardrobe, Abby joined Jane Elizabeth in early December 1844 for the journey. Although trains now whizzed along at the breathtaking speed of thirty miles an hour, the trip still took three days. They stayed at the Graham House in New York and had time for a "confab" with Sydney Gay, who was doing "noble" work on the *Standard*, before catching the Philadelphia steamer. Once aboard, they braved the December weather on the exposed Jim Crow deck in order to share the hardships of their black fellow passengers.

Having arrived in Philadelphia on the afternoon of December 5, Abby lodged with Elizabeth Neall and her father, Daniel, former president of the ill-fated Pennsylvania Hall. She scarcely had time to change from her traveling dress before she was escorted to a meeting of the Philadelphia Female Anti-Slavery Society. Looking at the friendly, expectant faces, she must surely have recalled her visit to the city six years earlier, when she had given her first public speech. Hesitant then, she now knew precisely what she must do. "The Philadelphians all think truth is as tender as eggs and should be handled much more carefully," she confided to Stephen. "They think no one can handle it properly but under their direction. I have been expecting many curtain lectures, but have made up my mind to receive [them] all in good part and then do just as my judgment and conscience shall dictate. I think I shall never be so *short* with people as you are, but have my own way pretty much after all."[2]

During her first weeks in Philadelphia she spoke in and around the city, following the schedule that Edward Davis had planned. "She is just what I wanted," he reported to Maria Chapman. "She will help to draw the line & will show up Liberty party." Most of her meetings were spent in debate with Thomas Earle. The older brother of her boarding schoolmates Pliny and Eliza, he was a well-trained lawyer and formidable opponent—"a sophistical reasoner whose arguments appear plausible to the superficial thinker," Abby said, while Jane Elizabeth described him as "so ingenious and crafty that it needs a tremendous thunder storm after every speech to clear the moral atmosphere." Apparently Abby's "storms" were effective, for a week after her arrival in the city Mary Grew told her that the Pennsylvania Anti-Slavery Society had dismissed Earle as its agent—an action that could be "attributed to your speech on Sunday last."[3]

Despite his dismissal, Earle and Kelley dominated a Christmas week convention of the society, arguing like "two Kilkenny cats" on every issue, Abby said. Advocating voting as the best means to bring about abolition, Earle persuaded the delegates to pass a resolution that called at least "for charity and forbearance among abolitionists who entertain differing views." The final victory was Abby's, however, for the convention agreed that the Constitution was a proslavery document and went on record in favor of disunion, leaving the Liberty party "twisting and squirming," she wrote Wendell Phillips.[4]

For the next four months Abby led a corps of lecturers through Pennsylvania. Accompanied by Erasmus Hudson and Benjamin Jones, a young Philadelphia Quaker, Abby and Jane Elizabeth held meetings in the southeastern part of the state, speaking in the rich farming counties of Bucks and York and the prosperous Pennsylvania Dutch settlements in Lancaster—where the people were "mostly of German descent and hence slow," Abby said—in industrial Carlisle, site of a military post, and in the state capital at Harrisburg. While traversing the wild and beautiful country along the Susquehanna River, they planned to cross the Mason-Dixon line for a meeting in Maryland. When sympathizers there could find neither a meeting hall nor lodgings for them, they contented themselves with speaking outdoors, fifty yards from the border.[5]

Early in the tour they ventured into the slave state of Delaware to attend the annual meeting of the Quaker-led Delaware Anti-Slavery Society. Speaking in the Town Hall in Wilmington until they were expelled by the authorities, Abby and Erasmus Hudson pulled few punches, calling slaveholders "man-stealers" and denouncing the church's role in maintaining slavery. Perhaps the assertion that most bothered their audience was a resolution promulgated by Abby that said that "prejudice against the colored population which deprives them of equal civil, social and religious rights is cruel, proscriptive and murderous and cannot be indulged by any friends of freedom and Christianity." Slaveholders angrily replied, and after two days of debate, which turned riotous at times, the convention adjourned inconclusively. Nevertheless, Thomas Garrett,* president of the society, who had been their host during the convention and was the leading stationmaster of the Underground Railroad in the slave states, assured Abby that the visit had "put many to talking and thinking on the subject of slavery" while her advocacy of the right of free discussion had "opened the eyes of honest politicians of both parties."[6]

Back in Pennsylvania Abby found the work less taxing than in other places. Jane Elizabeth, developing into a speaker of great power, divided lecture dates with Hudson and Jones, allowing Abby, who was still the chief drawing card, an occasional day off to rest her throat and catch up with correspondence.

"The Pennsylvanians are hospitable and friendly beyond anything I ever before met with," she wrote Stephen. "They carry us from place to place in their big waggons always having great numbers of fat horses. And their hearth stones are so entirely like *our folks* that I have not felt a stranger since I have been here." However, she found them stingy compared with New Englanders. "Quakers are brought up to contribute everything but money and it will take them a long time to forget this training."[7]

Still, she succeeded in selling five hundred copies of *The Brotherhood of Thieves*, a pamphlet that Stephen had written, and more than a hundred of *The Constitution, a Pro-Slavery Document*. "There is a great deal of curiosity to see what the worshipped fathers said in the sainted convention, especially when their veneration is denied," she told Wendell Phillips. The

---

* A legendary figure on the Underground Railroad, Garrett helped more than twenty-seven hundred slaves to freedom. Arrested in 1846 and ordered to pay a heavy fine, he reportedly told the judge, "Thou has not left me a dollar, but if anyone knows a fugitive who wants shelter and a friend, send him to Thomas Garrett." (McGowan.)

pamphlet sales brought in enough to cover the women's expenses, but she warned Wendell that she would soon ask the executive committee to vote a small salary for Lizzie, as she now called Jane Elizabeth, "as she had not yet learned like me to live on the odds and ends of trifles and she will need to replenish her wardrobe."

Because Maria Chapman was preoccupied with the *Standard*, Abby's business correspondence went to Wendell, who now had charge of lecturers for both the American and Massachusetts societies. The two got along famously. She asked permission to put Benjamin Jones on the payroll as an agent and negotiated a raise—from seven to ten dollars a week—for Dr. Hudson. Urging Wendell to come to Philadelphia in the spring because "we need a Bishop to confirm our converts," she began addressing her letters to "Rt. Rev. Wendell Phillips, Bishop of Boston."

Explaining that he was unable to leave Boston even for a night because of Ann's illness, Wendell cheered her on. "How gloriously you are doing!" he wrote. "Now poor dear Abby, bleed those fat Quakers & fill up our exhausted treasury." He signed his letter "Benedicite mea filia, Wendell, Bishop of Boston," adding a postscript to suggest that Charles Burleigh be made archbishop because of the length of his beard.[8]

The work of Abby and company did not always proceed smoothly. With churches and meetinghouses regularly closed to them, they spoke in stable lofts and mechanics' shops, in parlors of temperance taverns, and in the outdoor marketplace in Carlisle. In Chester County, near the Maryland border, rowdies drowned out their speeches by beating on tin pans and blowing horns and threatened to ride Abby and Jane Elizabeth out of the neighborhood on a rail. While Abby stayed home one night to write to Stephen, Lizzie and Benjamin were "completely baptized with eggs. 'Twas Lizzie's first introduction to a real mob." Eggs were thrown again in the courthouse in Harrisburg, and Abby's lecture was cut short after pepper scattered from the balcony set the audience coughing and sneezing.

Pennsylvania had the largest black population of any state in the North, and the lecturers could always count on an enthusiastic reception in black churches. "When we go from white audiences to colored, we feel that we are among the friends of good order and harmony," Lizzie reported to the *Standard* from Harrisburg. "They seem to be the only people in town who are determined to maintain freedom of speech and the right to peaceable assemblage."

During two visits to the state capital the abolitionists stayed at Mrs. Whitehill's boardinghouse, a favorite of the legislators, who needled them about their views at the breakfast table. The day after the pepper-throwing incident Hudson recorded a dialogue between Goodrich, clerk of the state senate, and Abby Kelley. After Mrs. Whitehill complained of the bold behavior of a young black waiter, Goodrich tauntingly suggested that he be sold into slavery.

"Ought not all impudent white boys be sold into slavery too?" Abby sweetly inquired.

"If all the impudent white women were sold the market would be well-supplied," responded Goodrich.

"And [with] all impudent white men the market would be glutted," said Abby.

Goodrich huffily terminated the conversation, but Mrs. Whitehill had the last word: She told the abolitionists to leave her boardinghouse.[9]

As a rule Abby paid more attention to black servants than white ones, but she was disturbed one day when the maid employed by her hosts in Chester County asked to speak with her. Newly arrived from Ireland, the girl was performing all the work in a large household where her mistress did nothing—"not even so much as to make her bed"—for wages of a dollar a week. After working hours she was confined to "a desolate kitchen" and treated as an outcast. Abby, who was proud of her Irish descent and aware of the growing prejudice against the Irish immigrants who were fleeing their homeland because of a potato famine, recognized a link between the maid's oppression and that of the slaves. "When I tried to console her and told her that we were trying to bring about a better state of things, a state in which she would be regarded as equal, she wept like a child," Abby reported to Stephen. "I think we should be faithful in the families where we go and bear testimony against this great wickedness. I have been negligent."[10]

Doubtless the maid's employer failed to appreciate Abby's intervention, but others she encountered thought she was doing "a noble work." While Eliza Follen wrote from Boston to bless her "for doing that which I would but cannot do," a Lancaster woman expressed "deep felt gratitude for enlightening my mind on the true principals for the Abolishment of slavery. Thou canst not imagine the great change in public opinion in this place since your visit." Even abolitionists like Sarah Pugh, who had dreaded Abby's presence, telling Maria Chapman that "very many here who are ready for strong meat would turn away in disgust if it were set before them in its raw state by A. Kelley," had been won over. As treasurer of the Pennsylvania society Sarah had ample opportunity to observe Abby's "unceasing devotion and self-sacrifice." Although "she has not brought peace but a sword, in private she wins all hearts by the warmth of her own and her truly feminine gentleness & sweetness," she said.[11]

Despite the accolades, Abby's Pennsylvania sojourn was not wholly a happy time. Her stay had started on a sad note when Francis Wright, ill for some months, came to Philadelphia for medical treatment. Abby stole time from meetings to keep vigil with Paulina at his bedside until he died on January 2. At Paulina's request, Abby spoke at his funeral, testifying to his faithfulness in leaving the church—much to the attending minister's confusion.

Overwhelmed by grief, Paulina remained in Philadelphia to settle Francis's affairs, putting aside some of his clothing—a 'Robe de Chambre,' a vest and some collars"—as a keepsake for Stephen, before joining Abby and Jane Elizabeth on their travels. Now that her husband was dead, there was nothing to prevent her from speaking in public, but her tour with Abby seems to have decided her against becoming an abolitionist lecturer. Instead she chose a career in health reform. Left with ample means, she went to New York City to study. After virtually stealing her education* because no medical school would admit her, she gave her first course of lectures in anatomy and physiology, for women only, in 1846.[12]

---

*Paulina Wright bribed librarians and doorkeepers in order to read medical books and study skeletons and bone collections. She also paid a doctor for private lessons. Her studies completed, she imported an anatomically correct mannequin from France, the first ever seen in the United States. When she displayed the mannequin at her lectures, some women dropped their veils while others fainted. (Nathan; Stanton, Anthony, et al., v. 1.)

Francis's death, the first loss of someone her age, destroyed Abby's feeling of invulnerability. On the day that he died, she read in the *Standard* that Stephen had been attacked by a mob. Suddenly it occurred to her that he, too, could die. Profoundly shaken, she did something unheard of. She canceled a meeting where two thousand people had expected to hear her and went to bed instead. After a troubled night she wrote Stephen in the morning. Theretofore she had believed that her faith would sustain her if anything happened to him. Now she knew better. "I thought I was much stronger," she wrote. "I never found it so hard before to be so far from you."

For two years they had been courting, largely by mail. Reams of paper had been consumed as they exchanged ideas, endearments, and reports of their work. While emotional Stephen often poured out his innermost feelings, Abby usually stuck to antislavery business, indicating her affection obliquely through advice about bathing frequently and washing his hair or, once, telling him to read a novel, Eugène Sue's *Mysteries of Paris*,* which she "would not recommend to young people, but [would to] one of your outstanding integrity."

Even when they met, she kept him at arm's length until Stephen charged that she was ashamed to acknowledge their relationship. In an unusually revealing reply addressed to "My dearest," Abby attempted to allay his fears. "As the thirsty traveler in the Sahara desert longs for the greenness and cool spring . . . so does my heart pant to stand before the world the wife of Stephen S. Foster. Why then should I want to conceal our connexion?" There were many reasons, including maidenly modesty. "I should not want to kiss you in company even if we were married nor should I wish to exchange caresses in the presence of others. It may be right to do so [but] that is not in harmony with my feelings. They're always ardent, and having been dammed up for so many years, it is difficult to restrain them."

Further, "My usefulness in the anti-slavery field would be lessened" if

---

* Translated into English in 1844, Sue's novel was popular in reform circles.

the engagement were made public. "People wish me married to get rid of me, and did they know of our relation, they would say I was under *obligations to take care* of [you], and if I did it not, they would call me unfeeling and brutal. Did you know how much I was condemned, and how much my influence was lessened by the reports that I neglected my dear mother?"

Abby's letter was the closest she had ever come to acknowledging sexual yearnings. The Graham way of life counseled abstinence before marriage and moderation afterward, while phrenologist Orson S. Fowler, who recommended three- to five-year courtships, divided the "bump of amativeness"—the love of the sexes for each other—into a lower portion for mere animal passion and an upper portion of pure Platonic affection, and it was clear to which Fowler gave a higher rating. Thus Abby, who had read his *Matrimony or Phrenology and Physiology Applied to the Selection of Congenial Companions for Life*, ascribed her ardent feelings to her longing for domestic life, the home and family she had forsworn when she dedicated herself to antislavery. Her fear that she would be unable to restrain her feelings was an important reason for refusing to see Stephen more often. But "I *can* and *ought* to *discipline myself*," she decided. "I will have a rule over my own spirit, treating you like a brother, and only like a brother, for in treating you otherwise I make myself unhappy in being separated from you."

A man of extreme mood swings, Stephen went from depression to elation when he received her letter. Finally convinced of her love, he moved to take control of their relationship. Now that he had learned "that you are as completely in my power as I am in yours," he had no intention of postponing their marriage indefinitely. "I've been thinking how much longer I ought to allow you to stroll around the country in company with all sorts of men. I have no idea of spending another *cold* winter so long as I have a *wife* who is bound to keep me warm and comfortable. I am heartsick of bricks and flatirons for winter companions. I shant allow you the veto forever.

"Now you are my *own*", he continued. "Perhaps you do not like the idea of being so thoroughly possessed by another, but I shall hold you *fast*. I know you are an *artful* girl & much skilled in managing; but you can never *manage* yourself away from me. I shall henceforth claim & hold you as my *own* property. I shall now *tyrannize* over you to my heart's content so you may prepare for it & make a virtue of submission. 'Wives submit yourselves unto your husbands' is the command." He concluded by threatening to send an announcement of their impending marriage to the newspapers, "so surrender yourself and submit quietly to my authority as a good dutiful loving wife should."

Undoubtedly much of this was intended as humor, or at least Abby chose so to interpret it. After deflating him by saying that his "bundle of softsoap" had just reached her, she devoted two pages to antislavery matters before taking up his proposal for an early marriage. She had agreed to an engagement only because she had "the highest and holiest confidence" in his devotion to the cause and had been sure that he would not "try to swerve me from this stern path of duty. Altho' I firmly believe you have been jesting, I warn you to be careful how you push your jokes too far. My domestic feelings are strong, but my moral organization is stronger and far more active."

Stephen could take what comfort he could from her playful threat to demand "after the fashion of chivalry," that he bring her "trophies of victory, shackles broken, whips dust-trodden, sword in the left hand and a proclamation of emancipation in the right, before your lady love shall yield to her good knight, altho' he holds her heart of hearts most truly."[13]

Obviously Abby still retained veto power. No more was said about an early wedding for a time although, in subsequent letters, Stephen made little attempt to conceal his dark moods. "Abby, I am *unhappy*. A chord of sorrow and sadness vibrates in my bosom," he declared some months later. "It is you that have made me this wretched—you *my beloved my own dear Abby* the one on whose gentle bosom I had hoped to recline my aching head & whose soft hand I had fondly expected would smooth my furrowed cheek." Because she had been ill when they had recently met, he was convinced that she was developing "that most insidious of all diseases, consumption." "Your life is in imminent peril," he continued. "No person can long endure what you are taking on. Make me one promise as sacred as our conjugal vows . . . that you perform no more labor than you would recommend to me. If you grant it and do it in good faith, you will relieve my mind of its present anxiety."

Abby's Quaker training in unsentimentality shaped her reply. "It is not that I *wanted* to laugh but because I could not avoid it, that I shook my sides most thoroughly on reading the last word of yours." His melodramatic preamble had caused her to fear that "some terrible thing had happened" until she had discovered that it was only "your old story of apprehension for my health." True, she had been fatigued when they met, but she was "never in more perfect health in my whole life than at the present moment." Her tone softening, she added, "I laughed yet I did feel very sorry that you should have been the victim of your own groundless fears. In relation to the promise you ask me to make, I make it *most heartily and cheerfully*. Now will you not promise me to cheer up, 'laugh and grow fat.' "

Some of Stephen's insecurity stemmed from the fact that Abby was a star in the abolitionist firmament, universally admired, if not always loved, while his confrontational style and flamboyant language antagonized many. His aggressiveness at meetings and his willingness to face mobs and jail, the very qualities that made him a hero to Abby, offended "the Boston friends" who, despite their radical politics, set great store by good manners. Garrison thought him "morbidly combative"; Quincy mocked him as "St. Stephen, the connoisseur in martyrdom." Even Phillips, the most sympathetic member of the Boston clique—"he likes to make everyone happy," Abby said—described Stephen as "wild and illogical" although recognizing his "devoted, noble, pure, eloquent, John-the-Baptist character."*

Stephen had found greater acceptance along the psychic highway in New York, where people felt less concern for decorum. Those who knew him intimately, like the Wrights, thought him a gentle, kindly man with a sprightly sense of humor. Before his first visit to Waterloo, Mary Ann McClintock had feared that his arrival would cause dissension. "Don't fear,

---

* Maria Child had a particular aversion to Stephen Foster. Dining with him in New York when she was editing the *Standard*, she commented on his "Calvinist visage": "Whew! It's as blue as brimstone fires. I would quit a boarding-house where his face dined often." More than a decade later she still found Stephen "as good as an unleashed bull-dog to keep me away from Anti-Slavery meetings. I could scarcely find words to express my disapprobation of that man's way of doing things." (LMC to L. Loring, Holland and Meltzer; LMC to MWC, July 26 [57], Meltzer and Holland.)

Mother," her daughter had assured her. "Thee will love him when thee gets acquainted with him."

Sure that the Bostonians would also love him when they knew him better, Abby brought up his name frequently in her correspondence with Maria Chapman. "What do you think of the 'Brotherhood of Thieves,' Foster's new pamphlet? Do give me your opinion," she wrote in one letter.

The Brotherhood of Thieves or a True Picture of the American Church and Clergy, written in the summer of 1843, was a seventy-five-page pamphlet that set forth the church's responsibility for slavery. After calling ministers "thieves, adulterers, man-stealers, pirates and murderers," he had proceeded to document his charges in a sober, well-reasoned style, pointing out that if slavery was "man-stealing," then southern clergymen were indeed "a brotherhood of thieves" with their northern counterparts scarcely less guilty. The pamphlet not only attested to slaveholders' cruelty by quoting from southern newspapers but also reminded readers that northern churches maintained segregated pews and graveyards and refused to admit aspiring black students to their seminaries. Abby distributed *Brotherhood* at all her meetings; over the next decades it was one of the American Anti-Slavery Society's best-selling tracts.

Maria had grudgingly approved of *Brotherhood* but, perhaps suspecting Abby's special interest in its author, had warned that "he has but little consistency or stability"; hence there was always reason "to dread that he will be fooled by the enemy." After writing a scathing account of Stephen's melodramatic behavior at recent meetings in Boston, she declared that he could always be depended on "to blunder forward *for the destruction of the American Society*." Abby tactlessly read him Maria's letter, thereby reinforcing his belief that the Boston clique regarded him as undesirable. Instantly regretting this, she tried to mend matters by asking Maria to have "a long conversation" with Stephen when he came to Boston. "I read him [your] letter which you may recall was terribly down on him. You undervalue him and are greatly prejudiced against him. This is a pity. He has done great service here."

Predictably the meeting between Stephen Foster and Maria Chapman was not a happy one. Stephen was still smarting when he reported on the interview to Abby. She tried to explain why Maria had failed to appreciate his character. She is "a great woman full of the wisdom of this world," but her very worldliness made her incapable of understanding "*our* wisdom," Abby wrote. To Maria, Stephen's practice of provoking his audience, thereby courting martyrdom, seemed either playacting or foolishness. But Christ had also been called foolish by his contemporaries, Abby reminded him. Thus "he who is led by the spirit of Christ" must expect to appear "a fool to the worldly wise."

Although Stephen and Maria never became friends, there was a gradual improvement in his relations with others in the movement. The Reverend Adin Ballou, founder of Hopedale and president of the New England Non-Resistance Society, traveled with Stephen to the 1844 anniversary in New York and quickly recognized his special qualities. "Foster knows nothing of fear, compromise or concession," Ballou astutely commented. "His moral indignation is intense and what he *thinks* and *feels*, he expresses. His philosophy is that of the old school revivalists—knock down, and then explain! Shock, madden, overwhelm, *stun* sinners, then apply poultices and opiates. A pure-hearted conscientious man, he must do his own work in his own way."

A fortnight later, at a meeting in Boston, Stephen won nods of approval even from some who had previously thought him a wild-eyed fanatic. The sessions had been continually interrupted by Abigail Folsom, an eccentric woman whom Emerson had dubbed "that flea of conventions." She took the floor at every reform meeting, talking endlessly and often irrationally. On this occasion she had mocked those appointed to committees, calling them "beautiful leaders," had warned people not to listen to the Hutchinsons' "siren songs," and had interrupted Wendell Phillips's plea for funds by shouting, "Don't give him a cent!" Losing patience, Wendell left the platform, determined to escort her from the hall. Seeing him approach, she began to sink to the floor. Quickly Stephen thrust a chair under her and, with Wendell and another man, carried her outside while she called over her shoulder, "I'm better off than my Master was. He had but one ass to ride—I have three."

Antiabolitionists in the audience, who had enjoyed Folsom's disruptive behavior, joined with the more ardent supporters of a free platform to protest her expulsion. When Stephen defended his action, saying that he could not allow "an insane woman to use up the time of a meeting like this," a voice from the balcony asked, "What is the difference, Mr. Foster? *You* carry her out because they say she is insane. *They* carry you out because they say you're insane." Stephen pointed out that when he interrupted meetings, he was dragged off to jail, while Folsom had received humane treatment. Nevertheless, Nathaniel P. Rogers, who had not yet fallen into disfavor, said that guaranteeing free speech was more important than raising money and protested against expelling people "on doubtful grounds." Abby Kelley joined the discussion by asking if "friend Rogers would not take the knife from the hand of a maniac," and Edmund Quincy pointed out that a jury had recently found Folsom insane and had committed her to the Worcester State Lunatic Hospital. Rogers's reply must have delighted the abolitionists' foes: "She may be crazy enough for a jury yet not crazy enough for an Anti-Slavery Society."

Later that year, when Stephen sided with the Boston leadership in its struggle against "no organization" in New Hampshire, Rogers wrote bitterly that Stephen Foster, who had once "set wild examples," had now grown "tame."[14]

No matter whether Stephen was wild or tame. The shock of Francis's death had made Abby realize how much she longed to see him. Soon she was asking Wendell "to send two more agents into Penna forthwith." The abolitionists she was working with in Kennett Square had pledged to raise five hundred dollars to sustain the lecturers and suggested sending Fred Douglass and Stephen Foster. "Others would be received, yet these would be the most acceptable," she reported.

So confident was she of Wendell's response that a day earlier she had written to Stephen: "Come directly. Don't wait a day after you can get packed up. The Kennett A.S. Society passed a resolution urging your presence here. You are considered *the man* and you must bring someone who will 'take.'" Of course, she added, "you and I won't have to be together and so no talk will come of our 'improprieties.'"

Wendell did not disappoint her. Although he thought it foolhardy to send Douglass so close to the Maryland border, where bands of kidnappers were always on the lookout for runaway slaves, he dispatched Stephen to Pennsylvania in February, with freeborn Charles Remond as his companion.

For the next months Abby and Stephen contrived to meet occasionally and to correspond frequently. Although the antislavery campaign still took precedence, she openly expressed her desire to be with him. "I frankly confess I cannot again be an old maid. I want to see my other half more than ever," she wrote in one letter. And in another: "Every day's absence but strengthens the longing of my heart for its cherished object. How happy will that day be which shall say that separation shall no longer be necessary." Writing to "My beloved," concluding letters with "Angels guard and keep you," referring to herself as "the mother of your anticipated children," she permitted herself to express the feelings she had so long held in check. Even after Stephen sent one of his "terrible" letters, accusing her of neglecting her health, she responded with unaccustomed gentleness, assuring him that she was well—"my cold is gone, my habits are regular"—and expressing concern for his well-being instead.

Love was in the Pennsylvania air that spring. Abby teased Jane Elizabeth about an old bachelor who was paying her attention until she noticed that Lizzie was pairing off more and more frequently with young Ben Jones. Elizabeth Neall wrote to say that she loved Sydney Gay, but her father disapproved because Sydney was not a Quaker. After Gay wrote to tell of their engagement, Abby sent a sentimental letter to Elizabeth and confided her own plan to marry Stephen, hardly a secret by that time.*

Abby and Stephen were "castle-building" in earnest. Where would they live? Stephen proposed buying a farm in New York State where he would also start a paper and lecture in his spare time. Abby squelched the idea with her usual frankness. "You cannot *buy* a farm. Will you *hire* one? If you do, you will get deep in the mud and I shall have to help you out. If you go to farming with no capital, you will have to struggle hard to make the ends of the year meet and will have no leisure to establish papers."

---

* In gossipy antislavery circles news of engagements traveled quickly. Maria Chapman also informed Abby of the Neall-Gay engagement, and Sarah Pugh, writing to abolitionists in Great Britain, asked "Do you know of [Abby Kelley's] and S. S. Foster's love story?" (MWC to AK, nd, 1845, AAS; S. Pugh to Webbs, April 21, 1845, BPL.)

Meanwhile, this unconventional woman who had just been mocked in the *United States Gazette* for her deviant behavior—"We wonder if she knows how to broil a steak or knit stockings"—was not only sewing bedroom slippers for Stephen but trying to scrape together money for a trousseau. "I must save my coppers to buy you some bed linen and books for that little library of mine, where you shall have the privilege of reading to your own wife while she makes your linen and mends your broadcloth," she wrote. "Then I will help you plant and hoe garden and gather fruit and we will go to meetings together to help each other lift up the souls of the multitudes."

Only when it came to setting a date for their wedding did Abby pull back. Early in the spring she and Jane Elizabeth had received a letter from the Ohio antislavery society, inviting them to attend the society's annual meeting and to present the program of the American Society at conventions throughout the state during the summer. The society would guarantee their expenses and a cordial welcome. The invitation was tempting. Ohio was a wide-open field, its abolitionists scarcely aware of the recent debates and decisions in the East. Before long Abby was writing to Wendell—"Reverend Brother"—to say that "Elizabeth and myself feel a concern, as the Quakers say, to go into Ohio next summer. We think it will be more profitable than to spend the summer in N.Y. What think you?"

Stephen, who had been unwell, decided to remain in the East. Beginning to think seriously of his responsibilities as a family man, he hoped to find some lucrative employment as well as a place where they could settle in the future. "I wish I could urge you to go to Ohio with us," Abby wrote. "We shall have multitudinous gatherings there, and it will not be possible for Lizzie and me to talk so much as they will need. But my first wish is to see you restored to health."[15]

In May Abby's team of lecturers went to New York for the anniversary of the American Anti-Slavery Society, the meeting that punctuated each year of the organization's work. Assembling in the Tabernacle, the delegates proceeded along predictable lines. Wendell Phillips convincingly propounded the doctrine of "No Union with slaveholders." Stephen Foster declared that southern clergymen sold their own slave children—and a group of ministers left the hall while he spoke. Frederick Douglass provided a dramatic moment when he revealed the name of his former owner, thereby inviting arrest as a fugitive.

The real surprises, however, were the women. Abby's talk on the labor to be performed in the coming year and the funds needed to sustain it was so effective that the *New York Herald*, archenemy of reformers, described her as "the lovely, intellectual, enchanting, fascinating Abby Kelley." A former slave whose name the secretary failed to catch—it was Sojourner Truth*—made her first appearance at an abolitionist meeting, speaking "with good sense and strong feeling." And Jane Elizabeth Hitchcock made such a vigorous attack on the Constitution that Garrison, hearing her for the first time, contrasted the "modesty and calmness of her demeanor" with the "clearness and cogency of her reasoning" and thought that she had dispelled forever the "absurd notions in reference to woman's sphere."

After the meeting Abby and Stephen spent a few vacation days with Olive and Newbury Darling in Connecticut, for she was at last eager to have him meet her family. While there, Stephen wrote to his older brother Galen to apprise him of their plans. "Abby sends you an invitation to her *wedding* which she says will come off about Christmas at Kennett, Chester Co. Pa. I shall not join her in this, at present, at least, for I think it a matter of great doubt whether she ever has one." However, he somewhat grumpily concluded, "She may possibly so far reconcile me as to induce me to become a party to [it]."[16]

---

* Sojourner Truth (c. 1797–1883) was emancipated by New York State law in 1827 and became a powerful, witty speaker for antislavery and woman's rights. Her best-known speech was "And aren't I a woman?"

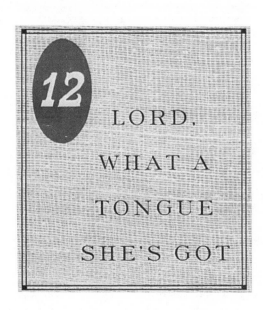

12

LORD, WHAT A TONGUE SHE'S GOT

journey to the West was still an adventure in the 1840s, but Abby found the trip more comfortable than she had anticipated. After traveling by train through New York State, she boarded an Erie Canal boat for the first time and delighted in the way it "slipped along so quietly and smoothly." Her only regret, she told Stephen, was that he was not with her so that she had to eat her Graham food "in dumb silence. 'Tis disagreeable, this eating alone. It is not good for *women* to be alone—I mean at the table."

Once she was in Ohio, antislavery friends carried her to New Lisbon (now Lisbon), the site of the convention. Ohio had a reputation for fertile soil where corn grew ten feet high, but the fields she saw from the buggy window were brown, the corn stunted, and the fruit in the orchards shriveled because a late frost had been followed by drought. With the practiced eye of a farm woman turned abolitionist agitator, she feared that many families would lose their income for the year—and "this will make it hard to raise money."

The Ohio American Anti-Slavery Society was a small sleepy organization with leanings toward the Liberty party until its officers invited Abby Kelley to address their annual meeting. On June 5, 1845, five hundred men and women, mostly Quakers with a scattering of black people, crowded into New Lisbon's Disciples' Church, the only building in town willing to admit them. Filling seats and aisles to capacity, they spilled over onto the front walk, where benches and an awning had been placed for the overflow. For three busy days Abby lectured, argued, and cajoled until she had converted her listeners to her own brand of radical antislavery. True, they tabled her resolution calling for disunion—that would come later—but they were won over by her attacks on the church and Liberty party, agreed to investigate Ohio's black laws, and voted to establish an antislavery newspaper.

Abby quickly discovered that the *Standard* and *Liberator* took from ten days to two weeks to reach Ohio's country towns. This was far too late to announce upcoming meetings or to give people "the news while it is still *news*," she wrote Wendell Phillips. If the West was to be abolitionized—and by this she meant not only Ohio's million and a half citizens but the people of Indiana, Illinois, and the new state of Michigan as well—a local paper was a necessity.

She had been in Ohio less than three weeks when the first issue of the *Anti-Slavery Bugle* appeared. Its masthead ascribed to Edmund Burke, read: "I love agitation when there is a cause for it—the alarm bell which startles the inhabitants of a city saves them from being burned in their beds", and its lead editorial promised to "sound the bugle-note of Freedom over the hills and through the valleys, blow[ing] a blast that will wake from their slumbers the tyrants at the South and their guilty abettors at the North."[1]

The *Bugle* started as a poorly printed four-page paper that lacked editor, subscribers, press, or type of its own. Abby made it her special charge, sending off urgent letters to Boston and New York. Wouldn't Oliver Johnson come west to edit the paper? Or Parker Pillsbury, now that the *Herald of Freedom* was discontinuing publication? What better way for the American Society to spend "time, money or talent than in establishing a strong post west of the mountains?" But Johnson and Pillsbury proved unavailable. Wendell Phillips was in the country for the summer, Maria Chapman preoccupied with the *Standard* and next winter's Christmas Fair, and Sydney Gay sourly reminded her that she had promised to build circulation for the *Standard*, which as usual was in dire financial straits.

Even before she had their replies, she convinced Benjamin Jones and Lizzie Hitchcock, who had come west for a summer's lecturing, to become temporary editors of the *Bugle* and had helped them establish headquarters in Salem, a pleasant, prosperous village ten miles north of New Lisbon. Dubious about his new role, Benjamin complained that the paper "had been undertaken under the influence of temporary excitement, thee raised the mercury by blowing upon the bulb of the thermometer—it now stands at summer heat, but it *will* fall in obedience to the laws of calorie, unless we can build up a better anti-slavery fire. Thee must do all that is possible. Make *special* efforts at every meeting to obtain subscribers and donations."[2]

Abby took up the challenge. By early July she had sent him the names of three hundred subscribers; at summer's end there were four hundred; by fall, seven hundred. In April 1846 the paper had a thousand subscribers and was well on its way to becoming self-sustaining.* That summer its editors were able to expand its pages from four to six columns and to buy a press. The *Bugle* continued to sound its uncompromising "bugle-note of Freedom" for the next fifteen years, remaining the chief organizing tool of the Garrisonians in the Old Northwest, as the region was still called. Abby, who had planned to spend only a summer in Ohio, remained there for a year and a half and returned whenever the paper needed her.[3]

The *Bugle* was not Abby's only concern. The local abolitionists all were second-rate speakers, she wrote Stephen. "They want you here and have asked if you could not be induced to come." Within weeks he was at her side, and together they spent much of the summer lecturing on the Western

---

* At its most successful, the *Liberator* never had more than twenty-five hundred subscribers.

Reserve, a three-million-acre tract bordering Lake Erie, before traveling to other parts of the state.

Admitted into the Union in 1803, Ohio was still largely agricultural. Canals and riverboats linked its major cities—the first rail line between Cleveland in the north and Cincinnati in the south was not completed until 1846—while in the sparsely settled countryside travelers were dependent on stagecoach or horse and buggy. On the Western Reserve, which had been settled by emigrants from Connecticut, villages resembled those in New England, but one-room log cabins chinked with clay and bark were still predominant in other places.

A generation behind New England and the mid-Atlantic states in its economy, Ohio also lagged culturally. A statewide public school system was not established until 1849; state-supported high schools opened four years later. Such distinguished visitors from abroad as Frances Trollope and Charles Dickens complained of the Ohioans' "incessant remorseless spitting of tobacco juice" and the smell of onions and corn whiskey that enveloped them. Abby Kelley detested tobacco and whiskey, too, but had grown accustomed to frontier manners in New York State. She found the "Buckeyes" rough but applauded their lack of pretension. "The most marked distinction between N.E. and Ohio is that here all their deformities are visible to the whole world. There they are colored and glossed over. I like this openness," she wrote.[4]

Abolitionism was popular in the state, particularly on the Western Reserve. Even in Cincinnati, whose prosperity rested on trade with the South, there was considerable sympathy for fugitive slaves who crossed from the Kentucky side of the Ohio River and traveled to Canada on the Underground Railroad. Along with Ohioans' dislike of slavery and sentimental regard for the runaways went a strong belief in white superiority, which was reflected in the state's onerous Black Laws. These laws not only denied blacks the right to vote and to testify against whites in court but required them to register with the authorities and post five-hundred-dollar security bonds before settling in the state.

Abby won some support when she preached against the Black Laws but found it difficult to convince Ohioans to give up their "hateful prejudice against color." "I have sat down and reasoned out this question of the equality of the colored man," a fellow lecturer confided. "I know that he is my equal brother. Then I go out, meet a colored man on the street, and in my heart cannot feel toward him as I feel toward the white man."

The Ohio antislavery society had divided in 1840, reflecting the split in the East, but there was less sectarian bitterness between the rival factions. After her first encounter with the Garrisonian leaders in the state, Abby told Maria Chapman that they reminded her of Pennsylvanians because they had "more affection than intellect or conscience." They had wanted to hire a local man as editor of the *Bugle* not because of his competence but because "he is such a nice man" and "now is poor" and "out of employment." "Our warfare with Liberty party is not relished," she added. "They have so many 'good friends' in it and they are 'such good abolitionists' that the party must be spared."

She soon set them straight. Accompanied by Stephen and other speakers she had corralled, she moved on from the Reserve during 1845 and 1846 to visit every major city in the state—Cleveland, Cincinnati, Columbus, Toledo, Akron, Dayton—and even ventured forty miles into Indiana. In a region where there were few amusements and fewer lyceums or libraries, "New England's eloquent daughter" became a stellar attraction. At a typical gathering called to celebrate August 1, the anniversary of the emancipation of the slaves of the West Indies, three thousand people converged on the village of Marlboro, in Stark County. Walking, riding horseback, driving wagons, some came from as far as seventy miles away—a day and night of steady traveling. Buggies for two held four; carriages for four held six; road wagons expanded to carry a dozen members of a farm family.

In a grove outside the village, local abolitionists had constructed a crude amphitheater, with benches arranged in a semicircle facing a speakers' platform. In the shade of the trees bordering the grove, a table set up by the Ladies' Sewing Circle offered needle boxes, workbags, aprons, bookmarks, each neatly embroidered with "THIS IS FOR THE SAKE OF FREEDOM" or "REMEMBER THEM IN BONDS." Nearby energetic matrons and their daughters bustled about an improvised kitchen and trestle tables, preparing to feed all comers. They also took charge of finding barns and haylofts in which to lodge overnight visitors.

On this occasion Abby and Benjamin Jones opened the meeting with reports of the benefits that emancipation had brought to the West Indies while Stephen, who had charge of the book trunk, found a place to display the antislavery tracts and periodicals they carried with them. On the second and third days he and Lizzie Hitchcock also took the rostrum to expose the proslavery character of the government, the corruption of the churches and the Liberty party. In keeping with the picnic atmosphere, songs punctuated the speeches: Whittier's hymn "The Freed Islands," "Come Join the Abolitionists," and a new addition to the antislavery repertoire, "We Go for Dissolution":

> We are coming, we are coming, freedom's battle is begun,
> No hand shall furl her banner ere her victory be won.
> Our shields are locked for liberty, and mercy goes before.
> Tyrants, tremble in your citadels, oppression shall be o'er.
> We go for Dissolution
> We go for Dissolution,
> And "No Union with slaveholders,"
> Shall ring through the land.

By the time the meeting adjourned, the *Bugle* had a hundred new subscribers and eighty dollars pledged toward its support.[5]

Wherever the team of abolitionists spoke, the press focused on Abby, the first woman to lecture in the West since Fanny Wright had spoken in Cincinnati a decade earlier. Headlining her appearance with reports of ABBY & CO., ABBY KELLEY AND HER SUIT, and ABBY KELLEY AND HER *PROCHEIN AMI*, STEPHEN S. FOSTER, the papers described "a woman of extraordinary intellect" with "rather handsome features," even though they thought she "had better go home and mend the holes in her stockings." Most correspondents referred to her as the "master spirit" or the "principal personage," putting down Stephen as "a mere ranter." "She makes no hesitation to jump up when he is speaking and take the floor from him right in the midst of his talk."

Some of the reporters' accounts were ingenious. One declared that her real object was the destruction of the churches. He knew this, he solemnly explained, because "her habits are the same as the Communitists: no flesh, no butter, no spices. She is practicing, as a method of regeneration, the modern infidel means of purifying the heart." "And that's not all," another added, tongue in cheek. "Instead of being content, like a Christian woman, with simply washing her face and hands, she carries her modern infidel method of regeneration and purifying the heart so far as absolutely to wash her whole body every day. And I am told she is so shameless that she freely admits it. I think it is intolerable heathenism for the woman to resort to pure water, instead of relying on the grace of God to keep her clean."

The comments on Abby's personal habits stemmed from her insistence on her own bowl of water—even if it was brought to her in an iron skillet—and a modicum of privacy for a daily bath, a requirement that was not always easily met in rural Ohio. Although she was entertained in well-furnished homes on the Reserve, in other places she was obliged to perform her ablutions at a well outdoors, while at night her sleeping quarters were separated from her hosts' by a quilt suspended from the rafters. Food, too, was a problem. In a region where pork and bacon were the chief fare, it was difficult to hold to a Graham diet. When fresh vegetables were unattainable, Abby lived on potatoes and eggs.

By the time she wrote to sister Olive in November 1845, she was "quite unwell," she reported. "This 'great West' is so tremendously big and there is so much to be done in it, that I have scarcely had time to take a long breath. For the first three months we were here we had meetings every day or went on long journeys, sometimes thirty or forty miles, and occasionally had to journey into the night so as to hold meetings [the next] day." Stephen, somewhat healthier than usual, was bearing the brunt of the speaking in order to spare her. Occasionally they took time off for sight-seeing, visiting ancient Indian mounds and fortifications. Abby longed to cross the border to Kentucky to see Mammoth Cave, but friends warned that her life would be in jeopardy if she entered a slave state—"so I suppose I can't go. What a glorious Union!!!" When they reached the center of the state, she spent a week with her sister Ruth Pollard and Ruth's husband, Warren, who were living "pretty comfortably" on a farm in Columbus, where Warren employed three field hands and Ruth had a girl to help in the kitchen and hired her washing done.

Afterward Ruth traveled with her to a log village outside Dayton to see their half sisters Nancy and Lydia and other Kelley relatives. Lydia was burdened with six children and a heavy-drinking husband. One widowed cousin took in washing and plain sewing while Nancy, "as fat as pork," went out to nurse for three dollars a week to support the "lazy loafer" she had married. Fastidious Abby told Olive that Nancy was almost as bad as he. "With their three children, they crawl into their nest and breed filth. 'Twas sickening." She was so disgusted with Nancy that when she learned that she belonged to a Baptist church, she didn't try to persuade her to leave it. "It may keep [her] from some temptations, and besides some people can't very clearly comprehend an argument," she told Olive.

In closing her letter, she reported on her wedding plans. Before coming to Ohio, she and Stephen had hoped to marry that fall in eastern Pennsylvania so that friends and some family members could be present. She had even had "a half proposition in my head to have a ceremony performed in a *church*—that all the world might know 'for certain' that S. S. Foster and Abby Kelley were not opposed to the marriage institution." But the Ohio field had proved so demanding that they had regretfully decided to marry "on the wing."

Because Pennsylvania did not require a minister or magistrate to officiate, they decided to marry in the little town of New Brighton, just across the Pennsylvania line. Although sad that none of their family could be with them, "We make this sacrifice for the slave's sake as we have others, with joy," Abby concluded her letter.

Accompanied by Lizzie Hitchcock, Ben Jones, and Samuel Brooke, the general agent of the Ohio antislavery society, they went to New Brighton the week before Christmas. They were married at the home of Milo Townsend, a fellow abolitionist, on December 21, 1845, shortly before Abby's thirty-fifth birthday. In the Quaker tradition they had drawn up their own wedding certificate:

> This is to certify that we Stephen S. Foster, Son of Asa and Sarah M. Foster of the town of Canterbury and State of New Hampshire, and Abby Kelley, Daughter of the late Wing and Dianna Kelley of the Town of Millbury and State of Massachusetts, have this day consummated a matrimonial connection in accordance with the divine law of Marriage, by a public

declaration of our mutual affection, and covenant of perpetual love, and fidelity, of our purpose to perform faithfully, all the relative duties of husband and wife.

About fifty people, most of them friends of the Townsends, were present for the evening ceremony. One wedding guest reported: "Stephen gave them his views relating to marriage, Abby spoke of her anti-slavery life—its toil and sacrifice. The assembly was more like a funeral than a wedding—not a dry eye present—the only refreshments—cold water!"

Returning to Ohio, the Fosters had a few private days together in Columbiana, a village near Salem, before resuming their meeting schedule. Writing to Abby a decade later from the farm where they had spent this brief honeymoon, Stephen called it the most "hallowed spot on the globe, for here I was first really introduced into the inner sanctuary of the marriage relation. Here it was that I first felt the full *force* & *power* of those genial rays which have beamed upon my pathway from a cloudless sky, turning darkness into day & soothing my lacerated spirit with a tenderness of affection of which I had never dreamed."

Always more chary of expressing her feelings, Abby contented herself with telling Sydney Gay, also newlywed: "Since our marriage our meetings have been much more successful than heretofore. . . . Had I known how much holier and happier and more useful married life is than single, I should not have tarried so long."[6]

After the *Bugle* published a terse announcement of the marriage, Ohio newspapers hailed it with mock applause. "None too soon!" one editor wrote. "Well done, Abby!" a second commented, trusting that the marriage would put a stop to her attempt "to overturn Uncle Sam's government" and would keep her at home taking care of babies. Perhaps her friends in the East feared some such change, for when Parker Pillsbury congratulated Stephen on his marriage to *"The Woman"* of the age," he abjured Abby to remain faithful to the cause. "I doubt if there [was] much joy in heaven when Theodore Weld ran away with the Grimkés & made one a mother, and both obscure & private women," he reminded her.

What should he call her? Sydney Gay asked. "Must I say my dear Foster, as you say 'My dear Gay'—[or] my dear woman, whatever your name is."

Abby jokingly signed herself "Mrs. S. S. Foster" in reply, but that was probably the only time she used her husband's name without her own. In other correspondence as well as in announcements of meetings she was "Abby Kelley Foster" or "Abby K. Foster," following the style that Maria Weston Chapman had introduced and that younger feminists like Elizabeth Cady Stanton adopted.[7]*

Maria, who was still annoyed because Abby had remained in Ohio instead of going to New York to gather subscriptions for the *Standard* ("There are souls to be saved everywhere," she had scolded), waited more than a month before commenting on the marriage and then only asked to be remembered "very cordially to your husband" before discussing antislavery business. Ignoring the slight, if indeed one was intended, Abby replied by telling her about Lizzie Hitchcock. Lizzie and Ben Jones had planned a long engagement but, after editing the *Bugle* together for some months, had decided that it would be "more convenient" to marry immediately. Following the Fosters' example, they had gone to New Brighton for a simple ceremony and were now back in Salem preparing to set up housekeeping on their editorial salary of four hundred dollars a year, a small sum even by Ohio standards. Lizzie, who had been pampered and protected ("wished and was gratified—spoke and was obeyed"), until Abby brought her into the movement, explained how she planned to manage: "Two rooms will answer—one for our office and parlor, which with a bed, will also serve for a bed-room at night, and the other for a kitchen and dining room. Fifty dollars will be sufficient to furnish them as the cooking-stove will be the most expensive article of furniture."

Moved by Lizzie's acceptance of her "sudden transition from elegance to meanness," Abby could not suppress "tears of gratitude for so rich a gift to our cause. She bears no love for the West, but stays here for the slave's sake," she told Maria. "Can the American Society make her a present?"

---

* Most feminists to be in the 1840s and 1850s objected to being called by their husbands' names. Maria Weston Chapman was never "Mrs. Henry Chapman," or Maria Child, "Mrs. David L. Child." Elizabeth Cady Stanton protested vociferously when Wendell Phillips addressed her as "Mrs. H. B. Stanton." (Hersh).

And if a gift was sent, "I pray you that she may never suspect that I have said anything about it."

Maria responded promptly. The Executive Committee of the American Society sent a hundred dollars to Lizzie Jones "as a means of aiding her to aid the cause" but also asked Abby for an estimate of her own expenses. A woman had contributed fifty dollars to the western mission, and Maria wanted to pass it along.

Abby, who saw no parallel between her situation and Lizzie's because she was inured to the financial hardships of antislavery work, told Maria to use the fifty dollars for agents' salaries. "I don't look out for rainy days," she explained. "My husband does because he feels it his duty. When I shall be compelled by circumstances to take a salary, I will frankly say so." She added, "If the Society has not the ability to pay Stephen's salary they need give themselves no uneasiness as we can get along without it. They had better pay Jones than him. Jones is going to housekeeping and we are not for the present—perhaps not under a year."

Stephen was equally generous. Although he accepted a salary because he felt it incumbent on a man to prepare to support his family, he too put others' needs before his own. Sending his expense account to Wendell Phillips, he told him not to pay the money due him if the society was short of funds or if Wendell thought "the amount charged too large for services rendered." Should he be paid, he wanted Wendell or Francis Jackson to place the money at interest until he needed it. The following summer, when Parker Pillsbury came to Ohio, Stephen discovered that Parker was being paid less than he. "Now I think this outrageous, as he does quite as much work as I do, besides doing it *very much better*," he wrote Wendell. "I hope, therefore, that you will raise his support, if it be at the expense of my own."[8]

Still on the defensive about remaining in Ohio when Maria and Sydney wanted her in New York, Abby told Maria that their work in the West had been "more effective than anything we have before done. Ohio is to the West what Mass. is to N.E. in point of influence and we trust our labors have given her a Mass. character." In at least one striking way, the new field differed from others they had worked in. Despite newspaper attacks, they had encountered little violence. Once some mischievous boys had cut off a piece of Benjamin's coat; twice Stephen had dodged stones or rotten eggs. But no one had laid a hand on any of the antislavery lecturers until Abby attempted to speak at a Quaker meeting.

Late in the summer of 1845 she had gone to Mount Pleasant, a Quaker settlement near the Ohio River, to attend the Yearly Meeting of the Society of Friends. The two-story brick meetinghouse, built in 1816, had once been the mother meeting for all Friends west of the Appalachians. However, the society now gathering there was Orthodox Friends. Abby knew that she would be unwelcome; even soft-spoken Lucretia Mott was not "in harmony" with them. Nevertheless, Abby took a seat in the meeting and, after waiting for the better part of a day, rose to remind her audience of Friends' historic commitment to abolition. She had scarcely begun to speak when an elder interrupted, ordering her not to disturb the meeting. But she continued, saying that she had a message to deliver. When a second elder and then a third told her to sit down, she invoked George Fox, who had felt called upon by God to interrupt church services. By this time tempers were rising. As she persisted, several men moved toward her, determined to escort her from the building. Remembering Stephen's technique, she immediately went limp. Amid great confusion she was carried bodily from the meeting and deposited none too gently on the ground outside. While an eastern Friend called the incident "disgraceful and even brutal," the Ohio press chortled. One reporter, although admitting that he could not vouch for it, wrote that Abby had "kicked tremendously at the good Quaker shins."

Her only other physical encounter during her eighteen months in Ohio took place in Lake County on the Western Reserve on a warm Sunday in July 1846. Shortly before sunset a constable arrived at the house where the Fosters were staying with a warrant for their arrest. The charge was Sabbath breaking; they had sold antislavery books at a Sunday meeting. When they refused to accompany the constable, he left to obtain reinforcements. Returning with two deputies, he seized Stephen, only to have Abby throw her arms around her husband and declare that although it was common to separate husbands and wives in the South, they could not do so in Ohio. The constable and his men finally managed to drag the limp couple through the doorway and deposit them, feetfirst, in a waiting buggy. As they drove off, neighbors who had gathered to see the excitement sang antislavery songs, while a carriageload of sympathizers followed them to their destination. This was only the beginning of the lawmen's travail, for the Fosters resisted every inch of the way. They refused to leave the buggy to be arraigned or, after being dragged out, to recognize the authority of Deacon Cunningham, the presiding magistrate. When asked if she pleaded guilty, Abby responded by reminding the appreciative crowd that a century earlier Quaker women had been "whipped until the skin was torn off for breaking the Sabbath." She had no doubt that the deacon would commit "similar barbarities" if public sentiment permitted.

Cunningham ordered them imprisoned in the local tavern to await trial the next day. The hapless constable and his posse carried them to a bedchamber, where, Stephen reported, they enjoyed a refreshing night's sleep while three deputies stood guard at their door. The following morning they were taken by force to the tavern parlor, where court was in session, and were formally charged with "breaking the Sabbath by performing manual labor in selling books." The Fosters stood mute, but antislavery people, some of whom had driven a dozen miles during the night, crowded into the room to speak in their defense. A lawyer who was not an abolitionist but who believed in civil liberty acted as counsel. He pointed out that it was common practice to sell books in church on Sundays and that Deacon Cunningham himself had frequently done so. In the face of the lawyer's charge that the Fosters' arrest arose out of "malice, spite and political bigotry," the embarrassed magistrate acquitted them. Following their release, they held an impromptu meeting in front of the tavern while their persecutors drove away, "writhing and gnashing teeth" because their prey had escaped them.

Their arrest permitted the kind of theatricality that both Fosters delighted in because it gave them a chance to demonstrate that church and state were united in opposition to abolition. The *Cleveland American* agreed that the incident had been "a great day" for Abby and Stephen. "To see them dragged through the streets and boosted into and out of the vehicle, pliant as inanimate carcasses—heavy as sin—meek as lambs—locked in each other's arms—were scenes that would have made Cruikshank ecstatic. And then such a non-resistant beating as they gave the magistrate and all concerned." After publishing Stephen's lengthy account of the incident, the editor added his own comment on Abby: "Lord, what a tongue she's got."[9]

The eagerness of some Ohioans to harass the Fosters was due in no small part to the outbreak of the Mexican War that summer. In May Abby and Stephen, accompanied by a large contingent from Ohio, had traveled to the New York anniversary. Worn out by the past year's exertions, Abby had not planned to speak at the meeting, but when the new magnetic telegraph brought word of the outbreak of hostilities below the Rio Grande, she could not contain her indignation.

"My place is not in the city, but in the back woods. While the newsboys are crying at every corner, I find that in this great Babel, the only sympathy felt about the war is with those who are buying and selling stocks," she began. Not only was the war an unjust attack of a large nation on a small one, but its purpose was to extend slave territory. "Our fathers were successful in the Revolution, because they were engaged in a holy cause, and had right on their side. But in this case we have not. This nation is doomed," she declared. Predicting that the slaves in the South would join with the Indians of the West—"who are only waiting to plant their tomahawks in the white man's skull"—she saw nothing but destruction ahead. She was reaching the climax of her speech, declaiming, "LET THE NATION BE ACCURSED SO THAT ITS PEOPLE MAY BE SAVED," when plumes of smoke curled up from the platform beneath her feet.

The audience watched, transfixed, until Stephen broke the spell and ordered everyone to leave the hall. The fire, of unknown origin, was quickly extinguished, but it brought Abby's speech to a dramatic end. At the next session the society went on record against the war, supporting Abby's motion "to use vigorous means to prevent enlistments."

The Garrisonians' opposition to this unpopular war found support in many parts of the North. At the convention of the New England Anti-Slavery Society in Boston the following week such illustrious fellow travelers as the Reverends William Henry Channing and Theodore Parker joined in an antiwar pledge that committed its signers to oppose the war "at all hazards, and at every sacrifice, to refuse enlistment, contribution, aid and countenance to the war." Two young Harvard alumni, James Russell Lowell and Henry David Thoreau, who had hitherto remained on the sidelines, now recognized the war as an effort to extend the Slave Power. Lowell, agreeing to serve on the *Standard*'s editorial board, wrote a series of satirical poems and essays that were later collected as *The Biglow Papers*. Speaking in the dialect of a Yankee farmer, Hosea Biglow was antiwar, antislavery, and prodisunion:

> *Ez fer war, I call it murder,—*
> *There you hev it plain an' flat;*
> *I don't want to go no furder*
> *Than my Testyment for that. . . .*
>
> *They just want this Californy*
> *So's to lug new slave-states in*
> *To abuse ye, an' to scorn ye,*
> *An to plunder ye like sin. . . .*
>
> *Ef I'd my way I hed ruther*
> *We should go to work an' part,—*
> *They take one way, we take t'other—*
> *Guess it wouldn't break my heart. . . .*

Thoreau, who was then living in a cabin on Walden Pond, did not attend the antislavery convention, although his sisters, Helen and Sophia, were present and signed the antiwar pledge. However, a month later he refused to pay his poll tax because the money would support the war. Arrested, he spent a night in the Concord jail and later wrote his influential essay "Civil Disobedience," in which he first espoused the doctrine of nonresistance.

The Fosters, accompanied by Parker Pillsbury, hurried back to the West for the annual meeting of the Ohio Anti-Slavery Society. Convening in Salem, the delegates voted to change the name of the society to the Western Anti-Slavery Society, so as to include all the states and territories west of the Appalachians. They readily agreed to sign and circulate a peace pledge; a month later a Western Peace Society was also formed.[10]

Local patriots objected to the Fosters' slashing attacks on the government and to their advice to young men to stay out of the army, but a large proportion of their listeners agreed that the war was an unsavory adventure waged for the benefit of the South and moved closer to the Garrisonian position. One of Abby's main supporters in the state was Joshua Reed Giddings, Whig congressman for the Western Reserve. A square-built, good-tempered man of fifty, self-educated and blunt-spoken, Giddings had served in the House of Representatives since 1838 and was now the leader of the small antislavery bloc in Congress. As soon as Abby arrived in Ohio, Giddings had invited her to his home in Jefferson and had shared a platform with her. To her surprise, she liked him, "in so far as I can admire a politician," she said. "He is as honest [as] a politician can be and more honest than I had expected to find him." Following their joint appearance in Jefferson, "Whigs came from far and near to induce us to visit their respective places," she reported. "We go in under the patronage of their tall man and then the way we deal out blows to right and left is a caution."

Giddings continued to cooperate with the Fosters even though their relationship proved politically embarrassing. After Abby had quoted him as saying that "the Union is a curse and ought to be dissolved," opposition papers attacked the congressman for his friendship with "dissolutionists and disorganizers." When he ran for reelection in 1846, the *Cleveland Plain Dealer* condemned him as "the *bosom* friend of ABBY KELLEY and [endorser of] the fanatical sentiments of that *woman* in reference to *dissolving this glorious Union.*" The paper found that "his Whiggery has *progressed* into the *rankest treason!*"

Replying to the attacks, Giddings refused to repudiate either Abby or the American Anti-Slavery Society, which, he said, "embraces some of the most devoted patriots and purest philanthropists of our nation." Although he disagreed with the society's interpretation of the Constitution, he said that he could foresee the time when the slaveholders' usurpation of power might make dissolution of the Union a necessity.

For her part, Abby proved more doctrinaire. After Giddings spoke in Congress in opposition to the "unholy and unjust war" with Mexico, Sydney Gay proposed that the American Society commend him. Garrison backed Gay's resolution, but Abby amended it, insisting that the word "false" be inserted so that the resolution read: "In the councils of our nation, one man at least, Joshua R. Giddings, is as faithful as his false position will permit him to be to his duty."

Maria Giddings, the congressman's twenty-year-old daughter, who was one of Abby's staunchest admirers, wrote to ask her father how he felt about the backhanded compliment. Giddings was philosophical. "I regard their position as *false*, but when I speak of them it's respectful, leaving it for the world to judge," he replied. "But the compliment was well intended and was received in the spirit in which it was given."

With the Fosters' help or in spite of it, Giddings was elected to Congress again. When he returned to Washington for the next session, one of his table-mates at Mrs. Sprigg's boardinghouse, where the antislavery Whigs stayed, was a freshman congressman from Illinois named Abraham Lincoln.[11]

The obverse of Abby's mistrust of politicians was her faith in women. "*One* woman is worth *two* men any day in a moral movement," she declared. "Not that they are naturally better or wiser, but because they have not, from the customs of society, been so much perverted." Girls had not been taught "the tricks and falsehoods of trade and politics into which a boy is baptized. Hence their moral perception is much clearer." Always on the lookout for potential leaders, she found a promising recruit in Betsy Mix Cowles, a forthright woman of thirty-five whose family had emigrated from Connecticut when she was an infant. Related by marriage to Alice Cowles, who had extended a hesitantly helping hand to Abby in 1840, she was a graduate of Oberlin and lady principal of the Grand River Institute, a private seminary. Giddings called her "the greatest woman on the Reserve," Abby told Maria Chapman. "She is the daughter of a Presbyterian minister, brought up in the hotbed of bigotry, yet with a soul as free and a mind as comprehensive as the Universe."*

---

* Betsy Cowles (1810–76) remained a leader of the Garrisonian abolitionists in Ohio until the Civil War and also played a major role in the nascent woman's rights movement, serving as president of the first woman's rights convention held in the state. After her death a historian wrote that although Joshua Giddings had represented the abolitionist sentiment of his district in Congress, Betsy Cowles, more than any other person, had created the sentiment that upheld him. (Stanton, Anthony, et al., v. 1; *BUGLE* April 27, 1850; Williams.)

Abby pursued Betsy, addressing her in language that sounds effusive now but that rang true in mid-nineteenth-century America. "My heart goes out to greet you. How I wish I could press you to my bosom," one letter began. Abby hoped to persuade Betsy to give up her position at the institute and become a full-time antislavery agent. Betsy had no taste for lecturing but took the lead in organizing women's antislavery societies and sewing circles.

These Ladies' Anti-Slavery Sewing Circles were particularly significant in Ohio, where, unlike the East, women were still dependent on their looms and nimble fingers for most household goods. A decade earlier they had sewn outfits for missionaries about to depart for Africa. Now, under Betsy Cowles's direction, the sewing circles made trousers and coats for underpaid antislavery agents and for fugitive slaves on their way to Canada. They also prepared flannel cloth, thread, bonnets, quilts, to be sold at antislavery fairs, which were a major source of funds for the *Bugle* and the state society.

Nor did the women neglect other aspects of antislavery work. At monthly and quarterly meetings of the ladies' societies, an address by an abolitionist lecturer was followed by singing. Betsy Cowles and her sisters were accomplished musicians who moved listeners to tears with the haunting lament of a slave mother:

> *Gone, gone; sold and gone*
> *To the rice-swamp, dank and lone,*
> *From Virginia's hills and waters—*
> *Woe is me, my stolen daughters!*

and then raised their political consciousness with a "dissolution song" that Abby had sent them. Betsy, who was also mindful of the need to combat prejudice, introduced a chorus of black teenagers from Cincinnati at the gatherings, rallied support for black parents' efforts to integrate a new public school in Massillon, and prepared articles and petitions against Ohio's Black Laws.

When opponents attempted to discredit her by calling her an Abby Kelleyite, Betsy welcomed the epithet and transformed it into a term of endearment. In an appeal for attendance at one Ladies' Anti-Slavery Society

meeting, she invited "those who call us Abby Kelleyites to come and see
what a company of such 'ites' will do if only one creates such a stir." Before
long others adopted the phrase, even speaking of their daughters as "little
Abby Kelleyites."[12]

Abby's most important convert during these Ohio years was Lucy Stone,
the young Massachusetts woman who had been too timid to join Abby in
the pulpit in 1842. Now a slender woman of twenty-six with bright red
cheeks and expressive eyes, Lucy was a student at Oberlin College, enrolled
in the Gentlemen's Course leading to a bachelor's degree, rather than in
the two-year Ladies' Course. Despite its liberal reputation, Oberlin was
controlled by evangelical ministers who had sided with "new organization"
in the 1840 split and believed that women should remain in their sphere.
One of the few Garrisonians on the campus, Lucy kept a picture of Garrison
in her room—her schoolmates said that she said her prayers to it—and
defended disunion and the antiwar position to all comers.

When the Fosters visited the college in the spring of 1846, Lucy helped
gain an audience for their meetings and volunteered to sell subscriptions
to the *Bugle*. However, it was difficult to discuss "the Church or Constitutional question," she wrote Abby, "because the women to whom I have
access, neither know or care anything about it. Would to God they did.
They are, however, interested in the question of 'woman's rights' and a
few are taking the *true* ground. I wish I *could tell* you how much *good* I
received from your visit here," she concluded. "My heart dances gaily at
the remembrance—it will be *long* before I shall be *so cheered* again."

Since Abby's only other contact at Oberlin was James Monroe, a young
Quaker whom she dismissed as "an amiable soul—pity he was not created
with a backbone," she welcomed Lucy's assistance and quickly tried to put
her to work. Lucy had already made a public speech at a celebration of
West Indian independence, to the consternation of Oberlin's Ladies' Board.
Abby urged her to do more. "Why delay? Is not now the accepted time?"
she asked.

Lucy, who had taught school for years in order to pay for her Oberlin
education, insisted on completing the final year of her course. She continued
to aid the Fosters, sending letters on their behalf to the *Oberlin Evangelist*
and answering attacks on them by Liberty party men who were now

supporting the Mexican War. When Oberlin officials refused to permit Abby and Stephen to speak on campus because they were "infidels," she deplored the decision but thought that the faculty was sincere—"all but one."

"No! No!" Abby scolded Lucy for her naiveté. "You believe them sincere. What reason have you for such belief? You are a good, confiding girl. After you have fought the wild beasts of Ephesus, or the worse than wild, the tame beasts of the pulpit, as long as I have, you will not be so easily taken with their cant and profession. Your eyes will be open some time, and not very far distant if you go into the battle."

To illustrate further the attacks on her, Abby mentioned another "fabrication" circulating on the Oberlin campus that was designed "to destroy my influence for saving my sisters from chains." It was said that she was pregnant and was immodestly continuing to lecture in defiance of all the rules of propriety and the danger to her unborn child.

"*I am no more going to have a baby than you are*," Abby assured Lucy. "And as I have not heard you were, I take it for granted you are not, though should I *hear* such a report I would not believe it, if you were an anti-slavery lecturer. No, in Heaven's name, I implore you to deny these malicious slanders. Do you believe we are wanting in ideas of decency, to say nothing of knowledge of physiology? You are not much acquainted with us, and therefore I don't blame you for supposing it might be true. If I am not mistaken in physiological facts, I never can be a mother while I work so hard in this cause. And I must exercise self denial for the sake of the mothers who are childless."

A month after this letter to Lucy the Fosters returned to Oberlin. They were permitted to speak in the college chapel because black people in the vicinity had asked to hear them.[13] Shortly after the visit Abby discovered that her knowledge of physiology was limited. She was indeed pregnant.

Her extraordinary exertions in Ohio—the daily lectures and the nights of travel—as well as her low-fat Graham diet had probably caused her to have irregular or scanty menstrual periods. The then-current medical wisdom that confused menstruation with ovulation had led her to believe that pregnancy was impossible. However, by late October, when she was three months pregnant, she could no longer ignore the changes in her body.

The Fosters had planned to wrap up their work in the West in the fall of 1846 and, after a brief rest, spend the winter in New York raising money for the *Standard*. Now all their plans were changed. They would have to give up their peripatetic way of life and establish a home. Stephen was still intent on buying a farm, but although briefly tempted by the fertile fields of Ohio and Pennsylvania, he and Abby agreed that "home" meant New England.

At the end of October Abby wrote to Sydney Gay to tell him that she must disappoint him. She and Stephen would stop in New York "to give you the reasons for our decision. Do not think we do the impolitic till you hear all we have to say," she begged. After explaining their situation to Gay, they went on to Boston to make plans for the months ahead.

From Massachusetts Abby still kept a watchful eye on Ohio. She urged Betsy Cowles to "keep up the agitation—don't let the waters become stagnant" and informed Maria Chapman that Lucy Stone would be available to lecture the following summer. Maria was "highly gratified with the prospect of having another representation of our sex in the field," Abby wrote Lucy, and hoped that she would go to work as an agent of the Massachusetts Society. "A particular reason for my wishing you to come forward now," Abby explained, "is that for the present I shall be out of public meetings. That which was reported of me falsely last summer is true now. Since my marriage, I have always desired to be a mother, but feared my health would prevent it. Now, altho' this wish is gratified I am at times half sad that I am not able still to stand in the fore-part of this mighty battle."[14]

CONFLICTING
CLAIMS

Despite some concern for propriety—pregnant women were not supposed to appear in public—Abby did not retire immediately on her return to Massachusetts but continued to attend meetings through January 1847. She had gained so little weight, she wrote Betsy Cowles, that "no one suspected me from my form and none but my most familiar friends saw the signs in my countenance." Even in February, three months before her baby was born, she was still "pretty trim only a little more flesh than usual."

She and Stephen took part in the annual meeting of the New England

Non-Resistance Society and gave a series of lectures in Boston, Worcester, and locations in between. Christmas week found them in Boston, where, for the first time in seven years, Abby attended the Anti-Slavery Bazaar at Faneuil Hall. Women had come in from the country to decorate the historic building with cedar boughs, wreaths, and loops of ground pine. Table after table was spread with elegant wares—paintings, rare books, silver jewel boxes, and embroidered screens contributed by abolitionists in the British Isles—as well as with the children's dresses, aprons, and purses made by local Female Anti-Slavery societies. The centerpiece of the glittering display was an elaborately wrought silver tea service that the women of Edinburgh had sent to William Lloyd Garrison, along with an "Address to the Women of the United States," which more than ten thousand Scottish women had signed.

On Christmas Eve Abby was asked to read the "thrilling" address to the assemblage and to follow it with a speech of her own. She was well launched into her speech when the gaslights suddenly failed, plunging the hall into darkness. With her usual aplomb she continued talking as if nothing had happened while the fair managers scurried around for candles to provide a flickering light.

Although she would never overcome her distaste for the consumerism that the fair encouraged, she could only agree that this year's was the grandest ever, and its proceeds of $4,525, which went to the antislavery society, were truly impressive. James Russell Lowell, who was reporting New England news for the *Pennsylvania Freeman*, sent a rhymed letter to Miller McKim giving the highlights of the affair:

> *The great attraction now of all*
> *Is the "Bazaar" at Faneuil Hall,*
> *Where swarm the Anti-Slavery folks*
> *As thick, dear Miller, as your jokes.*
> *There's Garrison, his features very*
> *Benign for an incendiary,*
> *Beaming forth sunshine through his glasses*
> *On the surrounding lads and lasses,*

There was Maria Chapman, too,
With her swift eyes of clear steel-blue,
The coiled-up mainspring of the Fair,
Originating everywhere
The expansive force without a sound
That whirled a hundred wheels around,
Herself meanwhile as calm and still
As the bare crown of Prospect Hill.

After describing Phillips, Quincy, and other luminaries, he turned to Stephen and Abby:

Hard by, as calm as summer even.
Smiles the reviled and pelted Stephen,
The unappeasable Boanerges
To all the Churches and the Clergies,

Who studied mineralogy
Not with soft book upon the knee,
But learned the properties of stones
By contact sharp of flesh and bones,
A kind of maddened John the Baptist,
To whom the harshest word comes aptest,
Who, struck by stone or brick ill-starred,
Hurls back an epithet as hard,
Which, deadlier than stone or brick,
Has a propensity to stick.
His oratory is like the scream
Of the iron horse's phrenzied steam
Which warns the world to leave wide space
For the black engine's swerveless race.

A Judith, there, turned Quakeress,
Sits Abby in her modest dress,
Serving a table quietly,

As if that mild and downcast eye
Flashed never, with its scorn intense,
More than Medea's eloquence.
So the same force which shakes its dread
Far-blazing locks o'er Ætna's head,
Along the wires in silence fares
And messages of commerce bears.
No nobler gift of heart and brain,
No life more white from spot or stain,
Was e'er on Freedom's altar laid
Than hers—the simple Quaker maid.

During the fair, which continued for eleven days, Abby chaperoned Maria Giddings, who was making her first trip to the East before going to Washington to spend the winter with her father. Abby, who found Maria's politics more to her liking than the congressman's, introduced her to the Boston friends and took her on sight-seeing expeditions to Plymouth and to Lowell, still considered a model factory town. She hoped that the New England visit would give Maria "strength sufficient to withstand the insidious influences she will meet at Washington and the more insidious because more disguised influences she will meet at home."

Late in January the Fosters went to Abington, a town south of Boston, to deliver a series of lectures. They spoke to sympathetic audiences for four days, but on the fifth a mob turned out to silence "those awfully wicked disturbers and infidels, S. S. and A. K. Foster." Abby dodged a shower of eggs, continuing to speak until clapping, stamping, and whistling drowned out her words.

Her last public appearance during her pregnancy was at the annual meeting of the Massachusetts Anti-Slavery Society, where she served on the business committee and urged support for the antislavery newspapers but left most of the talking to Stephen. His travels in the West had made him acutely aware of the importance that American men attached to voting. In Ohio he had experimented with a "Disunion ballot" which carried the names of men pledged to refuse any office that required them to support the Constitution.* He saw this as a valid protest vote that would stir up discussion, but the Boston clique and even his friend Pillsbury declared the scheme impractical, if not unprincipled. "Will friend Foster be found standing at the ballot box peddling votes?" a delegate asked. Stephen replied that he could see no difference between peddling votes and peddling books; he would be willing to stand at the ballot box and ask every Whig, Democrat, and Liberty man to take a ballot on which was written "DISSO-LUTION." The convention passed a resolution on the Mexican War, declaring that all who backed it were "traitors to liberty and the rights of man" but voted down Stephen's disunion ballot with near unanimity.[1]

As her letters from this period indicate, Abby greeted her pregnancy with mixed emotions. Along with "much delight and untold joy" at the prospect of having a child, she felt anxious about leaving the "battlefield" and guilty when she thought of the slave mothers whose children were sold away. "I felt sad at the thought of cooping up for a year or so altho' my feelings and reason bid me wish to be a mother," she wrote. "I am happy in my present situation only I am full of anxiety that the cause of liberty should move onward at an accelerated rate."

She spent the next months assembling the thousand and one things needed for housekeeping and baby. "I have been so long lecturing I have got all run ashore for night clothes, underclothes, & etc.," she wrote Betsy Cowles. "And I shall need to take a multitude of 'ittle stitches which you may know is a direfully large job for such little garments." In February she stayed with Stephen's parents on their farm in Canterbury, New Hampshire. Her first extended visit with Father and Mother Foster, as she called them, gave her a chance to become better acquainted with the elderly couple, then eighty-one and seventy-four respectively, and with members of Stephen's large family. From New Hampshire she spent a week in Cambridge with Eliza Lee Follen, dean of Boston's antislavery women and now a

---

* The so-called Australian ballot, a single ballot carrying the names of all candidates and printed at public expense, was not introduced into the United States until late in the century. Until then each party printed its own ballots and distributed them to voters at polling places.

counselor of the Massachusetts Society. White-haired Eliza, widowed by her husband's death in a steamboat accident six years earlier, was the author of numerous antislavery poems and tracts and another of Abby's ardent admirers. Leaving Eliza in mid-March, she went to Cumberland, Rhode Island, to see her sister Lucy, as well as Joanna and Diana Ballou, whose families had left the Hopedale Community. Lucy's husband had died while Abby was in Ohio and she was about to be married again, to Jason Barton of Middle Haddam, Connecticut.[2]

Meanwhile, Stephen was lecturing in Massachusetts and hunting for a farm in the Worcester area, where they had agreed to settle. Worcester's population had tripled and quadrupled since Abby had lived there. A manufacturing as well as an agricultural center, it now had a daily newspaper, the *Worcester Spy*, published by John Milton Earle, another member of the family that Abby had known since her youth, and was served by six railroad lines. Trains left the depot four times a day for Albany, New York City, and Nashua, New Hampshire; seven trains made daily trips to Boston, and stagecoaches ran to Millbury, Leicester, and other neighboring communities. Worcester's transportation facilities were an important factor in the Fosters' decision to settle there; besides, it was a good antislavery community, with a lively city society and two active county organizations.[3]

Ever since their engagement Stephen had been saving the small royalties paid him for *The Brotherhood of Thieves*, entrusting the money to Wendell Phillips or Edward M. Davis to place at interest until he should need it. But the two thousand dollars or so that he had accumulated did not bulk large in the 1847 real estate market. "I saw our place which suits me to a charm," he wrote Abby, "but the difficulty is to get hold of it. If you can manage to raise me ten thousand dollars, I will ensure you one of the pleasantest homes in all the town. Come, now, wont you work for me as you used to for the Anti-Slavery Society?" he joked. "You are the woman that never says 'I cant.'"

Abby was unable to help. She still had a small sum of money from her parents' estate, which had been invested in mortgages, but it was earmarked for home furnishings.[4] With the baby expected in May she must have been feeling anxious when Stephen at last wrote in early April to say that he had bought a house—the Cook place on Mower Street in the Tatnuck section of Worcester, not far from Abby's childhood home. Her anxiety gave way briefly to dejection. She remembered the old Cook place. She had been dreaming of a cottage requiring little housework and two or three acres for an orchard and garden. Instead Stephen had contracted to pay $3,450—$2,250 down with a $1,200 mortgage payable by 1849—for a dilapidated fourteen-room two-and-a-half-story house, with barns and outbuildings in a sad state of disrepair and thirty-nine acres of rocky, hilly land.

"My air-castles are all demolished in one blow," Abby wrote moments after receiving Stephen's letter. "Instead of a *few* acres, very many—for *first* rate soil, *third* or *fourth*—instead of *near* W[orcester] three or four miles out—instead of *fruit* land, what will hardly bear any at all. . . . You talk about tearing down a part of the house. I take it for granted it is the kitchen part as I know that to be very old. But would it not be better to build another house rather than add to the one now standing?" And, finally, because she knew the people living nearby to be bigoted, "Of all the neighborhoods in Worcester, Tatnuck is most repulsive to me."

Having thus demolished Stephen's air castles as well, she consoled him by agreeing that he had done all that he could "under the circumstances" and promised to stop grumbling and make the best of things. She then proceeded with page after page of orders and countermands. Instead of Stephen's cleaning and repairing a portion of the house immediately, as he had proposed, she thought he should wait for her arrival, the day after Lucy's wedding, when she would bring with her Amos Ballou's sister Avilda, who she had hired to stay with her for several weeks. "She is a very capable business girl and can turn her hand to everything—sewing, fitting up furniture, cleaning house, cooking. Avilda and I can make it *decent* and perhaps *comfortable*." Meanwhile, it would be well for Stephen to buy "a couple of sleeping couches—although I don't want them put up where there probably are bugs." On second thought, perhaps he should get only bedsteads and she would bring straw bedticks and comforters to go with them. "Indeed I think you had better not buy many things for the house till I can be with you, as you know I am an old maid," she warned. If Stephen would only "get a beginning of eatables," they could buy furniture when she came and "begin to have a home." They must also arrange to collect their far-flung belongings. The book trunk that they had carried through Ohio was at the Garrisons', filled with linens and clothing; the bundle of "little petticoats" she had made reposed on a shelf in the Anti-Slavery Office, and there were house furnishings stored in Millbury ever since her mother's death.

Before sealing the letter, she could not resist a final reproach. Lucy's husband to be had just bought "a fine house with a pretty yard and garden for the trifle of $560. It is all in readiness for their reception."

Stephen, who knew Abby well by now, was not disheartened. He had not dreamed of "a pretty yard and garden." He wanted a working farm and welcomed the challenge that his stony acres presented. "I like my place on further acquaintance," he wrote Edward Davis the day before Abby's arrival. "It is very much out of repair & will keep me busy for some time getting things to my mind. I shall do much of the work of repairing and cultivating with my own hands." Assisted by brothers and nephews, he performed a prodigious amount of work to make the house habitable by Abby's standards, as well as stocked the farm with cows, pigs, and chickens and planted his first crops.

The Cook place, as Abby continued to refer to it—it was years before she would speak of it as "our home"—was actually a handsome Federal-style house, built in 1797, with a brick facade, black shuttered windows, and a fanlight doorway. Its classically simple lines and its rambling rooms and wide brick fireplaces, which, today, have won it a place in the National Register of Historic Places, must have seemed hopelessly plain and old-fashioned in 1847, when gabled story-and-a-half Greek Revival houses, with cooking ranges and Franklin stoves for heating, were at the height of their popularity.[5]

However, Abby was not thinking about architectural styles when she reached Worcester on April 15. The biological clock was ticking loudly now. She had only weeks to convert this vast, leaky barn of a house into a suitable place for an infant. As far as can be determined, she did not consult a doctor during her pregnancy, nor did she want one at her confinement, she firmly told Stephen. Instead she had asked Paulina Wright, now a recognized expert on physiology, to be with her when she gave birth. But could she make elegant, affluent Paulina comfortable in the old Cook place? "I don't want her to come unless she can be happy," she wrote Stephen. No letters report on Abby's confinement. It is a safe guess, however, that Paulina arrived on time, hurrying from the annual meeting of the American Society in New York—the only anniversary meeting that Abby had missed—to assist in the birth of a baby girl on May 19, 1847. Abby and Stephen named her Paulina Wright Foster.[6]

The baby was enchanting—and demanding. Abby nursed her, probably at two-hour intervals, as prevailing folk wisdom dictated. Still, she cried, and her mother, who had solutions for most of the world's ills, felt helpless. Abby did not recover from childbirth as quickly as she had anticipated. Three months afterward she still suffered from hemorrhoids, a common complaint of pregnancy, for which she took daily sitz baths. She tried to conceal her discomfort from Stephen for fear that he would hire someone to take care of her. By her reckoning, there were enough people in the old Cook place that summer. Brother Newell Foster had closed his printshop in Portland, Maine, and with his wife, Eliza, and their children had come to Worcester to lend a hand. Brother Galen had arrived from Pennsylvania in June, to remain until the crops were harvested, and brother David and various Foster nephews came from time to time.

The farm required an immense amount of work. Whenever it rained, the fields were flooded. The first potato crop rotted before Stephen and company were able to dig drainage ditches. Only after the barn was repaired and the orchard manured could they take time to patch the leaky farmhouse roof or to set up a hogshead outside the kitchen to catch rainwater, thereby saving the women the long trip to the well.

Eliza and her daughter Helen took over the cooking and washing, leaving Abby a boarder in her own home, free to devote herself to the baby. Everyone meant well, but she felt some discontent when, early in August, she helped Stephen pack for a trip to Ohio. He was going to meet Garrison and Douglass at the annual meeting of the Western Anti-Slavery Society. Garrison was making his first trip to the West in response to Abby's prodding, and she yearned to be there. "How much pleasure it would give me to be at New Lyme and see all those bright faces," she wrote Stephen. "But my pleasure in our little one at home is much greater."

The baby—her name shortened from Paulina to Alla—now weighed twelve and a quarter pounds on the scale in the barn and was eating and sleeping better. Every morning, still following Graham's regimen, Abby plunged her into a bath of cold well water. "Sometimes she screams, but generally is quiet and only looks surprised. She does not cry as much as when you were home," she told Stephen. By September, when Alla weighed fourteen pounds, Abby was obliged to forgo the daily plunge because she could not pump and carry enough water to the house; instead she resorted to a sponge bath—in cold water. Afterward Alla lay on her mother's bed, "reading" the *Bugle* and watching Abby bathe, dress, and straighten up the room. Then, still content, she played on Eliza's bed while Abby went to the barn to milk the cows. Several times a day in fair weather Abby brought her outdoors, where she delighted in the chickens and took "particular notice" of the lamb and cows.

Alla's daytime naps, taken in a cradle in the sitting room, gave Abby a chance to read the *Liberator* and *Standard* and to catch up with long-neglected correspondence. At night she went to sleep without a protest. "Baby has not had a nervous turn since you left. I think it is because I am getting stronger nerves myself," Abby informed Stephen in September.

Late in the summer Abby felt energetic enough to make the three-mile trip into Worcester with Alla so that she could hear Lucretia Mott lecture. She had never heard her speak save for brief remarks at meetings, and she found her "decidedly more radical" than she had anticipated. At a crowded gathering in the Unitarian Church Lucretia endorsed every reform "from laying aside the whip stick in families" to nonresistance, temperance, antislavery, and woman's rights.

Abby drove into town again when Stephen's parents came for a fortnight's visit. This time Mother Foster carried Alla while Abby managed the horse's reins with one hand and held a sun umbrella over them with the other. After calling on friends, they went to the telegraph office to satisfy Mrs. Foster's curiosity about the new invention. The wagon was too uncomfortable for Father Foster, who remained on the farm and harvested the white beans. "He has scrutinized every spot on the place and says he likes it better than expected," Abby wrote Stephen. "I have often prayed that you and I may have as true a life and as great happiness in old age as our dear father and mother. How young and beautiful their love is."

The Kelley family turned up, too. Olive and Newbury came for dinner; Joanna stayed overnight while Amos was attending a cattle show in Worcester, and Diana, who was in Millville, was expected momentarily. Brother Albert and his wife, Deborah, visited, bringing their eight-week-old baby. Abby pitied Deborah, who was burdened by "four children the oldest not six, and the milk[ing] of four cows, besides her ordinary housework." With no one to assist her save Albert and a hired hand, she was "quite feeble." "If I had my usual strength I would go and help her," Abby said.

Glad as she was to see them all, she would have preferred to wait for these visits until she could live "less mixed up." She wrote Stephen: "I have an increasing dislike of this mixture. I am happy and try to make those about me comfortable, but we should all be better satisfied to have our birds' nest separate. Eliza has not furniture sufficient without using mine. I am willing to accommodate her, but her mode of doing things is unpleasant to me, as I presume mine is to her; tho' we love each other and live in much harmony. She is not careful of things."

At four months Alla continued to enchant. She played with a rattle and sucked her thumb, a habit her mother thought looked pretty now but might make trouble by and by. "She has so thoroughly entwined herself about me," Abby told Stephen, that she could not consider leaving her. "You have not been with her constantly and watched her every look and heard her every breath; seen intelligence dawning and expanding every hour. She does not look up to you as to me, so imploringly for her food and the supplying of her wants, reminding me constantly of her entire dependence, and that I am her natural guardian and under the most sacred obligations to make her happy."[7]

No doubt she meant every word of this, but as she regained her strength, she became increasingly torn between love for her daughter and the claims of the antislavery struggle. She was greatly disturbed when Stephen told her that Frederick Douglass planned to start his own weekly paper. After his British tour his friends abroad had raised more than two thousand dollars, enough to buy an excellent printing press. Garrison and Phillips had advised against the paper—"the land is full of the wrecks of such experiments," they warned—but during his travels in Ohio with Stephen he had decided to go ahead with the project. In order to avoid seeming to compete with the *Liberator*, he had announced that he would publish his *North Star* in Cleveland. Both Lizzie and Stephen predicted that his paper would put the troubled *Bugle* out of business.

Publishing his own paper appeared to Douglass another way of affirming the equality of black people. But his independent move implied to the Garrisonians that he had begun to question their principles. Fiercely loyal to the *Bugle*, Abby wrote Stephen, "I, for one, am not willing to trust the anti-slavery cause in the West to Douglass. I always have been and still am fearful of [him]. Do, I pray you, enforce on all the duty of sustaining the *Bugle*. Maybe we shall have to go out there next year to keep it afloat." Even when Douglass changed his plans and established the *North Star* in Rochester, New York, she refused to be mollified. "Is Douglass' paper going to injure the circulation of the *Standard* in New York?" she asked Sydney Gay. "I fear it."[8]

Now when Alla napped in the afternoon, Abby read, "laying in a store of book knowledge to fit me for greater usefulness." She corresponded with Joshua Giddings, who sent her government reports and records of debates in Congress, and with Mary Howitt, a British journalist who planned to write an article about her. Abby, who had a distaste for personal publicity, refused to cooperate with Howitt despite Maria Chapman's urging. As a result, the January 22, 1848, issue of *Howitt's Journal* carried on its cover a portrait of "Abby Kelley Foster, the Eminent American Anti-Slavery Advocate" but contained no biographical memoir inside.

After Stephen's return from Ohio Abby attended some local antislavery meetings, but she was obliged to forgo the Christmas Fair and the annual meeting of the Massachusetts Society in Boston because Alla was teething. "If she continues well, my intention is to wean her at nine months [instead of the customary twelve], and be ready to accompany my husband as early as March," she wrote Maria. "I should not wean her so early but am told by physiologists that is the best time." Stephen's youngest sister, Caroline, had agreed to care for Alla when Abby engaged "in the field warfare again," she told the Gays. "Stephen says I shall not be willing to leave her. We shall see whether I care so much for my baby as to forget the multitudes of broken hearted mothers."

As word of her plan got around, many women were critical. Lizzie Gay, a new mother herself, didn't like the thought of Abby's "deserting" her baby "even for the slave's sake. I should be too selfish to do so." Susan Cabot, Eliza Follen's sister, warned that "the training of an immortal spirit" was "a sacred work," and Lizzie Jones openly scolded: "For the sake of millions of suffering children whose mothers have left them in the care of aunts & sisters or hired nurses, I am sorry. Your influence on the course of human freedom will be good but your influence on home duties and home virtues will be bad. If you would wait until your child is old enough to wean it would be less reprehensible. I shall set a better example. If the little stranger that we expect to bless us shall live I shall not feel like leaving it to lecture in ten months."[9]

By the beginning of 1848 Abby was restless and bored, admitting later that her sojourn at home had been "perfectly killing." To keep busy, she initiated an antislavery fair in Worcester. Aware that her radical reputation would frighten away people, she persuaded Sarah Earle, wife of the editor of the *Spy*, to head the fair committee and circulated a call soliciting support for the event, to be signed by prominent local women. When she wrote to Lucy Stone to obtain her signature, she explained that she had not had time to transcribe the call but trusted that Lucy would endorse it anyway. "It is sound, of course, *because it was written by myself*. But conservative enough for such women as Mrs. Earle." She also arranged to have Maria send merchandise left over from the Boston bazaar. The fair, held in Brinley Hall, Worcester's largest auditorium, was a surprising success as antislavery propaganda and as fund raiser. Maria had predicted that the Worcester women would raise three hundred dollars, Abby hoped for five hundred, but when the proceeds were totted up, there was a thousand dollars to be turned over to the treasury of the American Society. The Worcester fair became an annual event, and Abby went on to mastermind a similar venture in Portland, Maine, arranging by mail to have the Portland women receive assistance and advice from the Boston Female Society.[10]

She was unable to return to the lecture platform as early as she had planned because first Stephen and then she came down with influenza, which reached epidemic proportions in eastern Massachusetts that winter. In May, looking thin and pale, she attended the anniversary meeting of the American Society in New York. Sitting on the platform with Lucretia Mott and other notables, she made her usual strong plea for contributions to the antislavery treasury. During the summer and fall she lectured on Sundays in towns near Worcester, speaking jointly with Stephen or with Lucy Stone, who was now an agent of the Massachusetts Society. In August she remained at home with Alla while Stephen and Lucy traveled to Cape Cod with Parker Pillsbury and William Wells Brown,* a talented ex-slave who had recently joined the Garrisonians. During a four-day convention in a grove in Harwich, the sight of Stone and Brown walking together ("a woman with a great black Negro" one man described them despite Brown's fair complexion) as well as Parker's and Stephen's sharp tongues so angered a crowd of twenty-five hundred people that the speakers were in danger of losing their lives. The trouble erupted on the last day of the convention, when Parker reported that a Cape Cod sea captain who was in the audience had accepted a hundred dollars to help a runaway slave escape and had then turned the slave over to the authorities. Eliciting from the captain that he was a member in good standing of the Baptist Church, Stephen proceeded "with the most scorching and terrible remarks" in support of a resolution "that our nation's religion is a lie." Suddenly "a troop of human tigers" rushed forward, shouting "Tar and feather them," "Haul them out," "Where's the darky?" Stephen managed to hurry Lucy away from the mob while the Cape Codders knocked down Parker and threw William from the platform. Sympathizers came to their rescue before anyone was seriously injured, but Stephen's good broadcloth coat was ripped from top to bottom. Reporting the attack in detail, the *Liberator* said that it was reminiscent of

---

* Brown subsequently became the author of histories, travel books, plays, and novels, his best known being *Clotel; or The President's Daughter: A Narrative of Slave Life in the United States*, believed to be the first novel by a black American.

the mob scenes in 1835, when Garrison had been dragged through the streets of Boston.[11]

Actually 1848 bore scant resemblance to 1835 except that it was also a difficult year for the Garrisonians. While revolutions raged in Europe, the *Liberator* focused on the end of the Mexican War. In the Treaty of Guadalupe Hidalgo Mexico was forced to cede more than a million square miles to the United States, a region encompassing the present states of California and New Mexico and parts of Utah, Nevada, Arizona, and Colorado. Should this vast new territory be slave or free? The debates in Congress spilled over into the streets and convention halls as politicians prepared for the presidential election. Years of antislavery agitation had convinced a sizable number of northerners to oppose the extension of slavery, and political parties began to divide along sectional lines. Antislavery Whigs, calling themselves Conscience Whigs, and antislavery Democrats— the Barnburners—seceded from their parties and, joined by some Liberty men, organized a Free-Soil party, whose motto was "Free soil, free speech, free labor and free men." The Free-Soilers did not propose to abolish slavery but only to prevent its expansion. Nevertheless, antislavery politicians and officeholders, men like Joshua Giddings and Salmon P. Chase of Ohio, Charles Sumner and Charles Francis Adams of Massachusetts, and William H. Seward, former governor of New York, flocked to join it. "Anti-slavery is at length a respectable element in politics," Seward said.

The Garrisonians saw the new party in a different light. The Free-Soilers advocated only halfway measures, continuing to support a union with slaveholders and rejecting a platform plank that called for equal rights for blacks. Despite these compromises, many honest antislavery men believed that for the first time they had an option and could vote without violating their consciences. Their candidate, Martin Van Buren, lost the election, but there was a considerable falling away from the ranks of the Garrisonians, particularly in the West.[12]

Abby received letter after desperate letter from Lizzie Jones predicting the demise of the *Bugle* and the end of the Western Anti-Slavery Society, which could no longer pay Benjamin's meager salary. The Joneses were living on the money Lizzie earned from the sale of antislavery books, including *The Young Abolitionist*, a book for children that she had just written. With a baby on the way Benjamin wanted to return to his trade as cabinetmaker so that they, too, could purchase a home. Without help from the American Society, *"our cause in the West is gone,"* Lizzie wrote. "Will you not speak to some of the friends in regard to this matter?"

To compound Lizzie's problems, the leadership forces of the American Society were decimated that summer. Garrison was spending four months at a water cure establishment in Northampton, seeking alleviation of chronic ailments. Phillips was laid up with a life-threatening attack of dysentery, and Maria Chapman—indispensable Maria—had sailed for England in July. Determined to give her children the kind of education that she had had, she remained abroad with them until 1855. Although a second team had taken over—Quincy editing the *Liberator* and Anne Weston and Helen Garrison filling in for Maria on the Boston fair—the Executive Committee of the American Society lacked a quorum and did not hold a meeting until the fall of 1848.

Abby was finally able to present the claims of the *Bugle* to the committee only to learn that the American Society was too deeply in debt to help out. If the *Bugle* were to survive, she would have to raise the money and find a new editor to replace the Joneses. Carrying on a three-cornered correspondence with the Western and American societies and with Oliver Johnson, she convinced Johnson to edit the paper *if* she could come up with six hundred dollars for his annual salary and a similar sum to pay off the Western Society's back debts.[13]

Late in March 1849 Abby brought Alla to New Hampshire, where Caroline Foster was to take care of her, and then headed for New York and Philadelphia. Encountering her on the way, Lucy Stone remarked that she looked ill. No, Abby answered. "But when I left my little daughter I [felt] as though I should die. But I have done it for the sake of the mothers whose babies are sold away from them."

Traveling alone for the first time since her marriage, she was more cheerful when she wrote Stephen from Sarah Pugh's home in Philadelphia. "How odd it seems to address you by letter. You have come to be so entirely a part of myself that I should not feel much more awkward in addressing a dissevered portion of my own body." It was exhilarating to be on her own again, she confided, "and being as outlandish as it happens to be convenient, no one saying, 'Why do ye so?' " Even if others disapproved of her, she did not mind. "They are nothing—no more than so many images in a Museum. I find on looking into my inner man, that this has *always* been the fact with me. I feel the presence only of those whom I intimately know."

The Philadelphia abolitionists were "struck with a panic" when they learned of Abby's intentions because their society was also in debt. However, she secured hundred-dollar pledges from Lucretia and James Mott, Edward M. Davis, and Robert Purvis, the wealthy black man who was president of the Pennsylvania Society. She then traveled to Bucks County to call on the Quaker farmers whom she had met five years earlier. "How hard it is for these rich Quakers to give up a single farthing," she told Sydney Gay. "The ways of Providence are indeed mysterious, else I should have been rich and they poor." By the end of April she was able to report to Wendell Phillips, then secretary of the Executive Committee of the American Society, "I have secured the $600 for which I left home, and hasten to inform you that the necessary correspondence may be had to put Johnson in the editorial chair of the *Bugle*."

Although the American Society was still a national organization, supporting the *Standard* and providing ideological leadership for the movement, it no longer employed a general agent or organized conventions, except for the annual anniversary meeting. With ten of the twelve members of the Executive Committee in Boston (only Sydney Gay and Sarah Pugh lived elsewhere) the society concentrated on New England, where Samuel May, Jr., served as general agent of the Massachusetts Society, supervising teams of lecturers in the state. In other regions the work was initiated by state and local societies. And by Abby Kelley.[14]

With her fund-raising tour for the *Bugle* completed she set out to find new areas where work was needed. "I have an idea in my head which I will submit to you," she wrote Wendell. "Let us determine to conquer some *particular* territory, say eastern N.Y. If we have a *special* work to do and set ourselves right earnestly to do it, we can always raise the necessary funds. In order to impress on people the fact that we are in earnest to do something the coming year, the Ex. Com. must give a bugle blast warning the abolitionists to come up to the annual meeting, prepared to lay out and see to the execution of the work."

Because she had recently met Ann Phillips and had been impressed by Ann's political astuteness as well as her courage in face of her debilitating illness, Abby added a postscript: "I will thank you to ask your wife if I am not right? If she says yes—as she will—then I shall have confirmation." Ann Phillips must have agreed with Abby, for at the anniversary meeting Wendell presided over a Committee of Thirty, which, after examining the "state and prospects of the cause," proposed a concentration of forces in eastern New York. "It is a welcome duty to tell friends that the aid of Mr. and Mrs. Foster can be had for this purpose," he announced.

After a flying trip home to see Alla, who looked "as plump as any Paddy* child," Abby and Stephen headed for Long Island, where few Garrisonians had ventured before and where they found people "as ignorant of antislavery as the Turks and as bigoted as *Quakers*." In Flushing, Oyster Bay, Glen Cove, and other villages on the North Shore, they encountered hallooing crowds of men and boys and showers of rotten eggs. One egg struck Abby in the face, but "fortunately it had a chicken in it and did not besmear me," she cheerfully reported. Although they secured a few subscriptions for the *Standard*, they were soon ready to move on to the Hudson Valley. "Long Island is a hard soil—Stephen says unclaimable. I say we should not give it up yet," she wrote Wendell and Ann.[15]

Working in Dutchess and Ulster counties for the balance of the summer and fall, they found the going easier. "Dutchess is unusually fine," Abby told the Phillipses. "It was settled mainly from New England, hence the population is intelligent and enterprising with far less bigotry than we generally find—not the least disposition to mobocracy or rowdyism. They subscribe for a good many papers and buy a considerable many books. Ulster on the opposite side of the river is more Dutch and they are not so much disposed to read but still are not reluctant to hear.

---

* Abby frequently used "Paddy," current slang for Irish, just as she spoke of Ohioans as "Buckeyes."

"You may think we get along slowly. We do but experience teaches us that it is best, when we go to a place which is entirely ignorant of our principles (as are all the places we now visit) to give them a course of from three to six lectures and then return in a few weeks and give them a few more, having as much personal conversation and getting as many subscribers for papers as we can. In this way we make a permanent impression. They see ours is the only course consistent with principle, if our real wish is to abolish slavery. We have made a good number of converts and trust they will stand."

Spelling each other on the lecture platform, the Fosters worked well as a team. In an unusual division of labor for the time, Stephen wrote reports of their meetings for the *Standard*—he made fun of Abby's literary efforts—while Abby kept track of finances. She carried with her a small linen-covered notebook in which she recorded in her neat handwriting every penny received, pledged, or expended, transcribing the relevant information for Wendell or Sydney. Because the purchase of the Worcester farm had left them in debt—"my creditors are as hungry as greyhounds"—she had reluctantly agreed to accept a salary of twelve dollars a week from the American Society. From time to time she requested Sydney to send some of their back pay to Newell Foster so that he could apply it to taxes or mortgage.

Abby also took charge of forwarding the names of new subscribers to the *Standard*. When Stephen was "ready to give up in despair" because they had not obtained twenty new subscriptions, the weekly goal he had set, Abby was confident that they would get "a large number" when they went over the ground a second time. And when she was in a panic before an important meeting, Stephen was the confident one. Although she could depend on him, other abolitionists continually disappointed her. Time and again when she planned a big meeting, promising that notables from New York and Philadelphia would speak, the notables let her down. For an August 1 picnic in the Hudson River town of Milton, she had invited half a dozen speakers, all of whom declined at the last moment.

"If I had belonged to the class lachrymose I should have got some relief; as it was I went to the grove in a most woefully feverish plight refusing to be comforted even by Stephen who is never disturbed or anxious," she told Gay. But the meeting turned out well, with more than five hundred people in attendance, most of them "children in the cause who were more than satisfied. So I had my anxiety for my pains and Stephen as his wont is, had the satisfaction of saying 'Now did I not tell you that all would be well.' He always trusts in God but keeps his stores of powder dry."

During the Fosters' four months in eastern New York the only lecturers who aided them were Ernestine Rose* and Lucretia Mott. Rose, an abolitionist and woman's rights advocate but not a Garrisonian, "made very acceptable speeches but they were not so useful as remarks from a person who sympathizes fully with us would have been." Lucretia, however, did "great service," Abby said. "Her labors here are invaluable."

Abby saw so clearly the tasks that needed to be done that she sometimes lost patience with colleagues. Although she knew that Sydney Gay was swamped by his editorial duties, as well as his responsibilities as a new father, his carefree attitude left her fuming. "You must have read my last letter with your elbows," she scolded when he garbled subscribers' names. Or "I have crossed you out of my book of abolitionists" after he failed to come to a meeting. "You have again told the people up here you would come and then did not even send an excuse for your absence. Nor was Parker [Pillsbury] here. He did not get our letter till his arrangements for going home were all cut and dried and I suppose he thought it of less consequence to disappoint the convention than his family."[16]

Abby was unfair to Parker, who had been in Ohio all summer and was permitting himself a scant few days at home before coming to New York at her bidding. Her gibe at him perhaps reflected her own conflicted feelings as believing as she did in the urgency of the work, she was nevertheless returning to the farm and Alla.

Since leaving Worcester in the spring, she had seen her daughter only

---

* Ernestine Rose (1810–92), daughter of a Polish rabbi, emigrated to the United States in 1836 and almost immediately joined the campaign for a married woman's property bill in New York. A freethinker who was willing to be labeled "infidel," she joined John Collins's Skaneateles community in 1843. Although an eloquent antislavery lecturer, she is best known for her leadership in the woman's rights movement. (Suhl.)

twice, briefly at the anniversary meeting and for a fortnight in September, when she brought her from New Hampshire to the farm. Saying good-bye then had been painful. "I always suffer very severely on leaving our little one but this time I became quite sick over this terrible separation. She is now in a most interesting period of her life," she wrote Betsy Cowles.

A sparkling child with dark hair and "wondrous long dark eyelashes," Alla did not lack for loving care. Besides doting grandparents and assorted aunts, uncles, and cousins in New Hampshire, she had a barnyard of pets at home: five kittens, nine pigs, three calves, one colt, and numerous chickens by Abby's count on one occasion. When she was away, Abby wrote Alla frequently. Faithful Caroline read her the letters and just as faithfully recorded her replies: "When I asked her what I should write mother, she invariably says Alla dont wet her pantalets, and when reminded that she does sometimes, says must not any more." Other letters from Alla-Caroline recounted the minutiae of daily life from bowel movements to mosquito bites to muddy aprons, not omitting the time she pulled up Grandmother's flowers or misbehaved in church. When a neighbor dropped by, Caroline reported the visit without comment: "Betsy Morrill called to see Alla. Says she is very [plain] and she dont know why she should not be as father and mother both are, that her intellect and faculties are not well developed and finally that she is nothing but a young one."

Even when Abby permitted herself time with Alla, she never forgot the cause. In the fall of 1849 she wrote to Anne Weston offering to help out with the Christmas Fair. She could be of little use decorating the hall— "where taste is required"—and she still had Quakerish scruples about raffles, a form of gambling, but "I can sell well for my common sense teaches me how it is done." If Anne needed her, she would board in Boston with Alla and Caroline "and so visit my little one during the Fair as I can occasionally snatch a little hour from my duties and shall be with her nights, mornings, &c."

Alla spent Fair Week in Boston with her mother and aunt and, after a brief stay in Worcester, was taken back to New Hampshire.[17] Late in January 1850 Abby went to eastern New York to consolidate the gains made in the fall. Stephen accompanied her until it was time to return home for spring planting. Intent on becoming an orchardist, he purchased some four hundred fruit trees in New York, including nursery stock to be used for grafting as well as pear, cherry, and apricot trees that would bear soon. He also planned to move one barn, build another, and regrade the front yard. Undismayed by his work program, he found the challenge invigorating. "There is something in the productions of this barren soil that I like better than anything produced in the fertile soil of the West," he wrote Abby.

The Executive Committee had given the Fosters a free hand in New York, authorizing them to employ lecturers where needed and to pay "such salary as shall seem just." Abby urged the committee to appoint a general agent to coordinate campaigns all over the North and thought that the post would be ideal for Stephen, who could do much of the work—the correspondence and record keeping—from the farm.

Stephen refused to consider the idea. "It was truly gratifying to me to hear of your success," he wrote in April. "I have often told you that you could accomplish more alone than with my aid. So you have additional evidence not only that I am not fit for general agent, but that I am not fit for lecturing agent. Of this I have long been conscious, & I now hope you will not again urge me into the field. I can labor, but I do not think either writing or public speaking is my province. I have a strong & growing dislike to both."

"You are gratified at my success and pretend to think it is because you were not here. But our success was better than what I have had here," Abby responded. "You need not try to invent excuses for withdrawing from the warfare till victory is won. 'Tis too late."

Despite her chiding, he continued to deprecate himself, writing in a later letter, "Your great success throws me entirely into the shade, and might awaken my envy, if it were not, after all, *my own*. As it is, I can only congratulate myself on the exercise of that good sense & sound discrimination which made you my *first choice* among all the women of my acquaintance & the good fortune which places such a *prize* within my grasp."

Abby continued lecturing until it was time for the anniversary meeting, where Stephen was to join her. She sent him a detailed list of instructions, asking him to bring her parasol, which was "in the next to upper drawer in the bureau," twice reminded him to bring her plaid shawl, and suggested that he carry their old carpetbag so that she could pack her winter cloak in it when they returned home. Nor did she neglect Stephen's apparel, for he was to order new clothes. "Pray attend to getting them in good season," she advised. "If you get some thin woolen stuff for pants pray have them lined with light colored cambric. But have a nice suit throughout." Familiar with the timetable of every steamboat and railway line entering New York City, she suggested that since his boat would arrive first, he come to the North River dock to meet her, "and then we will go together to find us a boarding place."

With the logistics settled, she made known her desire to speak at the meeting. Ordinarily she preferred to leave the oratory to Garrison and Phillips, confining herself to a plea for funds, but this time she had "something special to say." In addition to giving "due prominence to the idea of the equality of women," she wanted to speak of the huge financial investment that tied the North to the South and the political leverage that this conferred on the slave power. Writing to Sydney Gay, who as the lone Executive Committee member in New York was in charge of arrangements, she asked for a place in the program early in the day, modestly explaining, "I dont want my Graham bread to follow the delectable dishes which will be served."

Her speech was never delivered. As she joined the other speakers on the platform, she could see that there was trouble ahead. For weeks the pro-slavery *New York Herald* had been calling on its readers to break up the meeting. Now the seats and aisles of the Tabernacle were crowded with rowdies, under the direction of Captain Isaiah Rynders, a Tammany Hall leader who controlled the large Irish immigrant vote in the city through a judicious distribution of beer and political favors. Standing in the front of the auditorium, Rynders heckled the speakers, offering his own anti-abolitionist resolutions, while his followers hissed and cheered. After "Garrison's nigger minstrels" were shouted down, Rynders brought forward a "Professor" who attempted to prove scientifically that blacks were not men but monkeys without tails. Although Frederick Douglass and Stephen Foster took on the mob in debate, their victory was temporary. Rynders brought the sessions to a close with a resolution that the "humanity-mongers" confine themselves to a study of "the degradation among the

Negroes in the North." The abolitionists concluded their business in a boardinghouse run by William Powell, a black Garrisonian, where Abby, undaunted, proposed that the society seek funds for more extended operations in the coming year.

After stopping at home to see Alla, the couple went to Boston for the New England Anti-Slavery Society convention. If the *Boston Courier* is to be believed, Abby as well as Stephen had purchased new clothing. The paper described her with more than a touch of malice as wearing "a black silk dress cut in the French style of 1842—open in front and faced with lace edging. She wore a dickey and linen cuffs, black stockings and high treed shoes. Her hair was well oiled and 'done up' conformable to her age. Though not what one would describe as an ornament to the 'gentle sex,' she is quite good looking."[18]

Abby had three peaceful weeks at home before starting off for Ohio for the summer. She left reluctantly, she wrote Sydney, but there was no one else to do the job. "I have either got to go there or let the *Bugle* down."

Alla remained in Worcester because Sister Ruth Pollard, who was visiting in the East, had volunteered to take care of her and keep house for Stephen during Abby's absence. Everyone concerned soon regretted the offer. Accustomed to the Kelleys' housekeeping standards, Ruth was unable to cope with the more relaxed ways of Stephen's family. That summer his older brother Adams had come to help with the plowing and haying, bringing his wife, Sarah, and their five children. By midsummer, with other brothers and sisters visiting, Stephen was sleeping in a trundle bed on the parlor floor while Ruth struggled to keep the rooms clean and in good order. "I don't think they have swept the sitting room once nor the garret nor the old bed chamber," she wrote.

In a long letter she detailed the work she had done: making beds; turning the carpet; airing Abby's things; making Stephen pants and shirts. "On washing days I have helped all day & have ironed considerable more than my part." When neighboring farmers came to help raise the roof of the newly repaired barn, she and Sarah made baked beans and gingerbread for their dinner. The fact that the roof did not fit and the framing had to be done again did not help anybody's mood.

Alla was "very well," Ruth assured Abby. "When I asked her what I shall write she says tell her I help Aunt Sarah. She did one day wipe the knives forks & spoons. She and I have had some very good times." But Ruth, whose idea of a good time was to take Alla visiting, dressed in white, found it troublesome to take care of her when Sarah's youngsters and other cousins were underfoot. "She wants to run everywhere they do & eat everything & she gets as dirty in one day after having on clean clothes as a little Paddy." "I don't think Stephen appreciates what I have done," she concluded, for when she suggested that Alla be taken to New Hampshire, he replied undiplomatically that he didn't want Ruth to stay if she didn't want to, for Sarah could take care of Alla. "I told him she could not. I knew her clothes would be all out of order & everything."

By the end of July Stephen decided to bring Alla to Aunt Caroline while Ruth visited other relatives. "I will have all her clothes clean and packed before I leave," Ruth promised Abby. "Do not say a word to Stephen about what I have written for men never know as women are worth much."

More aware of the household tensions than Ruth realized, Stephen wrote Abby that Alla was "much happier since she got out of Ruth's leading strings. I like Sarah's management of her. She never crossed her, nor, I believe, did she ever have any difficulty in getting her to do as she wished. I learnt from Sarah that Ruth punished her by shutting her up & it vexed me beyond measure.

"I do not wonder that you want to see her for I think her truly an interesting child. Sarah says she is unusually reasonable for one of her age. She seldom asks me a second time for anything which I tell her that I am not able to buy for her." In another letter Stephen wrote, "I am happy to find that with all her buoyancy of spirits & apparent thoughtlessness she still has sympathies deep & tender." She had worried, along with the rest of the household, when Adams had "a severe attack of the bowels" and was moved almost to tears at the sight of Stephen giving his horse a whipping. "I have very pleasant times with her at night as she is then always in a mood to talk. She often tells me that I am a poor man because I have got but one little daughter, but if I had a whole lot of little daughters I should be a rich man. Do you think you will ever make me a *rich man* in your daughter's estimation?"

Abby ignored the question, but the correspondence made her conscious of all she was missing. While sending Alla "bushels of love and cartloads of kisses" and admonishing her to say "I would rather not" instead of "I won't," she told Stephen that she found it "a great sacrifice to be away at this period of [Alla's] intellectual moral and social development. I begin to think that I can do better than any other person, in forming her character. 'Tis of momentous importance that she should be under the proper influences. Children are like daguerreotype plates. They catch the images that are thrown upon them. The preaching and teaching does but little; 'tis the passing life that effects most."

Stephen's letters were so cheerful and affectionate that Abby accused him of sounding "like a lover to his mistress. I have come to the conclusion that you are trying to make up at this late hour for your entire lack of that quality in the days of our courtship." Stephen replied, "I never felt more like a lover than at the present time. I am looking forward to your return as a *new marriage* & it would be strange if the experience of four or five years did not enable me to conduct my part with somewhat more facility & grace. I have been under too good a teacher not to have made some improvement during this period, even if I am a dull scholar. Besides, my early love was the offspring of hope, my present, the fruit of knowledge. My lady love was an unsubstantial personage. My wife is a *real entity*. I *know*, now, *what* I love, & *why*."[19]

Tantalizing as this correspondence was, Abby did not permit thoughts of home to slow her down. Even on her journey to Ohio she made every moment count. After stopping overnight with Diana and Olney Ballou in western Massachusetts, where Olney was working as a builder, she had proceeded along New York's psychic highway to the Motts in Albany and then to Syracuse, where Samuel J. May met her at the depot and took her to his home. At a crowded meeting in Syracuse's Town Hall that night— where she had "nothing to regret but my fatigue and the extreme heat"— she raised $150, some of it from Gerrit Smith, who surprised her by pledging $25, his first contribution to the American Society in eight years, "and I hope an earnest of good things to come." The next day she spoke at a temperance meeting, encountering little opposition "altho there was a fearful amount of black coats and white cravats and any quantity of twaddle." Then to Buffalo by express train, pausing to purchase a life preserver before boarding a Lake Erie steamboat headed west. Not that she feared an accident in summer, she told Stephen, "but I have always wanted a life preserver and now we must take it with us when we go by water." Galen Foster met her at the wharf in Erie, Pennsylvania, where she repaid money she and Stephen had borrowed for the purchase of the farm. After a week of travel she reached Cleveland on June 22, 1850, and immediately plunged into the work: "scattering light, raising funds, obtaining subscribers."

Her three-month tour of Ohio was a triumph. In the fine summer weather she spoke outdoors most of the time or in the shade of a great tent similar to tents used by religious revivalists. Abolitionists hauled the tent from place to place with a three-horse team, pitching it on a village green or in a field at the edge of town. This "portable Faneuil Hall," which seated more than three thousand people, attracted crowds from all over the region. Families brought picnic lunches; children played tag around the guy ropes, and peddlers hawked their wares—including Cronk's beer, the *Bugle* noted disapprovingly.

Although the acoustics of the tent put a strain on her throat and lungs, Abby was at her populist best in the carnival atmosphere. Never a polished phrasemaker, she talked with fervor, "from the fullness of her heart." Describing the auction block and the "torturing lash," she offered an "affecting narrative" of the escape of a slave couple to the North. To heighten the drama, she paused while local abolitionists sang a song dedicated to the runaways, a plaintive air whose refrain was "Are we there yet?"

Nor were all her speeches tearjerkers. She silenced hecklers with sharp words, attacked the Free-Soilers, and, in the heart of Joshua Giddings's district, mocked his devotion to the Constitution. After expressing her "high personal esteem" for the congressman, she illustrated the "diabolism" of his position by supposing that a slave girl belonging to Henry Clay had run away. Having heard of Giddings's abolitionist sympathies, the girl made her way to his home with Clay in hot pursuit. "The poor panting girl rushes to him expecting to find protection" only to hear Giddings declare, "Fidelity to the Constitution forbids my defending or rescuing the slave." Barring his door, he "thrusts the despairing girl back into the clutches of her master." "Where was his pledge of fidelity to the slave now? Of what account was his burning eloquence in favor of Liberty and Justice?" she asked. Her listeners laughed, cried, and opened their purses.

In August Parker Pillsbury joined her, bringing a package from Stephen containing antislavery books as well as a pair of shoes she had forgotten. Henry C. Wright, whom she had scarcely seen since his days with the Grimkés, also accompanied her. With the two men sharing speaking engagements, she had time to visit abolitionists at home in her quest for money. Always at her best in face-to-face encounters, she made more than a thousand individual calls to convince the Ohioans that "money is the sinews of war" and that a reform movement, like any business, could not run without it. By the time the great tent was transported to Salem in September for the annual meeting of the Western Anti-Slavery Society, she had raised $870 and had increased the *Bugle*'s subscription list to 1,270, the largest ever. The paper was safe for another year.

Wherever Abby traveled, she acted as a magnet for women. When she held a three-day convention in Litchfield, a village on the Western Reserve, her host was Josephine Griffing, a thirty-six-year-old matron who had emigrated from Connecticut with her husband. Josephine had become a convinced Garrisonian during Abby's first Ohio tour four years earlier; she wrote for the *Bugle* and was an officer of the Western Society. Now, although she had a year-old baby, she agreed to join Abby as a part-time lecturer.*

During the Litchfield convention a group of Oberlin students drove over to hear Abby. Antoinette Brown, a friend of Lucy Stone's who was completing her theological studies and would later become a minister, accepted Abby's invitation to address the gathering, demonstrating "excellent abilities" and "rare intelligence," the *Bugle* reported. At the conclusion of her own appeal on behalf of slave women, Abby asked, as she often did, "Who

---

* Through the 1850s Josephine Griffing spoke against slavery in Indiana, Michigan, and Ohio. A founder of the Ohio Woman's Rights Association, she became its president in 1853. Moving to Washington at the close of the Civil War, she became a leader in freedmen's relief work and assisted in the formation of the Freedmen's Bureau. (James et al., eds.)

in this great assembly is willing to plead for the cause?" To her joy, a young woman stepped forward to say, "I will." Sallie Holley, an Oberlin senior and a native of upstate New York, insisted on completing her college course but promised to start lecturing as soon as she was graduated. Abby did not let her forget the promise.

Abby's sole disappointment that summer was with Lizzie Jones, who, after the birth of her daughter, had put aside antislavery work to give lectures on physiology. Profitable lectures. She had earned $340 in three months, Abby reported to Stephen. "Don't you know people will pay you for scientific knowledge when they will kill you for showing them their sins?" When Stephen teased that Ben must idolize Lizzie now that she was making him rich, Abby replied, "You would not like for me to be so miserly as she is. I would rather be poor than parsimonious."[20]

14

BLOODY

FEET,

SISTERS!

A t the conclusion of the annual meeting of the New England Anti-Slavery Society in May 1850, Abby joined Lucy Stone, Paulina Wright, Dr. Harriot Hunt,* and a handful of other women in a dingy anteroom of Faneuil Hall to discuss ways of giving a formal structure to the amor-

---

* Harriot Hunt (1805–75) had studied medicine privately and, starting in 1835, had built a successful practice in and around Boston. Eschewing conventional medicine, she based her treatment on good diet, exercise, and an insight into emotional causes of disease. (Hunt.)

phous woman's rights movement. The Woman's Rights Convention in Seneca Falls in 1848 had been followed almost immediately by a convention in Rochester. After an eighteen-month hiatus Betsy Cowles, Lizzie Jones, Josephine Griffing, and others of Abby's Ohio friends had called a meeting in Salem "to secure to all persons the recognition of Equal Rights." Now it was time for a national convention that would set goals and outline a program of work, the group in Faneuil Hall decided. Paulina, recently married to Thomas Davis, a wealthy Rhode Island abolitionist, had more leisure than the others and took on most of the organizational work. She prepared a call, which was signed by such prominent citizens as Ralph Waldo Emerson, Bronson Alcott, and the Reverend Thomas Wentworth Higginson, as well as by leading abolitionists, and engaged Brinley Hall in Worcester for October 26–27, 1850.

Although Abby had left the arrangements for the convention in Paulina's capable hands, she felt responsible for its success. She had been particularly provoked by Lizzie Jones's refusal to take time from her profitable physiology lectures in order to attend the gathering. So few women had experience on the platform that Lizzie's defection was a matter of real regret, she wrote Wendell Phillips when she hurried home from Ohio in early October. She also asked Wendell to lend her some lawbooks so that she could prepare herself to speak on woman's political and legal disabilities, a subject she had hitherto neglected, "being so entirely absorbed by the 'one idea.' " "I am anxious that the Convention should impress the age," she explained. "What I most fear is a lack of women who 'themselves must strike the blow.' "

Abby need not have been concerned. When she and Stephen, accompanied by eighty-five-year-old Asa Foster, drove to Worcester on October 26, the streets surrounding Brinley Hall were crowded, and every seat in the auditorium was taken. "Above a thousand persons were present," the *New York Tribune* judged, "and, if a larger place could have been had, many more thousands would have attended." Three of Abby's sisters— Olive, Joanna, and Diana—were there; so were her former schoolmates Elizabeth Buffum Chace and Rebecca Spring. Lydia Mott had come from Albany, and Mary Ann and Oliver Johnson had made the long trip from

Ohio.* Although men outnumbered women, Sarah Earle called the convention to order, retaining the chair until Paulina Wright Davis was elected president.

Paulina conducted the meeting with dignity and skill setting its tone by reading a poem from an anonymous contributor:

> *A Woman's Rights Convention!*
> *There's music in the word;*
> *Through every vein of living frame,*
> *My warm life-blood is stirred.*
>
> *A Woman's Rights Convention!*
> *Ring out the word on high;*
> *If my brother man will help me,*
> *To help myself I'll try.*

There was no dearth of capable speakers. In a ringing voice Lucy Stone proposed the circulation of petitions asking for suffrage and the right of married women to own property. Antoinette Brown refuted arguments from the Bible that were used to bolster women's subordinate status. Ernestine Rose pointed out that the Pilgrim Mothers had done as much to build New England as the Pilgrim Fathers. Abby Price of Hopedale talked on the injustice of excluding women from trades and professions, followed by Dr. Harriot Hunt, who spoke on medical education for women and read letters of rejection she had received from Harvard Medical School. After Sojourner Truth spoke, the gathering unanimously passed a resolution stating that slave women were "the most grossly wronged of all" and called on convention delegates to raise "the trampled womanhood of the plantation to a share in the rights we call for ourselves."

---

* Pregnant with her fourth child, Elizabeth Cady Stanton was unable to attend but sent a letter suggesting topics to be covered. Conspicuous by their absence, however, were most of the leaders of Boston's Female Anti-Slavery Society. Ann Phillips, Helen Garrison, and Thankful Southwick had signed the call, but as far as can be determined, the convention received no support from the Weston sisters, Eliza Follen, or Susan Cabot.

Abby Kelley's speeches were not reported, but one at least must have surprised the gathering, for Lucretia Mott felt called on to explain that her language "must not be construed to favor the use of violence and bloodshed" as a means of obtaining woman's rights. At fifty-seven, Mrs. Mott was the convention's most politic figure, steering a path between passionate Abby Kelley and those male speakers who talked of "giving" the women their rights or "permitting" them to receive them. When the Reverend William Henry Channing suggested that women did not need the vote but could influence political decisions through their superior moral power, she quickly contradicted him. And when Wendell Phillips denied that men were responsible for women's wrongs—"we have inherited these customs"—she gave him a light-handed but telling rebuke. Not all the men were conservative. William Lloyd Garrison, Frederick Douglass, and Stephen Foster unequivocally declared themselves in favor of woman's rights, and Charles Burleigh made the startling suggestion that men not only share child care but so simplify their diet and clothing that women would have more time for participation in public activities.

At the conclusion of the convention the assembly decided against a formal organization, chosing instead to appoint an eighteen-member Steering Committee and five subcommittees that would gather facts and guide public opinion toward establishing "women's co-sovereignty with men." Abby served on the Central Committee and the Committee on Civil and Political Freedom while Paulina, chairwoman of the Steering Committee, was empowered to call another convention in a year's time.

With the help of the press, which wrote satirical articles about the "Hens' Convention" and "Insurrection in Petticoats," the proceedings were brought to the attention of people all over the country so that for the first time the woman's rights cause became nationally known. Reading the accounts of the convention, an Englishwoman, Harriet Taylor,* wrote an article on

---

* Harriet Taylor married John Stuart Mill in 1851 and subsequently worked with him on his influential essay *The Subjection of Women*.

"Enfranchisement of Women" for the *Westminster Review*, encouraging British women to organize for their own rights.[1]

When the second National Woman's Rights Convention met in Worcester on October 15, 1851, there were three times as many participants as the year before, with women in the majority. Literary figures from New York and Boston graced the platform, alongside such seasoned veterans as Lucy Stone and Ernestine Rose. Lucretia Mott was absent, but Angelina Grimké had come out of retirement to deliver her first speech in thirteen years.

Tired after an arduous summer campaign in New York, Abby had arrived at Brinley Hall determined not to speak. For three days she listened to the discussions, obscurely troubled by the number of fashionably dressed affluent women and their emphasis on what seemed to her their selfish concerns. Perhaps it was an accident; but neither Sojourner Truth nor Frederick Douglass was present,* and no antislavery resolution had been offered. On the third night of the convention, which had moved to Worcester's City Hall to accommodate the overflow crowd, Elizabeth Oakes Smith, a contributor to such magazines as *Godey's Lady's Book* and one of the first women to lecture on the lyceum circuit, delivered a learned, polished speech on "Womankind."†

At its conclusion Abby could keep silent no longer. After paying tribute to the "genius" who had proceeded her, she said that the cause of woman's inequality lay deeper than anyone had yet suggested. It was true that women's opportunities were limited and that women were inadequately rewarded for their labor, but, she said, "I cannot, I will not charge it all upon men." Therefore, she presented a resolution: "That woman lacks her

---

* Sojourner Truth was lecturing in Ohio, Frederick Douglass editing his newspaper in Rochester, New York.

† Elizabeth Oakes Smith was not a universal favorite. When the third Woman's Rights Convention met in Syracuse in 1852, Paulina Wright Davis backed her for president. But Susan B. Anthony, attending a woman's rights meeting for the first time, objected to Elizabeth's and Paulina's low-necked dresses with flowing sleeves, declaring that women who dressed like that did not represent the "earnest, solid, hardworking women of the country." After some discussion Lucretia Mott was chosen president of the convention. (Stanton, Anthony, et al., v. 1.)

rights because she does not feel the full weight of her responsibilities; that when she shall feel her responsibilities sufficiently to induce her to go forward and discharge them, she will inevitably obtain her rights.

"Mary Wollstonecraft was the first woman who wrote a book on 'Woman's Rights'; but a few years later, she wrote another entitled 'Woman's Duty.' "* she explained. "We, who are young on this question of Woman's Rights, should entitle our next book 'Woman's Duties.' Impress on your daughters their duties; impress on your wives, your sisters, on your brothers, on your husbands, on the race, their duties, and we shall all have our rights.

"Man is wronged," she continued. He is "engaged in dollars and cents until the multiplication tables become his creed" while his wife and daughters remain "like dolls in the parlor." If women took more responsibility, their husbands would not be reduced to "mere machines for calculating and getting money." The cult of True Womanhood had circumscribed women, but it had also given them privileges that made them "lazy" and "indolent." "There are thousands of women in these United States working for a pittance who know they are fitted for something better and who tell me when I urge them to do business for themselves 'I do not want the responsibility of business. It is too much.' Well, then, starve in your laziness."

Then, as if sensing that she was losing the sympathy of her listeners, she broke off to say, "I hope that you do not feel that I speak to you in anger. I did not rise to make a speech—my life has been my speech. For fourteen years I have advocated this cause by my daily life. Bloody feet, sisters, have worn smooth the path by which you have come hither."

The audience was startled out of its complacency. "Great sensation," a reporter noted as Abby's words echoed through the hall—and "loud cheers" when she took her seat a moment later. Her speech was printed and distributed as a woman's rights tract, and "bloody feet" became a metaphor used for decades to describe the trials of the pioneers of the movement.

---

* Mary Wollstonecraft's *Vindication of the Rights of Women*, published in 1792, included the first detailed statement of women's wrongs and also criticized women as trivial, pleasure-loving, and weak in character. Abby erred when she said that Wollstonecraft had written a subsequent study on women's duties. (Flexner.)

Yet the speech set her apart from other leaders. She was calling for a radical change in the way women lived, for egalitarian marriage, with both partners sharing financial as well as community responsibilities—in short, a life such as she was leading. But the woman's rights platform concentrated on property rights, suffrage, equal education and equal pay, and even the right to refuse one's husband's sexual demands. Unfortunately Lucretia Mott was not present to mediate. Instead Ernestine Rose gave the obvious response— that rights come before duties—"and he who enjoys the most rights, has in return the most duties"—and the convention moved on to other matters. Although Abby continued to back the woman's rights cause, she did not make it her first priority until after the Civil War.[2]

The year between the two woman's conventions had been a busy one. George Thompson, the noted British abolitionist, had announced his intention to visit the United States. He had last been in America in the "mob year" of 1835, when antiabolitionist activity was at its height and he had been driven from the country by threats on his life. During the intervening years he had achieved prominence in England and India as a champion of labor reform and had been elected to Parliament. Tall, handsome, with a magnetic platform presence, he was a favorite of the Boston clique. Garrison had named his oldest son after him, Wendell Phillips called him "a universal idol" whose "vivacity, brilliance, and variety of accomplishments charm everyone," and Anne Weston was rumored to be in love with him. Despite his charisma, Thompson had failings that his American friends deplored. He drank too much tea, he took snuff and, some said, laudanum, and he was often financially embarrassed—a condition that apologists blamed on an extravagant wife. He was making this trip to the United States in order to lecture for pay as Dickens and others had done, to earn enough "to keep the pot boiling at home." The abolitionist leaders, who were disappointed that he would not be devoting himself to antislavery work and disgruntled at the thought that he might be using the cause for personal profit, proposed a compromise. If Thompson would make a tour of the Northeast speaking against slavery and giving only occasional paid lectures on other topics, his friends would solicit contributions for a "Thompson purse" to enable him to pay his debts.

To ensure large, generous audiences, someone had to take charge of

George Thompson. The Executive Committee appointed Abby Kelley. In January 1851 she left home to organize a two-month lecture tour in New York for the British spokesman. After passing through Springfield on her way west, she sent Wendell Phillips the first contributions to the Thompson purse—$28.75, most of it painstakingly collected $1 at a time. "*Our* friends in the city are few and not able to do much," she warned.

Her warning proved prescient. When Thompson arrived in the Massachusetts town shortly afterward, he was greeted by a full-scale riot. Echoing the anti-British sentiments of an earlier generation, proslavery demagogues joined with Irish immigrants who had their own reasons to hate Great Britain. They plastered the city with placards denouncing the "British spy," hung life-size effigies of George Thompson and John Bull from the trees on the town common, and prevailed on the proprietor of the hall engaged by the abolitionists to withdraw permission for its use. When Thompson wrote Abby from his hotel room that night, he could smell the burning tar barrels on the common as a mob set fire to the effigies to the accompaniment of shrieks and exploding firecrackers. "The mob is doing our work," he wrote.[3]

Indeed, it was. For as accounts of the rioters who had denied a British MP the right to speak appeared on the front pages of newspapers, curious crowds gathered at railway depots in New York to see him. They lined the roads when he traveled by carriage and filled the seats in the auditoriums Abby hired, even when an admission price of twelve and one-half cents was charged.

The Thompson entourage made up quite a party. In addition to Abby and Stephen, who was able to leave the farm in winter, Sojourner Truth joined them. A member of the Northampton Association until the community failed in 1846, she was embarking on her first extended antislavery tour, lecturing, singing her "homemade songs," and selling copies of the *Narrative of Sojourner Truth*, which a Northampton woman had written at her dictation. The Executive Committee had also engaged George Putnam, a Lynn abolitionist, to act as Thompson's secretary and to send progress reports to the *Liberator* and *Standard*.

Putting aside sectarian politics for the time being, Abby joined with the political abolitionists under the auspices of a committee calling itself Friends of Freedom to set up meetings for Thompson from central New York to the Canadian border. Gerrit Smith was host to the party in Peterboro where it had its first glimpse of the bloomer dress* that his daughter, Elizabeth Smith Miller, had introduced. Frederick Douglass participated in all the conventions and entertained Thompson at his home in Rochester. Samuel J. May took charge of the entourage in Syracuse, and Elizabeth Cady Stanton helped Abby arrange a meeting in Seneca Falls.

Audiences were enthusiastic and collections substantial, but Abby found that traveling with a celebrity sometimes had disadvantages. Thompson was a bit of a prima donna. Accustomed to the excellent railway system of his native land, he found travel by wagon over bumpy roads spine-jolting. He was too tired to attend the Seneca Falls meeting and too ill to speak at the first convention in Rochester, where six hundred people were waiting in the hall to hear him. Abby and Stephen—and Sojourner and Frederick—filled in for him, holding audiences together until the star was ready to make his appearance. If Abby felt critical of his self-indulgence, she never mentioned it in her reports to Wendell. Instead she enclosed drafts for two hundred, four hundred, six hundred dollars for the Thompson purse and reported enthusiastically on his success.

"*How can we ever value you enough?*" Wendell wrote when he acknowledged the contributions. "What a noble reception you have prepared for George."[4]

Although Thompson did not undervalue Abby's zeal, which, he wrote, "burns with a strength and clearness which not time nor persecutors can impair," he confided in letters to Anne Weston that Abby was not the woman he would have chosen for a traveling companion. A great favorite with the ladies, who flocked to his hotel room to beg for autographs and locks of hair, he enjoyed a pretty face and an occasional flirtation. Writing to Anne, who sent him books to read and canisters of imported tea so that

---

* The bloomer dress consisted of a loosely belted tunic, a knee-length skirt, and pantaloons reaching to the ankle. Designed by Elizabeth Smith Miller, it was enthusiastically adopted by her cousin Elizabeth Cady Stanton, Lucy Stone, and Susan B. Anthony. Its name came from Amelia Bloomer, who recommended the costume in her temperance paper, the *Lily*. (Stanton.)

he would not have to settle for the local product, he praised Abby's "masterly (no *mistressly*) speech on the growth and influence of the slave power" and commended the "faithful, indomitable, unwearied" Fosters, who were "generous and devoted friends of the American Anti-Slavery Society, quick to scent a plot & unmask false friends—good financiers."

Having said this, Thompson admitted to a distaste for Stephen, who on more than one occasion had "turned the milk to curds by an attack on church organizations," and to reservations about Abby, whose unswerving devotion to duty seemed formidable. "I love her dearly for her work's sake," he wrote Anne, while wishing that she had other attributes. "But nonsense—she is made to be a missionary in the anti-slavery cause, not to be a companion for a sentimentalist like me. She has a nobler work than to amuse my weary hours."

Unaware of Thompson's opinion of her—or perhaps not caring as long as he kept his speaking engagements—Abby was filled with "great joy" at his triumphs in the state. For years she had been promising her New York friends a glimpse of the antislavery celebrities. Now, as the tour drew to a close, she asked Garrison to join them for two weeks. In a reply addressed to "Most persevering, most self-sacrificing, most energetic, most meritorious of coadjutors,"* Garrison turned down her request on the ground of ill health but agreed to set aside a few days at the time of the May 1851 anniversary meeting. Thanks to Isaiah Rynders and the proslavery press, the American Society was unable to rent a suitable hall in New York City and had decided to hold its annual meeting in Syracuse.

The Syracuse gathering marked the culmination of Thompson's tour. With the Englishman as keynote speaker and Gerrit Smith on the platform, the sessions reminded participants of the early days of antislavery unity— with a single exception. When Edmund Quincy moved that the society endorse all antislavery newspapers that stood for disunion, Frederick Doug-

---

* Commonly used by the abolitionists to signify "helper" or "assistant," "coadjutor" was originally an ecclesiastical term meaning "one who assists a bishop."

lass rose to say that his views on the Constitution had changed. After careful study he now believed that the Constitution could be construed as an antislavery document. Further, he thought that "it was the first duty of every American citizen to use his political as well as his moral power for [slavery's] overthrow."

In the stunned silence that followed his announcement, Garrison exclaimed, "There is roguery somewhere!" Although he later said that he had not intended to impugn Douglass's integrity, and Douglass responded by overlooking the "hastily expressed imputation," neither man forgave the other. Their quarrel smoldered for two more years, erupting at last into a vituperative crossfire that severed relations between the black leader and the Garrisonians for the balance of the decade.

After the anniversary Abby returned to Worcester for a few weeks with Alla and Stephen. When in June a thousand people attended a grand Farewell Soiree for George Thompson at the Assembly Rooms in Boston and presented him with a twenty-two-hundred-dollar purse, much of which Abby had collected, she was back in New York "on an expedition of *observation, exploration and finance*."[5]

During her work in New York Abby unavoidably became involved in the feud with Frederick Douglass. Although she worked harmoniously with him during the Thompson tour as well as on earlier trips in the state, she could not rid herself of the belief that there was not room enough in the antislavery movement for three newspapers—four if she counted the *Liberator*—and she often found herself competing with Frederick for subscribers. As Garrison and Phillips had predicted, the *North Star* was having rough sledding. Douglass had been forced to sell his elegant press and to mortgage his home to keep the paper going. He might have been obliged to give it up had it not been for timely assistance from Gerrit Smith, who offered to merge his *Liberty Party Paper* with the *Star*, and from Julia Griffiths, a young white woman who had met Douglass in England and had come to the United States to help him. With a tenacity that resembled Abby Kelley's and business acumen not unlike Maria Chapman's, Julia had organized women's support groups for *Frederick Douglass's Paper*, as it was called after the merger with Smith, as well as helped with writing and editing. She is "a silly tool," Abby confided to Sydney Gay, adding with unsisterly abandon, "I wish all the old maids were either married or else good abolitionists."

As Douglass moved into the mainstream of antislavery work, he not only espoused political action and renounced nonviolence but decided that the Garrisonians' attacks on churches was harmful to the cause. The man who had agreed that the churches were "combinations of thieves, adulterers and pirates" during his first antislavery tour in Rhode Island now denounced Stephen Foster and Parker Pillsbury as "infidels" who did not accept the Bible and called the black Garrisonians—his former colleagues Charles Remond, William C. Nell, and Robert Purvis—"*practical* enemies of the colored people."

Increasingly Abby felt obliged to keep an eye on Frederick and "that miserable Julia Griffiths," who had brought Rochester's conservative women into a Ladies' Sewing Circle in opposition to the Garrisonian female society that Amy Post and her friends had formed a decade earlier. During the Ladies' Festival, held to raise money for *Douglass's Paper*, Frederick called a convention to organize a state antislavery society grounded in political action. Only Stephen's quick-wittedness on the convention floor, Abby told Garrison, saved "our good honest friends" in Rochester from being "duped." When the Executive Committee decided to hold the 1852 anniversary in Syracuse—the group was still barred from New York City—Abby gave six reasons why it should be held in Rochester instead. Not the least of these was to challenge Douglass in his own bailiwick and expose him as an enemy of the cause—"for he is an enemy," she reiterated.

The 1852 anniversary was fairly peaceful because all factions united to rescue a party of fugitive slaves, but the quarrel with Douglass turned nasty a year later, when the *Standard* called Griffiths "a Jezebel whose capacity for making mischief between friends would be difficult to match" and the *Liberator* hinted broadly that Frederick and Julia were having an affair that was causing "much unhappiness" in the Douglass household. The *Liberator* subsequently published a denial from Anna Douglass (a letter that those on the scene said had been "concocted by Frederick & Julia"), and Garrison issued a halfhearted apology for having written on personal matters; but the hostilities continued.

As far as Abby was concerned, Frederick lost his last claim to her friendship when, under the influence of the political abolitionists, many of whom had been "new org" men, he blamed Abby for causing the "first grand division" in the antislavery movement. In a major speech delivered before the Ladies' Anti-Slavery Society of Rochester, and repeated in other cities, he said that the 1840 split had rested on "a very minor question— Shall a woman be a member of a committee in company with men? Before I would have taken the responsibility of dividing the ranks of freedom's army, I would have suffered my right arm to be taken off," he averred. "How beautiful would it have been for that woman, how nobly would her name have come down to us in history, had she said: 'All things are lawful for me, but all are not expedient! While I see no objection to my occupying a place on your committee, I can for the slave's sake forego the privilege.' The battle of Woman's Rights should be fought on its own ground; the slave's cause [is] already too heavily laden."[6]

Abby replied only by working harder to bring young people into the Garrisonian fold. During the Thompson tour Aaron Powell, a student at the State Normal School, had disregarded his Quaker father's wishes and had attended one of Abby's meetings. Moved by what he heard, he became a Garrisonian. When he visited the Foster farm later in the year, Abby persuaded him to address a meeting. He spoke so well that she brought him to Boston the next day to introduce him to the Executive Committee. By the fall of 1852 he had dropped out of school to become a lecturing agent for the American Society.*

Susan B. Anthony was another of Abby's New York State recruits. A member of a progressive Rochester Quaker family, Susan was a sturdy, attractive woman of thirty-one when she first met Abby at the time of the Thompson tour. She spent a week with the Fosters and Thompson while they held meetings in Buffalo and Niagara Falls. Abby used all her per-

---

* Aaron Powell (1832–99) continued as an antislavery lecturer until 1865, when he became editor of the *National Anti-Slavery Standard*. He remained active in reform work for the rest of his life. (Powell.)

suasive powers to convince Susan to continue with her, but Susan, lacking confidence in her ability to speak, returned home. After several years of temperance and woman's rights work, she acceded to Abby's urging and joined the antislavery lecturing corps.

Nor had Abby forgotten Sallie Holley from Oberlin. As soon as Sallie returned home after her graduation, she received a letter from Abby offering her ten dollars a week and expenses to lecture for the American Society. "I will meet you in Syracuse, to begin our winter meetings," the letter concluded. On a Sunday evening in November 1851 Abby sat in a front pew in Samuel J. May's church, listening as Sallie, "with great power & pathos," told of the injuries done to the slave. Sallie's friend Caroline Putnam, who was sitting next to Abby, noticed that she frequently drew her handkerchief from her muff to wipe her eyes and thought she had taken cold. But after the meeting Abby put her hands on Sallie's shoulders and, in a voice choked with emotion, said that she had been weeping tears of joy, "thanking God that when I am so worn and weary and feeble, He has raised up one who can speak so nobly and winningly in this holy and persecuted cause!"[7]

Worn, weary, feeble at forty! Abby had spent a strenuous year, without permitting herself time for rest, and her friends had begun to notice the strain. Garrison, keeping a fatherly eye on his abolitionist family, wrote to scold her for putting her "valuable life" in jeopardy by working too hard. He had heard that she frequently spoke "from two to three hours." Not only was this a tax on the "bodily comfort" of her audiences, but it contributed to her "physical prostration" and would seriously affect her voice and lungs. "You are a very rare and very complete woman in everything but—a just consideration of your own health and strength," he concluded. "These are to be sacrificed, cheerfully and unreservedly, rather than one jot of principle, but this is not a question of principle, but of sound judgment."

Abby promised to heed his advice, but she could not take time to rest until she had trained Sallie Holley. Sallie was a natural orator who moved her listeners by describing the plight of the slaves, but she needed instruction in the nuts and bolts of lecturing: how to find a hall and attract an audience in a strange town, to keep track of subscriptions, book sales, and contri-

Abby Kelley at 41

New England Yearly Meeting Boarding School, Providence, Rhode Island, in 1831 (*Moses Brown School*)

Although Salley Holley, left, is not as well-known as Stone or Anthony, she was a popular antislavery lecturer from 1851 until after the Civil War. Betsy Mix Cowles, right, another of Kelley's proteges, was never comfortable as a public speaker, but she became the leading organizer of antislavery and woman's rights work in Ohio in the decades before the war. (*Oberlin College Archives*)

Elizabeth Margaret Chandler, who died in 1834 at the age of 27, was the first American woman to write antislavery poetry and essays. Her grave in Michigan became something of a shrine for abolitionist travelers. (*Library Company of Philadelphia*)

Laura Haviland, who had joined Chandler to organize the first antislavery society in Michigan Territory, worked with Abby Kelley to rebuild the society two decades later. Founder of an unsegregated school and conductor on the Underground Railroad, she continued her reform activities for many decades after the war.

Marriage Certificate

To whom it may concern.

This is to certify that we Stephen S. Foster Son of Asa, and Sarah M. Foster of the town of Canterbury, and State of New Hampshire, and Abby Kelley, Daughter of the late Wing and Diana Kelley, of the Town of Millbury, and State of Massachusetts, have this day (December 21. 1845) consummated a matrimonial connection in accordance with the divine law of Marriage, by a public declaration of our mutual affection, and covenant of perpetual love, and fidelity, of our purpose to perform faithfully, all the relative duties of husband, and wife.

In testimony whereof we hereunto affix our respective names.— Signed at New Brighton Beaver County Pennsylvania, December 21. 1845.

Stephen S. Foster
Abby Kelley Foster

The Marriage Certificate of Abby Kelley and Stephen Foster. (*The Worcester Historical Museum*)

Stephen Symonds Foster, dynamic antislavery lecturer, courted Abby Kelley for four years before she agreed to marry him. This daguerrotype was taken circa 1852.

Abby Kelley Foster in 1855

The Fosters' farm on Mower Street in the Tatnuck section of Worcester, Massachusetts. A portion of the stone wall that Stephen built can be seen right foreground. (*American Antiquarian Society*)

Main Street, Worcester, Massachusetts, in 1850, shortly after the Fosters moved there. (American Antiquarian Society)

Abby Kelley always welcomed black
women to the antislavery platform.
Sojourner Truth, opposite, made her first
antislavery tour with Kelley in 1851 and
traveled with her many times in later
years. (*National Portrait Gallery, Smithsonian Institution*) Sarah Parker
Remond, above left, was shy about public
speaking because of the inadequate
education she had received in Massachu-
sett's segregated schools. Encouraged
by Abby, with whom she toured in 1857,
she developed into an impressive public
speaker. She later went to Europe to
study and lecture. After attending medical school in Florence, Italy, she became a
doctor. (*Essex Institute*) Frances Ellen
Watkins Harper, above right, a poet, novelist, and orator, also lectured against
slavery with Abby Kelley. Charles
Remond, right, a popular lecturer and
Sarah Remond's brother, frequently
shared the platform with Abby Kelley.
(*Library of Congress*)

Charismatic George Thompson, British M.P. and reformer, was beloved by American abolitionists. This daguerrotype, showing him with Wendell Phillips and William Lloyd Garrison, was taken in 1851, the year that Abby Kelley escorted him on a profitable antislavery tour. (*Boston Public Library*)

Edward M. Davis was a wealthy merchant who supported the abolitionist cause and frequently assisted Abby Kelly.

Vassar College in the 1860s

The Reverend Samuel May, Jr., served as general agent of the Massachusetts Anti-Slavery Society from 1847 until the end of the antislavery struggle.

Thomas Wentworth Higginson, clergyman, author, and colonel of a black regiment during the Civil War, worked closely with the Fosters during their Underground Railroad days as well as in the woman's rights movement after the war.

Julia Ward Howe, author of the "Battle Hymn of the Republic," left, and Mary Livermore, lecturer and editor, right, were leaders of the Massachusetts Woman Suffrage Association. Abby Kelley disagreed with them frequently, finding them too conservative.

Alice Stone Blackwell, left (*Boston Public Library*), the daughter of Lucy Stone, and Lillie Buffum Chace, right, Elizabeth B. Chace's daughter, both worked for *Woman's Journal*. As members of the second generation of woman's rights advocates, they, along with Alla W. Foster, were known as "Suffrage Daughters."

Although Kelley never overcame a distaste for politicians, she cooperated with Congressman Joshua R. Giddings of Ohio, left, who headed the small antislavery bloc in the House of Representatives, and more grudgingly with Charles Sumner, right (*Boston Public Library*), leading abolitionist spokesman in the Senate.

Stephen Foster's portrait,
above, was made in 1869
(*Library Company of Philadelphia*), but when Abby Kelley
was asked for late pictures of
herself, she always said that she
was too busy to pose. The
daguerrotype of her, right
(*American Antiquarian Society*),
was probably taken in the
late 1850s.

On her seventieth birthday, Elizabeth Cady Stanton, left (*Rhoda Barney Jenkins*), announced that she weighed two hundred pounds. Lucy Stone, below, also gained weight as she grew older.

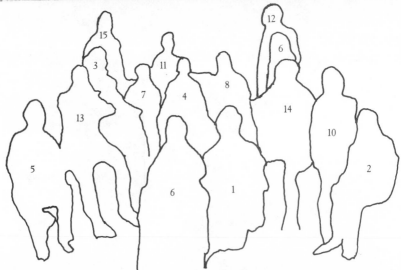

In July 1886, surviving abolitionists and their children held a reunion at the home of Lucy Stone and Henry Blackwell. Those present were: 1. Samuel Sewall 2. Theodore Weld 3. Elizabeth B. Chace 4. Abby Kelley 5. Samuel May 6. Harriet Sewall 7. Sarah Southwick 8. Lucy Stone 9. Zilpha Spooner 10. Henry Blackwell 11. Alla W. Foster 12. George T. Garrison 13. William Lloyd Garrison, Jr. 14. Wendell P. Garrison 15. Francis J. Garrison. (*Sophia Smith Collection, Smith College*)

butions and send regular accountings to Sydney Gay and Wendell Phillips. Besides, there was the big question of Sallie's political soundness. Her late father, Myron Holley, had been a founder of the Liberty party, and there was a danger that she might join the political abolitionists. Julia Griffiths had already told her that if she had any self-respect, she would not ally herself with infidels like the Fosters, and Douglass had asked Gerrit Smith to invite Sallie to become a correspondent for *"our* paper."

But Sallie, who worshiped Abby and believed that she could do no wrong, was not easily wooed away. After they spent three weeks lecturing together, Abby reported that her pupil could become the "most effective and eloquent woman that has ever graced our platform." Better schooled in literature than Abby was and by nature less combative, Sallie appealed to people who found her mentor too fiery. Abby recognized this and wisely refrained from trying to change her style. "She has so much poetry in her addresses that the sword is very much covered. Still this is her way and I want she should pursue it," she wrote Stephen. As far as ideology was concerned, Sallie listened thoughtfully when Abby explained "the folly of political machinery in carrying forward a moral reformation." After several weeks with her, Abby was confident that "no one would suspect she had leanings towards the Liberty party."

Sallie's indoctrination was never concluded because Stephen was taken ill and Abby was called back to Worcester. By then, however, she was sufficiently versed in Garrisonian principles to travel on her own, a fact that Douglass sourly attested to in a letter to Gerrit Smith: "She now wears the bonds that I have thrown off, being a pupil of Mrs. Foster and I fear goes it *blind.*"[8]

Stephen had been sick all fall, at first with "one of the worst colds that ever afflicted a mortal man," then with a pain at the back of his head that he thought might be brain fever, and finally with "night sweats and a terrible cough." Abby, who still embraced Sylvester Graham's dictum— "avoid medicines and physicians if you value your health"—had urged him to take a water cure at a new establishment in Worcester operated by a cousin of Susan Anthony's, Dr. Seth Rogers. Instead he had followed Rogers' regimen of cold tubs, wet sheets, and copious water drinking at home. Abby had not been seriously alarmed until Samuel May, Jr., wrote to tell her that Dr. Rogers said that Stephen must spend the winter in a warm climate if he were to avoid consumption. With the South out of bounds for abolitionists, the Executive Committee wanted to send him to Jamaica or another West Indian island. "It is their firm conviction that *you* need almost as much as he does the change in climate, the recreation and the rest," May wrote. Phillips, Jackson, and the others would give them up to two hundred dollars as "an outfit fund for the voyage"; besides, there was the possibility that they could earn salaries by lecturing on the island.

On her way home Abby consulted a clairvoyant healer about Stephen's health. Clairvoyants were practitioners of spiritualism, the latest "ism" to sweep the psychic highway. Their special powers, they claimed, enabled them to visualize the organs of sick persons and prescribe cures. Although Abby lacked "implicit confidence" in them, she had visited a seer three years earlier, when Alla was ill in New Hampshire. The clairvoyant, who had performed "wonderful cures" for other abolitionists, had diagnosed Alla's illness as worms and a "scrofulous humor in her blood" and had prescribed an antiworm drug and a syrup made up largely of sarsaparilla. Reassured because the medicines resembled those that her mother had dosed her with as a child, Abby had mailed them to Caroline in New Hampshire— and Alla had recovered.

The Dutchess County clairvoyant also came well recommended, and Abby reported her diagnosis to Stephen with some relish. "She says in the first place you talk too much and eat too much. Your stomach being weak, is unable to digest much food and none but the simplest with ease; and talking irritates your lungs and inflames your brain. Again you take your baths too cold. Such intense cold sends the blood with a rush to the chest and increases the irritation." The seer recommended wet bandages around the chest at night, warm douches in the morning, and sheet packs doused in seventy-degree water twice during the day. "I presume Dr. Rogers would laugh if he should know I had taken the pains to write the prescriptions of a clairvoyant," she concluded, "but it looks so reasonable that I thought I would submit it."

Abby's visits to clairvoyants had as much to say about the state of medical knowledge in Victorian America as it did about her credulity. With conventional practitioners still devoted to "heroic" measures, which killed as often as they cured, many people turned to alternative medicine, consulting phrenologists, hydropathists, faith healers, and the like in the belief that they were availing themselves of advanced scientific methods. Abby, who put her faith in diet, exercise, and water cures, was far less gullible than William Lloyd Garrison, whose hypochondria drove him from one quack doctor and miraculous nostrum to another.* Nor did she join the spiritualist movement, which had originated in New York State in 1848 with the Fox sisters, young women who professed to communicate with the dead through mysterious rappings. Many New York abolitionists, including Amy and Isaac Post, became "rappers"—Isaac published *Voices from the Spirit World* in 1852—and as the movement spread, Garrison received messages from the late Nathaniel Rogers, and Joshua Giddings "conversed" with the spirit of John Quincy Adams. After attending a séance on Cape Cod, Stephen told Abby that he "was not prepared to acquiesce in the correctness of [the] theory" although he saw "many things which are inexplicable." Later in the decade, when spiritualist journals threatened to supplant the *Liberator* in abolitionists' parlors, both Fosters criticized the new faith because it diverted energy from the struggle against slavery.[9]

By the time Abby reached home, Stephen had so far recovered that they agreed to forgo the Jamaica trip and spend the winter in New York, where the climate, they thought, would be milder than in New England. Stephen throve and gained weight during their busy months of lecturing, but Abby came down with a heavy cold. When she suffered from chills and fever, eating "hardly enough to keep a chicken alive," Stephen urged her to return to Worcester for a water cure, but she determined "to live it through" and finally succeeded. There was so much work to do and, as usual, so few people to carry on. Although she had been promised a team of lecturers, one by one they had disappointed her. Garrison's health again proved too

---

* In 1851 Garrison published an endorsement of Dr. Clark's Anti-Scrofulous Panacea, which had cured him of "a scrofulous diathesis." He wrote: "Your Panacea is very pleasant to the taste and permeates through the system in a very quickening manner. A doctor friend laughed. "Permeating the system! Why, it was the first time he had taken a glass of grog, and didn't know how good it was!" (Merrill and Ruchames, v. 4.)

delicate for the engagements she had planned for him, and both Phillips and Charles Burleigh were kept at home by sick wives. Even Sallie Holley, despite her "genius," needed constant coddling. When Sallie went home for a few weeks of rest, Abby feared that she was "too much in some traits of character like L. M. Child to be relied on."[10]

The all-absorbing issue in the early 1850s was the new Fugitive Slave Law, passed as part of a compromise between North and South. In return for the admission of California into the Union as a free state and a ban on the slave trade—but not slavery—in the District of Columbia, Congress drastically increased federal control over fugitive slaves. U.S. marshals were empowered to enter the free states in pursuit of runaways. If captured, the alleged fugitives were brought before U.S. commissioners for summary hearings. Without being permitted to testify on their own behalf, without a jury trial, they could be declared slaves and sent South solely on the word of a white man. Further, all citizens "were commanded to aid and assist" the marshals and were subject to fines and imprisonment if they refused.

The onerous law, which deprived everyone with a dark skin of basic civil rights, touched off a wave of panic in the black ghettos of the North. Only days after it became law, in September 1850, hundreds of families—runaways, relatives of runaways, and freeborn blacks—abandoned homes and jobs for a haven in Canada. Thousands followed over the next years while those who remained behind armed themselves with guns and bowie knives and determined to defy the law.

The Fugitive Slave Law presented the abolitionists with dramatic new opportunities for winning converts. The Slave Power was no longer an oratorical device; it was a flesh-and-blood reality, embodied in the U.S. marshals on the streets of northern cities. Slavery was no longer an abstract evil way down south in the land of cotton. It was made tangible at abolitionist meetings when newly arrived fugitives sang:

> *The hounds are baying on my track*
> *O Christians will you send me back?*

Outside of meetings, Wendell Phillips, Theodore Parker, and many others organized vigilance committees, which, working in concert with blacks, defied the U.S. marshals and sent fugitives on their way to freedom. In November 1850 the Boston Vigilance Committee rescued Ellen and William Craft, fugitives from Georgia, and put them on a steamer bound for England. Three months later black Bostonians marched into the courthouse where Shadrach, a waiter from a local coffeehouse, was on trial, and carried him away. In the fall of 1851 blacks and whites seized Jerry McHenry from a courthouse in Syracuse and conveyed him to Canada.

The vigilance committees posed a dilemma for those abolitionists who believed in nonresistance. Could they counsel blacks and their white allies, men like Phillips and Parker, who were not nonresistants, to refrain from the use of force? Samuel J. May, who, along with Gerrit Smith, had taken part in the Jerry McHenry rescue, confessed to Garrison that when he saw Jerry in the hands of the marshals, "I could not preach non-resistance to the crowd clamoring for his release. When I found that he had been rescued, I was as uproarious as any one in my joy."[11]

Abby was faced with the question during the 1852 anniversary meeting in Rochester. She was on the podium when the convention was informed of the arrival of U.S. marshals in the city. She immediately broke off her speech to make a solemn vow. No fugitive slave would be taken from Rochester. "I am prepared to throw my body in the way of the kidnappers and risk my life if need be," she declared. Then, while others left the hall to make sure that all known fugitives were safely hidden and to post placards warning against the slave catchers, she went on to reiterate that the only appropriate weapons in the struggle of right over wrong were still moral ones. Hers was the classic nonresistant position, which she maintained even when, later in the turbulent decade, many of her colleagues came to accept "righteous violence."

Stephen was more conflicted. Although his head counseled nonresistance, his viscera cried out for action. For the time being he solved his dilemma by assisting fugitives to escape on the Underground Railroad. The old Cook place, which lacked so many amenities, was well equipped with cellars and subcellars. In one of these, a vault ten by five feet that could be reached only by a trapdoor from above, was fitted out as a hiding place for runaways. Late at night a neighbor, often Thomas Wentworth Higginson, the young pastor of Worcester's Free Church, might deliver a fugitive to the Fosters.

When sure that the coast was clear, they would drive the escaping slave to Samuel May, Jr.'s home in Leicester or to another station on the underground route to Canada.

In earlier years the operation of an Underground Railroad station was hazardous for conductor as well as slave, but in the 1850s in New England towns like Worcester public sentiment was sufficiently on the side of the fugitive to obviate the need for secrecy. More often than not the runaways who were sheltered by the Fosters enjoyed the freedom of their farm. One visitor, probably Caroline Putnam, told of meeting a nineteen-year-old fugitive from Virginia who was so much a part of the family circle that Alla was teaching him to read. Her report of the encounter was published in the *Liberator*.

The Fosters, however, discreetly refrained from mentioning their illegal guests. Abby wrote of the fugitives they harbored only once, when she warned against a woman calling herself Orlena Tecumseh, who was not a runaway at all but "an opium eater and tobacco smoker" and "the boldest and most impudent beggar and most hardened imposter I have ever seen."*[12]

After the Rochester anniversary, Abby remained at home for more than a year, speaking locally during the 1852 election campaign and the months that followed. Although the Free-Soil party lost ground in the election, Gerrit Smith† and Thomas Davis, Paulina's husband, were elected to Congress, and Charles Sumner, Wendell Phillips's college classmate, was chosen to represent Massachusetts in the Senate. During her Worcester stay Abby brought Sallie Holley to Massachusetts, introducing her to the Boston clique and arranging to have her lecture with Lucy Stone and other agents of the Massachusetts Society. By the fall of 1852 Sallie was sufficiently seasoned as a lecturer to go off by herself on a tour of Pennsylvania and Delaware.

---

* In the 1890s, after the Fosters' deaths, the purchasers of their property named it Liberty Farm. Although it bears this title in the inventory of National Register of Historic Places, the name was never of the Fosters' choosing.

† Gerrit Smith resigned his seat in Congress before his term was over, apparently convinced that he could do little to abolish slavery while in office. (Harlow.)

Stephen had performed wonders with the farm, not only in the fields and orchard but in renovating the dilapidated house until it was almost acceptable to Abby. Money was still short. Abby's salary as a lecturer went to pay farm bills, but on more than one occasion she was obliged to borrow from Sallie, who had a private income. Stephen pointed out with unaccustomed cheerfulness that the experience of being poor was not "wholly useless as it will help us to sympathize with others who are in straightened circumstances."

In addition to lecturing, Abby busied herself with farm chores. Milkmaid to four cows, she rose before dawn in order to have the milk ready by 4:30 A.M., when it was picked up for sale in Worcester. When Parker Pillsbury visited, he found Abby in the kitchen, her range at full blast as she heated her "fleet of flat irons." "Mrs. Foster is proving herself a model wife of the house as well as the Queen of our female reformers. No farmer's wife is more devoted to domestic affairs or toils more diligently with her hands at the hardest of woman's work. Neither Mr. or Mrs. Foster need ever doom themselves to such labor," he reported in a letter to the *Bugle*. "With their commanding talents, they could grow rich were that their object. But they reason in a way peculiarly their own. They see that much hard labor needs to be done. They are willing to do their part. They take their lot with the rest of the *working world*."[13]

Responsible not only for Stephen and Alla's well-being but for hospitality to visiting family members and crews of workmen who were remodeling the kitchen, digging a well, or installing drains, Abby usually had a "girl" to help her. More often than not, the only employees she and Stephen could hire were the inexperienced Irish immigrants who now made up a quarter of the population of Worcester. Sharing the "Paddyphobia" of his contemporaries, Stephen deplored their ignorance, telling Abby in one letter that he did not want an Irishwoman to clean the house "without someone of taste & order to oversee." Although Abby used pejoratives like "Paddy," she was ahead of her generation in the way she treated the women who worked for her. She was not only "a very neat housekeeper," Sallie Holley reported, but "beautifully just to every member of the household. Her real reverence for humanity is shown by her ways toward the Irish girls who lived with her."

For the first time since Alla's infancy, Abby had a long, uninterrupted period with her daughter. In the 1850s children were still thought of as miniature adults, to be seen but not heard and to be trained by a judicious application of the rod. Although she had no child care manuals to guide her, Abby taught through affection and example, avoiding physical punishment and oppressive authority. Once when Alla was visiting the Ballous, a cousin asked, "Will your mother let you do this?" Surprised, six-year-old Alla replied, "My mother lets me do just as I please. If she wishes me to do a thing I generally do it." "The cousins could not understand how a child could be 'let' do just as she pleased. Alla, who had never heard of any other way, was equally unable to understand why all children should not be so 'let,'" Sallie Holley reported "Mrs. Foster is very conscientious not to use the least worldly authority over her child and she is richly repaid by the unbounded confidence and affection which the child reposes in her mother."

Abby also told Alla about the slave children who were taken from their mothers, explaining that her own mission was to preach to the "wicked" men responsible for slavery and to "make them good so that they would let the poor slave mothers go home." If Alla, too, wanted "to help the world grow better," she must learn "to be *very very* good" herself. Little Alla, who understood that her mother was working to free the slaves, was also an early believer in woman's equality. A favorite anecdote in reform circles had it that Alla was puzzled because her bedtime prayer always ended with *Amen*. "Ought they not to say *Awomen* sometimes?" she asked.

Abby's gentle but insistent doctrination seems to have been successful, for as an adult Alla expressed no resentment at having been left by her mother but only pride in Abby's devotion and self-sacrifice. "Had she been less noble, less brave, less tender of her child, she would have remained at home to enjoy her motherhood at the expense of other mothers," she told a woman's rights meeting after Abby's death. "She once exclaimed 'The most precious legacy I can leave my child is a free country.'"

Not all of Abby's teachings pointed a moral. As a small child Alla had the freedom of the fields and barns. Long before she could read, she knew the names of the garden and wild plants and was helping feed the chickens, cats, dogs, and an occasional orphaned calf. Meeting her for the first time when Alla was five, Sallie Holley found her "the very incarnation of sweetness and simplicity; though she is a child of decided character. I never saw a child of extraordinary parents that answered my anticipations before. She is just what you would expect from her father and mother."

Stephen, too, played an important—and unusual—role in Alla's upbringing. In Abby's absence he patiently answered his daughter's questions, tended her when she was ill, and consoled her when she missed her mother. When a stuffy nose made it difficult for her to breathe at night, he moved her cradle next to his bed, picking her up as she struggled for breath and rubbing her forehead with a damp cloth until she was able to sleep again. After her cousins had returned to school one fall, leaving her without playmates, he built her a swing in the kitchen; when she objected to going to New Hampshire, he bought her a harmonica to play on the train. "Alla talks much of you & says she has often cried because you were gone, but I have not seen her tears," he wrote Abby. "She is very happy & a great comfort to me in your absence."

Alla's trips to New Hampshire became less frequent as Stephen's parents grew older. After Sarah Foster had a stroke, Caroline was responsible for caring for her and was no longer available for child-sitting. Fortunately in 1851 Adams Foster bought a farm in Worcester, where Alla could stay when her parents went on short lecturing trips. Occasionally, too, one of Abby's sisters filled in. When Diana Ballou kept house for Stephen for ·a few weeks, he teased Abby by telling her what an excellent cook Diana was.[14]

In the spring of 1853 Abby left Stephen and Alla on the farm while she attended the American Society's anniversary, which once again convened in New York. The speechmaking had scarcely gotten under way when a breathless Susan Anthony interrupted the proceedings with a plea for help. She was one of several women attending the World's Temperance Convention at the Brick Chapel on Nassau Street. Although they had been elected as delegates, the male officials would not permit them to speak or vote. Abby and Lucy Stone clapped on their bonnets and hastened to Nassau Street. Abby, possessor of the loudest voice and the most experience of any of them, immediately attempted to take the floor. For more than ten minutes she stood in a back pew, repeatedly calling, "Mr. Chairman, Mr. Chairman," while the men in front of her shouted, "Order! Order!" and told her to sit down. When the credentials committee voted unanimously to reject the "Bloomer Delegation," Thomas Wentworth Higginson, a delegate from the Massachusetts Temperance Society, proposed that the women withdraw, to meet at Dr. Trall's Water Cure Establishment. As the women left, speakers denounced them, singling out Abby as a troublemaker who was "trampling the very son of God under her blasphemous feet."

In Dr. Trall's parlor that afternoon some fifty women and their male allies agreed that since the World's Convention had summarily excluded one-half of the world, they would organize a *Whole* World's Temperance Convention in New York in the first week in September. The Whole World's Convention, which was chaired by Lucretia Mott and supported not only by abolitionists but by such new woman's rights men as Horace Greeley and P. T. Barnum, was judged a great success. However, Abby did not participate. By the time it convened, she and Stephen were in the West, leading an antislavery tour to Michigan and Indiana.[15]

15
GENERAL AGENT

A fter hiring a Yankee couple to take care of Alla and the farm, Abby and Stephen left for the West in August 1853. Charles P. Hovey, the proprietor of a dry goods store on Boston's Summer Street, had contributed fifteen hundred dollars to the American Society to break new ground in Michigan and Indiana. Sallie Holley and Parker Pillsbury were going too. Garrison had agreed to spend a month in Michigan, and Abby was authorized to employ local agents as she saw fit.

After a "highly gratifying" meeting of the Western Society in Salem, Ohio, the Fosters left for Michigan. They spent a seasick night aboard a lake steamer—misnamed the *Superior*—then took a train from Toledo to Adrian in the southern part of the state. Admitted to the Union in 1837,

Michigan was largely wilderness still, with great stretches of virgin forest where only Indians and trappers ventured. In the southern counties bordering Ohio emigrants had cleared the forests and planted fields of wheat and corn. Adrian, with almost five thousand inhabitants, was a center of abolitionist and Underground Railroad activity, largely because of the efforts of two Quaker women, Elizabeth Margaret Chandler and Laura Haviland, who had organized Michigan Territory's first antislavery society as far back as 1832. Chandler, contributor of poetry and essays to the *Genius of Universal Emancipation* and the *Liberator*, was the author of the oft-quoted lines

> *While woman's heart is bleeding*
> *Shall woman's voice be hushed?*

which Abby had read as a young teacher in Lynn. After Chandler's untimely death in 1837, her grave on her brother's farm outside Adrian became something of an abolitionist shrine. Visiting it in October 1853, both Sallie Holley and William Lloyd Garrison penciled poetic tributes, Garrison's a sonnet "To the Memory of Elizabeth Margaret Chandler."

Abby, too, stayed with Elizabeth Chandler's brother that fall but left behind no verses. Her business in Adrian was to organize a new Michigan antislavery society to replace the long defunct one. With the help of Laura Haviland,* then a doughty widow of forty-five, the delegation of easterners convinced their Michigan friends to reject the political abolitionists and organize a state society based on "No Union with slaveholders."

For the next four months the Fosters toured southern Michigan, speaking in Ypsilanti, Battle Creek, Hudson, and other farming villages, as well as in such larger centers as Ann Arbor and Detroit. In Battle Creek Lydia Mott's sister Phebe Willis welcomed them, but in other places they were

---

* With seven children to support, Haviland (1808–98) was the founder of the River Raisin Institute, the first Michigan school to admit black pupils. She was also a conductor of the Underground Railroad, accompanying fugitives across the lake to Canada and making hazardous trips to Kentucky and Arkansas to bring out slaves. During and after the Civil War she taught and cared for freedpeople and was active in the woman's rights movement. (James et al., eds.)

on their own, the first Garrisonians to speak in the area. When she left home, Abby had determined not to work as hard as in the past. "I have not so much strength as formerly," she wrote Samuel May Jr. But she was quickly caught up in the excitement. "Just the same as of old—enquiry is on tiptoe, opponents deny our charges. We have only so many days and so we must drive the course through and talk in private all the time to convince individuals. Then when occasionally a leisure hour comes, we must read the papers."[1]

The Fosters held four or five well-attended meetings in Detroit's City Hall but were lambasted by the press, particularly the *Free Democrat*, organ of the Free-Soil party. Abby was described as "uninterestedly plain. Her character as expressed in her face is that of a cold, passionless, intellectual notoriety hunter. She is not a good speaker, not graceful, not eloquent and not pathetic even—the great *forte* of women speakers. Her efforts to cry, of which she made several, were all signal failures, resulting in the squeezing out of a very little moisture which, from the expression of her countenance, we judged to be vinegar or possibly nitrous acid. There isn't one lady in a hundred who, with her practise, wouldn't make a better speech than hers of last night." Stephen fared little better: "He is as destitute of intellect as his wife is of passion. His countenance is bad. His face is very large with a broad full jaw while his narrow excuse for a forehead is almost wholly engrossed by his eyebrows."

They also encountered the old charge of "no marriage." At one Sunday meeting a critic said that Abby had "formerly taken up with 'a great buck nigger' and after getting tired of him took up with Foster and, by and by [would] take up with someone else." That evening Stephen "called out the scamp and made him tremble," Abby reported.

Separated from Canada only by the Detroit River, Detroit was a terminus of the Underground Railroad with a sizable community of free blacks and fugitives. Black leaders called a meeting in the African Methodist Church to reply to the "coarse and vulgar assaults" on the Fosters. One of their resolutions said: "We view Abby Kelley Foster and her husband as true friends of the slave and therefore have no dislike as to the shape of his head or the length of her face, but we do have a great love of hearing the word which comes out of their mouths."

William Lloyd Garrison, who followed the Fosters to Detroit, was dismayed by the antagonism they had aroused and by the consequent lack of hospitality proffered to him. Instead of preparing the way for his visit, "Stephen and Abby appear to have given me an Irish hoist, 'a peg lower,' "* he wrote to his wife. When he was unable to obtain a hall to speak in, he, too, lectured in the African Methodist Church.

After Garrison went home, Abby and Stephen visited country towns to organize local antislavery societies and sell subscriptions to the *Bugle*, thus "touch[ing] both hearts and pockets." Travel in Michigan in winter was difficult. Snowstorms often blocked the stagecoach routes, and the state's few railroads were dirty as well as dangerous. Benjamin Jones, who joined them in February, complained of the chewers and spitters who littered a railroad car until it was "a perfect Lake Superior with here and there a used up quid, like an island. It was pitiful to see women with their skirts held up, looking for a place to sit." On their way to Ann Arbor the engine of their train ran off the track and rolled down a steep bank, landing bottom up. Fortunately the passenger cars remained intact, and Abby and Stephen were able to make their way through the snowdrifts to their destination.

Transportation in Indiana was even more primitive. Pillsbury, who preceded the Fosters there, warned of broken-down bridges and roads that were little more than cart tracks. Returning to his lodgings after a night meeting, he had to walk ahead of his host's buggy, holding a lantern aloft to enable the driver to avoid streams and gullies. One night, when a lantern was unavailable, he led the way through the woods with a lighted candle.[2]

Late in February 1854, while Stephen attended a Free-Soil convention, Abby went to Indiana alone, responding to pleas from three men who were on trial for aiding fugitives and who hoped that she would build up sufficient antislavery sentiment to save them from jail. She found log homes, log meetinghouses, and log furniture, which was unattractive as well as uncomfortable. "I go into queer houses in this new country," she wrote Alla. "This is indeed a poor one, tho' not so poor as some others. There are but

---

* "An Irish hoist" seems to have been a forerunner of today's Polish jokes.

three rooms besides the pantry. So I have slept in the same chamber with a man and his wife. I could get along very well, only that I am dreadfully bitten by fleas. I cannot even sleep o' nights with any comfort." Then, because she could never pass up an opportunity to edify her daughter, she added, "You must not think because the people here have queer log houses that they are not good and wise. The people where I now am are very kind, and know a great deal more than some folks who live in very fine houses."

Writing frequently to "my very dear daughter," Abby also sent gifts that might interest her: a "pretty" California gold quarter dollar and a subscription to the *Little Pilgrim*, a new children's magazine that promised "pure morality with pure literature." Interspersing news with loving admonitions, she advised the six-year-old to keep her hair well brushed and to help Aunt Sarah. In Alla's painstakingly printed replies, which her cousin Emma helped write, she reported the farm news: "Uncle Adams has got ten chickens and we have two hens sitting. . . . We have begun to drop potatoes. I drop them and grandfather covers. . . ." as well as "Do you know where my white woollen stockings are?" and "I shure would like to see you."[3]

Unlike Michigan, whose pioneers had come from New England and New York, Indiana had been settled in good part by families from Tennessee and Kentucky. Hating black people "with a perfect passion," they had enacted the most oppressive black laws of any state in the Old Northwest. Nevertheless, after holding "grand meetings among the Hoosiers," Abby reported to the *Liberator*, "I have never been to any new field where there was a more candid spirit of enquiry. Though it is a newly-settled section, and therefore possessed of little wealth it puts to shame many of our older fields. Nearly two hundred dollars have been put in our hands for the treasury and upwards of eight anti-slavery papers have been subscribed for." People sympathized with the men jailed for helping the runaways and were eager to hear her message. After "a thorough agitation" she felt sure that they would be ready to repeal "the execrable black code." "Did my strength permit I should remain in Indiana during the entire summer and lecture in the villages during the busy season." As it was, Stephen had already returned home for his spring planting, and later, in

April 1854, Abby headed east to report on her work at the anniversary meeting in New York.[4]

The anniversary coincided with the final congressional debates on the Kansas-Nebraska Act. The bill establishing the two territories repealed the Missouri Compromise of 1820, which would have banned slavery in the region. Instead territorial settlers were to be permitted to decide the question for themselves. By thus establishing a new principle of squatter sovereignty, Congress initiated years of guerrilla warfare in Kansas, pushing the nation a step farther toward civil war. The Garrisonians pointed out that the act was yet another demonstration of the strength of the Slave Power and the impotence of political abolitionism.

On May 30, 1854, the day that the Kansas-Nebraska Act became law, Abby and Stephen were in Boston at a convention of the New England Anti-Slavery Society. They found a city under siege. Anthony Burns, a presser in a tailor shop on Brattle Street, was being tried as a fugitive slave. Shortly after his arrest Thomas Wentworth Higginson had led an assault on the jail in an attempt to rescue him. When the attack failed and a deputy was killed in the melee, President Franklin Pierce telegraphed to say, "Incur any expense. The law must be executed." As a result, ropes were stretched across Courthouse Square and regiments of soldiers guarded every entrance to the building.

In Melodeon Hall, a short distance away, the antislavery convention proceeded against this background of high excitement. Stephen Foster proposed that a committee of abolitionists meet with the Free-Soilers, who were also in session, to form an organization to protect New England citizens from kidnappers. But unity between the two groups proved impossible to achieve. When Henry Wilson, a Free-Soil leader, asked for abolitionist support in the next election, Abby reminded him that Free-Soil votes had helped elect Massachusetts's governor, whose judiciary was responsible for Burns's incarceration. A better way to abolish slavery, she declared, was "for our Free Soil friends to come to [our] meeting and contribute ten thousand dollars to the American Anti-Slavery Society."

After a three-day trial the U.S. commissioner in charge of the case ordered Anthony Burns returned to his master in Virginia. Abby was in Boston again on the day of his rendition, attending a New England Woman's

Rights Convention. The convention accomplished little because the women adjourned to State Street to watch Burns's mournful march from the courthouse to the waterfront. Two thousand troops—cavalry, marines, artillery, National Guard—were on patrol. Flags were hung at half-mast; buildings along the line of march were draped in mourning black. All over the state church bells tolled, and effigies of President Pierce and the U.S. commissioner were burned on village greens. In the city fifty thousand spectators hissed and shouted, "Shame!" until a marine band tauntingly responded by playing "Carry Me Back to Old Virginny."

"There was a lot of folks to see a colored man walk through the streets," Burns wryly remarked after he was placed aboard a revenue cutter for the trip South. "'Twas the saddest week I ever passed," Wendell Phillips said. "I could not think then of the general cause, so sad [were] the pleading eyes of the poor victim."

The Fugitive Slave Law had been upheld, but it was a costly victory.*[5] Recognizing the opportunity for enlarging the scope of its operations, the Executive Committee voted to appoint Abby Kelley general agent of the American Society. She declined the honor but agreed to become general financial agent. Traveling through New England, she found old friends returning to the fold and new ones coming forward. John Greenleaf Whittier raised money for the *Liberator* and the Boston Vigilance Committee, writing that "we must forget past differences and unite our strength." An aroused Angelina Grimké hoped that "the arrest of every fugitive may be contested *even unto blood*," and Henry David Thoreau, described by the *Standard* as "a sort of literary recluse," came out strongly for disunion at an abolitionist picnic on the Fourth of July.

The picnic, an annual event, was held in a pleasant grove outside Framingham. Special trains from Boston and Worcester brought people to the grove; benches were lined up under the trees, and a placid pond formed a backdrop for the speakers' platform. Abby and Stephen arrived early,

---

* The cost of U.S. marines, soldiers, and revenue cutter was estimated to be a hundred thousand dollars. (Sterling, *Forever Free*.)

probably bringing Alla, for the picnic was a family affair with swings for the children, boats on the pond, and a refreshment stand for those who had not brought dinners.

Heading the finance committee, Abby made her usual appeal for funds, Stephen called on the friends of liberty to resist the Fugitive Slave Law, "each one with such weapons as he thought right and proper," and Wendell Phillips, Sojourner Truth, and Lucy Stone held the audience in thrall with their "soul-eloquence." After an hour's break for refreshments Henry Thoreau castigated Massachusetts for being in the service of the slaveholders and demanded that the state leave the Union. "I have lived for the last month—and I think that every man in Massachusetts capable of the sentiment of patriotism must have had a similar experience—with the sense of having suffered a vast and indefinite loss. I did not know what ailed me. At last it occurred to me that what I had lost was a country."

Thoreau's speech is still reprinted, but William Lloyd Garrison provided the most dramatic moment of that balmy July day. Placing a lighted candle on the lectern, he picked up a copy of the Fugitive Slave Law and touched it to the flame. As it burned, he intoned a familiar phrase: "And let all the people say *Amen*." As the shouts of "Amen" echoed, he burned the U.S. commissioner's decision in the Burns case. Then he held a copy of the United States Constitution to the candle, proclaiming, "So perish all compromises with tyranny." As it burned to ashes, he repeated, "And let all the people say *Amen*." While the audience responded with a tremendous shout of "Amen," he stood before them with arms extended, as if in blessing. No one who was present ever forgot the scene; it was the high point of unity among the Garrisonian abolitionists.[6]

People were still talking about Anthony Burns in late October, when a heavyset stranger registered at the American House in Worcester. What was Asa O. Butman, the United States marshal who had arrested Burns, guarded him in jail, and escorted him back to Virginia, planning now? Abby was lecturing in Rhode Island, but Stephen immediately went into action. As a nonresistant he had not joined the Worcester Vigilance Committee, headed by Thomas Wentworth Higginson. While the committee distributed handbills warning "LOOK OUT FOR KIDNAPPERS," and discussed treating Butman to a coat of tar and feathers, Stephen led a handful of nonresistants to the American House. "Our plan," he wrote Abby, "was to present ourselves in as large numbers as possible and fastening upon him an indignant gaze to follow him wherever he went till he should leave town." Soon some fifty men, black and white, had gathered in front of the hotel for an all-night vigil. They rang the house bell from time to time to expostulate with the landlord about his unwelcome guest until finally Butman appeared in the doorway. When he threatened them with a pistol, the watchers had him arrested.

By the time he was arraigned the following morning, the courtroom and streets surrounding it were jammed with spectators. When his trial was temporarily adjourned, some half dozen black men broke into the room in which he was held and commenced beating him. The city marshal interfered, arresting one of the assailants, but he could not disperse the crowd outside, which was shouting, "Bring out the kidnapper" and "Kill the scoundrel!" After a conference between city officials and community leaders, Butman, flanked by Higginson, Foster, and several of their followers, appeared on the courthouse steps. The abolitionists had promised Butman safe passage out of the city if he would agree never to return. Slowly an ill-assorted group made its way toward the depot. Higginson linked arms with Butman while Foster walked behind, one hand on the marshal's shoulder, the other thrust out to fend off the crowd that followed. The crowd grew until there were a thousand men and boys throwing rocks and shouting threats. At one corner a black man succeeded in planting "a tremendous blow" on Butman; others landed kicks and spattered him with eggs.

"Scenes of peril are not new to me," Stephen wrote Abby the next day, "but in all my past experience I have seen nothing like this. For a time it seemed impossible to save him from the fury of those he had so deeply injured."

At last Butman and his escort reached the depot, to find that the Boston train had gone and another was not expected for an hour. After locking the terrified marshal in the station privy, Stephen addressed the crowd. Butman had pledged never to return to Worcester. Such a promise, he said, was a victory for freedom, and he hoped no one would mar the triumph by further acts of violence. Finally, after another rush by the infuriated crowd, a hack was procured. Butman was shoved inside and driven safely to Boston.

Stephen was exultant. Worcester's citizens had proved that they would not permit slave catchers in their city. Butman had been forced to face their indignation and had become a suppliant at the feet of the abolitionists. All this had been accomplished through the application of nonresistant principles. "My heart sits more lightly in my bosom, & I breathe more freely now than at any time since the sad tragedy which made Anthony Burns a slave," he wrote Abby.

His enthusiasm was scarcely dimmed when he, his friend Joseph Howland, and five others—nonresistants and blacks—were arrested and charged with inciting to riot. The *Worcester Spy* had praised his behavior, but the proslavery press elsewhere demanded punishment for Butman's expulsion, and Stephen was a logical scapegoat. Refusing to give bail, he was locked up to await trial. When Sallie Holley called at the farm that week, Alla met her at the door to announce with smiling face, "Father's in jail."

During nine days of preliminary hearings Stephen took over the courtroom. He started by demanding that Abby act as his lawyer. When the judge denied his request—no woman had ever practiced law in Massachusetts—Stephen handled his own defense. Cross-examining witnesses— the landlord of the American House, the city marshal, the city watchman, and even the mayor—he elicited descriptions of his forceful mediation during the riot. In a closing statement to the court he declared, "I am a nonresistant, but if I could ever be converted to the doctrine of violence, I would, upon the issue of slavery, go for a bloody revolution." Although a grand jury subsequently indicted the black defendants for assault, Foster and Howland were acquitted.[7]

The winter of 1855 found Abby unwell. At the anniversary in May she looked so pale and thin that her friends were alarmed. Before the sessions were over, Wendell Phillips had collected pledges of more than five hundred dollars from members of the Boston clique and from Edward M. Davis, to permit her to take a year's leave from antislavery work without feeling financial pressure. Raising the money was much easier than persuading Abby to rest. "You must give up working and talking," Wendell urged in a series of friendly, scolding letters. "You owe it to humanity to save yourself.

Dismiss from your mind all anxiety about farm cares and Stephen's affairs. Don't worry about him or your little girl. There's one thing you owe that little girl which no one but you can pay her; it is to *live* & to *live in health* if possible. Be a good girl and do as you're bid."

Soon after the anniversary Abby and Stephen were hosts to a great family party to celebrate Asa Foster's ninetieth birthday. All ten of his living sons and daughters and their families came—from Maine, New Hampshire, Connecticut, Pennsylvania, Ohio—to mark the day. "Very earnest, upright looking people—everyone respectable and conscientious," according to a friend who was present. "All the children will sit down to dinner with the father, and at tea, all the grand-children. Little Alla was in great glee, so happy at this rare visit from so many cousins. Old Mr. Foster was one of General Arnold's bodyguard in the American Revolution, though but a mere lad. What a change he has lived to see in this great country! Steamboats, railroads, telegraphs, and all manner of mechanical improvements and inventions."

By the time the last guest had departed and the last dish had been replaced on its shelf, Abby was ready to take Wendell's advice. For much of the next two years she remained at home, refusing speaking engagements, skipping meetings, and limiting correspondence. During the summer she spent her days outdoors, carrying pails of water to her strawberry plants, raking the garden to clear it of stones—"very hard work," she told Stephen—and gathering fruits and vegetables for winter preserves. Wearing new bloomers when she climbed a ladder in the orchard to harvest apples and pears, she was "gazed at more than is agreeable." By fall she had gained six pounds and was feeling much stronger; even her voice was less hoarse.

When the annual plea for help came from the Western Anti-Slavery Society, Stephen went to Ohio in her stead, leaving her in charge of the farm. She hired new hands, supervised repairs to chimneys and drains, marketed the wheat and rye, throwing herself into the work so energetically that Stephen could barely conceal his annoyance. "I am happy to hear that you are getting along so well at home, but you cannot appreciate the importance of my presence there," he wrote. "That the men will be faithful I have no doubt, but that they will do all that needs to be done is by no means probable unless I am there to direct. You are a capital housekeeper & can make a very creditable anti-slavery speech, but I have little confidence in your ability to manage a farm."

Despite this put-down, the letters he wrote during his two-month absence demonstrated anew his dependence on her: "It is unaccountable to me that I should have left home without your likeness & Alla's. But you have always attended to everything pertaining to my personal comfort & so from habit I left all for you. I am sorry you should have forgotten a matter so important to my happiness." When he visited the place where they had spent their honeymoon, he reported that "the tenants of this house have changed, but my memory will cling to it as the real *birth-place* of a relation the loss of which would render life worse than a blank." After "a delightful visit" with Lizzie Jones and a friend, he told Abby that he "had been so long famishing for want of the society of refined, virtuous & loving women & as they seemed so much like your *very self* I found it difficult to maintain toward them that reserve that usually marks my intercourse with the other sex. It only wants your presence here to make my happiness complete."

Concerned with Alla's as well as Abby's health, he urged outdoor exercise for them both, proposing that they "practice calisthinics (if I spell the word right)" every morning. He thought Alla's physical training more important than her studies: "She had better learn to pick apples than to spell." But he cautioned, "Only be careful & not fall from the trees."

Abby's replies to "My very dear husband" were characteristically matter-of-fact. The cows had gotten into the corn. She was having the fence repaired. She rejoiced that he was making "grand speeches" and urged him not to work too hard. Although both commented on politics, critics of these two "fanatics" would have been surprised at the amount of time they devoted to discussing a new method of canning fruit.[8]

Abby had little chance to feel lonely during Stephen's absence. His hard work on the farm had paid off. Even to her critical eye their house was comfortable enough for visitors. Among her first guests had been William and Helen Garrison and their children. The senior Garrisons spent only a weekend, but Willy, Jr., and ten-year-old Fanny stayed for a month. Willy, who had spent most of his sixteen years in the city of Boston, had "a grand time" on the farm, riding horseback and helping with the harvest. "We have a great deal of fruit here, apples and pears in abundance," he wrote his parents. "I have picked 12 qts. of blackberries and Fanny has picked nearly as many huckleberries."

Although the fall brought less visitors, there were seldom fewer than eight at Abby's dinner table. Susan B. Anthony, who was taking the cure at Dr. Rogers's Hydropathic Institute, came several times. Abby thought her "an exceedingly interesting woman. She has grown, intellectually, more than any other person of my acquaintance within the last four years."

Sallie Holley and her companion Caroline Putnam were also regular visitors. Caroline, who could not bring herself to speak in public, felt inadequate until Abby found work for her. The American Society had begun publishing a series of short, simply written pamphlets to explain its position on the Constitution, the struggle in Kansas, and other issues. The program was patterned on the work of the American Tract Society, which published five million religious tracts yearly, for distribution in churches and through house-to-house canvassing by colporteurs, or city missionaries. Abby saw the tracts as a way of reaching people who did not attend meetings—"evangelizing the slaveholding barbarians" and bringing them to a state of "anti-slavery grace." During her years at home she pushed the program, persuading Wendell, Tom Higginson, and Stephen to write for it—Stephen's was a twenty-page pamphlet titled *Revolution the Only Remedy*—and recruited Caroline Putnam, Joseph Howland, and others as colporteurs.

To the colporteurs, she explained that the tracts must not be left on doorsteps. Potential readers should be visited again and again; if "disposed to receive the word," they must be given additional reading matter until they were "cured of the[ir] heresies." Although the tracts were free, she advised the colporteurs to obtain something from each person they talked to: "Aid for the cause. Money, labor, a good word. Get them to do something and they will love it."

For the next decade Caroline Putnam toured the North with Sallie Holley. While Sallie lectured, she trudged from house to house with a satchel filled with tracts. In one of many adulatory letters to Abby, she recalled: "The morning we took leave of you, you were writing by the little stand in your sitting-room and as you kissed me goodbye you said 'write to us often, will you not?' But does it matter to you whether you have my inconsequential letters? To you, whose footsteps unfalteringly keep pace with the sublime martial music of duty." Abby's example gave Caroline courage for those moments when "I stand on the steps of this door or that, with my little handful of Tracts thinking over the message I am to stammer out to the inmates when bidden to enter. How their objections & incredulity—and indifference and ignorance will tempt me to despair of any good that I can do." Despite her self-doubts, Caroline became the American Society's most successful colporteur, distributing thousands of tracts and sending in substantial contributions to the Tract Publishing Fund.[9]

In the fall of 1855 Susan, Caroline, and Sallie left Worcester to attend a Massachusetts Woman's Rights Convention in Boston. Almost everyone active in the movement was there—except Abby. Her poor health justified her absence, but had there been hints that she would not be welcome? Although the scanty records of the woman's rights movement of this period make no mention of a conflict, the Reverend Theodore Parker devoted one of his Sunday sermons at the Music Hall to the "reproach and odium" heaped on great reformers who were ahead of their time. After instancing Jesus, Socrates, and William Lloyd Garrison, he turned to "a woman who has traveled all over the North, laboring for woman's cause. She bore the burden and heat of the day. She was an outcast from society. Other women hated her; men insulted her. Every vulgar editor threw a stone at her, which he picked up from the mire of the street. The noble woman bore it with no complaint; only now and then, in private, the great heart of Abby Kelley would fill her eyes with tears at the thought of this injustice; but she never allowed her tears to blind her eyes, or quench the light which was shedding its radiance down her steep and rugged path. But when the cause had won something of respect, a great convention of women were summoned to meet in the heart of this Commonwealth; and those who had control of the matter thought it would not do to have woman's stoutest champion sit upon the platform. She must sit below it, lest it hurt the cause and peril the rights of woman to have woman's noblest champion sit in woman's honored place!"

Although no correspondence has been found that sheds light on Parker's sermon, "those who had control" of the convention included Paulina Wright Davis, still chairwoman of the movement's Central Committee, and Lucy Stone, its secretary. Criticism of Abby was not likely to have originated with Lucy, who, although she had given up her antislavery agency to become a well-paid lecturer on woman's rights, continued to work with Abby and had met her on numerous occasions. Nor would Lucy's recent marriage* to reformer Henry Blackwell have caused a breach, for Henry admired Abby, whose "earnest eloquence," he said, had converted him to abolitionism when he heard her speak in Cincinnati in the 1840s. Only a year before the Boston convention, when he rescued a slave child from her mistress, he had renamed the child Abby Kelley.

More probably Abby's absence from the convention was a product of her changed relationship with Paulina Wright Davis, whose second marriage had brought her wealth and social position and a strong taste for respectability. Summering in Newport, Rhode Island, an elegant seaside resort, and wintering in Washington with her congressman husband, Paulina now saw "no necessity of burdening our movement with all the unpopularities of the abolitionists," she wrote Elizabeth Cady Stanton. "I am determined to do my utmost to remove the idea that all the woman's rights women are horrid old frights with beards and mustaches." Although Abby Kelley hardly fitted this stereotype, Paulina had turned from her to bring forward women like Caroline Dall, a writer of some repute, and Elizabeth Oakes Smith, whose "extraordinary dress [and] aping of court ceremonies"† still made her unpopular with other women leaders.[10]

The rift with Paulina was no doubt painful, but it was compensated for by an outpouring of affection from others. Lizzie Jones visited Abby twice during 1855 and 1856, and they were soon exchanging confidences, as they

---

* When Lucy Stone and Henry Blackwell married on May 1, 1855, she insisted on retaining her own name; the phrase "Lucy Stoner" came to mean a married woman who keeps her birth name. (Blackwell.)

† Caroline Putnam had so described Smith at the 1855 Boston meeting, adding that Elizabeth Peabody, the educator, called Smith "thoroughly self-intoxicated." (C. Putnam to AK, Sept. 24, 1855, AAS.)

had a decade earlier. Lizzie had given up her moneymaking dreams and had returned to antislavery and woman's rights work. "I am more of a philosopher than I once was. We live on the income we have, tho' we live economically." Still ambitious, however, she was trying to prepare herself to become a lyceum lecturer by studying history, a project constantly interrupted by meetings, guests, and the care of her eight-year-old daughter. Practical Abby suggested that she hire a servant, but Lizzie preferred to do her own work, "partly from prudential considerations & partly because I do not want the privacy of our home infringed upon."

Wendell and Ann continued to send loving messages, promising to visit when Ann's health improved, and even Edmund Quincy wrote to say that Abby was "so good" that he felt "like a miserable wretch when I think of what you are doing & suffering & then think of my own shortcomings." Charles Hovey, long a benefactor of the Garrisons, gave a practical demonstration of his admiration for Abby and Stephen by putting them down in his will for $1,000 apiece. "In these days of spirit rappings I feared you might find this out & wish me done," he wrote Stephen, "so have concluded to pay you and your wife the annual interest during my life time." Enclosing a draft for $120—"being 6 prct on $2,000 of which please pay ½ to your wife"—he assured them that the gift would not lessen "by one cent" his contributions to the cause.

Some of this admiration was dissipated when Abby felt well enough to return to meetings again and spoke on what she saw as a tendency to compromise abolitionist principles. Agitation against slavery had begun to take a backseat to the controversy over "bleeding Kansas." The territory was a battleground where settlers from the Northeast, under the auspices of the New England Emigrant Aid Society, fought against guerrilla bands from the slave state of Missouri. Many abolitionists, including some who had been nonresistants, joined the fray. Thomas Wentworth Higginson and Dr. Seth Rogers led armed Worcester men to the territory. The Reverend Henry Ward Beecher's congregation presented each member of an emigrant party with a Bible and a Sharps rifle. Shipments of these new breech-loading rifles, which could fire ten shots a minute, became known as Beecher's Bibles; even Wendell Phillips contributed a hundred dollars toward their purchase.

The struggle to determine whether Kansas would be slave or free had given impetus to the new Republican party, a coming together of Liberty men, Free-Soilers, and antislavery Democrats. They opposed the extension of slavery in the territories but had nothing to say about its abolition in the South or about the rights of black people.* In Abby's eyes, the Republicans were no better than any other political party—worse, indeed, than the Liberty party, which had supported emancipation and equal rights. Stephen, for his part, urged the formation of an antislavery political party whose candidates would be pledged to disunion. "The people must vote," he insisted, as he had many years earlier. "We must provide ways for them to vote without sacrifice of principle." Abby made no secret of her disagreement with her husband's "hobby," as she called it, but felt impelled to come to his defense when colleagues refused to listen to him.

The New England Society convention in May 1856 was one of those occasions. A week earlier Charles Sumner, a leader of the Republican minority in Congress, had delivered a powerful speech in support of the Free-Staters in Kansas. Afterward he had been attacked by a South Carolina congressman who beat him over the head with a cane until he fell to the floor, bleeding and insensible. His life was still in jeopardy when the convention assembled at the Melodeon. After listening to speakers eulogize Sumner, Stephen took the floor. "Who is Charles Sumner that this Society should espouse his quarrels?" he asked. As a politician who had sworn allegiance to the government he was thus in union with slaveholders. "The men at Washington who do not want to get caned for a speech ought to leave the company of villains and come home."

Shocked by this unfeeling attack on the hero of the hour, delegates hissed, and both Garrison and Phillips were quick to answer him. When Stephen continued to criticize the senator and the Republicans, Garrison declared that he was taking up too much time. This brought Abby to her feet. "The cause of freedom demanded" that Stephen be given opportunity to answer

---

* Republicans supported Black Laws and opposed black settlers in Kansas.

his critics, she asserted. Abolitionists had a duty, unpleasant though it might be, to rebuke the Republicans when they compromised the truth.

Stephen received additional time to speak, but his only supporters were Charles Remond who proposed taking Sharps rifles from Kansas and using them in South Carolina, and Charles Hovey, who praised Stephen's "true eloquence."

Divisions in the abolitionist ranks accelerated after the Republicans nominated John C. Frémont as their candidate in the 1856 presidential election. There was little in the career of Frémont, a western explorer and the first civil governor of California, to recommend him as an antislavery champion, but many abolitionists rallied to his standard. For the first time in her life Maria Child was "infected with *political* excitement. I would almost lay down my life to have [Frémont] elected," she wrote. Even William Lloyd Garrison believed that the Republican party was "the legitimate product of the *moral* agitation of the subject of slavery for the last quarter of the century." On the eve of the election he wrote in the *Liberator*, "If there were no moral barrier to our voting—which there is—and we had a million ballots to bestow, we should cast them all for John C. Frémont."

Democrat James Buchanan won the election, but the Republicans carried nine northern states, substantially increasing their strength in Congress and in state legislatures. When, two days after Buchanan's inauguration, the Supreme Court handed down its Dred Scott ruling, which said that blacks could not become U.S. citizens and were "so far inferior that they had no rights which the white man was bound to respect," the nation—and the abolitionists—became further polarized.[11]

Abby made few public appearances during this period because of a disagreeable new health problem. For years, particularly during her western trips, she had been plagued by toothaches. The dentists of Ohio, who often combined barbering with dentistry, knew only one remedy for an infected tooth: pull it. By the time she consulted a dentist in Massachusetts, where a dental school had recently opened and nitrous oxide (laughing gas) was being successfully used for anesthesia, her teeth were beyond repair. After months of stressful surgery—she fainted during one operation—all her teeth were extracted, and false ones were prepared. Full dentures were common enough among her contemporaries,* but Abby was only forty-six when her last tooth was pulled.

Her dental work was still in progress when she attended the annual meeting of the Massachusetts Society in January 1857. Maria Chapman, who had returned from Europe a month earlier, took one look at Abby's sunken cheeks and pain-etched face and offered to raise money to send her abroad for the winter. Wendell seconded the proposition, telling Stephen that Abby would be a fool not to accept, but Abby turned down the offer.

In an uncharacteristically despondent letter to Wendell, written while she was waiting for her dentures, she expressed a feeling of alienation from the abolitionist family. In the first place, she mistrusted its motives. "Were I to allow myself to think the interest and anxiety of my anti-slavery friends, for my health, arises from affection for myself—my eyes would run over and my voice choke. But this cannot be, for except anti-slaverywise, I am a stranger to you all. I regard [Maria's offer] only as a matter of business—that it is for the cause's sake alone that you over value me."

Adding to her dark mood was her acceptance of the conventional wisdom that a woman in her mid-forties was old, with little to look forward to save "turning the corner," a Victorian euphemism for menopause. Never mind that Wendell at the same age was embarking on a career as an orator that was to bring him national renown. Misquoting Shakespeare, she reminded him: " 'My spring of life is fallen into the sear and yellow leaf.' People must not expect me to be so strong in the decline as in the meridian of life. I am getting old.

"Still I hope I am capable of some little service, and unless convinced that my efforts hinder and not help the cause, I shall endeavor to perform it. I shall get my under teeth this week, and, as soon as I am able to talk well with them, I purpose to sally forth and try what I can do."

Before returning to the field, however, she wanted to clarify her political position. Although her associates thought her "a *dogged* fool" for damning

---

* Garrison acquired full dentures in 1865, when he was sixty. (Merrill and Putnam, v. 5.)

the "idols of Republicanism," she insisted that the Republicans, whatever their seeming virtues, were politicians who sustained a slaveholding government. "We have nothing to do with motives. Our business is to cry 'unclean, unclean—thief, robber, pirate, murderer'—to put the brand of Cain on every one of them. We cannot afford to blunt the edge of our rebuke by bestowing compliments on the good points of their characters. We have no time."

Basically Wendell agreed with Abby's analysis of the Republicans despite his sympathy for his old friend Charles Sumner, whose seat in the Senate chamber was still empty. Treating her letter with the seriousness that it deserved, he set out to reassure her by proposing that the Executive Committee appoint her general agent of the American Society. The post, which had not been filled for more than a decade, would utilize her organizational talent and intimate knowledge of the field while permitting her to remain at home much of the time.

"I cannot tell you how much pleasure it gives me, as indeed to all, to have you willing to assume the post," he wrote in May 1857. Even dour Samuel May "*smiled* a most cordial delight as he hastened to record the vote." Her mode of operation and her salary were for her to decide: "Whatever you deem best will be satisfactory to us." However, it was "the especial wish of all the com^ce that you would spare yourself as much as possible—& refrain for your health's sake from all exhausting labors public or private."[12]

Looking over the field from Worcester as she accustomed herself to her new dentures, Abby found the work better organized than it had been in some time. Elizabeth Buffum Chace headed antislavery operations in Rhode Island. Holley and Putnam were traveling in the West, and Susan B. Anthony was in charge in New York. Shepherding three lecturing teams through the state during an unusually severe winter, Susan reported to Abby: "*My spirit has grown in grace*. The experience of the last winter is worth more to me than all my temperance and woman's rights work."

In response to pleas from the Joneses, Abby made plans for a late-summer campaign in Ohio and neighboring western states. The program would cost more than twelve hundred dollars, but, she told the Executive Committee, she would raise the money herself. In early July 1857 she left home on "a tour of finances." In Philadelphia, her first stop, she met with leaders of the Pennsylvania Society only to learn that they had not collected "their money harvest for the season" and did not want her to "glean" until later in the year. "I think their policy is very bad but they are not to be reasoned out of it," she wrote Maria Chapman.

After the meeting she spent a day with Lucretia and James Mott, who had just moved to a farmhouse outside Philadelphia, next door to Edward and Maria Mott Davis's summer place. "Her throat [is] far from well & she is quite hoarse," Lucretia wrote to her sister. "All her teeth have been extracted & a temp[orary] set in—she is fine look[in]g yet."

Abby took advantage of her day in the country to ask Edward Davis, hitherto a generous contributor, for money. She had expected a thousand dollars but came away empty-handed. "[He] will not, probably, give a Dollar to any anti-slavery society this year, tho' last year he expended between Three and Four Thousand for Republicanism," she told Wendell Phillips.

On her way to New York Abby stopped at Eagleswood, a communal settlement on Raritan Bay, New Jersey, founded by Rebecca Spring and her husband. The commune had been abandoned, but Eagleswood remained as a boarding school operated by Theodore Weld and Angelina and Sarah Grimké. Abby was not sure how she would be welcomed by the two sisters, who were now gray-haired and in bloomer dress, but they greeted her cordially and put their names down on her subscription paper. She was less successful in New York, where she spent long, hot days calling on potential donors. After a ferry ride to Brooklyn and "a most tremendous walk," she found the home of the Reverend Samuel Longfellow, brother of the poet, only to learn that he was out of town. The cousin of a Worcester friend was away for the summer; one Manhattan merchant was too busy to see her; another, proving to be "utterly proslavery," told her that "women should stay at home and look after their families."

Without a single new name on her pledge list at the end of a day, she waited in the Anti-Slavery Office until Henry Blackwell came to escort her to Orange, New Jersey, where he and Lucy Stone had bought a home. "A neat little cottage—a fine yard and garden well cultivated with abundant fruit trees," Abby told Stephen. Lucy, seven months pregnant, was "as bright and happy as a bird." After breakfast the next morning a neighbor took Abby to call on people who Lucy thought might contribute. But one man was away, and another "would not if he could emancipate the slave." Concluding that little could be accomplished in the vicinity of New York during the summer, Abby returned home.

In Worcester she appealed to merchants and professional men who had supported the Garrisonians in the past. She had always been successful when she went "a soliciting," owing in no small part, Stephen said, "to her charming powers of conversation." But this year was different. When she called on a busy doctor, using as her opening gambit a wish to see him head her subscription list "in a handsome manner," he praised her "noble energies" but gave nothing.[13]

By the time she went to Abington for the annual celebration of West Indian emancipation, she was seriously concerned. August 1 turned out to be one of those magic days, cloudy in the morning but with clear skies and a fair breeze by midday. People strolled to the lake and picnicked under the trees, before settling down to an afternoon of oratory. The speeches were the usual fare, some moving, some dull, until Abby took the rostrum.

"The first speech I ever made to a public audience was for funds," she recalled. "Twenty years have passed, but still the slave wears his bonds. Neither you nor I understood at that time, the length, the height, the thickness of the prison wall. We did not dream that the wall that hems in the slave is the boundary of the United States. We did not dream that the wall was garrisoned by forty thousand churches, [by] the United States Army with musket loaded and bayonet pointed. Although the strength of that wall [has] never been measured we know that its foundation is of sand, and that waves of public opinion have loosened [it] somewhat. . . .

"A short time since, I consented to take the general agency of the American Anti-Slavery Society. I will not be a general without soldiers; and my soldiers and their families must not be left to starve. I have resolved to enlist in the anti-slavery service every man and woman who has the gift of tongues, and they shall lash the waves of public sentiment; and the walls of slavery shall tremble. We must have the material means.

"My soldiers must have money. If it can be raised in no other way, it shall be by mortgaging the little farm that I in part own. I have pledged myself to raise $10,000 to carry on this work. I will give a hundred dollars, and if necessary a thousand, and if that will not do two thousand, and I do not know but that will drain my coffers.

"Some may think I am speaking under the impulse of excitement, and I wish to assure you it is not so. It is after consultation with my husband who volunteers to work for nothing this year. I feel that to leave my daughter a home, to leave her even a dollar when by sacrificing that home I could leave her freedom, I should be violating a trust that God has committed to my care. My husband and myself have made up our minds that money shall never be lacking while we have a dollar in our pockets."

When she sat down to loud applause, Wendell Phillips seconded her powerful appeal, recalling his first sight of Abby, "a young devoted girl," who had consecrated herself "in the bloom of youth, its ingenuousness, its enthusiasm, upon the altar of the slave. The clear, sweet tones of that now wearied voice, how fresh they are in my ears! Year after year have I watched it wearing away—life and health the cheerful price she paid—and I dare not let that man pass without bitter rebuke who throws in the way of those bloody and toil worn footsteps one single obstacle to success."

When Abby walked down the aisle with her collection box, people gave more generously than they were accustomed to. She raised almost five hundred dollars in Abington, but it was still a pitifully small sum when compared with the need.[14] She fared better in Boston, where Maria Chapman gave her letters of introduction to wealthy sympathizers. Abby told Stephen, "She knows what cord to touch in every heart. It is wonderful how she sees into everybody and knows better than themselves what motives actuate them." With Maria's advice she secured a pledge of five hundred dollars from a member of the Boston Female Society although "she is quite foggy on some points." Her husband, "a regular aristocrat" who gave thousands to the Republican party, refused to contribute. Although he agreed with Garrisonian principles, including disunion, he feared to act against "the class with whom he associates." However, when she said goodbye, she fancied he looked "relenting."

James Russell Lowell, who had drifted away from antislavery work to teach at Harvard and edit the new *Atlantic Monthly*, gave her fifty dollars and an introduction to Henry Wadsworth Longfellow. The poet had been in disfavor with the Garrisonians since the publication of his "Building of the Ship," whose lines "Sail on, O Ship of State!/ Sail on, O Union, strong and great!/ Humanity with all its fears,/ With all its hopes of future years, Is hanging breathless on thy fate!" had been interpreted as an answer to disunionism. Because a recent edition of his poetry had omitted his early antislavery verse, Garrison declared that he had "prostituted his fine poetical genius." Knowing this, Abby must have had misgivings when she walked down Brattle Street to Longfellow's Cambridge home. She was not surprised when "he gave politeness, but no money. He is a small souled man as his face indicates," she told Stephen afterward.[15]

By the time Abby returned to Worcester in late August, she had raised more than two thousand dollars, a substantial sum in 1857 dollars. However, her ten-thousand-dollar goal was becoming daily less attainable. On August 24 the New York branch of a western insurance company had failed, precipitating a financial panic. After a decade of unparalleled expansion, the nation's economy was suddenly in trouble. The onset of the panic had been so unexpected that Abby saw no reason to change her plans. She and Stephen were expected at the annual meeting of the Western Society on September 5. Afterward they were to travel through Ohio and Michigan with a large contingent of lecturers. The trip was to culminate on October 28 in a much-ballyhooed Northern Convention in Cleveland, where abolitionist leaders from the East would join them. The Northern Convention, so called to remind people of the slaveholders' Southern Conventions, had been in the planning stage for months. A committee headed by Garrison, Phillips, and Higginson had collected more than sixty-five hundred signatures to a call "to consider the practicability, probability and expediency of a separation of the Free and Slave States."

After the Western Society meeting, Abby's teams of lecturers spread out across the region. Abby traveled with Parker and Stephen, Susan Anthony with Aaron Powell and William Wells Brown, while the Joneses and Josephine Griffiths headed the Ohio contingent. The speakers' corps included some new faces, notably Lucy Colman, a friend of Amy Post's from Rochester, and black Sarah Remond, Charles Remond's younger sister. A strikingly handsome woman of thirty-three, Sarah had long wanted to become an abolitionist lecturer but had held back because thanks to Massachusetts's segregated schools, she thought that she lacked a proper education. Encouraged by Abby, who traveled with her in Massachusetts as well as in Ohio, she developed into an impressive public speaker.

Holding more than forty meetings in Ohio, Michigan, and western Pennsylvania, "the campaign continues to sweep bravely onward," Abby reported to the *Standard*. She found particularly receptive audiences among those who had voted Republican in the presidential election and now were disillusioned by the Ohio legislature's failure to repeal the Black Laws or protect fugitive slaves. Even the "ten thousand ridiculous stories" that usually circulated were heard less often, she said. When an opponent did attempt to debate with her, she "coolly, systematically and thoroughly dissected him while the audience applauded the operation."

Joseph Howland, who was making his first trip to the West, painted a less rosy picture. He reported that the abolitionists were vilified as "Free-lovers, infidels and last and mightiest, Abby Kelleyites. . . . Solemn-faced ladies ask us to explain why we associated with such a vile woman and why she had left her pretended husband Stephen Foster and whether it was seven or nine that she had at various times cohabited with."

When Abby and her fellow lecturers reached Cleveland on October 26 expecting to meet a large delegation of easterners, they were shocked to learn that the Northern Convention had been called off. In the months that they had been in the West, the nation's financial panic had become a depression. Banks had closed, businesses failed, mills shut down, and crowds of unemployed workingmen gathered outside factory gates. Because of the state of the economy, Garrison, Phillips, and the others had decided to postpone the convention. They had telegraphed the editor of the *Bugle* some days earlier, but the wire, unaccountably, had never been delivered.

Disappointed, the lecturing force gathered in a hotel room to decide what to do. Sizable numbers of westerners were heading toward Cleveland. The meeting hall was engaged; the press, alerted. To call off the convention now was surely a step backward. They decided to go ahead, if not with *the* Disunion Convention, then with *a* convention, which could take up important business. For two days the lecturers from the East and the delegates from Ohio and Michigan met in a poorly lit, half-empty hall, where there was almost as much criticism of the Boston leaders as of the Slave Power. Parker Pillsbury was particularly sharp, accusing them of acting arbitrarily and in bad faith, comparing their "apostacy" with that of the "new organization" in 1840. His attack was so vehement that Charles Hovey later told Abby that he had been "surprised to see such a speech from Pillsbury. Had it been from your husband I should not have thought it so strange as he so often gets into scrapes."

As the senior representative of the American Society in Cleveland, Abby tried to confine the discussion to antislavery matters. Insisting that the delegates could work successfully without Garrison and Phillips, she condemned "man-worship" and criticized people "for putting out their thinking as they do their washing, to be done by others." The financial panic offered a fresh opportunity for antislavery work. "When physical prosperity is at an end, moral prosperity will begin," she predicted.

Warming to her subject, she struck a new militant note. "Ours is a revolution, not a reform. We contemplate the entire destruction of the present National government and Union. *We must fire up the opposition* and create such a spirit of resistance that our opponents will be pushed to extremes. This is the work we have to do. Every year brings us nearer to the impending crisis."

Her theme was repeated in the convention resolutions. One declared that the Union was "a crime and a curse. We hereby proclaim our purpose in the name of Freedom and of God to seek its destruction." Another, despite the fact that many delegates were nonresistants, urged slaves "to strike down their tyrant masters by force and arms," adding, "We will give them every aid and comfort in our power in the same spirit which brought Lafayette and Kosciusko to the support of our Revolutionary fathers."

Despite the convention's small size and relative unimportance, its strong statements received broad coverage in the press. More than one editorial writer thought the resolutions treasonous and declared that their proponents should be hanged. Perhaps the convention edged North and South closer to their collision course. Certainly it widened the breach between the increasingly conservative members of the Boston clique and their radical opposition, represented by Pillsbury and the Fosters.[16]

16
THE IRREPRESSIBLE CONFLICT

eturning to Worcester, Abby spent time readying her household for the winter before going to Boston to mend political fences. Members of the Boston clique were still smarting at the criticism leveled at them in Cleveland, but Abby assured Maria Chapman that Parker's speeches had been intended as hyperbole, while Stephen had been misquoted in the newspapers. As for herself, although she regretted the Executive Committee's decision to postpone the convention, she did not question its right to do so.

The depression was having a serious impact on the society's treasury. Even when armed with Maria's letters of introduction, Abby was able to raise only eighteen dollars during two days of making calls. Trying to rally members of the Executive Committee, she had a set-to with Samuel May, Jr., who was "all despondency." "Mr. May is a truly good man," she told Maria, "but not infrequently is all in a 'muddle.' He now understands me and feels, I trust, that I am the general agent of the American Society and not an independent force."

Despite her efforts, receipts fell off so sharply that by December the Executive Committee had decided on a program of retrenchment. Abby had the unpleasant task of telling Lucy Colman and William Wells Brown that she could no longer keep them on the payroll and of warning other agents that their salaries might be slashed at any time. The expenses of the New York office were cut by two thousand dollars; that meant dismissal for one of the *Standard*'s coeditors, Oliver Johnson or Sydney Gay. Abby preferred to lose Johnson, who had been "republicanized," but Gay solved the problem by resigning to work on the *New York Tribune*.[1]

Although Charles Hovey warned her that business was so bad that his store was selling merchandise below cost, Abby pinned her hopes for revenue on the Christmas Bazaar. She urged Maria to increase her stock of mittens, socks, and other useful articles and to ask abolitionists to do their winter shopping there. She had not attended a bazaar in several years, but she agreed to be present and to bring Stephen and Alla.

As usual she sent Stephen instructions: "[Alla] had better bring her blue de lain and white and striped aprons and two pairs of stockings. Capes on dresses like her plaid are much worn and I think with her narrow chest it may be best to have some to cover her form. Mrs. Conant may make them and the trimming that was on her cloak may look well on them. The pieces are in the green box in the play chamber. If fringe is needed I can get it here."

The question of where the Fosters would stay during Bazaar Week was a sticky one. Garrison, always sensitive to criticism from his associates, had recently published an anonymous letter in the *Liberator* that attacked Stephen for speeches he had made in Michigan two years earlier. Abby recognized that the publication of the letter was Garrison's way of getting back at Stephen for his statements in Cleveland. At least the letter should have been prefaced by an editorial disclaimer, and she intended to tell

Garrison so. Before she had a chance, however, Helen Garrison had insisted that Abby stay with the Garrison family when Alla and Stephen arrived. "She and Mr. G. are oppressing me with kindness and will not consent that I should stay anywhere but with them," Abby wrote Stephen. Realizing that the invitation was a gesture of reconciliation, she reluctantly agreed to bring Alla to the Garrisons' home on Dix Place while Stephen boarded around the corner with Francis Jackson. "I did not like to come here," she told Stephen in a second letter, but "there is a determination on their part to keep up the old friendship. Wisdom demands that we should bear much for the cause sake, from those who have the same great object at heart."[2]

The bazaar netted thirty-five hundred dollars, less than the year before but enough to make a limited winter campaign possible. At the January 1858 meeting of the Massachusetts Society, Abby made a rousing speech proposing an antislavery revival. "We want every Abolitionist from every little town to ask the General Agent to send a lecturer to his town, and engage to raise his salary and expenses." Her proposal met with only a halfhearted response as discouraged speakers cited the financial panic and the rise of interest in Republicanism and spiritualism as reasons why a revival would fail. It remained for Stephen Foster, however, to say flatly, "It cannot be done. The community cannot be aroused as they were in the early days of the cause. Our people believe in a government of force. They wish to vote. They wish to testify, once a year at least, that there are so many men who go against slavery. All cannot do the same things which Mr. Garrison and Mrs. Foster can do, and which they do so well. But [they] can carry a ballot, and they long to carry one for freedom."

In the free-for-all discussion that followed, Garrison defended the abolitionist movement as practical and efficient while Phillips made a plea for the "old fanaticism." "With all Foster's ingenuity, he has never been able to construct a political platform upon which a sympathizer could stand, nor one even upon which he can stand himself," Thomas Wentworth Higginson said: "The *moral* position of this Society is the highest and noblest possible; but their practical position does not take hold of the mind of the country."

Struggling to rekindle enthusiasm, Abby made a final appeal for support.

She was not asking people to make sacrifices, she reminded them. "That which we gain in education, in enlightenment, in the salvation of our own souls, more than repays all we give."[3]

This was the last speech that Abby made for many months. Alla, now in her eleventh year, was seriously ill. She had developed into a most satisfactory child, amiable, intelligent, and responsible. A journal she kept while her mother was away showed her rising at six, making two beds, and sweeping the chamber before breakfast, then helping Aunt Sarah with butter and jelly making. She raised canaries, had her own garden plot, and wrote stories that her parents thought "first rate." Her school reports were excellent—her spelling better than her father's—and despite her mother's Quakerish reservations, she was looking forward to music and dancing lessons.

Abby had been somewhat concerned about Alla's narrow chest and round shoulders, and Stephen had repeatedly reminded her to stand up straight. But neither had been prepared for the day when it was not a question of standing straight but of standing at all. A spinal curvature, probably scoliosis, had abruptly transformed Alla from an active child to a frightened invalid.

Forgetting her prejudice against doctors, Abby hurried to consult Dr. Henry I. Bowditch, a member of the Garrisonian family and professor of clinical medicine at Harvard Medical School. After examining Alla, Bowditch sent her to Dr. J. B. Brown, a specialist in diseases of the spine, who prescribed bed rest until she could be fitted with surgical corsets.

For almost a year Abby never left Alla's side. While waiting for the corsets to be made, she took her to Newell Foster's home in Maine, where her cousins could divert her during her dreary stay in bed. Back in Boston in February 1858, they divided their time between Francis Jackson's and the Garrisons'. "Her case is alarming," Abby told Maria Chapman, "but I am in good heart, never for a moment believing that she is to be cursed with a life-long sickness or deformity." After each visit to the surgeon Abby sent Stephen progress reports. The corsets were "very disagreeable" at first, but Alla was gradually learning to walk short distances without help. The doctor had prescribed a tonic to improve her appetite. Meanwhile, would Stephen send additional nightgowns and nightcaps? It was difficult to wash clothes in other people's homes.[4]

In April they were able to return to Worcester, where Abby nursed Alla during long months of recuperation and Stephen helped with daily "magnetic" massages, thus imparting some of his "robust vitality" to her weak nervous system. Keeping up her spirits was a task made more difficult because Emma Foster, the cousin who had been Alla's companion since early childhood, suddenly developed tuberculosis and died in August. By then Alla was well enough to play outdoors without supervision and Abby invited Fanny and Frank, the youngest Garrisons, to spend a month on the farm with her.

Although Abby had not formally resigned as general agent, she had time to think only fleetingly of antislavery work. Fretting at her inability to accomplish anything, she begged Wendell and Ann to visit so that she could at least "wash the disciples feet" in return for "the many washings" she had received. Conscious of Ann's need for privacy, she described the parlor, bedroom, and well-ventilated attic she would set apart for them "remote from the rest of the family [where] you will not be disturbed by our noise." She begged them to tell her what she could do to make them comfortable, "for whether I can manage well in some departments, I can never provide 'creature comforts' for others unless I have directions."

Ann never managed to visit Worcester, but the two families kept up a running joke about the time when she *would* come to the farm and feast on "rich cake and strong coffee" with Stephen while Abby kept to her Graham diet. When, like most farmers, the Fosters ran short of cash during the winter, they turned without hesitation to the Phillipses for a loan, which they repaid after the harvest was in, not only with money but with barrels of Stephen's choice apples and pears.[5]

Although Stephen attended conventions in the fall, Abby did not return to meetings until January 1859. There had been no bazaar that Christmas. Maria Chapman had decided to give it up in favor of a Subscription Anniversary—a fashionable soiree with music, tea, and conversations, patterned on fund-raising ventures in England. Members of the Boston Female Society who looked forward to their annual stint at the fair tables were angered by Maria's unilateral decision. Abby sympathized with them, confiding to Ann Phillips her distaste for "one woman power." But when the Subscription Anniversary brought in more than six thousand dollars, almost double the amount raised the year before, she could only agree that Maria had achieved another "splendid success."[6]

The annual meeting of the Massachusetts Society saw a division between "the laughing and weeping philosophers," those who believed the cause advancing or declining. Leading the optimists, Garrison was cheered by the fall elections, in which Republicans had captured almost every northern legislature and had won virtual control of the House of Representatives. The doomsayers, including Higginson, Pillsbury, and the Fosters, put no faith in the Republican party. For more than two decades Garrison had taught that politicians were, by their very nature, compromisers. Basing herself on this teaching, Abby warned that the Republicans, "so near to us," must be rebuked "for their unfaithfulness to the principles we hold in common." She also took the opportunity to rebuke "those who sit in the editorial chair and never [go] out in the field except by invitation" and hence are not able to gauge public opinion. Although she thought that the present was "the most dangerous crisis to which Anti-Slavery has ever been subjected," she predicted that the time was not far distant when abolitionists would again stand together "hand to hand and heart to heart" and agree that the Republicans, like their predecessors the Liberty party and Free-Soilers, were more dangerous than an out-and-out proslavery party.

Although others criticized Garrison more harshly, Abby's were the words that stung. Disturbed by the lugubrious picture she had painted, he attempted, he said, "to give a more cheerful tone to the meeting [by indulging] in a little pleasantry." Instead of replying to Abby's criticism, he spoke of "her cracked voice and gray hairs." His tasteless attempt at humor brought Parker Pillsbury to his feet to rebuke Garrison for his "cruel" attempt to make Abby a laughingstock. Recognizing that he had lost the sympathy of his audience, Garrison immediately denied any attempt to ridicule "one I so loved and honored as A.K.F. who has not a gray hair in her head I am told."* Determined to keep the discussion on a political rather than personal plane, Abby ended it by declaring that she had taken no offense

---

* A photograph taken more than twenty-five years later showed that Abby still had dark hair.

at Garrison's remarks. "What if Garrison should snap me up as if I were a puppy," she told Stephen. She would still remember that he was the slave's best friend.*[7]

The winter and spring of 1859 proved to be dreary for Abby. Alla was attending school, but it would be years before she could give up the surgical corsets. Even then, her parents were beginning to suspect, she would always have a decided hump on her back. The progress of the cause was equally depressing. The Garrisonians were pressing for personal liberty laws that would prevent slave catching in the North. Susan Anthony was hard at work on the project in New York, Sallie Holley in New England, and the Joneses in Ohio, but the laws failed to pass in any northern legislatures. Decades of antislavery agitation had made people aware of the danger of the Slave Power, but increasingly they were putting their faith in the Republican party as an instrument of change.

Without Abby's dynamic presence, no major campaigns were scheduled, no series of conventions under way. Her despair at the slowed pace of the movement deepened when Charles Hovey died suddenly in April, at the age of fifty-two. He had been not only a generous friend but an important political ally. A self-made man who had never joined the Boston clique, he had criticized Garrison's reliance on the Republicans and had insisted that the Fosters' point of view receive a hearing.

Unable to attend the May anniversary in New York because of Alla, Abby was still mourning Hovey when she read the reports of the meeting in the newspapers. Wendell Phillips had delivered a militant speech. Aroused from her despondency, she ran to show the paper to Stephen, shouting, "Hovey's mantle has fallen on Wendell. We still have a radical in the Com[mittee]." Thanking Wendell, she shared her feelings about Hovey, asking, "Who will carry out all his great and glorious plans—his ideas of the brotherhood of the human family?"

Charles Hovey's will, to a considerable extent, provided an answer to

---

* Garrison's "little pleasantry" and Parker's and Abby's replies were not reported in either the *Liberator* or *Standard* accounts of the meeting.

Abby's question. In addition to individual bequests to the Garrisons, Fosters, and others, he had set up a trust fund to promote the antislavery cause and such kindred reforms as woman's rights, nonresistance, and temperance. No less than eight thousand dollars were to be spent annually for newspapers, books, and lecturing agents who would work for the abolition of slavery, basing themselves on the principle of "No Union with slaveholders" and a belief that "the natural rights of men and women are equal." Hovey had designated as administrators of the trust fund not only Garrison, Phillips, and Jackson but Abby and Stephen Foster and Parker Pillsbury. Thus the radicals would have a voice in disbursing a substantial sum of money each year.[8]

Late in May Abby and Stephen brought Alla to Boston, combining a visit to her surgeon with the convention of the New England Anti-Slavery Society. Once again Abby stayed with the Garrisons, leaving Alla in Helen's care while she attended the sessions at Mercantile Hall. A motion eulogizing Hovey was one of the few to receive unanimous approval. Otherwise the convention was virtually a replay of the Massachusetts Society's meeting four months earlier. Stephen condemned "those professed abolitionists" who looked to the Republican party for salvation; Pillsbury and Charles Remond supported him. Garrison and Burleigh dissented while Phillips, playing his usual role of peacemaker, agreed with "a large part" of what both factions said. Although there was no clear-cut consensus, the convention narrowly approved a resolution of Stephen's that criticized the Republican party.

Bothered by a hoarse throat, Abby spoke little. She made her usual appeal for contributions, reported briefly on the good work being done in Ohio, and once attempted to amplify a statement of Stephen's that she thought had been misunderstood. Deciding to forgo the final evening session because she was returning to Worcester on the early-morning train, she was not in the hall when Garrison replied to his critics.

After asserting that the radicals' charges against the abolitionist leadership were "false, unjust and entirely uncalled for," he asked for a reconsideration of Stephen's resolution and was sustained by a large majority. Perhaps encouraged by this endorsement, he then launched an attack not on Stephen, who was generally regarded as a crank, but on his popular wife. Abby, he said, had been obtaining money under false pretenses. While publicly be-laboring the Republicans, she had continued to call on them for contri-butions to the antislavery society.

His censure of Abby came as a bombshell. Charles Burleigh, ordinarily Stephen's severest critic, was the first to ask if Garrison had meant to accuse Abby of "fraudulent intentions." While others questioned him from the floor and buttonholed him in the lobby, Garrison denied imputing "inten-tional dishonesty" but insisted that Abby's behavior had been "unwar-rantable and highly inconsistent" and would be condemned by any impartial jury.*

Asleep at the Garrisons', Abby knew nothing of the discussion until Stephen arrived early next morning to fill her in. Her first impulse was to flee. She and Alla dressed hurriedly, refusing Helen's offer of breakfast, and disappeared through the front door just as their host came down the stairs to greet them. They had time for a brief call at the Phillipses' before catching the 8:00 A.M. train to Worcester.

Back home Abby felt as if she were living in a disagreeable dream. For more than twenty years she had steeled herself to ignore name-calling. But how could she overlook an accusation of dishonesty from the man she revered as the founder of abolitionism? Never mind that Samuel May, Jr., said Garrison had made "an ill-considered speech" and that Abby had "great provocation." Or that Wendell called Garrison's charge "wholly unwarranted" and had asked him to retract it. Or that the Board of Man-agers of the Massachusetts Society, as a demonstration of sympathy, had invited her to fill the seat left vacant by Hovey's death.

Abby was not comforted. She refused to join the Board of Managers and refused to reconsider her refusal even after Wendell told her it was her "post of duty" to stand in Hovey's place, "a post that your knowledge, your experience qualifies you to fill—which the present state of your health & family gives you such leisure as you never had before to attend to—

---

* Again neither the *Liberator* nor the *Standard* reported Garrison's remarks or the discussion that followed.

which the harmony of the cause & its best interests demand you to accept."

Abby declined the seat on the board not because she was hurt, she told Wendell—"I buried my personal feelings before I entered public life"— but because Garrison had destroyed her antislavery usefulness. "My husband thinks with you that I make too much of this matter. Neither of you has had any considerable experience in raising funds. If so you would know what would help, what would hinder and what would destroy you." How could she ask strangers to give to the cause when its foremost spokesman said she was dishonest? The only way out would be a public apology.

An apology was not forthcoming. Pressured by mutual friends, Garrison wrote to Abby almost two months after the incident. He had heard that she believed that he had accused her of dishonesty. "God forbid! I believe you to have always been actuated by the highest and purest motives, however lacking in judgment or consistency. Of all the women who have appeared on the historic stage, I have always regarded you as peerless—the moral Joan of Arc of the world. My admiration of your character and heroism, of your self-sacrificing spirit and exhausting philanthropy has been limited by nothing but the power of speech to express it. Our friendship has been intimate and unbroken for more than a quarter of a century—through how many fiery trials and strange vicissitudes!—and no one out of my family has been nearer or dearer to me than yourself."

But Abby was not seeking private vindication. Garrison had publicly accused her of fraud. "This accusation is upon the wings of the press and is ready to meet me when ever I shall attempt to serve the slave, in the only way that I can now serve him—financially," she replied. "I had intended to go West this autumn to aid the Western A.S. Society. But I am most effectually shut off from this work. Not only the enemies but the friends of the cause will distrust me. Your charge remains unretracted, unexplained, and in full force where it can harm my influence."

In a second and then a third stiff-necked letter, Garrison denied her remonstrances, attributing her problem, as he often did when friends disagreed with him, to "a morbid condition of the mind. Your paralysis of effort—your conclusion that by my injustice you can do no more for the slave indicate that you are not in spirit as you have been, either through bodily infirmity or some mental hallucination."

No, he insisted after she had sent him another twenty-page letter, "I have no 'retraction' to make, no 'apology' to offer, because I do not feel that I have been a wrong-doer." Abby wrote across the top of this reply, "No. 3, which has never been answered because I cannot afford to again defend myself against the charge of falsehood," and then put it in a drawer in her desk.

The pain did not subside. Invited again by the Board of Managers to take Hovey's seat, she quoted from the correspondence with Garrison to show that "a leading member of your body" still believed her behavior "utterly indefensible." Thus she could not join the board "either with comfort to myself or with profit to the cause." Even two years later, when Willy Garrison, now a man of twenty-three, visited the farm in an attempt to make peace, she rejected his kind offices. "I still stand before the world accused by my old friend with a very high crime. How then is it possible for us to meet on terms of social intimacy?"[9]

Undoubtedly Abby was being overly sensitive. Had she not been worn down by Alla's illness and Emma's death, she might have written off Garrison's attack as political and responded in kind. Wendell, eager to keep harmony in the abolitionist family, accused her of being unwilling to tolerate differences of opinion. But Wendell would soon realize that principles rather than shadings of opinion were at stake. After more than a quarter century of struggle Garrison and others in the Boston clique had come to view the Republican party as their own creation. They were ready to forget their stand against politicians, overlook the party's failure to demand emancipation, and coast along with it to electoral victory. This position, however, was unacceptable to many rank-and-file Garrisonians, particularly the black abolitionists. The Republican party "styles itself 'the white man's party,' " Robert Purvis reminded them. It had no place for him. Nor could slavery be abolished without destroying "that twin relic of barbarism—prejudice against color."

Since Abby was the best-loved member of his opposition, it was no accident that Garrison had singled her out for criticism. Nor was it surprising that among the letters of support arriving at the Worcester post office, there was no loving note from Maria Chapman. Rather, in a characteristic behind-the-scenes maneuver, Maria used her friendship with Harriet Martineau to attack Abby and her associates. Some months earlier Maria had arranged to have the *Standard* pay Martineau fifty pounds a year for semimonthly letters on European affairs. Following the Garrison-Kelley rift, the British sociologist used her *Standard* articles to advise the American abolitionists to stop bickering. Without mentioning names—"you know who I mean and they will know it"—she criticized "the fretful narrow spirit, and inexperience of a small number of devoted members" and advised them to defer to "the proved leaders of the cause" or "withdraw and work in their own way."

This officious advice from an observer three thousand miles away widened the gap between the contending forces. While Abby told Wendell that "Harriet Martineau, alias M.W.C. to the contrary notwithstanding," she was not going to withdraw from the struggle, her friend Joseph Howland sent a letter to the *Standard* criticizing Martineau and those "proved leaders" who defended the Republican party.

The Executive Committee had recently given Howland a three-month appointment as a lecturing agent. After his letter was published, the committee informed him that his services were no longer needed. When Wendell Phillips attempted to soften the dismissal by giving Howland a month's salary in lieu of notice, his motion was voted down.

Wendell then wrote to the *Standard* to protest both Martineau's "injudicious advice" and Howland's "captious charges." The difference between the contending abolitionist factions was merely a matter of semantics, he asserted. While Abby or Parker Pillsbury called the Republicans "enemies," he preferred to speak of them as "obstacles" or "hindrances." But even if there were significant differences, the antislavery platform was large enough to accommodate everyone. "I hope no one will leave our ranks," he concluded, "least of all those who are dear to us beyond expression—identified with many brave deeds and sacrifices—gems of our crown, right arms of our strength—'leaders' themselves, approved by long years of matchless devotion."

Maria Chapman did not reply openly to Wendell Phillips, whose prestige in and out of the movement had never been higher, but she managed to have a last word in private. At an Executive Committee meeting when Wendell, fortuitously, was absent, she put through a resolution praising

Harriet Martineau and inviting her to exercise "the largest liberty of thought and expression" in her *Standard* correspondence.[10]

Abby had spent most of the summer of 1859 "journeying, visiting and sea-siding" for the benefit of Alla's health. When she returned home, she found an urgent plea from the Western Society. Reluctant to turn to the Executive Committee, she appealed to Wendell. "I am a sort of medium between the West and the East anti-slaverywise," she wrote. The Ohioans wanted Parker Pillsbury to lecture but "felt delicate" about asking for him because he had resigned his agency following Garrison's attack on Abby. Would it be "proper, legal &c" for the Hovey fund to send Parker to the West and to pay for a new set of types for the *Bugle*? After the Hovey Fund agreed to aid the Western Society, Abby and Stephen made frequent trips to Boston for trustee meetings, seeking help for other pet projects. Over the next years the fund supported Susan Anthony's work in New York, paid for an antislavery book depository that Lydia Mott established in Albany, and supplied money for the preparation of new tracts.[11]

During the New England Society meeting at which Garrison had chastised Abby, she had probably been too preoccupied to notice a tall, spare stranger who sat through most of the sessions in Mercantile Hall and who was heard to say on leaving, "These men are all talk. What is needed is action!" John Brown went into action in October, seizing the federal arsenal at Harpers Ferry, Virginia, in the hope of touching off a slave uprising. The uprising was aborted when U.S. troops captured Brown and his men and put them on trial for treason. Wounded, Brown lay on a cot in a crowded Virginia courthouse for six weeks, using every opportunity to testify against slavery. His last words before his execution were a warning that "the crimes of this guilty land will never be purged away but with blood."

Thomas Wentworth Higginson, Gerrit Smith, Theodore Parker, and other abolitionists had secretly supported Brown, giving him money and advice. Frederick Douglass and Wendell Phillips had been aware that he was planning some action. But for those Garrisonians who still held to a belief in nonresistance, Brown's deed posed a moral dilemma. While deploring his use of force, they could not but admire his courage and selflessness.

Abby expressed her conflicted feelings by saying that she "agreed with John Brown in a certain sense and in another sense disagreed." At a meeting in Worcester she defended Brown against Adin Ballou, who still headed the nonresistant community at Hopedale. When Ballou chided her for abandoning moral suasion, she asked him what he would do if his wife were in the hands of a slave driver and Worcester men were heading south, muskets on their shoulders, to save her. Would he say, "Don't go, but stay here. I have a lesson to teach you against shedding blood?"

On the day of John Brown's hanging the American Society called for meetings across the North as "a moral demonstration against the bloody and merciless slave system." In Worcester bells tolled and the black community wore mourning to express its bereavement. While Ballou stayed at home to write an editorial asking "Are Non-Resistants for Murder?," Abby tried to reconcile her pacifist beliefs with her admiration for Brown. "John Brown conscientiously believed in the rightfulness of using the sword," she explained. "All we can say to the people is 'Oppose slavery with all your soul and strength and use such means as you can conscientiously and effectively adopt.'" Stephen described his own position more succinctly: "I claim to be a Non-Resistant, but not to be a fool. John Brown has shown himself a *man*, in comparison with the Non-Resistants."[12]

During the winter of 1860 John Brown's raid continued to agitate the country. Angry southerners, blaming the abolitionists and fearing slave insurrections, called loudly for disunion. In the North Republican politicians hastened to disassociate themselves from the martyred man. Abraham Lincoln, who hoped to be the Republican candidate for president, described Brown's deed as "peculiar," an "absurd" attempt by a white man to foment a slave revolt, while William Seward, another presidential aspirant, said that John Brown had been justly hanged. At the Republican National Convention, which nominated Lincoln, the party's platform declared Brown "the gravest of criminals."

The election year excitement emboldened Stephen Foster to attempt to form a radical political party pledged to the immediate abolition of slavery. Rejecting the idea of disunion, he took as his motto "Revolution, Not Dissolution." To the dismay of some of his associates, including his wife, he presided over a convention in Boston to organize a New England Political

Anti-Slavery Society. Wendell Phillips attended the meeting and gave it "a terrible overhauling." Abby stayed home.

Ill for much of the winter, Abby was nevertheless present at the major antislavery meetings, sitting on business committees with William Lloyd Garrison and Maria Chapman and speaking occasionally. At the Fourth of July picnic in Framingham, which was advertised as a celebration of "The Insurrection of 1776," she challenged Senator Henry Wilson, the ranking Republican present, to explain the party's position on slavery. She was answered not only by Wilson but by Garrison, who said that although he was critical of some Republican policies, he preferred the party to the Democrats. Although Abby's throat troubled her, she could not let this pass. The Republicans opposed slavery in the territories "where it does not exist," she said, but were "pledged to support slavery where it exists, in fifteen states of the Union, to give up fugitive slaves, and to put down slave insurrections. The Republican party does deceive people, does lure within its embrace large numbers of people who have a desire that slavery should be abolished. Therefore I regard it as more dangerous by far than the Democratic party, which deceives nobody."

In the few minutes left before the excursion trains departed, Stephen agreed with Abby's analysis of the Republicans but asked, "What are you going to do?" His solution was to invite his listeners to a Political Anti-Slavery Convention in Worcester in September.

Poorly attended, the convention was a fiasco. Lucy Stone, in one of her first public appearances since the birth of her daughter three years earlier, defended the Garrisonians and their interpretation of the Constitution. Thomas Higginson urged support for the Republicans in the upcoming election, declaring that "before we could have Foster for President, however desirable that would be, we must have Lincoln," to which Stephen replied, "I love my friend Higginson, but if there is anything I loathe it is his opinions." Frederick Douglass, who was still at odds with Garrison, supported Stephen, characterizing him as "a man of inflexible will and high moral principle, and one of the ablest speakers in the anti-slavery ranks." Instead of a political party, the convention settled for an Anti-Slavery Education Society, which would teach people the principles of democratic government and their duty to enforce them.

Abby was conspicuous by her absence from the convention. "I regret to say that she does not feel the importance of this movement," Stephen confided in a letter to Elizabeth Cady Stanton. "She has no faith that anything good can be accomplished by political parties. But we agree to differ on that as on many subjects."[13]

While Stephen organized in Worcester, Abby had gone to Ohio with Parker Pillsbury for the annual meeting of the Western Society. Estranged from so many of her colleagues in the East, she felt "a gush of sympathy and joy" when she was welcomed by the Joneses, Josephine Griffing, and other friends of freedom. In a speech summing up her antislavery philosophy, she recalled her first visit to Ohio fifteen years earlier, when an end to slavery had seemed imminent. "In our inexperience we did not realize how difficult it is to produce an entire change in the feelings of a whole community. First we had to create in the minds of the people the *idea* of the equality of the black man and white." Not until this idea was accepted could there be genuine emancipation. Although the Republicans were no better than past political parties, she hoped they would come to power, for then people would be undeceived and a new powerful antislavery movement could come into being. "Then we will have emancipation indeed—wrought by working a thorough change in the minds, hearts and consciences of the people."

All that fall Abraham Lincoln stumped the North, his supporters parading through the streets, singing, "Ain't You Glad You Joined the Republicans?" and "Old Abe Lincoln Came Out of the Wilderness." Abby Kelley traveled on the Western Reserve, seeking support for the *Bugle*, "the only paper in all the Western country that is [for] true freedom." Several years of crop failures as well as desertions to the Republicans had left the paper in dire financial condition, but Abby promised to build up its subscription list or sustain the paper herself. Accompanying her, Lizzie Jones was "happily disappointed" that Abby's impaired health detracted so little from her meetings. In a letter to the *Bugle* Lizzie analyzed "that wonderful power she has over an audience. First she understands perfectly the politics of the country and has been conversant with every leading event during the last thirty years. Then her strong sense of justice, her Christian principles and the terrible indignation that fires her soul, manifest themselves in retributive judgment upon the demagogue and compromiser. Every man listens like a culprit at the bar—he hopes to escape by quibble or evasion, but it is of no avail. The only prospect of salvation is in immediate repentance."

Despite her understanding of politics, Abby had no crystal ball. She could not foresee the day when Abraham Lincoln, dubbed "the slave-hound of Illinois" by Wendell Phillips that summer, would become the "Great Emancipator." His election pleased her, she wrote Wendell, because once the Republicans were in power, their failings would be evident. "We shall hardly need to wait a year to see Garrison endorse resolutions strongly condemnatory of the Republicans. [Then] our long quarrel might be dropped and we be all brought together again."

Her wistful prophecy failed to come true. Immediately, in the months before Lincoln's inauguration,* the abolitionists encountered mob attacks as serious as any they had previously experienced. As the South prepared for secession, northern factory owners and factory hands, their livelihoods depending on trade with the South, turned with a special fury on Wendell Phillips, who continued to support disunion. After reading of the menacing crowd that followed him home night after night, Abby wrote to say, "Three cheers for the most ultra of the ultras—the ripest of the fanatics." Although she did not believe that such "good luck" as the dissolution of the Union was imminent, she urged stepping up antislavery agitation to keep the incoming administration from a compromise with the South. Agricultural Ohio, not as susceptible to southern economic pressure as New England, was in "a listening condition," she told Wendell. "Pray help us to the means of agitation" through the Hovey Fund.

Events moved more rapidly than she had anticipated. The week after Lincoln's inauguration, when she spoke in Chapin's Hall in Cleveland, she predicted civil war. She would shed no tears over the war, she declared, for "when rogues fall out, honest men get their best dues. Out of the present

---

* Presidents were inaugurated on March 4 until the ratification of the Twentieth Amendment on January 23, 1933.

strife will grow a new Union in which the rights of all will be respected."

The Cleveland speech marked the end of her Ohio tour. After six months she was too weary to continue. Before heading for home, however, she pledged to make up the *Bugle*'s deficit out of her own pocket if necessary. But when Fort Sumter fell in April, followed by President Lincoln's call for seventy-five thousand volunteers, patriotic fervor was so strong that the Western Society voted to suspend the paper "temporarily." The *Bugle*'s May 4, 1861, issue was its last.

The end of the *Bugle* marked the end of an era for Lizzie and Benjamin Jones, who, after going to Ohio at Abby's bidding, were preparing to return to Pennsylvania. In a final issue of the paper Lizzie again paid tribute to Abby, "this dear friend of all down-trodden humanity":

"With the same earnestness and self-denial that characterized her first appearance in public, and her subsequent career, when she stung this guilty nation by her scathing rebuke of oppression, she came to us this season to do a missionary work that no other person could have done. She came without any compensation, save the approval of her conscience, and has borne her expenses out of her own purse, and I need not tell abolitionists that one who has worked for the slave a quarter of a century, does not own a purse very cumbersome. Her labor has been invaluable. She has talked publicly when she could and in private has strengthened many a faint heart. She has encouraged the weary and has striven to infuse into all a portion of the sublime faith and moral grandeur that have been the inspiration of her own life."

The *Standard* reprinted Lizzie's article with a laudatory preface from Oliver Johnson. The *Liberator* did not mention it.[14]

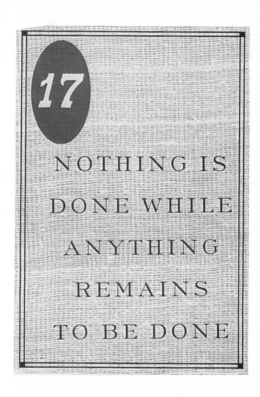

17

NOTHING IS DONE WHILE ANYTHING REMAINS TO BE DONE

All during the summer of 1861 flags waved and blue-coated volunteers marched through the streets until even abolitionists felt stirrings of patriotism. The federal government was waging war against the Slave Power. As a slave said, "When my master and somebody else quarrel, I'm for the somebody else." Nor was there much doubt that the "somebody else" would win. The North had triple the manpower of the South, with factories and railroads to back up its military might. The abolitionists' chief worry in those first months was that victory would come too quickly to bring freedom to the slaves.

To avoid dampening popular indignation against the South, the American and New England antislavery societies called off their May anniversaries. After the outbreak of hostilities Massachusetts abolitionists did not meet until the Fourth of July in Harmony Grove in Framingham. The day was delightful, sunny but with a breeze that carried the fresh smell of pine woods. More than two thousand people filled the benches in the amphitheater and settled back for speeches and song. Chairman Edmund Quincy was greeted with laughter and applause when, capturing the holiday mood of the day, he announced: "The American Anti-Slavery Society has for its Office Agent—guess who? Abraham Lincoln. For its General Agent in the field—Lieutenant General Scott, commander-in-chief of the armies of the United States. They are doing the will of the abolitionists."

Speaking from the platform where he had burned the Constitution seven years earlier, William Lloyd Garrison was hopeful about the outcome of the war, putting his faith in the "diabolism" of the South. Only slightly less optimistic, Wendell Phillips welcomed "emancipation by war" and prayed for Jefferson Davis "so he doesn't run away too soon." After the dinner recess only Stephen Foster sounded a dissonant note, proposing that abolitionists refuse to support the war until the government proclaimed emancipation for the slaves. When half a dozen speakers argued against it, his resolution was voted down.

The time for adjournment drew near. People were closing picnic hampers and collecting hats and shawls when Abby attempted to end the day on a note of unity. The discussion reminded her of a woman who watched her husband fight with a bear and didn't care a straw who won. Just as the woman cried, "Go it, bear! Go it, man!" so Garrison, relying on the diabolism of the South, and Phillips, on Jefferson Davis, were essentially endorsing Stephen's resolution. "There is no confusion of heart, there is no confusion of sentiment," she concluded. "When you sift the matter to the bottom, we all stand upon the platform of the American Anti-Slavery Society."[1]

Over the next years, however, it became increasingly difficult to paper over the differences among the abolitionists with an anecdote. Optimism faded as the war went badly for the North; each defeat and each stalemate made emancipation more remote. Union officers were routinely returning runaway slaves to their masters while General George McClellan, commander of the Army of the Potomac, ordered his men to put down slave rebellions "with an iron hand." Twice Union generals proclaimed freedom for the slaves in their departments; twice Abraham Lincoln revoked the orders, actions that led Stephen Foster to label the president "a greater slavecatcher than Jefferson Davis"—and Lincoln's hometown newspaper to call Foster "a rabid traitor."

Still, despite the administration's caution, the war was bringing about changes. Wherever Union armies marched in the South, slaves dropped their hoes and ran off to join them. When one, two, then half a dozen slaves appeared at Fortress Monroe in Virginia, General Benjamin Butler, hitherto a proslavery Democrat, declared them "contraband of war," like any other property belonging to the enemy, and put them to work. Lincoln accepted Butler's decision, and Congress followed with the Confiscation Act, calling for the confiscation of all property, including slaves, that was used "in aid of the rebellion." Confiscation did not mean emancipation, but when a Union fleet captured South Carolina's Sea Islands in November 1861, the Lincoln administration found itself with eight thousand contrabands and the need to develop a policy toward them. Within months the contrabands had become freedpeople, who worked in the fields to raise food for themselves and cotton for the army.

Abolitionists were divided about their own policy. Garrison, along with most of the Boston clique, wanted to soft-pedal criticism of the administration and work with more respectable characters than himself to influence public opinion. He secretly teamed up with Samuel Gridley Howe and other middle-of-the-road reformers to organize the Emancipation League. Our best plan, wrote Maria Chapman, who was in on the secret, is to "Start the thing by others & then fall in. I have long been in touch with leading N.Y. merchants—the fire is lighting at every corner."

The league initiated a propaganda campaign aimed at selling the idea of emancipation as a military necessity. In addition to lectures and newspaper articles, it sponsored a petition asking Congress to free the slaves and pay compensation to loyal slaveowners. Calling for emancipation for selfish reasons instead of demanding it as an act of justice was a violation of antislavery principles, the Fosters and others insisted. And compensation for "those mythical persons—the loyal slaveowners" had always been anathema to the abolitionists. "Not for my right hand," Stephen declared, would he sign such a petition. Nevertheless, the *Liberator* and *Standard* printed it in every issue, and countless well-meaning people affixed their names to it.

Before he was aware of the work of the Emancipation League, Stephen had sent Wendell Phillips a thoughtful letter urging him to lead a movement to arouse public opinion and compel "a timid reluctant Administration" to proclaim emancipation. Stephen wanted lecturers, "great and small," canvassing every town and village, conventions in key cities—in short, a return to the old days of antislavery agitation. Although Wendell agreed with his criticism of the go-slow policy of the president, he was never comfortable in the role of organizer. Instead he embarked on a series of lectures, even traveling to the Midwest, where he found large receptive audiences. Pulling no punches in his denunciation of Lincoln, he moved closer to men like Charles Sumner, Henry Wilson, and Thaddeus Stevens of Pennsylvania, who were beginning to be known as the Radical Republicans in Congress. He was so successful that Ann was afraid that he was compromising his position as a moral spokesman. "I fear you are nearly popular because you have gone to the worldly men," she wrote when he went to Washington to speak in the Capitol.

While the *Liberator* and *Standard* supported the Emancipation League, other abolitionists joined wholeheartedly in the war effort. To Abby's dismay, the Ohio Society ceased to hold meetings. The press and type of the *Bugle* were disposed of, and the great tent that had sheltered so many stirring gatherings was cut up and sold as secondhand canvas. Thomas W. Higginson became colonel of the First South Carolina Volunteers, the first regiment of ex-slaves to be mustered into the army, with Dr. Seth Rogers as his regimental surgeon. Edward M. Davis served under General John C. Frémont in the Department of the West but had resigned after a year because the war was not being fought on moral grounds. J. Miller McKim had left his post with the Pennsylvania Anti-Slavery Society to work in the freedmen's aid societies that were assisting the newly freed people in Union-held areas in the South.[2]

Abraham Lincoln's conduct of the war only confirmed Abby's distrust of politicians. While most women she knew, including nonresistants, were knitting socks for soldiers or picking lint and rolling bandages, she remained aloof. At the New England Society's meeting in May 1862, she denounced the administration and those abolitionists who supported it. They had lost sight of their first principles, she scolded, and were trying to save the country instead of the slaves. Emancipation as a military necessity would leave the colored race still hated until "the poison of this wickedness" destroyed the nation. "Advancing age always tends to conservatism," she declared, in a dig aimed at Garrison and his willingness to compromise. "We should pray to be preserved in the freshness of our fanaticism."

The debate that she touched off was so engrossing that the dinner recess was postponed in order to allow everyone a chance to speak. Many, including aging Thankful Southwick, agreed with her, although no one went as far as Stephen, who, with his usual extravagance, offered to fight under the banner of the South if Jefferson Davis would proclaim emancipation.

The evening session was marked by an emotional dialogue with young Thomas Earle, son of Abby's Worcester friends, who was a lieutenant in the Massachusetts Twenty-fifth Regiment. Earle described how he and his comrades had defied a colonel by refusing to return a fugitive slave to his master.

"Shame on those who fight for such a government!" Abby called out.

Stung by her comment, Earle stood his ground. "Where would you have been today, Mrs. Foster, if we had not gone to fight for our country?" he asked. "Pennsylvania ravaged, New York ravaged, Worcester burned, your farm destroyed!"

Abby remained unmoved. "Mr. Earle has sustained me in my exclamation. Shame on those who fight for such a government! It is in complicity with the rebellion for [by proclaiming emancipation] it might put an end to the war in twenty-four hours, if it would."[3]

Her participation in the New England meeting was unusual because she had still not fully recovered from her strenuous labors in Ohio the year before. Her energy level low, her throat raw, she was scarcely able to carry out her domestic duties. Alla, leading the life of a normal fourteen-year-old, required less supervision, but she still needed fittings of her surgical corsets. On one of these trips Abby probably consulted a doctor about her own health. She was told that she had dyspepsia, a catchall diagnosis that could encompass anything from indigestion to depression to stomach ulcers.

Whatever the nature of her illness, it kept her from the lecture platform and from most meetings.

Even her eyesight was impaired so that Stephen, the family worrier, feared that she was going blind. But Abby bought the strongest magnifying glasses she could find and continued to follow the war news in the newspapers. Some slow progress was being made. Congress had freed the slaves of the District of Columbia—after how many millions of signatures on how many thousands of petitions for over thirty years—but had paid compensation to their owners, and the president had followed this by proposing to ship the freed slaves to Haiti or Liberia. Nor did she cheer loudly when Lincoln issued his Emancipation Proclamation. The document proclaimed that all slaves in areas still in rebellion were "forever free," but it did not free a single slave, for it applied only to the region controlled by the Confederacy, where it could not be enforced, and did not affect slavery in the loyal border states. "How cold the President's Proclamation is—graceless coming from a sinner at the head of a nation of sinners," Sallie Holley wrote Abby. "A little glad I was," Parker Pillsbury damned it with faint praise while Charles Remond reminded those who hailed the proclamation that "at no time have the spite and hatred toward the colored man been more venomous."[4]

As increasing numbers of slaves were set free by Union armies, antislavery women began to join their nonpolitical sisters in organizing the Sanitary Commission, a precursor of the Red Cross, and in freedmen's aid societies, which were supplying teachers, rations, and clothing to liberated areas from Washington, D.C., to South Carolina and Louisiana. Susan B. Anthony found this kind of war work unsatisfactory. Schooled by Abby in her first days on the antislavery platform, she believed that the activities of the Sanitary Commission and freedmen's aid societies were "common charity, common benevolence," which could safely be left to others. The distinctive work of "we who call ourselves radical abolitionists," she said, was to end slavery and to convince the nation of the common humanity of black people.

She and Elizabeth Cady Stanton, who was also at loose ends, decided to form a women's organization to work for the abolition of slavery, guaranteeing freedom by an amendment to the Constitution. On behalf of the Woman's Central Committee, which, in an initial burst of patriotism, had called off conventions for the duration, they summoned the "loyal women of the nation" to meet in New York during anniversary week of 1863.

Loyal to whom? Abby wrote Susan: "Will you let me know distinctly if you propose to commit yourselves to the idea of loyalty to the present Government? I can not believe you do. If the present Administration had done its duty, the rebellion would have been put down long ago. It needs strong rebuke instead of unqualified sympathy and support."

Agreeing with Abby, the thousand women who met in New York voted to support the government only "in so far as it makes a war for freedom." They organized a Woman's Loyal National League, with Stanton as president and Anthony as secretary, and pledged to collect a million signatures on a petition asking Congress to pass a Thirteenth Amendment to the Constitution that would outlaw slavery everywhere in the United States.

Opening an office in New York City, where the Stantons were now living, Susan set about mailing petitions, counting and collating them when they came back, and dispatching speakers to rally women to the good work. The campaign went more slowly than anticipated because people did not see the need for it. "Has not the president proclaimed freedom?" they asked. "Is he not doing the work as fast as he can?"

Short of money for printing and postage, as well as for a meager salary for herself, Susan went to Boston to ask the Executive Committee of the American Society for help. Turned down flatly, she took the next train to Worcester. "Left Boston in despair," she wrote Elizabeth, "but Stephen & Abby said it must not be. So he went in to Boston to see Garrison & Phillips, & returned with hopeful word." Stephen had convened both the Executive Committee and the Hovey trustees and had insisted on the importance of Susan's project. Although one member of the Executive Committee—probably Maria Chapman—had declared that she would throw the money into the sea before she would use it for this purpose, the others had finally been won over. The American Society pledged three thousand dollars to the women and promised to support the petition drive in the *Liberator* and *Standard*, while the Hovey trustees paid Susan a salary of twelve dollars a week.

Emboldened by this success, the three old friends sat in the Fosters' parlor and mapped out a campaign to assure the drive's success. "We have thought up twelve lecturers—who will make four lecturing corps—to undertake four different districts or states—hold single lectures in small towns, then meet in a grand mass meeting at some central point. We want in each corps a *white* man, *black* man & a woman—and to make the *woman* possible we must have Lucy Stone & Lizzie Jones. The Fosters commission me to make sure of Lucy," Susan wrote Elizabeth.

Abby and Stephen were once more trying to return to the old days, when the goal was to change people's consciousnesses. But by the end of 1863 most reformers were concerned with military rather than moral victories. The elaborate campaign that they worked out with Susan proved to be a pipe dream. Only a small group of lecturers, including Stephen and Aaron Powell, spoke on behalf of the women's petitions, while Abby and others, glad to have antislavery work to do, collected signatures in their communities. The Loyal League never reached its goal of a million, but by the summer of 1864 the women had collected four hundred thousand names, no small achievement. The rolls of petitions, arranged state by state, were carried into the Senate chamber by two tall black men and deposited on Charles Sumner's desk. Early in 1865 Congress passed the amendment, which abolished slavery in all the states and territories of the United States.[5]

The petition drive was just getting under way when the American Anti-Slavery Society celebrated its thirtieth anniversary in Philadelphia in December 1863. Almost everyone who had ever been involved with the movement—"old org" and "new org," Liberty men, Free-Soilers, Republicans—came to the meeting or sent messages of congratulations. There was real cause for rejoicing. Three million slaves were nominally free. The War Department had so far recognized the claims of blacks to citizenship as to permit the enlistment of black men in the Union army. Months earlier a New England convention had adjourned for an hour to permit the abolitionists to watch the Massachusetts Fifty-fourth, the first black regiment from the North, parade from the Boston Common to the waterfront, following the route that a manacled Anthony Burns had taken nine years before. In Philadelphia delegates to the Third Decade meeting visited Camp William Penn, where, on land leased from Edward M. Davis, black Pennsylvanians were receiving basic training.

When the meeting opened in Concert Hall, a squad of black soldiers were seated on the platform with a huge American flag as backdrop, while an auction block taken from a Virginia slave pen served as the speakers' rostrum. Before the meeting was called to order, Abby and Stephen talked with old friends: Lizzie Jones, whom they had not seen since Benjamin's death a year earlier; Amy Post and the McClintocks from upstate New York; Lucretia Mott and Mary Grew; Erasmus and Martha Hudson; Lucy Stone; Susan Anthony; and scores of others. One spectator remarked that it was less a public gathering than a family reunion.

However, some members of the family were absent. Maria Chapman had dropped out of antislavery activity, declaring that abolitionists had completed the "preparatory work" and should no longer "herd apart from the rest of the world." Spending much of her time in New York furthering her son's career as a stockbroker,* she retained her seat on the Executive Committee only in order to vote on crucial issues. Wendell Phillips and Parker Pillsbury had also absented themselves—the one claiming a conflicting lecture engagement and the other pleading illness—as their protest against the president's policies and Garrison's support of them.

Thus it was that after an ebullient Garrison had declared that if Congress abolished slavery, "I pledge that there shall be no more anti-slavery agitation" and hoped that the society would dissolve at its next meeting, Abby Kelley was the first to answer him. In one of the longest speeches she had made in some time, she said that despite the good things that were happening, she did not believe in instant conversion. Emancipation because of military necessity would not mean the change in public sentiment that the society had been working toward for thirty years. "Let us not be too confident," she warned. "Napoleon spoke a great truth when, receiving the congratulations of his generals on their success in Russia, he said 'I want you to remember that nothing is done while anything remains to be done.' Nothing is done while anything remains to be done, so far as the death of American slavery is concerned. I am willing to wait another ten years, if need be, in order to insure its destruction."

---

* Henry Chapman became president of the New York Stock Exchange in 1873.

Garrison immediately replied by thanking God that a miraculous change *had* taken place, but others, particularly Frederick Douglass and Charles Remond, spokesmen for the black abolitionists, agreed with Abby. In a powerful speech Douglass reminded the gathering that the American Society had been organized not only to end slavery but to elevate black people. "When we have taken the chains off the slave, we shall find a harder resistance to the second purpose of this great association," he said. As an instance of the continuing prejudice against blacks, he recalled the race riot in New York City the previous July, when, for four bloody days, a mob had taken over the city, hanging black men from lampposts, beating black women, dashing out the brains of small children, burning and looting until dozens were dead and thousands homeless. No, there had not been a miraculous change in public sentiment. "The work of the American Anti-Slavery Society will not have been completed until the black men of the South, and the black men of the North, shall have been admitted, fully and completely into the body politic."[6]

Within days of the Third Decade meeting, Abraham Lincoln lent support to Abby's and Frederick's warnings with a Proclamation of Amnesty and Reconstruction outlining the shape of things to come. A rebel state could be readmitted to the Union after one-tenth of its voters—white and male—had taken oaths of allegiance to the Union. The states would be required to accept the abolition of slavery but would be permitted to make their own "temporary arrangements" for the freedpeople. The nature of these arrangements became clear when General Nathaniel P. Banks, military governor of Union-held Louisiana, put freedmen to work for their former masters at wages as low as three dollars a month, forbade them to leave the plantations without passes, and ordered Union soldiers to enforce his regulations. Although Banks claimed that this apprenticeship system was "a first step in the transition from slave to free labor," the radical abolitionists and the Radical Republicans in Congress saw it as little better than slavery.

At the annual meeting of the Massachusetts Anti-Slavery Society in January 1864, Phillips attacked Lincoln's program for reconstruction as a step toward a "sham peace" and called for continuation of the war until the freedman was established "on his own soil, in his own house, with the right to the ballot and the schoolhouse within reach." Sharply disagreeing, Garrison supported Lincoln and backed his reelection as president. While newspapers chortled over the dispute between "these two bald-headed veteran disunionists," the Fosters applauded Phillips.

"We radicals have breathed more freely since your speech," Stephen wrote him after the meeting. "Your chart of the channel through which we are now sailing corresponds so entirely with our own that we do not fear to trust the ship to your hands." Abby added a postscript: "My joy exceeds all expression. Tell Ann I give her all the credit for the crystal clearness of your vision at this most important era. It is the best medicine my dyspepsia has had for three years. I think I shall be so set up that in a few months I shall be quite recovered." She signed her note "Yours for the most glorious country the sun ever saw."

By the time of the meeting of the New England Society in May Abby was well enough to take part in the debate. When Garrison urged the reelection of Abraham Lincoln, she reminded the society that it had always opposed the lesser evil. "A choice of candidates!" she exclaimed. "Twenty-four years ago today in Faneuil Hall, the question of how we shall vote was under consideration. We took the ground that we would do right, let the consequences be what they may. Our business is to preach absolute righteousness, absolute justice. Accept no small evils which are sure to prove to be large ones. Are we to give up our old position? Then we become not an Anti-Slavery Society but a political party."

Despite Abby's warnings against involvement in politics, Stephen and Parker Pillsbury—with Wendell Phillips's blessing—went to Cleveland immediately after the meeting, to attend a convention that nominated John C. Frémont as its presidential candidate. A week later Garrison was in Baltimore to witness the Republicans nominate Abraham Lincoln for a second term. All during the long, hot summer, while Grant was bogged down in Virginia and Sherman marched through Georgia, the abolitionists fought a no-holds-barred war of their own. Although the Fourth of July and first of August picnics were called off in order to play down their differences, former friends sniped unmercifully at one another. True to her principles, Abby supported neither candidate, but this did not stop her from criticizing Garrison as "recreant to the ideas of his youth." Susan, Elizabeth, and most black abolitionists backed Frémont and Phillips; Maria Chapman and most of the Boston clique backed Lincoln and Garrison.

Oliver Johnson's coverage of the campaign in the *Standard* was so biased that Wendell Phillips called the paper a "partisan Lincoln sheet" and forbade the treasurer of the American Society to send money for its support. At a hastily called Executive Committee meeting a scant majority rescinded this order but warned Johnson to be impartial in the future.

The *Liberator* was equally pro-Lincoln, but since it was Garrison's personal organ, it was more difficult to attack it. For several years, however, the Hovey Fund had been paying for one hundred copies of the weekly, to be distributed to opinion makers. Now the fund trustees, with Wendell, Abby, and Stephen insisting, canceled this subsidy because the *Liberator* had "no more claim to be circulated by the committee than any other Republican paper." After Sherman captured Atlanta in September, Lincoln's popularity soared and Frémont withdrew from the race. Lincoln was reelected by a substantial majority, but the internecine warfare in the abolitionist camp showed no sign of abating. Following the passage of the Thirteenth Amendment Garrison and his supporters declared that their mission had been gloriously fulfilled and that the antislavery societies should dissolve. Not so, said Phillips and the Fosters. No reconstruction of the nation would be acceptable without full equality for the freedpeople, including land and the vote. They pointed to Louisiana, which was asking to be readmitted to the Union, although Banks's regulations deprived the ex-slaves of political and civil rights. Louisiana's admission would set a precedent for other Confederate states, and the freedpeople would be at the mercy of their former masters. Garrison defended Banks and supported the admission of Louisiana to the Union on the same basis as Connecticut and Pennsylvania, states that also excluded blacks from voting.[7]

The annual meeting of the Massachusetts Anti-Slavery Society in January 1865 was carefully stage-managed by both factions. Surely it was no accident that three ex-slave children from Louisiana sat on the platform as symbols of the victory that had been won. After they sang "I Was Born a Little Slave," bringing tears to the eyes of their listeners, the oldest boy read a speech praising General Banks. The Garrison group won that round but lost the next one. The Board of Managers had decided on a one-day meeting because there was no new business to transact. However, the Hovey trustees engaged the Melodeon for a second day and presented the case for black suffrage. Giving the freedman the vote, Phillips said, "would give him tools to work with and arms to protect himself." Garrison boycotted the session but wrote in a *Liberator* editorial that his opponents wanted "to display their folly and give vent to their personal spleen under the guise of being deeply concerned lest the rights of the colored people should be compromised."

Personal spleen there undoubtedly was. Abby, who at an earlier meeting had vowed to talk until midnight to block a resolution to give money to the *Liberator*, now objected to the reelection of Maria Chapman and Anne Weston to the Board of Managers because "they believe the work of the Society already done." Stephen said that Garrison was ready "to make a compromise with the devil" when he supported General Banks, while George Thompson, newly returned to the United States, called Stephen's charge "calumnious and malicious." But after the name-calling had subsided, Frederick Douglass, Charles Remond, and Frances Ellen Harper, a black poet and lecturer, backed the Foster-Phillips-Pillsbury group by insisting that the antislavery societies continue until suffrage for the freedpeople was won. Garrison's resolutions of the day before were tabled; Phillips's proposals passed unanimously.

The assassination of Abraham Lincoln and the surrender of the Confederates in April 1865 gave special importance to the American Society's anniversary meeting in May. A majority of the Executive Committee backed Garrison when he favored the immediate dissolution of the society, declaring it "an anomaly, a solecism, an absurdity to maintain an anti-slavery society after slavery is dead." But when Phillips called for continuing until "absolute equality before the law" for black people had been achieved, the majority of the meeting supported him. After Garrison said that securing the ballot for freedpeople was not proper antislavery work, Frederick Douglass recalled his first assignment as an antislavery agent when he had accompanied Abby Kelley and Stephen Foster to Rhode Island to war against the Dorr constitution because it contained "the odious word 'white.'" When the constitution was defeated, "we thought it was a grand *anti-slavery* triumph and it was. Slavery is not abolished until the black man has the ballot."

When the vote was taken, three-fourths of the delegates favored continuing the antislavery society. After Garrison refused reelection, Phillips was chosen president, Pillsbury became editor of the *Standard*, and Abby Kelley and Caroline Remond Putnam, sister of Charles and Sarah Remond, replaced Maria Chapman and Anne Weston on the Executive Committee. "Well, if Phillips, P. P. and the Fosters chose to wear 'the old clothes' of the American Anti-Slavery Society after they are thrown aside, let them," Oliver Johnson commented to Maria Chapman. "It will be the old story of the ass in the lion's skin."

With the voting concluded, Abby made her first fund-raising speech in several years. "Public sentiment must receive a deep and radical regeneration," she declared. "In order that this may be effected, mass meetings and conventions must be held, publications circulated, and all the various agencies for influencing the public mind put into requisition."

She made the same plea at meetings of the New England and Massachusetts societies over the next months, when Garrison and his associates urged dissolution and were again defeated by substantial majorities. After the Thirteenth Amendment was ratified in December 1865, Garrison withdrew from the regional societies and discontinued publication of the *Liberator*.

During 1866 southern legislatures, organized under the presidential reconstruction program, not only rejected black participation but drew up Black Codes that severely restricted the liberty of the freedpeople. And in Washington, where President Andrew Johnson was making racist and drunken speeches and vetoing bills that would have offered protection for the ex-slaves, the news was not much better. But when the Radicals in Congress called on the radical abolitionists to continue their agitation, Abby Kelley was too ill to respond.[8]

At fifty-five she could no longer conceal from herself that something was dreadfully wrong, that some monstrous growth was taking over her body. Writing to Wendell for advice about making a will, she confided, "I hardly have a desire to live another six months under such suffering as I have endured for the last. My husband and daughter have both been trying to induce me to apply to some physician, but I have so little faith in physicians, I have not done it. But now I am so ill I can do nothing, not even have the oversight of my family, and I have decided to see if the doctors can help me".

Her old friend Erasmus Hudson had given up both antislavery lecturing and the practice of medicine to design orthopedic devices, particularly artificial limbs for amputees, a business that boomed during the war when he worked under contract with the U.S. surgeon general. When Abby consulted him, he sent her to Dr. Gilman Kimball of Lowell, a pioneer gynecologist. The two men confirmed her fears. She had a "dropsical affection" caused by a tumor on her ovaries. Most ovarian tumors were benign and tended to shrink after menopause. But if the tumor pressed on neighboring organs, causing pain, surgery was a hazardous possibility. Dr. Kimball had been performing ovariotomies since 1855, but despite his considerable skill, 40 percent of his patients died of postoperative infection.

Considering this grim statistic, Abby decided to postpone an operation and see what diet, light exercise, and a tonic would do to dispel the pain. "Stephen has exhausted all of his energies in trying to build me up," she wrote Wendell from her sister's Rhode Island farm in November. "I am getting better," she cheerfully insisted. "The main difficulty remains, but I am so much stronger and have so much less suffering I think I shall throw it all off."

For the next two years Abby's friends rejoiced in her presence at meetings, marveling at her ability to participate despite her obvious ill health. The struggle in the South had shifted when Congress nullified the black codes and passed the Fourteenth Amendment, guaranteeing citizenship—but not suffrage—to the freedpeople. While the amendment was slowly making its way through state legislatures for ratification, the Reconstruction Act of 1867 required U.S. military commanders in the South to enroll black men as well as white in upcoming state elections. These steps toward justice for the freedpeople were met by a rising tide of violence in the South.

After a brutal incident in Tennessee, Abby warned the members of the New England Anti-Slavery Society against complacency: "When in all the rural districts of the South, men, women, and children are held, worked and treated as slaves, I contend that we have not freedom. When some hundred people, assembled at a hall, were attacked by a gang of white men—respectable men, the chivalry of the South—the lights extinguished and atrocities perpetrated—women killed, and others worse than killed—and nothing done to punish the fearful crimes, who will say the Negro is free? We, as Abolitionists, come here to give him suffrage that he may be free, and when that is guaranteed him, beyond all possible peril, then I will vote to dissolve."

"She spoke with divine energy of soul and consecration," said Caroline Putnam, still one of Abby's most faithful admirers. "Those of us who felt that her wasting illness would not spare her long on earth were deeply thrilled with the throbbing of her great womanly heart." Sarah E. Wall, a Worcester abolitionist, was similarly moved. "To me it was touching to hear one who had already sacrificed life to the cause, avow her determination to spend her last breath if need be to secure protection to the outraged colored women of the South," she wrote to the *Standard*.[9]

Not all of Abby's friends were pleased with her political stance in these postwar years. The woman's rights leaders who had submerged their own interest in the wartime struggle had joined other reformers in an American Equal Rights Association, whose goal was universal suffrage, encompassing women as well as men. They were shocked to discover that the Fourteenth Amendment spoke of "male inhabitants" whereas all previous references to voting in the Constitution mentioned "persons" without specifying sex. Quick to see that the phrase would set back the fight for woman suffrage indefinitely, Elizabeth and Susan appealed to their influential friends. But Charles Sumner, who was leading the congressional fight for black suffrage, only shook his head. He had spent some nineteen pages of foolscap trying to get rid of the word "male" without success, he told them. Similarly Wendell Phillips insisted: "This is the Negro's hour." Thirty years of agitation and four of war made black suffrage timely, but the nation was not ready for woman suffrage as well.

For once, Phillips and Sumner realized, principles and expediency coincided. The ballot was vital to the freedmen, who were being cheated of wages and physically abused by their former masters. It was also vital to the Republican party, which needed the freedmen's two million votes in order to retain control of Congress. Without black suffrage the former slaveowners would be back in power in Washington and in legislative halls in the South. Woman suffrage had no such immediate compelling significance—or backing in Congress. To tie it to black suffrage, Phillips said, would be "to have a wagon with uneven wheels."

Although Abby had helped organize a Massachusetts chapter of the Equal Rights Association, she agreed with Wendell that black suffrage was the immediate priority. Through 1866 and 1867 she supported this position, even when it brought about sharp exchanges with both Stephen and Parker, who sided with the women.

"O, Abby, it is a terrible mistake you are making," Lucy Stone wrote her in despair. "You, and Phillips & Garrison and the brave workers, who for thirty years have said 'let justice be done if the heavens fall' now believe that the nation's peril can be averted if it can be induced to accept the poor half loaf of justice for the Negro, poisoned by its lack of justice for every woman of the land. Tears are in my eyes, and a wail goes through my heart akin to that which I should feel, if I saw my little daughter drowning with no power to help."

Writing with difficulty, for even a letter took a toll on her diminished energy, Abby sympathized with Lucy but suggested that her despair was caused by overwork. "Yes, dear Lucy, I have been a hundred times in that same despairing condition. I was over-done and I continued to over-do, and now I am reaping the consequence. Pray be warned and save yourself for woman and the world," she counseled. Recalling that her own entry into the abolitionist field had stemmed from a strong belief in woman's equality, a reform that she had always considered "broader, more comprehensive, more important than antislavery," she explained that "the only question has been which shall take precedence in time. The slave is more deeply wronged than woman and while a nation can keep him a chattel it cannot be induced to allow political rights to woman. I should look on myself as a monster of selfishness if, while I see my neighbor's daughter treated as a beast—as thousands still are all over the rural districts of the South—I should turn from them to secure my daughter political equality. If you see a different path to pursue, I say to you today as I said to you nearly twenty years ago, 'pursue it,' and God bless your efforts now as heretofore."

Retaining her youthful love for Abby, Lucy had concluded her letter with "a kiss for the hem of your garment." But there were no similar affectionate remonstrances from Susan B. Anthony or Elizabeth Cady Stanton. Susan had angrily pledged "to cut off this right arm of mine before I will demand the ballot for the Negro and not the woman," while Elizabeth's speeches and writings about degraded, ignorant "Sambo," whose interests were put ahead of intelligent, refined white women, were increasingly racist.

In New York in May 1867 for a medical consultation Abby attended the first anniversary meeting of the Equal Rights Association. She had not planned to speak, but when Elizabeth said, "The Negro should not enter the kingdom of politics before woman, because he would be an additional weight against her enfranchisement," she walked up to the rostrum. "Were the Negro and the woman in the same civil, social and religious status to-day, I should respond aye, with all my heart to this sentiment," she said. "What are the facts? The Negro is treated as a slave to-day in the South. Without wages, without family rights, whipped and beaten, given up to the most horrible outrages, without that protection which his value as property formerly gave him. Have we any true sense of justice, are we not dead to the sentiment of humanity if we wish to postpone his security till woman shall obtain political rights?"

Abby spoke with her usual vehemence, but she looked so ill that when the Reverend Henry Ward Beecher followed her to the platform, he commented with a striking lack of sensitivity that although he had entered public life at the same time as Mrs. Foster, "I am not so much worn by my labors as she seems to have been."[10]

Over the next months Abby grew worse. Her body distorted, in constant pain, she finally agreed to surgery. Standard medical practice called for operating in a patient's home rather than in a crowded hospital, where the chance of infection was greater. Therefore, on the morning of July 30, 1868, Dr. Kimball, Dr. Hudson, and Miss Sawyer, a nurse trained in surgical procedures, assembled in the Fosters' bedroom for "the fearfully hazardous operation of ovariotomy." So great was the concern among "the anti-slavery comrades" that Hudson reported on the operation for the *Standard*. He found Abby "in a very cheerful and hopeful frame of mind, full of courage. With the most cheerful resignation [she] laid herself upon the operating couch. At her request I etherized her, and in ten minutes she was in an easy unconscious state. The time consumed by the operation was some twenty-five minutes when she was gently removed to her bed. The weight of the morbid mass and its contents was thirty-five pounds. In about one hour she awoke to consciousness, in a blissful state of mind.

"It is now forty-eight hours since the operation. She is cheerful and hopeful, her expression natural, voice strong, and her condition highly favorable for a speedy recovery. Nevertheless she is far from being out of danger by inflammation [but] I entertain the most sanguine expectations of her recovery. Her own *faith*, noble courage and cheerfulness are her sureties."

The *Standard*, displaying Hudson's report prominently on its editorial page, followed with later bulletins from the good doctor. On August 10 Abby "continued steadily and slowly to convalesce." Two weeks later "our noble friend has passed the critical period [and] is now able to rejoin her rejoicing family circle."

Hearing the good news from Dr. Hudson, Ann Phillips was among the first to congratulate Abby and to "thank God that you are given again to us & the world. What a great blessing we esteem it no words can tell. Now be sure & rest long enough. Don't do anything for a long while but just pet yourself & grow strong. Stephen, be sure & dont let her lift her hand except to please herself," she counseled.

Samuel May, Jr., one of the few members of the Boston clique who remained friendly with the Fosters, confirmed that Abby was "doing remarkably well, beyond the expectations of all. The anxious question now is, has she vital force enough left to overcome the effects of the operation. She has taken the most nourishing food possible & some resort to brandy has been found necessary."

Before the end of August Abby was able to walk downstairs by herself. "She sprang—almost—from her chair," May reported. "I look upon her as one raised from the dead." Nurse Sawyer departed, and Sarah Wall came to help with the housekeeping.[11] But Abby took little time to "pet" herself because there was work to be done. Alla was going to college.

At twenty-one Alla was a sturdy young woman with a good mind, a pretty face, and a small, misshapen body. During Abby's years of pain, the driving force that had kept her going was her desire to see her daughter complete her studies so that she would be capable of supporting herself when her parents were dead. However, educational opportunities for women in Massachusetts were scarcely better than they had been forty years earlier. Worcester's high school did not admit girls until 1872, and no college in the state would accept female students. Fortunately there was an alternative that had not been available to Abby—a college for women established by Matthew Vassar on a country estate two miles from Pough-keepsie, New York.

Opening in 1865 in an ornate four-story building, Vassar College offered both a classical and a scientific education which, its founder promised, would equal Harvard or Yale's. It also guaranteed strict supervision of students under the watchful eye of a Lady Principal, who insisted that they dress for dinner and, on occasion, personally measured the length of their skirts. That the president and most of the faculty were men must have displeased Abby, but she approved of Maria Mitchell,* professor of astron-omy, who came from a Quaker-abolitionist background and was known to defy parietal rules by keeping her pupils in her observatory long past the 10:00 P.M. curfew.

Alla left for Vassar in September with a trunkful of clothes and her parents' anxious good wishes. When she reported that no one had met her at the Poughkeepsie railroad station on arrival and that she had ridden to the college at night with a strange hackman, Abby was upset. "In such cases, girls have sometimes been carried to a brothel and imprisoned beyond the reach and knowledge of their friends," she fretted. In this first letter to her suddenly grown-up child, she reiterated a promise that Alla could take the full four-year course—"the funds can be furnished"—and ex-pressed her desire that Alla "should have as thorough an education as you

---

* Born on Nantucket, Maria Mitchell (1818–89) discovered a new comet in 1849. Continuing her stellar research at Vassar, she was recognized as a great teacher who influenced many to adopt science as a career. The first woman to be elected to the American Association for the Advancement of Science, she was also a feminist and a founder of the Association for the Advancement of Women. She and Abby often met at woman's rights meetings during the 1870s and 1880s. (James et al., eds.; *Woman's Journal*.)

have the strength to obtain. As to the question between the Classical and Scientific course you must decide for yourself. Your father says 'tell her if she can enjoy the Greek and succeed in it I should like that she should take it.' " With perhaps a remnant of Quakerish disapproval of the classics, Abby added, "I prefer the Scientific for a person of your organization."

After Alla's departure Abby, feeling that she "had so much to do and so little strength to do it," accompanied Stephen to Canterbury, New Hampshire. His father had died at the beginning of the war, but his mother had survived until the previous spring, dying in her ninety-sixth year. Now that their crops were harvested for the season, Stephen's brothers and sisters were assembling at the old homestead for a reunion. Thinner than she had been in some time, Abby needed to refurbish her wardrobe before going. Sarah Wall—"good kind soul"—remodeled her plain black silk, trimming it with lace from an old dress of Alla's until it was "quite passable. I have it on at this important gathering," she wrote Alla from New Hampshire. She felt stronger, and "all the ten brothers and sisters are very well and in high spirits." It was the last full-scale reunion for the Foster family. Two months later Newell, youngest of the brothers, was attending a meeting in Boston with Abby and Stephen, when he collapsed in the auditorium and died the next day, victim of a heart attack at the age of fifty-four.[12]

The meeting was the founding convention of the New England Woman Suffrage Association, the first regional suffrage association in the nation. As one of its organizers Abby was in an uneasy alliance with Republicans, who were striving to wean the women from the Stanton-Anthony position and convince them that black suffrage must come before women's. Although she still distrusted politicians, Abby found herself in agreement with such old adversaries as Senator Henry Wilson and arguing toe to toe with Lucy Stone. For the better part of one evening session she and Lucy debated. "Hearts and minds swayed first to this side and then to that, as these two women, so loved and honored for their lives of self-denying labor, set forth the grounds on which their respective opinions were founded," the *Standard* reported.

At last, when it was close to midnight, Abby's arguments prevailed. The new association appointed both Lucy and Stephen to its executive committee and elected Julia Ward Howe president. A respectable clubwoman, best known as the author of "The Battle Hymn of the Republic," Howe was a new convert to woman suffrage who was willing, she said in a gracious acceptance speech, "that the Negro shall get the ballot before me."

Abby's speeches at the convention brought her into mainstream politics for the only time in her life. She was still in Boston when Senator Wilson called on her to ask her to help secure the passage of the Fifteenth Amendment to the Constitution, which would guarantee suffrage for blacks. "In an hour's conversation [he] set forth the prospect for carrying the amendment through Congress, and its chances of ratification in the States" she told Gerrit Smith. "Altho' he trusted it could be carried, he had grave doubts, unless our [antislavery] society would inaugurate a series of measures for bringing up the public sentiment to a higher level."

After consulting with Wendell and with Aaron Powell, who had become editor of the *Standard* when Parker left to work with Elizabeth and Susan, Abby planned a yearlong campaign to bring pressure on Congress and the state legislatures. The campaign opened with an appeal to the Senate, surely written by Abby, which reminded its members that "in the moral world nothing is settled until it is settled right." Copies of the *Standard* were sent weekly to members of Congress and to state legislators, who would be voting on ratification. Lobbyists were dispatched to doubtful legislatures to ply "every shaky member with such arguments as shall bring him up to the point of duty" while black speakers from the South traveled to key northern states to give firsthand reports on the reign of terror back home. "To accomplish this work of thorough agitation," she estimated that ten thousand dollars was needed, she told Gerrit Smith in one of her first appeals for money.

Besides Smith and other wealthy abolitionists, Abby turned to the Ladies' Committee, which was planning the annual Anti-Slavery Subscription Festival. Although receipts had fallen off during the war years, the festival was still the American Society's chief money raiser. To make the affair political as well as social, Abby shrewdly suggested inviting John Willis Menard of Louisiana and the Reverend James Sims of Georgia to the festival and to the meeting of the Massachusetts Society the next day. Young black men, they had been elected to office under the Reconstruction Act of 1867—Menard to Congress and Sims to the Georgia legislature—but had been denied their seats. Both were dramatic examples of Reconstruction gone wrong and the freedmen's need for the Fifteenth Amendment.

The night of the festival was pleasantly warm for January. A full moon lit up Boston Common as Abby and Stephen walked along Tremont Street to Horticultural Hall. Along one side of the meeting room, members of the Ladies' Committee received contributions and pledges; on the other, they presided over a refreshment table where guests could purchase ice cream and cake while greeting their friends. The social hour was followed by the reading of poems by John Greenleaf Whittier and Julia Ward Howe and by short speeches by Menard and Sims as well as local talent. "We all agreed that it was the most delightful gathering of its kind that we had ever known," wrote Charlotte Forten, a black committee member. When she and others opened their money boxes the next day, they found that they had taken in $5,125, the most that had been raised since the beginning of the war. "Abby Kelley Foster, well nigh spent in many years of arduous service, and the past year almost miraculously saved to life, was not only able to be present, but by her still great power and efficiency, contributed more perhaps than any other to the auspicious pecuniary results," the *Standard* reported.[13]

At the Massachusetts Society meeting the next day the sessions were unusually harmonious. Even Stephen was on his best behavior, making jokes at his own expense while announcing that he now believed that the society's main business was the fight for the ballot for the freedman. Abby followed with a plea for funds needed to step up the campaign for the Fifteenth Amendment in doubtful states. "The Society must not and cannot die until its work be accomplished," she insisted.

The most impressive speeches at the meeting came from black people: Frances Ellen Harper, describing prejudice in the North as well as the South, and Menard and Sims, with their accounts of violence in their home states. Their presence in Boston—where no hotel would rent them a room—had been as effective as Abby had anticipated. They had dined with leading Republican politicians, talked with officials at the State House, and Sims had even preached a Sunday sermon in Mount Vernon Church. In succeeding months he continued to speak in the North under the auspices of the American Anti-Slavery Society.

Congress passed the Fifteenth Amendment in February 1869. For another thirteen months it traveled from state to state for ratification. Although Abby was not well enough for stump speaking, she kept in touch with abolitionists across the country, calling on them to lobby their legislators and to support the *Standard*, which was giving away thousands of copies of each issue. At the anniversary meeting in May, when she and Stephen stayed with the Hudsons and Alla came from Vassar to join them, she took the floor several times, cross-questioning James Sims and Henry Turner, another black man who had been expelled from the Georgia legislature, in order to make the point that with the Fifteenth Amendment they would be able to maintain themselves in office. She also made clear that she had no illusions about her new political allies. "I give no thanks to the Republican party for having granted suffrage to colored voters, any more than I thank them for having stricken off the shackles in the first place, that they might save the Union. As a party, it has never done anything for the colored man for the sake of justice, for the sake of humanity," she insisted. But by appealing to its self-interest, by showing that black suffrage was necessary to save the party, "we shall be able to accomplish our object."

Abby did not attend the annual meeting of the American Equal Rights Association, held on the same day as the American Society's business session. Stephen went, however, setting the tone for an acrimonious discussion by demanding that Elizabeth and Susan step down as officers because they supported "educated suffrage" rather than equal rights. When Susan said that suffrage must go to "the most intelligent first" and Elizabeth added that she did not believe in allowing "ignorant Negroes and foreigners" to make laws for her to obey, Frederick Douglass upbraided them for their racism. He reminded them that suffrage for the black man was "a question of life and death in fifteen states of the Union" while the ballot for women had no such urgency. Paulina Wright Davis, Ernestine Rose, and several younger women supported Susan and Elizabeth, but the majority voted with Lucy Stone, who now favored the Fifteenth Amendment—"thankful if *any* body can get out of that terrible pit"—although she regretted that Congress had not passed a similar amendment enfranchising women. The meeting marked the end of the Equal Rights Association and the beginning of a split among woman suffragists that lasted for more than two decades.

Abby remained aloof from these hostilities as best she could, her mind still on a single track. Nineteen states had ratified the amendment at the time of the May anniversary, but by summer's end the number was only twenty and the *New York Tribune* warned, "The Amendment is in danger." All that fall she anxiously followed its fate: twenty-two ratifications, twenty-five, then twenty-seven. She was still touring to raise money in January 1870 when one more state was needed to make the required three-fourths.*

At last in February the long wait was over. After Texas had become the twenty-eighth state to ratify the Fifteenth Amendment, the Executive Committee of the American Society held an emotional meeting. Abby came from Worcester, Caroline Remond Putnam from Salem, and Sallie Holley, who was visiting in Boston, was invited to join them. With Wendell Phillips in the chair, the committee agreed that since the primary purpose of the antislavery movement—"to secure for the black race equal rights with the white as citizens of the United States"—had been accomplished "as far as law can do it," the society would hold a victory celebration in New York and then vote to disband.

After Secretary of State Hamilton Fish formally proclaimed that the Fifteenth Amendment was part of the Constitution, April 9, 1870, was chosen as the date of the final meeting. Whereupon Abby Kelley broke all precedent by ordering a new dress, one that departed so sharply from her usual made-over black or gray that Alla teased her about trying to look young and stylish. "How funny you must look in it," she wrote with the frankness that only a college girl could use toward her dowdy mother. The color and cloth were "especially undesirable," she judged, although "it cannot be worse than that red calico. Bows on the belt! O tempora, O mores!"

Alla's criticism did not mar the occasion when "the anti-slavery comrades" gathered in Apollo Hall for a day of "gladness and sadness." From the opening hymn—"Our nation's free!/ Our nation's free!/ How bright

---

* From March 1869 to February 1870 the *National Anti-Slavery Standard* published a weekly scorecard showing the number of states that had ratified the Fifteenth Amendment.

its future destiny!"—to the final resolution to disband, which passed unanimously, the meeting was remarkable for its unity. Lucretia Mott, the oldest person present, Wendell Phillips, Frederick Douglass, Charles Burleigh all marveled at the progress that had been made, differing only on whether thanks should go to God or to man. Speaking briefly, Abby paid tribute to the absent William Lloyd Garrison, who had started the great struggle. Then, unable to resist a captive audience, she reported on the future of the *National Anti-Slavery Standard*, the paper she had helped keep afloat for thirty years. Dropping the first words of its name, it would become the *Standard*, an independent journal of "Reform and Literature," edited by Aaron Powell—and it would still need support.

Although she also mentioned a homestead bill that, if passed by Congress, would give land to the freedpeople, Stephen was the only speaker who dwelt on the work that remained to be done. Explaining that he felt more at home fighting battles than celebrating victory, he reiterated Abby's appeal for land for the freedman—"without which he would not be free to vote"— but saw the crusade of the future as a contest with "the spirit of caste.

"Nothing is so insipid and disgusting to me as to walk up and down New York streets, where every man is white, and all look as if they came out of the same bandbox. I want the hand of the Lord to shake this pale face of ours out of its self-conceit. . . . I blush in the presence of the Indians. . . . Then there are the Chinese. The very report of their coming has frightened half of your Republican Senators out of their faith in universal suffrage. These are the future labors to which you are summoned. Do not imagine that you have the right to take off the harness," he concluded.

Stephen was correct, but for this one day, Abby gloried in the success of the movement and all the changes that had taken place in her lifetime. "Have we not moral as well as physical rail-roads and telegraphs?" she asked. "I feel as if I had lived a thousand years."[14]

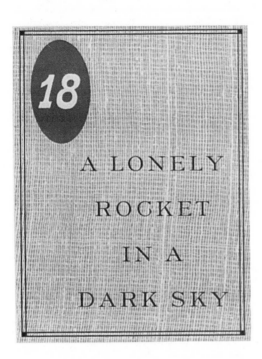

18

A LONELY ROCKET IN A DARK SKY

" Y our father has [won] for the first premium on apples and pears a plated ice pitcher and a plated cake basket, each valued at fifteen dollars, besides one dollar on Hubbard squashes," Abby reported to Alla. "So your long cherished desire for an ice pitcher is gratified. I have not yet seen them but they are said to be very good."

Throughout Alla's college years Abby wrote weekly, usually on Fridays, and Alla replied with equal regularity. The handful of letters that have survived reflect affection and respect, with no attempt on Abby's part to coerce and no attempt to rebel on Alla's. Gone was the didactic tone that Abby had employed in Alla's childhood. Now she was writing to an equal, sharing the details of life on the farm, reporting on family and friends and,

357

less often, on the reform work in which she was involved. Could Alla advance her Christmas vacation by a few days in order to celebrate her parents' twenty-fifth wedding anniversary? "We feel a desire for *a visit*, a *real visit* from you." Would she like to go to Boston for the Woman Suffrage Bazaar? "I shan't go," her mother added. "I am not well enough. And if I were, I don't like Bazaars enough to think it would pay."

On a trip to Boston in 1870 Abby had talked with Louisa May Alcott, whose *Little Women*, published the year before, was a staggering success at home and abroad. "I upbraided her for not allowing Jo to remain an old maid," Abby wrote Alla. "She replied that it was not her fault that she married. She left her as she should be, in sublime maiden-hood, blessing the whole world and being blessed in return, but her friends set up such a howl against it, and the publisher joining the chorus, saying it won't sell half as well, the change was inevitable. But by and by her old maid will come. So she promises."

Alla's clothes, too, required considerable discussion. Made by a dressmaker in Worcester during college vacations, her wardrobe had to be planned in advance. Abby sent her a pattern for a basque, clipped from the *Worcester Spy*, and discussed the pros and cons of a grenadine, a silk dress covered by a thin gauzy material. Abby thought the grenadine too hot for summer, but if Alla wanted it, she would rip her own old black silk to use for the undergarment. The black silk was still serviceable "to wear under a shawl at home and to wear into the city or to other places where the waist could be covered," so Alla must let her know her wishes as soon as possible.

For her part, Alla reported on her courses: "English Literature drives me nearly frantic. I have [written] nine pages on Chaucer, though the minor authors take only three or four. . . . We have delightful experiments in Natural Philosophy. . . . German is no play." She enjoyed a lecture on Sir Philip Sidney given by George William Curtis, a lyceum lecturer but was disappointed when the faculty twice refused to let Wendell Phillips speak on campus because he was too radical. Although she did not have her parents' capacity for indignation, she was exasperated by this and other narrow aspects of Vassar life, as when drama students put on a bowdlerized version of *Romeo and Juliet*, omitting Romeo altogether because "Miss

Lyman will not allow any one to dress in male attire." When, during Alla's junior year, Miss Lyman died, President Raymond* asked the students to wear a crepe mourning badge for thirty days. "I do not bow to the decision of the majority in this case," Alla told Abby, although she contributed to a fund for flowers for the Lady Principal's funeral.

Occasionally Abby ventured to suggest a campaign for students' rights. "You think very little would be gained by a small number leaving the college because of its oppression," she wrote in 1870. "We think you are entirely mistaken. Should only one leave for good reason, and publicise in a few respectable journals the reasons for so doing, it would effect a radical change." Alla would not hear of it. "I am so proud of you and father, that you are both so devoted to all the reforms. I am sure that I shall never do anything half so useful. But the children of good and great people are apt to [be] ugly or forceless, and I think you and I should be thankful that I am not any worse."

A serious, if not a brilliant, student, Alla was elected to Phi Beta Kappa when she graduated from Vassar in 1872. That fall she went to Cornell University for graduate study in history, one of the first women to enter the new university.† When newspapers reported that Cornell women were lagging behind their male classmates, Stephen Foster wrote to ask for his daughter's grades and was pleased to learn that she had a 4.25 average out of a maximum of 5. After a year at Cornell she returned home to support herself by teaching high school students while she completed a dissertation. She received a Master of Arts degree from Cornell in 1876.[1]

Although they missed Alla, Abby and Stephen were neither lonely nor bored. Stephen was still performing backbreaking labor on the farm, where two decades of plowing and composting had transformed thin, stony soil into fields of high fertility. The farm was barely a paying proposition, but Stephen hauled early vegetables to market in June, sold eighty quarts of

---

* Hannah W. Lyman was Lady Principal, John H. Raymond, president of Vassar.

† Cornell University opened in 1868, and the first women were permitted on campus in 1872. (*Woman's Journal*, June 14, 1873.)

milk daily in summer, and harvested bushels of pears and apples in the fall. The fruit trees that he had carried from New York State, planted, grafted, and pruned were now in their prime, winning prizes annually at the county fair in Worcester and commanding top prices. As the season wound down, he and Abby made cider with the windfalls and packed barrels of fruit for special friends. With obvious pride Stephen itemized the contents of a barrel intended for Wendell and Ann. "First are the pears, some of which will be good, if not too much jammed. The apples are of various kinds. First are Primates, Leland's Spice, Shepard with a few Greenings, which are large but will not keep. Next come the Porters— then a few specimens of Baldwins, Hubbardston, Nonsuch, Northern Spy, Yellow Bellflower, Peck's Pleasants, & perhaps one or two other kinds— all specimens on which I took a premium at our recent Fair. In the bottom are Greenings which will keep till Winter, as will all the kinds which lie buried below the Porters. Say to Ann that she need not fear to eat freely of them, as they cannot harm a stomach that can bear *cake & coffee*."

Abby was no longer strong enough to milk the cows or harvest the fruit, but she was still a country woman who appreciated the cycle of the seasons that drew her to the vegetable garden in spring and to the meadow where wild raspberries and blackberries ripened in midsummer. Gathering and preserving the berries were women's special province, part pleasure, part chore, as, in Sallie Holley's words, they "picked and pickled and dried and pied and puddinged and preserved and stewed and stuffed."[2]

Occasionally, when the upkeep of the farm became burdensome, Abby and Stephen considered moving to more urban surroundings. Lucy Stone and Henry Blackwell, who had bought a house in Dorchester, overlooking Boston Harbor, reported that there were bargains to be found in their neighborhood. The Fosters went to Dorchester to inspect the area but quickly returned to Mower Street. Their once-ramshackle building was now pleasant and comfortable, its brick facade scrubbed, its leaky windows puttied, its floors made level. Stephen had even installed a bathtub, a much appreciated luxury after a lifetime of heating water on the stove and filling a tin tub. Shade trees had grown up around the house, and a lawn sloped down to a magnificent stone wall that bounded the property. Stephen had built the wall over the years, prying the stones from the furrows as he plowed and painstakingly laying them atop one another until the wall was six hundred feet long and "wide enough and solid enough for President Grant's four-in-hand to drive upon," Thomas Higginson declared.

As Worcester grew from town to city, Tatnuck had lost some of its remoteness. There was a post office now within walking distance, and the Worcester Horse Railroad stopped twice daily at the Fosters' corner, making it convenient for visitors. Abby's guest list had changed with the changing times. Sallie Holley had discontinued antislavery lecturing after the ratification of the Fifteenth Amendment and had joined Caroline Putnam in Virginia, to run a school for freedpeople. The Holley School, as it was known, received a barrel of Stephen's choice apples every fall, but the two women no longer traveled to Massachusetts. Others came in their stead. Theodore Weld, who, with Angelina and Sarah, had moved to Hyde Park, south of Boston, stayed overnight when he lectured in Worcester—"A great feast to us," Abby wrote when she begged Angelina to come, too. Erasmus and Martha Hudson came from New York from time to time; Elizabeth Buffum Chace and her daughter, Lillie, a contemporary of Alla's, stopped in Tatnuck on their way to woman's meetings in Boston, and Wendell Phillips never failed to call when in the neighborhood. He continued to be the Fosters' most faithful correspondent—more than a score of scrawled notes from him in this period attest to their enduring friendship—but Ann's health had steadily worsened, and she no longer joked about visiting. During summers, when they stayed in Princeton, ten miles from Tatnuck, Wendell always contrived to come to the farm, even if it meant arriving on the 9:00 A.M. train and departing at 4:00 P.M. For her part, Abby called on them when in Boston; Ann, who seldom received visitors, made an exception for Abby and even asked to meet Alla.[3]

New friends who were glad to exchange Boston's summer heat for cool country air included the Reverend John T. Sargent, president of the Massachusetts Anti-Slavery Society during its last years, and his wife, Mary, who had taken charge of the antislavery festivals after Maria Chapman's default. A Unitarian minister who had lost his pulpit after inviting Theodore Parker to speak, Sargent credited Abby and Stephen with bringing him into the antislavery movement. During a ten-day stay on the farm he painted an idyllic picture: "Only think what a recreation it is, to ruralize and have daily converse with such a man and such a woman, amid their ripening and gathering sheaves, the singing birds, the fruits of [their] orchard, the quiet of the lovely vale."

Comparing Stephen the abolitionist lecturer with Stephen the farmer, Sargent wrote, "How he shook those skunks of Southern oppression! How he made the feathers fly from all vultures south of the Mason Dixon! He went right into the affair with sleeves rolled up, as it were, just as he hoes corn, prunes a vine or digs potatoes. Southern pretensions fell down before him like the weak stubble and meadow hay under his scythe. And what he did not do or finish, you may be quite sure his wife did and does."

Had Abby been a hostess with social pretensions, she could have looked on the Sargents as a great catch, for in winter their spacious home on Chestnut Street was headquarters for New England intellectuals. On the first Monday of every month they were hosts to the Radical Club, a coming together of aging transcendentalists, liberal theologians, writers, and reformers, including Ralph Waldo Emerson, Bronson Alcott and his daughter Louisa, Samuel Longfellow, Thomas Higginson, Elizabeth Peabody, and Julia Ward Howe. The Reverend John Weiss read a paper on "The Immanence of God," to which Wendell Phillips responded with a defense of orthodox religion; Emerson spoke on "Greatness"; the Reverend William Ellery Channing warned of the coming struggle between labor and capital; and a Harvard scientist outlined Darwin's theory of the origin of species. The club was loosely organized, without bylaws or constitution, but Mary Sargent contrived to invite all progressive-minded visitors to the city to attend. Thus at any meeting guests might include Ellen and William Craft, the former slaves who had been helped to freedom by Boston's Vigilance Committee and were now returning to their native Georgia to establish a communal farm; Edmonia Highgate, who had been teaching freedpeople in Mississippi; Charlotte Forten, Lucretia Mott—and Abby Kelley.

Abby attended the meetings of the Radical Club whenever she came to Boston, bringing Alla with her during college vacations. She made some "interesting remarks" after Bronson Alcott and Robert Dale Owen discussed utopian governments, and she talked at length when Aaron Powell read a paper on "The Lesson of Quakerism." As a birthright Quaker she was more critical of the society than Powell or other club members had been. When a young woman, she recalled, she had been "without God, without hope in the world, with no anchor for [my] soul" until she encountered the "living work" of the antislavery movement. "Inspired by the doctrine that he who loves God will love his neighbor, *there* I saw Christianity and went to work in accordance with it," she said. Impatient with the abstract tone of the discussion, she added that she was still working hard for the black people of the South and thus had no time for theological speculation. "My life has always been a life of labor," she concluded. "I am not intellectual nor aesthetic and could not answer questions belonging to those departments."[4]

Although Abby may have felt uncomfortable discussing philosophy with Emerson or Alcott, her ideas on religion did not differ widely from those of the transcendentalists. She had long ago given up a belief in a personal God, substituting the Good or, as a poem she still remembered from boarding school phrased it, "Thou great first cause, least understood." When Alla was a child, she had spoken to her of this "great first cause" as God because it was "a good name answering to our Christian idea of its omnipotence, omnipresence, omniscience and all beneficence." In the future, Abby believed, "We shall grow more like Him and know him more and more." Alla later said: "She was sure of this continued existence. A life of labor, not of rest, for she believed that only by struggle could spiritual and intellectual powers be developed. Her religious belief was a part of her very being and gave a calmness and peace to her later life which enabled her to live or die with equal resignation."

At the Radical Club and other gatherings Abby made an accommodation of sorts with William Lloyd Garrison. Encountering him at the old Anti-Slavery Office, she had been unable to resist inquiring about Helen and the children. "I had a pleasant interview with her," Garrison told his wife. "She being in a tender state of mind and rejoicing to hear of Fanny's engagement, Wendell's prospective marriage and your improving condition." Once the ice was broken, they met with fair frequency at the Sargents' and at woman's rights meetings. Relations remained lukewarm, however, until they found themselves equally concerned about conditions in the South.

As the radical abolitionists had predicted, the freedpeople were rapidly losing their rights. Without land, tools—or repeating rifles—they were hard put to defend themselves against the Ku Klux Klan and other terrorist groups. After the closely contested presidential election of 1876 congressional leaders struck a bargain. Republican Rutherford B. Hayes was installed as president in return for his promise to withdraw from the South the federal troops that had been the ex-slaves' only bulwark. When Garrison sent a letter to the *New York Times* sharply criticizing Hayes's conciliatory policy toward the "old slave oligarchy," Abby wrote to thank him for "his very forceful and much needed letter." He replied with praise for her "discerning spirit and true standard of judgment," signing his letter "Yours for 'the good old cause.' "[5]

Since there was little she could do for the freedpeople, Abby turned to other work. "Worcester is in the most deplorable condition on temperance," she wrote a friend. "A most besotted city and hardly an influential name to work against the curse. Almost every professional man, also those in public positions are moderate drinkers, and some, even habitual drunkards." Radical temperance men and women were needed to fight the apathy, she declared, for there was no middle ground between the unrestricted sale of liquor and absolute prohibition. While Stephen "thumped and thundered" at local temperance meetings, she joined other women on visits to rum sellers. When, in 1875, after four years of agitation against the dramshops, the Massachusetts legislature passed a local option law that permitted voters to decide whether their communities should be wet or dry, she was the first woman to stand at the polls distributing ballots that opposed all liquor sales. Despite her efforts, Worcester remained wet, although she and Stephen succeeded in closing down the tavern in Tatnuck, near their home.[6]

Temperance remained high on her agenda, and she joined the Woman's Christian Temperance Union* when a Massachusetts chapter was organized, but Abby's main preoccupation in the 1870s was woman's rights. The movement was now divided into two broad organizations: the National Woman Suffrage Association, headed by Susan B. Anthony and Elizabeth Cady Stanton, and the American Woman Suffrage Association, with Lucy

---

* Founded in 1874 in Cleveland, Ohio, the WCTU still has some fifty thousand members. (Flexner; *New York Times*, Sept. 14, 1989.)

Stone, Henry Blackwell, and Julia Ward Howe at the helm. The goal of both organizations was suffrage, but their tactics and organizational structures differed. The more militant National Association lobbied Congress for a Sixteenth Amendment to the Constitution, sponsored demonstrations at the polls, and spoke out on a range of women's issues—wages and working conditions, education, marriage, even the touchy subject of divorce. Less strident, the American Association avoided side issues and concentrated on winning suffrage, state by state. Critics accused the National Association of favoring free love; the American Association was said to be an adjunct of the Republican party. To publicize their views, Susan and Elizabeth edited a short-lived paper called the *Revolution*; the better-financed American Association issued the *Woman's Journal* from 1870 until well into the twentieth century.

Had Abby been in good health and a resident of New York or Washington, where most National Association meetings were held, she might well have joined forces with Susan and Elizabeth—once she had managed to forgive them for their apostasy during the Fifteenth Amendment campaign. But since she was not well enough to travel, she remained loyal to Lucy and the affiliates of the American Association, the New England and Massachusetts suffrage associations. Their meetings were stodgy compared with antislavery meetings. Usually they opened with a prayer from a woman preacher and closed with the singing of the "Doxology." The secretaries who took minutes referred to "Mrs. S. S. Foster," "Mrs. Samuel Howe," and even on one occasion called Lucy Stone "Mrs. Blackwell," once an unforgivable affront in Lucy's eyes. Unlike the abolitionists' gatherings, where anyone had been permitted to take the floor and opposing views were encouraged, the suffrage women allowed only paid-up members to speak and vote. It remained, therefore, for Abby and Stephen—"those indefatigable stirrers-up of public feelings, and woeful destructives of the public's self-complacency," as Samuel May* described them—to stimulate debate. There was seldom a meeting where one or the other did not propose

---

* After the death of his father in 1870 May dropped "Jr."

strongly worded resolutions and aggressive action. When a speaker resolved that opposition to woman suffrage was "inconsistent with Republican principles," Stephen amended the resolution to "They who seek to deprive woman of the ballot are tyrants and despots." Lucy, Henry, and Julia Ward Howe argued against the change, but Abby insisted that "severe language" was necessary to every reform. "[William] Ellery Channing convinced the intellect of the sin of slavery, but William Lloyd Garrison was needed to sting the conscience into action," she reminded the meeting.

Abby criticized a resolution that thanked Massachusetts's governor for his halfhearted support of woman's equality; there would be time to thank him when he had done something useful, she said. When a woman proposed "asking" a public figure for assistance, she amended it to "demanding." Time and again she called for stronger resolutions: "The whip needs a snapper" or "Harmony! I don't want harmony. I want truth."

Following a *Standard* report that said that Stephen had called suffrage opponents "sneaking villains," he wrote an amused letter of correction. "That I am fond of epithets in dealing with 'wickedness in high places' and have great faith in their utility, I cheerfully admit. Whenever I have occasion to use an epithet, my aim is to select one which accurately describes the particular characteristic which I wish to make odious. [Sneaking villains] has no such descriptive character, but applies equally well to a great variety of crimes and for this reason [is] of little value." He went on to defend his "moral caustics" by comparing them with Jesus' excoriation of the scribes and Pharisees as "Ye serpents, ye generation of vipers."[7]

After the Republican party had failed to keep its promise to the women in the 1872 campaign, the Fosters offered "stinging denunciations" of the party—to the discomfort of Henry Blackwell, who had worked hard for Grant's election. Lucy, plump and motherly-looking with a white lace cap covering her smooth gray hair, was no longer the rebel of earlier years. Although she, too, must sometimes have wished that the Fosters would be quieter, she never failed to remind the women of a new generation of "the reverence due them for their devotion to the cause of liberty."

Other women were less forbearing. Mary Livermore,* who had not been an abolitionist and had led the Sanitary Commission during the war, was coeditor of the *Woman's Journal*, along with Lucy and Henry. She was one of the few who dared challenge Stephen, calling him "intolerant and unreasonable" and saying that suffragists must exercise "a Christlike spirit." Abby, who was usually on her husband's side these days, replied, "Rebuke of sin was one important exercise of a Christlike spirit. Plain denunciation of wrong is a duty now, no less than in antislavery days."

Although they risked antagonizing the younger women by their pungent phrases, more was at stake than semantics. The movement was making slow progress, they thought, because the women were "too tenderhearted" to accomplish anything. Each year they presented petitions asking the legislature for a change in the state constitution to permit women to vote, and each year they were turned down. A handful of lecturers traversed the state, finding their widest audiences in Worcester County, where Abby worked to arrange meetings, but new tactics were needed to prevent the movement from stalling. It was time, Abby declared, for "a Bunker Hill battle in the Woman's Rights contest."[8]

In 1872 she and Stephen decided to bear witness in a dramatic way—by refusing to pay taxes on their jointly owned farm until Abby was permitted to vote. The timing was propitious. The centennial of the Boston Tea Party was to be commemorated in 1873, and the nation was planning a mammoth one hundredth birthday celebration three years later. Few would need to be reminded of the revolutionary slogan "Taxation without representation is tyranny." Nevertheless, at the annual meeting of the Massachusetts Woman Suffrage Association in 1872, when Abby proposed that all sign a pledge to withhold their taxes "till the aristocracy of sex" was eliminated from state law, only Sarah Wall and Margaret Flagg, a Worcester widow, were willing to affix their names to it.

---

* A tall, square-jawed woman with curly auburn hair, Livermore resigned from the editorship of the *Woman's Journal* in 1872 and became so popular on the lyceum circuit that she was known as Queen of the Platform. (James et al., eds.)

A tax protest was not altogether a new departure. A younger Lucy Stone had refused to pay taxes on her New Jersey cottage in 1858* and had stood by when a tax collector auctioned off three tables, four chairs, and a steel engraving of Gerrit Smith. A neighbor had bid them in and returned them to Lucy, but the incident had been unsettling. Respect for property and for paying one's debts was so firmly embedded in the Protestant ethic that few had emulated her.

Having braced themselves for the contest, the Fosters were let down when more than a year passed with nothing happening. They had been notified that the farm would be sold if they did not pay up, but no date for a sale had been set. Eager to get on with the protest, Abby called on the tax collector to suggest, with as straight a face as she could command, that the sale take place on the Fourth of July, "a peculiarly appropriate time for the enforcement of the principle of taxation without representation." With an equally straight face, the official replied that he had such a backlog of cases that he would not reach hers until the following spring. Fearful that the town fathers had decided not to prosecute, Stephen demanded that the matter be disposed of immediately. "If we are wrong in resisting the law we ought to suffer. If right, we can afford to, as it is only through suffering that the few can lift the many to a higher plane," he wrote to the *Woman's Journal*.

Worcester's officials were in a disagreeable position. Undoubtedly they had little desire to make headlines by seizing the home of a well-known, elderly couple. On the other hand, there were a considerable number of citizens who demanded that those "fanatics" be made to obey the law or take the consequences. At last a "City Collector's Notice" was published in the local papers. The Foster homestead in the Tatnuck district would be sold at public auction on February 20, 1874, unless they paid taxes of $69.60 plus interest and costs.

---

* In 1915 a thousand suffragists watched as a bronze tablet was unveiled on Lucy Stone's New Jersey home. Its inscription: "In 1858 Lucy Stone, a noble pioneer in the emancipation of women, here first protested against their taxation without representation." (Blackwell.)

Although Abby had been looking forward to the confrontation, surely she felt a pang when a deputy collector nailed a sign to her front door: WILL BE SOLD AT PUBLIC AUCTION. But she and Stephen immediately went into action, calling a Convention on Taxation Without Representation, to be held in Worcester the day before the sale. All the old-time reformers were invited to participate. Pleading a previous engagement, Thomas Higginson wrote: "These sales of property are to the Woman Suffrage movement what the Fugitive Slave cases were to the Anti-slavery movement. They are the nearest we can come to 'the blood of the martyrs.' " Also regretting his inability to be present, Garrison wrote of his "profound respect" for their action, "for I know you are not actuated by personal pique, or factious whim, or desire of notoriety, but simply by the truest self-respect, the finest sense of justice, the loftiest patriotism, and the highest appreciation for the principles of liberty and equality."

The convention, held in Washburn Hall, was a lively one, with Samuel May presiding, Alla acting as secretary, and Lucy Stone making a moving speech about Abby: "This woman who towers head and shoulders above every woman in the state, who gave the strength of her youth and the wisdom of her mature life, and all her substance to free the slave, now feeble by advancing age and by hard service for her country, tomorrow will have her house sold over her head because, like Jefferson and Adams and Hancock, she believes taxation without representation is tyranny."

In the past month the tax protest had received unexpected support from two spunky elderly women from Glastonbury, Connecticut. Julia Smith, aged eighty-two, and her sister, Abby, seventy-seven, had never attended a woman suffrage meeting, but when Glastonbury officials raised their taxes, they refused to pay them because they had not been permitted to vote on the town budget. In January 1874 a tax collector had seized seven of their cows to cover the delinquency. These were not ordinary cows but pets that answered to the names of Daisy, Minnie, Bessie, and so forth and would not permit anyone but the Smiths to milk them. After the editor of the *Springfield Republican*, recognizing a colorful story, described the cow auction, newspapers across the country carried articles on the sisters, and the *Woman's Journal* initiated a campaign to "BUY BACK THE COWS!"

At the Fosters' invitation, the sisters had come to the meeting. Abby

Smith, making her first public speech, said, "They can't shut us up as they did our cows." In the excitement of the moment Henry Blackwell proposed that all women refuse to pay taxes, but when Abby Kelley suggested that men, too, refuse, he hastily withdrew his proposal. The meeting rejected a resolution of Stephen's declaring that "taxation without representation is robbery" and the men responsible for it "are guilty of the highest public crime known to human law" but voted unanimously to condemn the proposed action of the city of Worcester as "unjust and in violation of principles of government."[9]

In Garrison's letter to Abby he had hoped that "there is not a man in your city who will meanly seek to make [your] property available to his own selfish ends. Let there be no buyer at any price." But when the auction was held at City Hall, one man was mean enough to bid on the farm. Osgood Plummer, a Worcester resident who wanted to teach Stephen Foster that it was "better to obey than *defy* the laws under whose protection he lives," was awarded the Fosters' farm—house, barns, fields, and orchards— for one hundred dollars.

At the conclusion of the sale Stephen sought out Plummer, calling him a robber and warning that he and his family would remain on the farm until forcibly removed. Were he not a nonresistant, he added, he would shoot down any intruder, but as it was, he and Abby would rely on "the force of inertia. There's power in the eye of an honest patriotic woman," and through this power he hoped to win.

Shaken by the encounter and foreseeing years of litigation, Plummer reneged on his purchase. "As I have no desire 'to rob him of his hard earnings' as he terms it, I propose to allow the city to take legal possession," he wrote the tax collector. Under the law the city would hold the deed for two years. If the Fosters did not pay their back taxes by then, they would be evicted.

Meanwhile, an editorial in the *Woman's Journal* headed "ABBY KELLEY FOSTER IS HOMELESS" brought a flood of offers of help. "Of course I need not tell either of you at this late date how I appreciate this last chapter in lives full of heroic self sacrifice to conviction. Ann and I look to you with admiring & grateful sympathy," Wendell Phillips wrote. "Come to us for at least a temporary shelter," John and Mary Sargent urged. They admired the "grand position" Abby had taken, with Stephen "arm in arm with you as ever. What a rare duality of force this is! Would there were more men and women—more husbands and wives who would so cooperate!"

Writing of those "oldtime thunderers" Stephen S. Foster and Abby Kelley Foster, newspapers were surprisingly sympathetic. The *New York Evening Post* declared that their "deed of heroism has no parallel." The *Springfield Republican* proposed that women be permitted to vote in municipal elections, and the *Independent* predicted that when women became martyrs for the vote, the end of male suffrage was near.

Not everyone applauded, of course. A Worcester woman told sixty-three-year-old Abby that when she was evicted, she could go to the Home for Aged Women. No, Abby responded at a meeting in Boston. "If I am turned out of the house which we have built, which is hallowed to me by joy and sorrow, by life and death, no roof shall ever shelter me. I will go up and down the streets of Worcester and upbraid every man that I meet with his sin against justice."

Worcester's tax collector had additional business with the Fosters. The initial auction had been held to satisfy unpaid real estate taxes, but they also owed a personal property tax, levied on livestock, wagons, and farm machinery. In June 1874 and again the following year a deputy sheriff seized one of their cows to satisfy the debt while a local paper recommended the auctions because "Mr. Foster's cows are all good ones and there is opportunity for someone to get a fine animal."

In subsequent years, when the farm was auctioned again, Stephen bid it in, and the city took its taxes out of the money he paid. "He did not pay the tax, but resisted its collection by all the peaceful means at his command," Alla explained in a letter to the *Spy*. "He no more paid the tax than does the plundered western traveler pay the highwayman to whom he hands his purse."

Abby and Stephen struggled to keep the protest alive. Abby gave interviews, Stephen wrote letters to the newspapers, and both reminded their listeners at meetings that they were fighting the battles of the American Revolution again—"only with better weapons and on a higher plane." When the suffragists held a Fourth of July picnic in the grove at Framingham, it seemed almost like the old days. Two thousand people turned out to hear a brass band playing "Cheer, Cheer, the Day Is Dawning" (to the tune of "Tramp, tramp, the Boys are Marching") and a new suffrage song composed by the Hutchinsons, "Vote It Right Along!" Seated on the platform with William Lloyd Garrison, Abby proposed a resolution: "That no honorable man can support a government that disfranchises his wife and daughter and degrades them to the political companionship of paupers, idiots and criminals." Stephen followed by declaring that he would not vote until his wife could; he hoped to bring about the emancipation of women by moral force.

Except for Lucy Stone, who made an emotional speech backing the Fosters and Smith sisters, they found few supporters. Mary Livermore described Abby as "a lonely rocket shot into a dark sky" but did not agree with her tactics. "To give blow for blow and to heap anathemas on those who do not see grand truths as I do is not my course," she explained. "I have to keep myself sweet in spirit, tolerant, kindly, full of faith in man and Almighty God. The difference between Mrs. Foster and myself is not one of principles—simply methods of work." Even Garrison, speaking in the grove for the first time in ten years, disagreed with Abby, saying that the suffragists must use different tactics and styles of arraignment from those the abolitionists had used.

The Fosters had hoped for a mass protest. Thirty-four thousand women owned property in Massachusetts. The justice of permitting them to vote in town meetings, where tax rates were set, was clear to many. Had a thousand property-owning women—or even a hundred—refused to pay taxes, they might have won at least a partial victory. But only Sarah Wall, whose property was also sold at auction, joined them. There were not many heroes, Lucy Stone sadly reported.

When the American Woman Suffrage Association prepared an exhibit for the great Centennial Exposition in Philadelphia, Lucy collected the tax protests of Sarah Wall, Abby Kelley, the Smith sisters, and her own and had them framed. The walnut cabinet in which they were displayed was hung so high on the wall of the Woman's Pavilion that few could see it.[10]

In 1880 the Fosters settled their tax bill with the city and regained the deed to their property, abandoning the protest only when Stephen was too ill to continue. He had suffered a paralytic stroke four years earlier. Although he had recovered sufficiently to attend some meetings, by the end of the decade he was an invalid.

When Stephen's health improved slightly, Abby joined Lucy in organizing a woman's suffrage jubilee to commemorate the first Woman's Rights Convention in Worcester thirty years before—"The public beginning of the woman suffrage movement," the *Woman's Journal* said in an answer to the National Association's claim that the movement had begun at Seneca Falls in 1848. Of the nine women who had met in the anteroom of Faneuil Hall in 1850, only Abby and Lucy were still alive, but women who had attended the convention came from all over New England for a grand reunion. Greeting each other in Worcester's Horticultural Hall, the common salutation was "How gray you've grown!" Abby, looking older than her seventy years although her hair was still dark, listened to speaker after speaker ring changes on her bloody feet metaphor as they reminded the women that it was she who had smoothed the way.

The mood of the meeting was optimistic, Two women sang "On to Victory," to the tune of "Hold the Fort":

> *Thirty years of toil and struggle,*
> *Pleading for the Right;*
> *Thirty years! But Truth is mighty,*
> *Lo, the goal's in sight.*

Lucy Stone and others spoke of the gains of recent decades. Following the Fosters' tax protest, Massachusetts and eleven other states had passed school suffrage laws, which permitted property-owning women to vote on some educational issues. It remained for implacable Abby to characterize these laws as "insulting" and to declare that she had "no thankfulness" for them. Thomas W. Higginson was reminded of antislavery days, when he and Abby differed on what he thought details and she matters of principle. By temperament he belonged to "the half-loaf party," he said, and Abby "to that which will accept nothing short of the whole."[11]

After the meeting Abby went home to nurse her invalid husband, "who was more to her than her own soul," she had told the women. Alla was on call, ready to assist when needed. She had spent a year in Cincinnati teaching at a Young Ladies' School—"It was like plucking out right eyes for us to let her go," Abby said—but after her father's stroke she returned east. Teaching history at Roxbury High School and later at the renowned Girls' High in Boston, she came to Worcester on weekends and during vacations. She took her father for rides, wrote his letters, and kept him entertained, but Abby did not want her to be with him constantly, thinking it "too heavy a drain on her strength and sympathies."

Instead Alla became her parents' representative at woman's meetings, social affairs, and bazaars, joining such other "suffrage daughters" as Alice Stone Blackwell and Lillie B. Chace. She went to a reception at the New England Woman's Club in honor of Mary Grew, president of the Pennsylvania Woman Suffrage Association, and she traveled to Rhode Island for a New Year's Eve party at the Chaces', where guests played crambo, a rhyming game, wore paper hats, and exploded "those popping things" at midnight.

Alla's most melancholy task as stand-in for her parents was attending memorial services. One by one the old abolitionists were dying: Helen Garrison in 1876; Charles Remond and Charles Burleigh in 1878; Angelina Grimké and William Lloyd Garrison in 1879; Maria Child and Lucretia Mott in 1880. "We are going away, all of us & I rejoice that I was one with you in your work," Wendell Phillips wrote the Fosters after he spoke at Garrison's funeral.

The imminence of death made some old-timers and their children anxious to secure the movement's place in history. Garrison's sons were working on a multivolume biography of their father when William Henry Channing called on the Fosters to implore them to "finish the work given you to do. Sit down with your daughter and *tell the stories* just as they suggest themselves to preserve your testimony to the grand historic import of the antislavery movement." The resulting book, he said, would provide a unique record of the "blending of Puritan and Quaker intensity of conviction" and would leave the Fosters exhilarated by their recall of the "glory and beauty" of their past.

Stephen was sufficiently interested to ask Parker Pillsbury for newspaper accounts of his early mobbings and arrests, but Abby still rejected personal publicity. When Frank and Wendell Garrison asked for photographs to include in their father's biography, she sent them a recent picture of Stephen, but the only picture of herself she could find was a daguerreotype made some twenty years earlier. "I have had so busy a life," she explained, that "I have never taken time to sit for a picture except a friend has compelled me. Besides"—and perhaps there was a touch of vanity here—"since my severe illness of a dozen years ago I am so changed that most of my friends prefer a picture of me taken before that time." When the Garrison biography was published in 1885, it included a portrait of Stephen with gray hair and chin whiskers and a youthful, smiling Abby.[12]

Most of the Fosters' contemporaries had a firm belief in immortality, feeling sure that death meant "translation" to a better world where they would meet the friends who had predeceased them. "My father was different," Alla told Lillie Chace. "The longer he lived the stronger became his doubts. His only relief was in labor, and when health failed, and he could do nothing to better the condition of humanity, his agony was intense. He was not sure of immortality, but he longed to end this life of suffering, even if his spirit were to be annihilated."

Visiting the farm in the summer of 1880, Wendell Phillips found Stephen "frail and broken" but with "the same stern loyalty to principle, the same readiness for self-sacrifice and the same intense longing to be useful." "Tell Stephen to take courage," he wrote Abby, "& we'll agree that if he survives me that he shall say a good word for me; & if I outlive him I'll testify the truth in his behalf—that's about an even contract."

A year later Abby summoned him to fulfill his part of the bargain. Stephen Foster died at dawn on September 8, 1881, his death, the *Worcester Spy* reported, caused by "general nervous prostration, from excessive brain work, resulting from the force and vigor with which he put his whole soul into every enterprise, giving little heed to relaxation and repose." Later that day Abby and Alla mailed postal cards to friends and colleagues to inform them that there would be a memorial service in a fortnight.

The memorial meeting, held in Horticultural Hall in Worcester, was all that Stephen could have desired. A life-size portrait of him wreathed with ivy—"a very natural likeness"—stood on the right side of the platform, a massive basket of flowers on the left. Abby and Alla were center stage, flanked by sisters Joanna and Lucy and four of Stephen's sisters and brothers.

All the surviving abolitionists in the region had come: Wendell Phillips and Lucy Stone, Parker Pillsbury and Elizabeth Chace, William Bowditch, Thomas Higginson, Samuel May. Instead of the usual platitudinous oratory with its inflated claims for the deceased, speaker after speaker testified to Stephen's uniqueness: "born of the Old Testament, a Hebrew of the Hebrews, a moral John Brown." May, who had been sorely tried by Stephen in the past, called him a "most original man, absolutely true to conscience and absolutely true in obeying its dictates. He was not gentle, but he was never vindictive; he dealt in truth, never abuse." Parker Pillsbury, his oldest friend, recalled the day—"forty one years ago this month"—when Stephen first entered a church and demanded to be heard on behalf of the slave. Lucy remembered a mob attack when his immediate concern had been for her safety, and she praised his work for woman's rights. "He was our adviser and reprover. He reproved what he called our timidity. 'Why don't you fight for your rights in the way your opponents ought to be fought?'" he had asked. She also lauded his marriage, which "demonstrated the possibility of a partnership of equals, neither affirming mastership, never a thought of superiority or dictation or control."

Wendell Phillips, the final speaker, agreed with Lucy's estimate of "that perfect marriage. The happiest of homes, the sweetness of that domestic life. In private [Stephen] could pass easily from grave to gay, enjoying wit and every kind of intellectual life." But in public he was "an agitator at a time when nothing else but an agitator could serve. He never uttered anything but the holiest and loftiest indignation from the depths of the most compassionate and gentlest of souls. How many are better for his having lived!"

In an obituary in the *Woman's Journal* Higginson described Stephen as a nonresistant "in whose hands the olive-branch became a war club, [who] struck down every opponent with a merciless stroke and a heart full of the kindliest affection." He wielded "his sledge hammer as if it were a rapier. Five minutes after, he was the kindest and gentlest of men. In our milder moral conflicts of these days, more than one participant must miss the tonic of his grasp, his voice, his look. No doubt each age raises up for itself the moral leaders that it needs, but it seems to me, at this moment, an enfeebled world without Stephen Foster."[13]

Satisfied that Stephen had received the appreciation that was due him, Abby set about putting her life together again. Frederick Douglass, who had been unable to attend the memorial service because of his appointment as recorder of deeds for the District of Columbia, wrote to express his sympathy, adding, "I know you to be a philosopher, and as heroic as Dear Stephen, fully able to look with steady eye the sternest facts of life." She replied to say that although she was "lonesome and saddened," it had been Stephen's desire during his long illness "to be called away," so that she was reconciled to his loss. Then, with a flash of her old spirit, she expressed her disappointment with the freedpeople's slow progress toward equality. "Yet we rejoice in every little gain and know the time must come when the old heathenish, hellish prejudice shall disappear. God speed the right," she concluded.

Despite her interest in the freedpeople's fate, Abby could do little. Willy Garrison had been shocked by her frailty when he saw her at Stephen's memorial service. "The scabbard of her body was almost outworn, inadequate for the keen and active brain that filled it," he said. She had never fully recovered from the 1868 operation or, indeed, from her strenuous labors in earlier decades. Now she had a new ailment, catarrh—probably chronic bronchitis—which caused difficulty in breathing. Her feebleness may have been intensified by the belief that threescore and ten was a normal life-span and that little more could be expected after that milestone. Whatever the reasons, physical or psychological, it was quickly apparent that she could not remain alone in the too big, too empty house on Mower Street.

Family and friends were nearby. Adams Foster was dead, but Sarah Foster still lived on their Tatnuck farm while her daughter Ann Maria was rearing a family on the adjoining property. There might have been a place for Abby there, but she was never entirely comfortable with the Foster family's style of housekeeping. Instead she turned to her sister, Lucy Barton, an energetic widow of sixty-two who, with her daughter Flora, was operating a boardinghouse in Worcester at 100 Chatham Street, about five miles from the Foster farm. Abby would become their star boarder.

During the next year and a half Abby sold eleven acres along Tatnuck Brook to a neighbor who needed the water rights for his mill and her house, barns, and remaining acreage to Oliver Stark, a bootmaker, and his wife, Melissa. After agreeing to move out by April 1, 1883, she spent her days sorting through the possessions of a lifetime. When she heard that Frank Garrison was collecting *Liberators* to give to libraries, she offered her copies of the paper. Apologizing for their poor condition, she explained that she and Stephen had always invited their farm hands, "who had little care for cleanliness," to read them so that her copies were "much soiled. But such as they are I did not like to waste." Nor, recalling her thrifty Quaker forebears, did she like to discard beds, sofas, quilts, dresses, crockery. A barrel of clothing was shipped to Sallie Holley's school in Virginia; other furniture and bedding went to Lucy Barton's and to Alla's room in Boston, but some favorite pieces as well as scraps of cloth to be used for reupholstering and dressmaking were stored in the Starks' attic while "good clean 'middling' bags" were left in their granary. For more than a year after her move she and Alla returned to the attic regularly, bringing their lunches so that they would have a full day to sort through the stored goods and retrieve pieces that friends could use.[14]

The sales of the property had brought $8,061, more than double what she and Stephen had paid in 1847. With this money and other savings invested in mortgages that paid 5 and 6 percent interest, she had an income of close to $500 a year. This did not permit extravagant living, but as a scrupulously kept account book for the years 1881–84 attests, it was adequate for her needs. She spent $5.50 for board, another 30 or 40 cents for washing, and up to $15 annually for coal to heat her room. The account book listed numerous small items for clothing repairs: buttons and thread, 9 cents; lace, 15 cents; ruffles, 25 cents; bustle, 58 cents as well as a rare payment to Sarah Wall for dressmaking. Abby spent 25 cents for garters, 65 cents for a hairbrush, 25 cents for cough syrup, and $1 for Murdock's Liquid Food, a food supplement that Alla bought for her in Boston.

Postage, once a high-budget item, was now inexpensive; her weekly letters to Alla carried a 2-cent stamp, and she often used the new penny postal cards for brief messages. The most expensive personal item in the three years covered by her account book was a parasol that cost $2.20. Her sole luxury was the rental of a horse and carriage—$1.50— to pick up visitors at the depot and to make occasional trips to neighboring towns.

By the summer of 1883 she felt settled enough in her new quarters to resume her correspondence with the Phillipses. "How happy it is that now that dear Stephen is gone you have so happy a home," Wendell responded. "Ann says 'I love that sister & would like to see her.' Remember if you do ever get to town to be sure to come & see us. We will talk of old folks & old times and be happy over lots of blessings after all the weariness & sufferings, losses & changes." But soon the loving messages from Wendell ceased. Following a heart attack, he died on February 2, 1884, his last words, "What will become of Ann?"

"This week has seemed longer than any other since I came here," Abby wrote Alla. "I have been so full of thoughts of the present, past, and future, so closely pressed upon me by the unexpected death of Mr. Phillips. I did not think of his going so soon." Too unwell to attend the funeral although Sarah Southwick invited her to stay with her in Boston, she was "glad that no attempt at eulogy was made in the church. Did not he speak to all ears in the city? Yes, to the state, to the country, and the world." Sadly she wrote a note to Ann and asked Alla to inquire at the young Garrisons to learn how she was faring.

Never demanding about her surroundings, Abby declared herself content on Chatham Street, where Lucy and Flora did their best to make her comfortable. They saw that she had proper meals, wadded paper and felt around her windows to keep out the winter cold, turned her carpet and gave her room a thorough spring-cleaning. Lucy made Abby's out-of-town visitors welcome, encouraging them to stay the night if she had a spare room, and invited the Foster relatives for Thanksgiving dinner. Albert Kelley and his daughter, another Lucy, came to call occasionally, and Joanna Ballou, their only other surviving sister, arrived for a fortnight's visit. Abby, had been looking forward to seeing Joanna but found her stay upsetting. At eighty-three Joanna was still loquacious and opinionated. "Her disagreeable peculiarities have become stronger and sharper," Abby confided to Alla. Besides, "she is so deaf that it is difficult for me to talk with her at all."

Far pleasanter were the visits from nieces, grandnieces, and nephews— Darlings, Fosters, Kelleys, Kinneys—who spent hours with Abby in the sitting room, took her for rides, and even tried to get her to go to Barnum's circus when it played in Worcester. Once when Henry Kinney, Ann Maria's son, drove Abby to Sarah Foster's for dinner, the outing almost ended in disaster. His lumbering farm horse fell down, tipping the carriage—and Abby. Henry unhitched the horse, rescued his aunt, and procured a ride for her in a passing buggy. But although Abby reported that she had a good dinner, "nicely served," and "lots of chit-chat" with Sarah, she had pulled a muscle in her side that left her stiff and sore for a long time. "My system is so low that a slight bruise, even, lasts for weeks," she wrote Alla. "The lack of any firmness of body or mind is one principal reason of my dreading to go abroad or undertaking to do anything."[15]

Alla, who sometimes thought that her mother was giving in to her infirmities, encouraged her in weekly letters and continued to represent her at meetings, teas, and memorial services. She served on the finance committee of a Suffrage Subscription Festival, where the Hutchinsons sang "Clear the Track for Woman Suffrage" and the walls of the hall were decorated with quotations from Shakespeare: "Sir! Here's a Woman Will Speak" and "Happily a Woman's Voice May Do Some Good."* With old feuds forgotten, she attended a memorial meeting for Maria Chapman, the unveiling of a statue of Harriet Martineau, and a reception for a visiting British abolitionist. "What a pity that your bowels are so sensitive. It would have been delightful for you to meet Mrs. Burleigh and Mary Grew again," she wrote after one social occasion.

The correspondence between mother and daughter had undergone a change since Alla's college years. Now in her mid-thirties, Alla sometimes wrote as if she were the parent and Abby the child. She hoped that Abby took fresh air daily, recommended that she gargle with hot water when she had a cold, and suggested that she take up knitting. "Why not make a pair of socks for Callie's baby? Susan [Darling] can perhaps give you instructions if you do not know how to shape them. I shall need new

---

* In *The Merry Wives of Windsor*, act II, scene II, the correct quotation is "Sir, here's a woman would speak with you." "Happily a woman's voice . . ." is from *The Life of Henry the Fifth*, act V, scene II.

mittens by-and-by. So you see that work in abundance awaits you, should you find the occupation agreeable."

On occasion Alla interceded for Lucy when boarders complained of Abby's eccentricities. Fastidious though she had always been, Abby saw nothing wrong about using her spitbox in the sitting room when she had a bronchial attack or even cleaning her dentures there. "Will it not be best," Alla tactfully inquired, "now that you have a fire in your room, to make a rule not to bring the box out, but go in there whenever you need to use it? If [Aunt Lucy] had not boarders, she would not object at all she says; but she must be careful not to annoy them. I find it safer, in boarding, to do all the business of my life in my own room, with my door shut."

In other letters Alla described the lectures and concerts she attended— "I consider music one of the necessities of my life"—and reported on her collaboration with a Vassar friend who was pioneering in the field of public sanitation. Ellen Swallow Richards, the first woman graduate student at the Massachusetts Institute of Technology, was developing techniques for studying room ventilation, water quality, and sewage disposal. Alla assisted her, investigating the sanitary properties of sinks and wall coverings for Richards's book *Home Sanitation: A Manual for Housekeepers.* "I have learned many new things this year," she wrote her mother. "Our old home was not in suitable condition in many ways. The cellar should have been concreted or cemented. Then the pipes from the bath-tub and sink must have brought up unhealthy gases, having no 'trap' to cut them off. Our rooms were never properly ventilated. If you had given as much attention to health as to reform, it might have been better for your bodies if not for your souls. Father was very indifferent to sanitary laws, but you were always much interested."

Abby accepted the change in roles with good grace. "How glad I am that you have such fine opportunities for information in Boston," she responded after Alla had described a lecture. She had plenty of fresh air, she assured her daughter, because she took frequent carriage rides. "I pay only a Dollar or a Dollar and a half for a good carriage and go then for a five miles ride, carrying four of us at once." She meekly consulted Alla about a new dress before going to Canterbury to see Caroline Foster and again when they planned a White Mountains vacation. Sarah Wall made the dress for the second trip, but Abby asked Alla how wide the velvet ribbon should be, adding, "The dress is dark drab. It is not the color I should have chosen had I time to think about it." Although still unsure of her taste in clothing, she was positive about the kind of inn they should stay in—"plain people, of common sense and decent table where I shan't have to perk up . . . access to a fire in cold weather, and above all no midges or mosquitoes."

As old age brought some forgetfulness, Abby feared that she was losing her mind. She castigated herself when she failed to write to Alla one Friday and apologized for her "flickering brain" after misdating a letter. "I read the papers and saw the dates, but they did not impress me," she explained. "I am often in that condition—knowing, and still not being sufficiently impressed to take in the fact. A state like being half way between sleeping and waking. I hope it is not leading to the condition I have all along feared and dreaded."

Abby need not have feared senility. Her handwriting was as firm and legible as it had been fifty years earlier, and her thoughts were still clearly expressed. If Alla had seriously pictured her mother in a rocking chair, placidly knitting, she was doomed to disappointment. Despite her impaired vision, Abby pored over newspapers and journals, reacting to events with her habitual vehemence. She was particularly concerned about the South, where the Fifteenth Amendment was being ignored with the acquiescence, if not the support, of the Republican party. She mourned because there was no Wendell Phillips to deliver a "terrible rebuke" to the Supreme Court when it declared the Civil Rights Act of 1875 unconstitutional. She was unsparing of her criticism of Thomas W. Higginson—"always a compromiser"—for an article on blacks' loss of voting rights in the South that she thought was "calculated to befog." She praised George Hoar, a Worcester man who had succeeded Sumner in the Senate, for his "bold, clear, uncompromising position" on most issues. "If you have not read Hoar's speech in the Springfield Convention, pray read it directly," she wrote Alla. "He ignores the woman question, of course. As a party man he could do nothing else. But if he succeeds in making the Negro equal before the law, thereby saving the true democratic principle of government, he will have done a grand work. If it is not done, we shall as a nation go to wreck."

She had little interest in the outcome of the 1884 presidential election, seeing "no difference of consequence" between Cleveland or Blaine, but she followed political battles in Great Britain, where Prime Minister William E. Gladstone had pushed through bills granting manhood suffrage and land reform. Gladstone was "a remarkable statesman, if statesmanship consists in carrying a government forward, with gradual improvements and with as little friction as foresight, wisdom and prudence will allow," she told Alla. "He is evidently satisfied of the correctness of democratic principles, and will do all in his power to introduce them so fast as it can be done without revolution. But he must vote for many things which he can but condemn in his own soul to keep Victoria and her class quiet." Gladstone again confirmed her view of politicians: "No person can be a real follower of Christ and be a statesman. The real Christian will be crucified all the day long."[16]

In addition to the letters to Alla, Abby sometimes attempted longer pieces of writing. So many people had asked for her reminiscences that in 1885 she started to put them down. The task was difficult because she had little material to jog her memory. "I never kept a diary, or any incidental notes of my life. I never kept any articles from newspapers either commendatory, or condemnatory, and seldom kept a letter," she explained. In twenty neatly written pages she recalled her "severe trials" during her first years as "a public-speaking woman." Dates and place-names were sometimes wrong, but the assaults on her character by clergy and laymen, the loneliness and ostracism were set down in detail. Afterward she had grown a thick skin, schooling herself to ignore her persecutors, but those first years in Connecticut were still painful to recall. The effort of thinking about them brought a "rush of blood to my head which is very distressing and puts an end to all thought," she told Alla.

Although she gave up the autobiographical memoir, she occasionally determined to set the record straight on aspects of the antislavery movement. The publication of William Lloyd Garrison's biography brought on a reassessment of the abolitionists, largely unfavorable. Usually Willy or Frank replied to the critics, but when their father was attacked for his insensitivity to the "Woman Question," she felt obliged to speak, "if it be only a cry I can utter."

Her seventy-fifth birthday found her at her writing table, recalling for a new generation the barriers that women had faced a half century earlier. Briefly she described her "terrible service" in the lecture field when "unsavory eggs, the contents of stables and out-houses" were hurled at her, and ministers called her "Jezebel" and "fornicator." "Wherever the *Liberator* went the question was fully examined. We were standing against the whole world on the woman question. No other association received women on equal terms with men. No other women were on the public platform," she wrote. Gradually "the furnaces of truth" melted the shackles that bound women, and "little by little, one by one, [they] came forward. To-day, behold the multitude that cannot be numbered!" she concluded with a flourish.

Lucy Stone wrote to say that the *Woman's Journal* was "very glad" to publish her article "Mr. Garrison and His Critics." However, by the time it appeared in the January 30, 1886, issue, Abby was laid up with "a dreadful attack of catarrh" brought on by her writing efforts. "I cannot convince you of the labor and dreadful excitement it caused me," she told Alla.

During 1885 and 1886 Abby corresponded with Frank Garrison about the situation in the South, went to Leicester to celebrate Samuel and Sarah May's fiftieth wedding anniversary, and mourned the death of Ann Phillips. Hearing from Lizzie Jones, who still wrote occasionally for the *Woman's Journal*, she invited Lizzie's daughter, Ella, to spend a few days in Worcester when she came to New England.

Perhaps it was while they were arranging for Ella's visit that Lizzie sent Abby the letter that John Greenleaf Whittier had written to Benjamin Jones in July 1840, the letter that accused Abby of "blowing up" the American Society and compared her with Eve and Helen of Troy. Abby probably had heard of the letter long before, but seeing it in the poet's handwriting reminded her anew "of the days when woman's souls were tried" not only by their enemies but by their professed friends. "Whittier's Quaker education left him without excuse," she told Lucy Stone when she sent the letter to the *Woman's Journal*. Lucy agreed that the letter should be published "to show the weight which women had to lift up," but she was preoccupied with a forthcoming meeting of the American Woman Suffrage Association, and the letter never appeared.

Lucy did make time in her busy schedule for a long-planned reunion at her Dorchester home in July 1886. Elizabeth Chace, now in her eightieth year, traveled from Rhode Island, Abby and Alla from Worcester, while Sarah Southwick and Harriet Sewall represented the Boston Female Anti-Slavery Society. Eight-six-year old Theodore Weld, Samuel May, and Samuel Sewall, Garrison's sons, and cohost Henry Blackwell made up the rest of the party. Abby sat next to Wendell Garrison at lunch and had "much cheerful and pleasant conversation," but when a photographer lined them up on Lucy's porch for a group picture, she looked thin and drawn alongside plump Lucy and buxom Elizabeth Chace.

When she wrote to thank Lucy for the outing, their mutual health was on her mind. She reproached herself for permitting Lucy to carry her carpetbag at the railroad station. "Don't you know that it is necessary to husband your physical resources, in order to have them fully in hand for the guidance of your mental powers? Now, I pray you look strictly after your health." Then, seeking a tactful way to tell Lucy to lose weight, she commented on Elizabeth Stanton, who had announced on her seventieth birthday that she weighed two hundred pounds. "I don't believe as much fat as E. C. Stanton boasts can be carried by any body but a 'Dutchy' woman. Yankees have too much conscience and spiritual responsibility to health to carry such a burden."[17]

After a vacation in the White Mountains with Alla, Abby felt well enough to agree to write a sketch of Stephen's life for the forthcoming edition of *The National Cyclopaedia of American Biography*. She saw this as a chance to secure his place in history not as a fanatic but as a thoughtful man who had pursued his own idiosyncratic path to reform. Parker Pillsbury, who had recently reprinted *The Brotherhood of Thieves*, sent her his recollections of the youthful Stephen; for the rest she went through old letters and her memories.

Always thorough in anything she attempted, she became obsessed with the task of doing justice to Stephen's complex personality. Observing the intensity with which she worked, sister Lucy thought that it was taking too strong a hold of Abby's emotions—"like a new sorrow and crucifixion"—and begged her to slow down. But Abby, writing and rewriting in what must have been close to panic, could not rest until she had found the appropriate words—and they would not come. Finally, after giving a brief account of Stephen's career, she characterized him by quoting from Oliver Johnson's recent book *William Lloyd Garrison and His Times*, in which Oliver had called Stephen "guileless and ingenuous" with an "absolute faith in moral principles" and an "honesty and candor" that could not be doubted. To recapture the special quality of his oratory, she concluded with a stanza from James Russell Lowell's 1846 poem which described Stephen as "A kind of maddened John the Baptist/ To whom the harshest word comes aptest,/ His oratory is like the scream/ Of the iron horse's frenzied steam."

After recopying the sketch and mailing it to the printer, she wrote a postal card to tell Parker that it was completed. When she gave the card to Lucy to mail, she trembled so much that Lucy feared she would fall. The next morning she remained in bed, ate some porridge, but was too tired to get dressed. When she still could not rouse herself the following day, Lucy telegraphed Alla to come. Abby opened her eyes when her daughter arrived, as if to ask why she was there, then closed them for the last time. It was January 14, 1887, the day before her seventy-sixth birthday.*

"She slept her life away without pain," Lucy Stone wrote Elizabeth Chace. "Her face had the old, sweet serenity of the earlier time. The troubled and careworn look was gone and only peace and rest were visible."

At Abby's request the funeral service, held at her sister's home, was private, with only relatives and close friends in attendance. Although they knew her dislike of eulogies, the mourners could not remain silent. Samuel May, conducting the service, recalled Abby as he had first seen her: "a face beautiful in feature, in intellectual and moral expression, a voice clear, full, musical, penetrating; a slender graceful figure, simply arrayed.

"Few Americans can be named—statesmen, scholars, orators, no matter how gifted—who did so much for the abolition of American slavery as did the woman whose worn-out frame lies before us. She was one of the few—

---

* The cause of death was "asthenia," which medical textbooks of the day defined as exhaustion of the circulatory system.

the marked few—whose words startled and aroused the land; who compelled attention (and that not by mere vehemency of speech, but by genuine earnestness of heart and soul); who made the guilty tremble; who forced sleeping consciences to awake, and forbade that they should sleep again until slavery ceased.

"There were indeed other women who early and late befriended the slave's cause. But that cause could not have gone forward as it did, but for Abby Kelley Foster. No one of them ever did take, ever could have taken the place she so marvelously filled; could ever have done the amount of telling, incisive, incessant work which she did for so many years; work so laborious, persistent, continuous, undismayed, as most persons now would pronounce impossible, and as most men, of however sturdy make, could not have been able to endure.

"We all have heard of self-sacrifice. In Mrs. Foster we saw it. She was its impersonation—she was itself. From the hour when she left her chosen work of teaching, and through all her life, a period of fifty years, she laid herself a willing offer upon the altar of humanity and truth, of her country's and of mankind's highest and enduring welfare. She took on herself the sorrows, pains, heart-anguish, stripes and wounds of her suffering sisters and brothers."

"Mrs. Foster stood in the thick of the fight for the slaves, and at the same time, she hewed out the path over which women are now walking toward their equal political rights." Lucy Stone took up the story. "The world of women owe her a debt which they can never pay. The movement for the equal rights of women began directly and emphatically with her. Other women had spoken in public. The sisters Grimké had taken a noble part but circumstances soon withdrew them from the public field, and it was left for Abby Kelley to take on her young shoulders and to bear a double burden, for the slave's freedom, and for equal rights for women. She who fought this dreadful battle is now at rest. She had no peer, and she leaves no successor."[18]

NOTES

ABBREVIATIONS USED IN NOTES

AAS	Kelley-Foster Papers, American Antiquarian Society
AEG	Angelina Grimké
AK	Abby Kelley
BFASS	Boston Female Anti-Slavery Society
BPL	Anti-Slavery Collection of the Boston Public Library
BUGLE	*Anti-Slavery Bugle*
CATALOGUE OF OFFI-CERS AND STUDENTS	Catalogue of Officers and Students, New England Boarding School, Providence, R.I.
CLEMENTS	William L. Clements Library, University of Michigan
COLUMBIA	Gay Papers, Columbia University
ECS	Elizabeth Cady Stanton
EXECUTIVE COMMIT-TEE MINUTES	Minutes of the Executive Committee, American Anti-Slavery Society, BPL
FAMILY RECORDS	Kelley-Foster Papers, American Antiquarian Society
FOSTER REM	Alla W. Foster, "Reminiscences of Mrs. Abby Kelley Foster," *Woman's Journal* (Feb. 7, 1891)
GIDDINGS, OHS	Giddings Papers, Ohio Historical Society
HAVERFORD	Quaker Collection, Haverford College Library
HOUGHTON	Houghton Library, Harvard University
HSP	Historical Society of Pennsylvania
JGW	John Greenleaf Whittier
KENT STATE	Kent State University Library
LHS	Lynn Historical Society
LIB	*Liberator*
LMC	Lydia Maria Child
LOC	Library of Congress, including Frederick Douglass Papers, Blackwell Family Papers, National American Woman Suffrage Papers, Stanton Papers
LS	Lucy Stone
MHS	Massachusetts Historical Society
MWC	Maria Weston Chapman

NASS	*National Anti-Slavery Standard*
NAWSA	National American Woman Suffrage Papers
NYHS	New-York Historical Society
OBERLIN	Oberlin College Archives
OHS	Ohio Historical Society
PAS	Papers of the Pennsylvania Abolition Society
PFASS	Philadelphia Female Anti-Slavery Society
RIHS	Rhode Island Historical Society
ROCHESTER	University of Rochester Library
RUTGERS	E. C. Stanton Papers, Douglass Library, Rutgers University
SBA	Susan B. Anthony
SCHLESINGER	Schlesinger Library, Radcliffe College
SCHOMBURG	Schomburg Center for Research on Black Culture
SMITH	Sophia Smith Collection, Smith College Library
SSF	Stephen Symonds Foster
SYRACUSE	Gerrit Smith Papers, Syracuse University
U. MASS	University of Massachusetts Archives
WHM	Kelley-Foster Papers, Worcester Historical Museum
WLG	William Lloyd Garrison
WP	Wendell Phillips

INTRODUCTION

1. Abraham Lincoln to Daniel Chamberlain, April 6, 1865, quoted in Thomas W. Higginson, "Anti-Slavery Days."
2. Nevins.
3. *Woman's Journal*, Jan. 22, 1887.
4. LIB, Jan. 8, 1847.
5. AK to Betsy Cowles, [October] 1, 1849, Kent State.
6. WP to AK, [spring 1851], AAS; WLG to AK, March 25, 1851, July 22, 1859, AAS.
7. LIB, Dec. 8, 1847.
8. AK to Darlings, July 22, 1838, WHM; WP to LMC, Feb. 21, 1842, in Lewis, ed.

CHAPTER 1: THE EDUCATION OF ABBY KELLEY

1. NASS, Oct. 8, 1840; Foster Rem.
2. The Kelley-Foster Papers in the American Antiquarian Society include handwritten genealogical data and summaries of deeds, hereafter cited as Family Records, AAS; Parmenter; AK to George Bradburn, April 15, 1841, AAS; Smith and Hindus; Baldwin.

3. Foster Rem; Family Records, AAS; Lincoln.
4. Family Records, AAS; Foster Rem.
5. Bidwell; Earle.
6. Foster Rem; Abby Hopper Gibbons, in Emerson, ed.; Elizabeth Buffum Chace, in Wyman and Wyman.
7. Foster Rem; Stanton; Wyman; BUGLE, Nov. 7, 1857.
8. Norton and Berkin, ed.; Rufus Jones; Drake; Brinton; Women's Book of Records for the Monthly Meeting, Uxbridge, RIHS.
9. Family Records, AAS.
10. Wall; Lincoln; Foster Rem; Women's Book of Records, loc. cit.
11. Archives of New England Meeting Society of Friends, RIHS; Catalogue of Officers and Students; Sanborn; WLG, in LIB, Oct. 13, 1832.
12. Author's visit to the boarding school, now the Moses Brown School; interview and correspondence with Frank E. Fuller, school historian, 1984–89; Fuller, ed.; Augustine Jones; Kelsey; Wyman and Wyman.
13. Thompson; Tolles.
14. Griscom; Fuller, ed.; Kelsey.
15. Kelsey; Fuller, ed.
16. Kelsey; Sanborn; James et al., eds.; Wyman and Wyman.
17. Foster Rem.

CHAPTER 2: A WIDER WORLD

1. Foster Rem; Catalogue of Officers and Students; Eliza Earle to AK, Feb. 28, 1837, AAS; quotation from I Kings 17:14 and 17:16; Family Records, AAS.
2. Millbury; Henrietta Sargent, in NASS, Sept. 2, 1841; Eliza Earle to AK, Feb. 28, 1837, AAS; Archives of New England Meeting, RIHS.
3. Faler; Dawley; Hawkes; Hacker; maps of Lynn from LHS.
4. AK to Darlings, Dec. 10, 1837, WHM; Hacker; Archives of New England Meeting, RIHS; Anna B. Smith to AK, Nov. 1838, AAS; Anna B. Smith to AK, March 7, 1839, WHM; Lydia Keene to AK, April 26, 1839, AAS.
5. Nissenbaum; Schwartz; Anna B. Smith to AK, Nov. 1838, AAS.
6. Koppelman; Chambers-Schiller, *Liberty, a Better Husband*; AK to SSF, April 7, 1847, AAS, es.
7. Mordell; John Pickard.
8. Anna B. Smith to AK, Nov. 1838, AAS; Catalogue of Officers and Students; Merrill and Ruchames, eds., v. 1; William Bassett to AK, Nov. 12, 1838, Nov. 6, 1839, AAS.
9. LIB, Aug. 18, October 6, 1832.
10. "Declaration of the Anti-Slavery Convention, Assembled in Philadelphia, Dec. 4, 1833" (broadside); Sterling, *Lucretia Mott*.

11. Lutz; LIB, 1833–36; Welter.
12. Records of Lynn Female Anti-Slavery Society, LHS.
13. Records of PFASS, PAS Papers, PHS.
14. Records of Lynn Female Anti-Slavery Society, LHS; Ann G. Chapman to AK, Aug. 13, 1836, AAS; AK to H. G. Chapman, Feb. 22, 1837, BPL.
15. LIB, Aug. 13, 1836; Records of Lynn Female Anti-Slavery Society, LHS.
16. LIB, Aug. 4, 1837.
17. Records of Lynn Female Anti-Slavery Society, LHS; AK to MWC, Nov. 25, 1837, BPL.
18. Family Records, AAS.
19. AK to Darlings, Dec. 10, 1837, WHM; James; Chambers-Schiller, *Liberty, a Better Husband*; LIB, Jan 9, 1857; Heilbrun.

CHAPTER 3: WOMEN FIND THEIR VOICES

1. LIB, May 18, 1837; Lucy Foster to AK, March 27, 1837, AAS; Benjamin Thomas; Luke 10.
2. AK to H. G. Chapman, Feb. 22, 1837, BPL; Faler; Dawley; Percival; Foster Rem.
3. E. Wright to Mary Grew, April 18, 1836, Mary Clark to PFASS, April 20, 1836, MWC to PFASS, Aug. 3, 1836, Jan. 12, 1837, PFASS Papers, HSP; LIB, March 4, 1837.
4. Identification of the "minds" can be found in biographies of contemporaries as well as in LIB. For Mary Parker, see Merrill and LIB. For Balls, see LIB, Dec. 14, 1833, Dec. 13, 1834, Sept. 19, 1838, ff., *Death Records*, Department of Vital Statistics, Boston; [M. W. Chapman] "Right and Wrong in Boston Female Anti-Slavery Society." For Child, see Meltzer and Holland. For Maria Weston Chapman and Weston sisters, see Pease and Pease; Chambers-Schiller, "The Cab"; Munsterberg; AK to MWC, Nov. 25, 1837, BPL; AK to Anne Weston, June 17, 1837, BPL. For Mott, see Bacon, *Valiant Friend*.
5. For Grimké sisters, see Barnes and Dumond; Birney; Lerner; Lumpkin; Benjamin Thomas; AEG to Jane Smith [November 1836], Clements; Abby A. Cox to PFASS, Feb. 15, 1837, PAS Papers, HSP; AEG to Jane Smith, Dec. 17, 1836, Jan. 20, Feb. 4, 1837, Clements.
6. AK to AEG, March 20, 1837, NYHS; AEG to AK, April 15, 1837, AAS.
7. Minutes of Lynn Female Anti-Slavery Society, April 19, 1837, LHS; LIB, June 2, 1837.
8. WPA, *New York Panorama, New York City Guide*; LIB, June 2, 1837, May 19, 1837.
9. Minutes of Anti-Slavery Convention of American Women, in Sterling, ed., *Turning the World Upside Down*; LIB, June 2, 1837; *Memorial of Sarah Pugh*. For ages of women, see Hersh; James et al., eds.; Sterling, *We Are Your Sisters*.
10. U.S. Department of Commerce; Sterling, *Speak Out*.
11. Swerdlow; AEG to Jane Smith, March 22, 1837, Clements; Anne Weston to Deborah

Weston, Oct. 22, 1836, BPL; *Colored American*, April–June 1837; AEG to Jane Smith, May 20, 1837, Clements.
  12. LIB, June 2, 1837; *Memorial of Sarah Pugh.*
  13. Minutes of Anti-Slavery Convention, loc. cit.; E. Neal to AK, March 12, 1843, AAS.
  14. LIB, June 2, 1837; AEG to T. Weld, May 18, 1837, in Barnes and Dumond, eds.; Martineau, *Martyr Age*; *New York Commercial Advertiser*, reprinted in LIB, June 2, 1837.
  15. Juliana Tappan to AK, June 15, 1837, AAS; AK to Anne Weston, June 17, 1837, BPL; Lumpkin; Minutes of Lynn Female Anti-Slavery Society, June 21, 1837, LHS; AK to Anne Weston [June 1837], BPL.
  16. LIB, Jan. 17, 1840; Birney; AEG to Jane Smith, June 26, 1837, Clements; Lerner.
  17. Melder; Minutes of Lynn Female Anti-Slavery Society, June 21, 1837, LHS; Stanton, Anthony, et al., v. 1; Blackwell.
  18. Sklar; Rossi; AEG to Amos A. Phelps, Aug. 17, [1837], BPL; JGW to Grimkés, Aug. 14, 1837, and T. Weld to Grimkés, Aug. 15, 1837, in Birney.
  19. AK to Darlings, Dec. 10, 1837, WHM; LIB, Oct. 13, 1837; *Woman's Journal*, Jan. 30, 1886.
  20. AEG to Jane Smith, Oct. 6, 1837, Clements.
  21. LIB, Oct. 13, 1837; AK to WLG, in LIB, Sept. 22, 1837; AK to WLG, Oct. 20, 1837, BPL.
  22. MWC to AK, Nov. 25, 1837, AAS; AK to Darlings, Dec. 10, 1837, WHM; AK to MWC, Dec. 9, 1837, BPL; William Ladd to AK, April 18, 1837, AAS; AK to Darlings, Dec. 10, 1837, WHM.

CHAPTER 4: THE CALL

  1. Birney; Lerner; Lumpkin; AEG and T. Weld to AK, May 3, 1838, AAS; LMC to E. Carpenter, March 20, 1838, Meltzer and Holland; AEG to T. Weld, [April 29, 1838], and Whittier poem, in Barnes and Dumond; Anne Weston to Deborah Weston, March 7, 1838, BPL; WLG to Helen Garrison, May 12, 1838, BPL.
  2. M. Pennock to AK, March 18, 1838, WHM; Birney; Lerner; Lumpkin; Barnes and Dumond; marriage certificate, Clements; MWC to E. Pease, Aug. 30, 1838, BPL.
  3. *History of Pennsylvania Hall*; Proceedings of the Second Annual Anti-Slavery Convention of American Women; WLG to Sarah Benson, May 19, 1838, BPL; Birney; Lumpkin; LIB, Sept. 19, 1838; Stanton, Anthony et al., v. 1; W. P. and F. J. Garrison, v. 2; Bacon, *Valiant Friend*; Sterling, *Lucretia Mott*; *Pennsylvania Freeman*, quoted in Samuel Pickard; Sarah Douglass to AK, May 18, 1838, AAS.
  4. Anne Weston to Mary Chapman, May 23, [1838], BPL; Charles Burleigh to Edward M. Davis, May 28, 1838, Houghton; James Mott to Anne Weston, June 7, 1838, BPL; WLG to George Benson, May 25, 1838, BPL.
  5. AK to Darlings, July 22, 1838, WHM.

6. LIB, June 8, June 29, July 6, 1838; Burleigh to Edward M. Davis, May 28, 1838, Houghton.

7. *Christian Mirror*, quoted in LIB, July 6, 1838; Isaiah 3:12; LIB, July 20, 1838.

8. James Mott to Anne Weston, June 7, 1838, BPL; Sarah M. Grimké to AK, June 15, 1838, AAS; AEG to Anne Weston, July 15, 1838, and Oct. 14, [1838], BPL.

9. Foster Rem; Austin; Bartlett.

10. LIB, Sept. 26, 1838; WLG to Helen Garrison, Sept. 21, 1838, BPL; Lynd, ed.; Curti; LMC to AK Oct. 1, 1838, AAS; Brock; Stewart, *Wendell Phillips*.

11. AK to Darlings, July 22, 1838, WHM; AK to T. Weld, Jan. 14, 1839, Barnes and Dumond; Lerner; Lumpkin; Birney; Sarah M. Grimké to AK, June 15, 1838, AAS; AEG and T. Weld to AK, Feb. 24, 1839 WHM.

12. O'Connor.

13. Foster Rem; I Corinthians 1:26–27.

14. William Bassett to AK, Nov. 12, 1838, Nov. 6, 1839, AAS; Anna Breed to AK, Nov. 1838, AAS; Lydia Keene, Anna Breed, et al. to AK, April 26, 1839, AAS; Mary Robbins to AK, Jan. 21, 1839, AAS.

15. LIB, Nov. 2, 1838; LIB, Feb. 8, Feb. 15, Feb. 22, 1839; March 1, March 15, 1839; Mary Robbins to AK, Jan. 21, 1839, AAS; LIB, March 22, April 26, 1839; Ruchames.

16. D. W. Ballou to AK, Jan 9, [1839], AAS; LIB, March 29, 1839; Kraditor; Anne Weston to Deborah Weston, March 23–26 [1839], BPL; LIB, May 3, 1839.

17. Anne Weston to Deborah Weston, March 23–26, [1839], BPL; LMC to LM, March 5, 1839, Meltzer and Holland; LM to AK, March 18, 1839, AAS.

CHAPTER 5: A PUBLIC-SPEAKING WOMAN

1. Anne Weston to Deborah Weston, May 15, 1839, BPL.

2. LIB, May 10, May 17, May 31, 1839; *Christian Mirror*, quoted in LIB, May 24, 1839.

3. Anne Weston to [sister], March 1, 1839, BPL; Lucia Weston to Anne Weston, [1839], BPL; AK to Anne Weston, May 29, 1839, BPL; Lumpkin; Birney.

4. Bridgwater and Kurtz; AK to Anne Weston, May 29, 1839; BPL; LIB, Oct. 23, 1840.

5. Wyman and Wyman, v. 2; LIB, Oct. 23, 1840.

6. Hannah Smith to AK, July 25, 1839, AAS; AK to WLG in LIB, Sept. 20, 1839.

7. Jonathan Leonard to AK, May 3, 1840, AAS; biographical note on Erasmus Darwin Hudson, Sr., U. Mass; AK to E. D. Hudson, Aug. 6, 1840, U. Mass; E. D. Hudson journal, Feb.–April 1840, U. Mass.

8. Olive Darling to AK, Sept. 12–18, 1839, AAS; Lucy Kelley and Joanna Ballou to AK, Sept. 8, 1839, AAS.

9. Olive Darling to AK, Sept. 12–18, 1839, AAS; Foster Rem.

10. Kraditor; AK to Elizur Wright, in LIB, Sept. 6, 1839.

11. *Connecticut Observer*, quoted in LIB, March 27, 1840; AK to WLG in LIB, April 10, 1840.

12. AK to WLG in LIB, April 10, 1840.

CHAPTER 6: WAR TO THE KNIFE'S POINT

1. Kraditor; LIB, April 10, 1840.

2. Alanson St. Clair to Amos Phelps, March 30, 1839, BPL, quoted in Kraditor; Elizur Wright to H. B. Stanton, in LIB, Dec. 6, Dec. 20, Dec. 27, 1839; Jan. 3, Jan. 17, 1840.

3. Munsterberg; MWC to Deborah Weston, April 18, [1839], BPL; MWC on draft of letter to Mary Parker, Lucy and Martha Ball, nd, BPL; MWC to Deborah Weston, March 14, 1839, April 18, [1839], BPL; MWC to Deborah Weston, May 9, [1839], March 14, 1839, BPL.

4. The struggle in the Boston Female Anti-Slavery Society is given in detail in "Right and Wrong in the Boston Female Anti-Slavery Society," written by MWC and published as a *Liberator* extra, 1840; H. B. Stanton to E. Wright, April 11, 1839, Wright Papers, LOC, quoted in Kraditor.

5. [Chapman], "Right and Wrong"; Anne Weston to Mary [Weston], Jan. 9, 1839, BPL; LIB, Jan. 10, 1840; MWC to Deborah Weston, May 9, [1839], BPL; LMC to Lydia B. Child, Dec. 12, 1839, in Meltzer and Holland.

6. The identification of the black women on both sides of the controversy has been made from mentions in LIB: Dec. 14, 1833, Sept. 19, 1838, April 3, 1840, ff.; in private letters: Anne Weston to Deborah Weston, April 18, 1837, Dec. 15, 1839, ff., BPL. Deborah Weston to Mary Weston, Jan. 5, 1840, BPL, uses "nigger"; MWC to E. Pease, Aug. 30, 1838, BPL on "sangre azul." Susan Paul's light skin is mentioned in Southwick, Martha Ball's in LIB, Sept. 19, 1838. Anne Weston to Deborah Weston, Oct. 22, 1836, BPL, quotes Henrietta Sargent on Snowden. See Quarles, *Black Abolitionists* for discussion of white abolitionists' color prejudice and paternalistic attitude toward their black associates.

7. Proceedings of Anti-Slavery Convention of American Women, 1837, 1838, 1839; [Chapman], 'Right and Wrong."

8. LIB, June 7, June 14, 1839, April 3, 1840, ff., reports black meetings in support of Garrison. The twenty-six signatures of "Women of Colour" are in varying handwritings, but the covering note appears to have been written by Anne Weston, BPL.

9. Martha Ball to Elizabeth Pease, May 6, 1840, BPL; Lucretia Mott to MWC, Dec. 16, 1839, May 13, 1840, BPL; Anne Weston to Deborah Weston, Dec. 15, 1839, BPL.

10. AK speech to BFASS, LIB, Oct. 23, 1840.

11. H. B. Stanton to Amos Phelps, Feb. 15, 1840, BPL, quoted in Kraditor; LMC to Ellis Gray Loring, May 7, [1840], Meltzer and Holland.

12. *Massachusetts Abolitionist*, quoted in LIB, May 29, 1840; LIB, April 24, 1840; Oliver Johnson; Wyatt-Brown.

13. LIB, April 24, May 1, May 15, May 22, 1840; E. Quincy diary, May 11–13, 1840,

MHS; Anne Weston notes of 1840 meeting, BPL; Anne Weston to MWC, May 13, 1840, BPL; Southwick; NASS, June 14, 1840; WLG to Helen Garrison, May 15, 1840, Merrill and Ruchames, v. 2; Wyatt-Brown; Executive Committee Minutes, 1839–40, BPL.
14. JGW to "Dear Sister," June 30, 1840, in John Pickard; JGW to Benjamin S. Jones, July 18, 1840, WHM; *New Haven Record*, quoted in LIB, June 5, 1840; *Journal of Commerce*, quoted in LIB, May 29, June 12, 1840.

CHAPTER 7: THE NOTORIOUS ABBY KELLEY

1. LIB, May 29, June 5, June 12, Aug. 14, 1840; NASS, June 14, 1840; Sarah M. Douglass to Charles Whipple, April 26, 1841, BPL; *New Haven Register*, quoted in LIB, June 12, 1840.
2. AK to Darlings, June 12, 1840, AAS; Merrill, ed., *Behold Me*.
3. LIB, June 5, 1840; AK to Darlings, June 12, 1840, AAS; LIB, July 17, 1840.
4. AK to Darlings, June 12, 1840, AAS; AK to Hudson, June 1840, U. Mass.
5. LIB, July 10, Aug. 14, 1840; NASS, July 30, Oct. 8, 1840; AK to Hudson, Aug. 6, 1840; U. Mass; AK to Darlings, June 12, 1840, AAS; Schlesinger.
6. LIB, July 24, July 31, 1840; NASS, July 23, 1840; Bartlett, *New Light;* Stewart, *Wendell Phillips*; Bacon, *Valiant Friend*; Cromwell; Stanton; Stanton, Anthony, et al., v. 1; LIB, July 24, Dec. 4, 1840; Lucretia Mott to MWC, July 29, 1840, BPL.
7. Alice Welch Cowles to Henry Cowles, July 9, 1840, Oberlin; Fletcher; Foster Rem; AKF, "What Hinders Us?"
8. AK to Hudson, Aug. 6, 1840, U. Mass; WPA, *Connecticut*; Foster Rem; LIB, Sept. 20, 1840; *Watchman and Wesleyan Observer*, quoted in NASS, Oct. 8, 1840.
9. Foster Rem; AKF, "What Hinders Us?"; I Corinthians 14:34–35; Revelation 2:20; Jeremiah 9:1; Horney; Sophia Rundlett to AK, June 15, 1841, AAS; Mary Moses to AK, Aug. 16, 1841, AAS; Wyman and Wyman, v. 2.
10. AK to Hudsons, April 12, 1841, U. Mass; Hudson journal, 1840–41, U. Mass; LIB, Sept. 18, 1840.
11. LIB, Oct. 9, Oct. 16, Oct. 23, Oct. 30, 1840; E. Quincy to AK, Aug. [1839], WHM; E. Quincy to Caroline Weston, Feb. 9, 1841, BPL; LIB, Oct. 23, 1840; NASS, Nov. 19, 1840.
12. AK to SSF, Jan. 30, 1843, AAS; Meltzer and Holland; *Woman's Journal*, July 18, 1885; MWC to AK, Oct. 3, 1840, AAS; T. W. Higginson; Southwick; LIB, Jan. 5, 1855, Dec. 4, 1840, Jan. 1, 1841; W. P. and F. J. Garrison, v. 3.
13. William Bassett to AK, Nov. 12, 1838, Nov. 6, 1839, AAS; Society of Friends; AK to Uxbridge Monthly Meeting of Friends, March 22, 1841, and AK to WLG, Sept. 20, 1841, in LIB, Oct. 8, 1841; Records of Uxbridge Meeting, June 25, Oct. 29, and Nov. 26, 1841, Archives of New England Meeting, RIHS; AK to LMC, Dec. 17, 1841, Holland and Meltzer; Pillsbury, *Acts*; Emerson, ed.; Wyman and Wyman.

14. Jerusha Bird to [MWC], Nov. 1, 1840, BPL; James Jackson to Oliver Johnson, Aug. 2, 1840, BPL; Esther Moore to WLG, Nov. 15, 1840, BPL; George Bradburn to AK, March 29, 1841, WHM; LIB, Jan. 15, 1841.

15. LIB, April 2, 1841; *Connecticut Observer*, quoted in NASS, March 18, 1841; AK to Hudsons, April 12, 1841, U. Mass; Strother; NASS, May 20, 1841.

16. Oliver Johnson; AK to Hudsons, April 12, 1841, U. Mass; Executive Committee Minutes, May 1841; E. Loring to AK, Sept. 27, 1841, AAS; LMC to E. Loring, June 17, Nov. 24, 1841, Feb. 15, Feb. 28, 1842, April 6, [1842], [Oct. 29?, 1842], Nov. 23, 1842, March 6, 1843, Meltzer and Holland; LMC to WP, May 3, 1842, Meltzer and Holland; LMC to E. Loring, May 17, [1841], May 27, 1841, Holland and Meltzer; AK to LMC, Oct. 27, 1841, Dec. 13, 1841, Dec. 17, 1841, Holland and Meltzer; NASS, March 24, April 22, May 13, May 20, 1841, Jan. 20, 1842, May 4, 1843; E. Quincy to Chapmans, May 18, [1841], BPL.

17. LIB, May 21, 1841; AK to N. P. Rogers, July 8, 1841, NYHS; Merrill and Ruchames, v. 3.

CHAPTER 8: A NEW HAMPSHIRE FANATIC

1. Pillsbury, *Acts*; Filler; LIB, June 4, 11, 1841.

2. Pillsbury, *Acts* and "Stephen Symonds Foster"; Burkett; Pease and Pease; Stearns; Family Records, AAS; Wyman; Stephen S. Foster, Alumni file in Dartmouth College Archives; Joel Bernard; obituary, *Worcester Daily Spy*, Sept. 9, 1881; AEG to SSF, July 17, [1837], AAS. I am indebted to Joel Bernard for the phrase "rural intelligentsia," which he in turn credits to David F. Allmendiger, *Paupers and Scholars: The Transformation of Student Life in Nineteenth-Century New England* (New York, 1975).

3. AK to N. P. Rogers, July 8, 1841, NYHS; SSF to AK, Sept. 27, 1855, AAS; AEG Diary, Clements; Chandler's "Mental Metempsychosis," in *Genius of Universal Emancipation*, Feb. 1, 1831; LIB, June 18, 1841.

4. AK used the phrase "home, sweet home" in AK to N. P. Rogers, July 8, 1841, NYHS, NASS, Jan. 13, 1842, ff.; AK to MWC, Aug. 10, 1841, BPL; MWC to AK, Aug. 16, [1841], WHM; E. Quincy diary, Aug. 17–18, 1841, MHS; LIB, Aug. 27, Sept. 10, 1841; Henrietta Sargent in NASS, Sept. 2, 1841.

5. AK to WLG in LIB, Sept. 10, 1841.

6. Wyman; Pillsbury, *Acts*; Pease and Pease; Joel Bernard; AK to George Benson, Sept. 13, 1841, BPL; E. Loring to AK, Sept. 27, 1841, AAS.

7. Gettleman; Lemons and McKenna; U.S. Congress; Schlesinger; P. Foner, VI; Quarles; Douglass; NASS, Nov. 4, Nov. 25, Dec. 23, Dec. 30, 1841, Jan. 6, Jan. 13, 1842; LIB, Dec. 31, 1841, Jan. 14, 1842; Strother; Hudson journal, Nov. 21, 1840, U. Mass.

8. NASS, Jan. 19, 1842; LIB, Feb. 11, Feb. 18, 1842; Anne Weston to Deborah Weston, Feb. 4, 1842, BPL; *Bay State Democrat*, quoted in LIB, Feb. 18, 1842.

9. Anne Weston to Deborah Weston, Feb. 4, 1842, BPL; Dickens.

10. LIB, March 4, 1842; Family Records, AAS.

11. LIB, Feb. 11, 1842, Jan. 12, 1855; Anne Weston to Deborah Weston, April 11, 1842, BPL; Alice Stone Blackwell memoirs, NAWSA, LOC.

12. Emerson, ed.; Sarah Pugh to Richard Webb, June 17, 1842, BPL; LIB, May 20, May 27, June 3, 1842; NASS, May 19, June 2, 1842; Executive Committee Minutes, May 1842, BPL; E. Quincy, in NASS, June 2, 1842.

13. LIB, June 3, June 10, 1842; Foster Rem.

14. LIB, June 17, 1842.

CHAPTER 9: ALONG THE PSYCHIC HIGHWAY

1. Cross; Carmer, "Listen for a Lonesome Drum: A York State Chronicle," quoted in Cross; WPA, *New York: A Guide to the Empire State*; AK to SSF, June 7, 1843, AAS.

2. J. A. Collins to AK, July 16, 1842, WHM; LIB, Aug. 12, 1842; NASS, Aug. 11, 1842; Seneca, N.Y. paper, quoted in LIB, Sept. 23, 1842; *Tocsin of Liberty*, quoted in LIB, July 27, 1842; *Seneca Observer*, quoted in LIB, Sept. 2, 1842; AK to MWC, Aug. 13, 1843, BPL; LIB, Oct. 28, 1842; AK to LIB, Sept. 30, 1842.

3. NASS, Nov. 3, 1842; *Utica Daily Times*, quoted in LIB, Nov. 18, 1842; AK to WP, Oct. 28, 1842, AAS.

4. Hewitt; WLG to Helen Garrison, Nov. 21, 1842, BPL.

5. WLG to Helen Garrison, Nov. 27, 1842, BPL; Pillsbury, *Acts*; Joel Bernard; LIB, Sept. 30, Nov. 25, Dec. 30, 1842; Matthew 23:29, 33.

6. LIB, Dec. 23, Dec. 30, 1842; NASS, Dec. 15, Dec. 22, 1842.

7. Cornell; Merrill and Ruchames, v. 4; Harper, v. 1; Abigail Mott to AK, Aug. 18, 1842, AAS; Sterling, *We Are Your Sisters*.

8. James et al. eds., AK to SSF, Jan. 30, [1843], AAS; P. Wright to SSF, [January 1843], AAS; P. Wright to AK, Dec. 25, 1842, AAS; P. Wright to SSF, Feb. 27, 1843; AAS; P. Wright to AK, [1843], AAS; AK to SSF, March 4, 1843, AAS; Wrobel; AK to SSF, March 28, 1843, AAS; Davies; AK to SSF, Jan. 30, 1843, AAS; P. Wright to AK, Dec. 25, 1842, AAS; LIB, Jan. 5, 1844; AK to SSF, March 24, 1843; AAS; AK to SSF, Aug. 13, 1843, AAS; AK to SSF, Nov. 22, 1843, AAS.

9. AK to SSF, Jan. 30, 1843, [Jan. 1843], March 4, March 28, Aug. 13, Nov. 22, 1843, AAS.

10. F. Douglass to AK, June 19, 1843, AAS; AK to E. D. Hudson, Feb. 7, 1843, U. Mass; E. D. Hudson to AK, March 2, 1843, AAS; James Gibbons to AK, Sept. 23, 1842, July 22, 1843, AAS; A. Chase to AK [June 1843], AAS; Jacob Ferris to AK, July 3, 1842, AAS; Samuel Porter to AK, Sept. 16, 1842, AAS; AK to Samuel Porter, Sept. 13, 1842, Rochester.

11. Judy Wellman to author, Jan. 24, 1986; Sterling, *Turning the World Upside Down*; Amy Post obituary, Jan. 30, 1887, Rochester; A. Post to AK, Dec. 4, 1843, AAS.

12. A. Post to AK, Dec. 4, 1843, AAS; E. McClintock to AK, Jan. 10, 1843, AAS; AK

to MWC, Dec. 15, 1842, Aug. 13, 1843, BPL; Merrill and Ruchames, v. 3; Chambers-Schiller, *Liberty, a Better Husband*; E. Neall to AK, March 12, 1843, AAS; Jeannette Brown to AK, July 19, 1843, AAS.
13. Cross; Harlow; *Seneca Observer*, quoted in LIB, Sept. 2, 1842; NASS, April 10, 1843; LIB, May 5, 1843.
14. LMC to E. M. Davis, March 7, 1843, Holland and Meltzer; LMC to Ellis Loring, March 6, 1843, Meltzer and Holland; NASS, May 4, 1843.
15. NASS, May 18, 1843; LIB, May 17, 1843; L. Mott, April 4, 1843, in Hallowell; *New York Express*, quoted in LIB, May 17, 1843; *Washington Globe*, quoted in LIB, June 2, 1843; AK to SSF, March 28, 1843, AAS; Laura to AK, July 29, 1843, AAS.
16. Ballou, *Autobiography*; Lucy Kelley West to AK, July 31, 1843, AAS; AK to SSF, June 1, 1843, AAS.

CHAPTER 10: ANTISLAVERY POLITICS

1. AK to LIB, May 5, 1843; Kraditor; E. Neall to AK, March 12, 1843, AAS; AK to NASS, April 10, 1843; LIB, Aug. 12, 1842; AK to MWC, Jan. 23, March 28, Oct. 19, 1843, BPL.
2. Harlow; G. Smith to AK, July 24, July 27, Aug. 24, Aug. 30, 1843, AAS; AK to G. Smith, July 26, July 29, Aug. 7, 1843, Syracuse; G. Smith to SSF, Oct. 23, 1843, AAS; AK to SSF, Nov. 22, 1843, AAS.
3. Stewart; Friedman; Pease and Pease; Chambers-Schiller, "The Cab"; E. Quincy to R. Webb, Jan. 29, 1843, BPL; Executive Committee Minutes, 1843–44, BPL.
4. MWC to AK, July 26, 1843, AAS; AK to MWC, May 5, 1843, BPL; MWC to D. L. Child, May 14, 1843, in Merrill and Ruchames, v. 3.
5. WLG to Henry Wright, Merrill and Ruchames, v. 3; P. Foner, v. 1; AK to MWC, Aug. 2, 1843, BPL; J. A. Collins to MWC, Aug. 23, 1843, BPL; Anne Weston to MWC, Feb. 5, 1841, BPL; AK to Hudsons, Feb. 27, 1843, U. Mass; AK to SSF, March 28, 1843, AAS; LIB, Sept. 29, 1843; MWC to AK, Sept. 3, 1843, AAS; AK to MWC, Aug. 28, 1843, BPL; Douglass.
6. LIB, Sept. 28, 1843.
7. A. Brooke to MWC, Oct. 5, 1843, BPL; AK to MWC, Sept. 4, 1843, BPL; AK to WLG, Sept. 4, 1843, BPL; LIB, Sept. 15, 1843; NASS, Aug. 24, 1843.
8. AK to SSF, Sept. 4, 1843, AAS; AK to MWC, Sept. 4, 1843, BPL; AK to WLG, Sept. 4, 1843, BPL; WLG to AK, Sept. 8, 1843, WHM; Anne Weston to Caroline and Deborah Weston, Sept. 9–11, 1843, BPL.
9. AK to MWC, Dec. 2, 1843, BPL.
10. WPA, *New York: A Guide to the Empire State*; AK to MWC, Aug. 28, Oct. 10, 1843, BPL; AK to SSF, June 13, 1843, AAS; *Woman's Journal*, Aug. 14, 1880. Altschuler and Saltzgaber contains full text of the Rhoda Bement trial. Ansel Bascom to AK, Feb. 16, 1844.
11. Griffith; Stanton; Altschuler and Saltzgaber.

12. MWC to AK, Jan. 1, 1844, AAS; Massachusetts Anti-Slavery Society Annual Reports, Twelfth Annual Meeting; W. P. and F. J. Garrison, v. 3; Madison; Sterling, *Forever Free*; LIB, May 20, 1842, ff; LIB, May 12, May 19, 1843, Sept. 6, Sept. 13, 1844; Bartlett.

13. AK to MWC, Feb. 5, 1844, Houghton; Ballou, *History of Milford*.

14. AK to SSF, Feb. 25, 1844, AAS; Abby Southwick to AK, Feb. 4, 1844, AAS; LIB, Feb. 16, 1844, Aug. 8, 1851, June 20, 1851; Anne Weston to Deborah Weston, April 11, 1842, BPL; J. Fiske to AK, March 10, 1844, AAS; AK to SSF, Feb. 25, 1844, AAS.

15. E. D. Hudson journal, 1844, U. Mass; Sterling, *We Are Your Sisters*; AK to WP, April 16, April 28, 1844, Houghton; Samuel Philbrick to AK, March 8, 1844, AAS; LIB, April 19, 1844; AK to WP, Sept. 28, 1844, Houghton; Bartlett; Stewart, *Wendell Phillips*; Sherwin; WP to AK, Jan. 27, [1845], AAS; LIB, April 5, 1844.

16. MWC to AK, [Oct. 1843], AAS; AK to WP, April 20, 1844, Houghton; Gay to AK, April 30, 1844, AAS; NASS, May 23, May 30, 1844.

17. LIB, May 10, May 17, May 24, 1844; WLG to James Yerrinton, May 7, 1844, in Merrill and Ruchames, v. 3.

18. AK to E. D. Hudson, July 23, 1844, U. Mass; AK to SSF, July 23, 1844, AAS; AK to NASS, Dec. 19, 1844; AK to SSF, April 22, 1844, AAS; Diana and Joanna Ballou to AK, Aug. 7, 1844, AAS; AK to WP, Sept. 23, 1844, Houghton; *Portsmouth Journal* and *Exeter News Letter*, quoted in LIB, Sept. 27, Oct. 4, 1844.

19. AK to SSF, July 23, 1844, AAS; AK to WLG, Sept. 26, 1844, BPL; MWC to AK, Sept. 30, 1844, AAS; LIB, Nov. 8, Nov. 29, Dec. 13, 1844; NASS, Dec. 26, 1844; WLG to Richard Webb, March 1, 1845, in Merrill and Ruchames, v. 3. The Rogers episode is extensively covered in Stewart, Merrill, John Thomas, Perry, and Friedman.

CHAPTER 11: THE PATH OF TRUE LOVE AND OTHER MATTERS

1. E. M. Davis to MWC, [September] 1844, BPL; MWC to AK, Sept. 30, 1844, AAS.

2. LIB, Aug. 23, 1844; AK to SSF, Dec. 29, Nov. 13, 1844, Jan. 3, 1845, AAS.

3. E. M. Davis to MWC, Dec. 10, Dec. 16, 1844, BPL; AK to SSF, Dec. 29, 1844, AAS; J. E. Hitchcock to MWC, Dec. 15, 1844, BPL; M. Grew to AK, Dec. 13, 1844, AAS.

4. NASS, Jan. 16, 1845; AK to SSF, Dec. 29, 1844, AAS; AK to WP, Dec. 25, 1844, Houghton.

5. E. D. Hudson journal, 1844–45, U. Mass; NASS, Jan.–April, 1845; AK to SSF, March 4, April 2, 1845, AAS.

6. E. D. Hudson journal, Jan. 1845, U. Mass; NASS, Jan. 23, 1845; Thomas Garrett to AK and J. E. Hitchcock, Jan. 18, 1845, AAS.

7. AK to SSF, Jan. 3, 1845, WHM.

8. AK to WP, Jan. 7, Jan. 21, Feb. 18, Feb. 22, 1845, Houghton; WP to AK, Jan. 27, 1845, AAS.

9. E. D. Hudson journal, 1845, U. Mass; AK to SSF, March 14, 1845, AAS; NASS, April 24, 1845.

10. AK to SSF, March 14, 1845, AAS.

11. Eliza Follen to AK, Feb. 12, 1845, AAS; M. M. Moore to AK, April 4, 1845, WHM; Sarah Pugh to MWC, June 15, 1844, BPL; Sarah Pugh to Webbs, April 25, 1845, BPL.

12. Anne Weston journal, BPL; AK to SSF, Jan. 3, 1845, AAS; AK to SSF, April 2, 1845, AAS; Nathan; LIB, June 5, 1846; James et al.

13. AK to SSF, Jan. 3, 1845, WHM; AK to SSF, Aug. 13, 1843, April 22, 1844, July 30, 1843, AAS; Fowler; SSF to AK, Aug. 10, 1843, AAS; AK to SSF, Aug. 13, 1843, AAS.

14. SSF to AK, March 18, 1844, AAS; AK to SSF, April 4, 1844, WHM; Benjamin Thomas; E. Quincy to Caroline Weston, June [1843], BPL; AK to SSF, April 22, 1844, AAS; WP to E. Pease, June 29, 1842, BPL; AK to SSF, Aug. 13, 1843, AAS; AK to MWC, Aug. 13, 1843, BPL; Foster, *Brotherhood*; MWC to AK, Sept. 9, 1843, WHM; MWC to AK, Oct. 12, 1843, AAS; AK to MWC, Nov. 9, 1843, BPL; AK to SSF, Nov. 22, 1843, AAS; *Practical Christian*, quoted in LIB, June 7, 1844; NASS, June 7, Aug. 8, 1844; LIB, June 14, June 21, 1844; NASS, Jan. 16, 1845.

15. AK to WP, Jan. 21, 1845, Houghton; AK to SSF, Jan. 20, Feb. 5, March 11, 1845, April 1845, March 25, 1845, Feb. 5, 1845, AAS; AK to Elizabeth Neal, April 5, 1845, Columbia; AK to SSF, Feb. 5, 1845, AAS; *United States Gazette*, quoted in NASS, May 8, 1845; AK to SSF, March 25, 1845, AAS; Jesse Holmes to AK and J. Hitchcock, March 7, 1845, AAS; AK to WP, March 23, 1845, Houghton; SSF to Galen Foster, May 18, 1845, AAS; AK to SSF, April 2, 1845, AAS.

16. LIB, May 9, May 16, May 23, 1845; NASS, May 15, May 22, 1845; *New York Herald*, quoted in NASS, May 15, 1845; SSF to Galen Foster, May 18, 1845, AAS.

CHAPTER 12: LORD, WHAT A TONGUE SHE'S GOT

1. AK to SSF, June 9, 1845, WHM; LIB, June 27, 1845; BUGLE, June 20, 1845; AK to WP, June 14, 1845, Houghton.

2. AK to MWC, July 17, 1845, BPL; AK to WP, June 14, 1845, Houghton; AK to Gay, July 6, 1845, Columbia; MWC to AK, Sept. 16, 1845, AAS; B. Jones to AK, July 14, 1845, AAS.

3. AK to Gay, July 6, 1845, Columbia; AK to Elizabeth Gay, Nov. 10, 1845, Columbia; AK to Gay, April 1, 1846, Columbia; BUGLE, June 12, Aug. 21, 1846.

4. AK to SSF, June 9, 1845, WHM; WPA, *Ohio Guide*; Trollope; Dickens.

5. Litwack; BUGLE, Oct. 6, 1860; AK to MWC, July 17, 1845, BPL; BUGLE, July 25–Nov. 13, 1846; LIB, July 11, July 25, Aug. 29, Oct. 10, Oct. 17, Oct. 24, 1845; LIB, June 27, 1845; BUGLE, Aug. 15, 1845.

6. BUGLE, Nov. 14, Nov. 21, 1845; *Western Christian Advocate*, quoted in BUGLE, Nov. 21, 1845; LIB, Oct. 17, 1845; *Indiana Freeman*, quoted in LIB, Nov. 7, 1845; Foster Rem; AK to Olive Darling, Nov. 8, 1845; WHM; AK to Elizabeth Gay, Nov. 11, 1845, Columbia; marriage certificate, WHM; Sarah Pugh to Elizabeth Pease, Jan. 20, 1846, BPL; SSF to AK, Aug. 31, 1855, AAS; AK to Gay, Jan. 22, Nov. 28, 1846, Columbia.

7. BUGLE, Jan. 9, Jan. 30, 1846; Pillsbury to Fosters, Jan. 9, 1846, AAS; Gay to AK, Feb. 11, [1846], AAS; AK to Gay, June 10, 1846, Columbia.

8. MWC to AK, Feb. 1, 1846, AAS; AK to MWC, Jan. 14, Feb. 18, 1846, BPL; SSF to WP, Feb. 17, Sept. 14, 1846, Houghton.

9. AK to MWC, Feb. 18, 1846, BPL; LIB, Oct. 17, Nov. 7, 1845; BUGLE, Oct. 17, 1845; WPA, *Ohio Guide*; Hallowell; BUGLE, Nov. 21, 1845; Charles Perry to Thomas Gould, Sept. 24, 1845, Haverford; *Cleveland American*, quoted in BUGLE, July 31, 1846; SSF to LIB, Aug. 14, 1846.

10. LIB, May 22, 1846; NASS, June 5, 1846; Lowell; Hough; BUGLE, June 12, June 26, Oct. 23, 1846.

11. Stewart, *Giddings*; Gamble; LIB, July 9, 1845; AK to Gay, July 6, 1845, Columbia; LIB, Sept. 26, Oct. 10, 1845; BUGLE, Sept. 19, Sept. 26, Oct. 3, Oct. 17, 1845; AK to Gay, July 25, 1845, Columbia; Giddings Scrapbook, OHS; Maria Giddings to AK, Feb. 27, 1847, AAS; LIB, May 22, 1846; Giddings to Maria Giddings, June 19, 1846, Giddings Papers, OHS; Baker.

12. AK to LS, April 20, 1846, NAWSA, LOC; Williams; AK to MWC, Feb. 18, 1846, BPL; AK to Betsy Cowles, Jan. 28, March 15, June 29, Nov. 8, 1846, Kent State; BUGLE, June 5, Sept. 11, Oct. 23, 1846, Jan. 1, Jan. 22, 1847; AK to LS, Aug. 2, 1846, NAWSA, LOC; Jane Neely to AK, Feb. 25, April 8, [1846], AAS.

13. Blackwell; LS to Fosters, March 25, 1846, AAS; AK to Betsy Cowles, March 15, 1846, Kent State; AK to LS, April 20, 1846, NAWSA, LOC; LS to AK, July 3, 1846, AAS; AK to LS, July 17, Aug. 2, 1846, Aug. 15, [1846], NAWSA, LOC; BUGLE, Oct. 9, 1846; LIB, Oct. 23, 1846.

14. Dr. Anne F. Sterling to author, 1986; *Boston Globe*, Jan. 10, 1986; AK to Gay, Oct. 28, 1846, Columbia; AK to Betsy Cowles, Feb. 9, 1847, Kent State; AK to LS, March 28, 1847, NAWSA, LOC.

CHAPTER 13: CONFLICTING CLAIMS

1. AK to Betsy Cowles, Feb. 9, 1847, Kent State; LIB, Dec. 18, 1846; Jan. 1, Jan. 8, Jan. 29, 1847; NASS, Dec. 31, 1846; LIB, Feb. 5, 1847; Massachusetts Anti-Slavery Society Annual Reports.

2. AK to Betsy Cowles, Feb. 9, 1847, Kent State; Eliza Follen to AK, Feb. 27, [1847], AAS; AK to SSF, April 7, 1847, AAS.

3. Lincoln; Hersey; O'Flynn; Howland.

4. SSF to WP, Feb. 17, 1846, Houghton; SSF to E. M. Davis, April 13, 1847, Houghton; SSF to AK, Feb. 7, 1847, AAS; Julius Ames to AK, Nov. 28, 1846, AAS.

5. AK to SSF, April 7, 1847, AAS; deed, April 27, 1847, WHM; SSF to E. M. Davis, April 13, 1847, Houghton; National Register of Historic Places Inventory, Department of Interior, Family Records, AAS; Frank Clarkson to author, Sept. 1988.

6. AK to SSF, April 7, 1847, AAS; AK to WP, May 5, 1847, Houghton; LIB, May 14, 1847; Family Records, AAS.

7. AK to SSF, Aug. 18, Aug. 24, Sept. 3, Sept. 9, 1847, [Sept. 1847], Sept. 28, 1847, AAS; Newell Foster and AK to SSF, Sept. 12, Sept. 26, Sept. 29, 1847, AAS.

8. P. Foner, v. 1; AK to SSF, Sept. 28, 1847, AAS; AK to Gay, Feb. 1847, Columbia.

9. AK to SSF, Sept. 9, 1847, AAS; Giddings to AK, Feb. 2, 1848, AAS; Mary Howitt to AK, Sept. 2, [1847]; *Howitt's Journal*, Jan. 22, 1848, BPL; AK to MWC, Dec. 17, 1847, BPL; AK to Gay, Sept. 19, 1847, Columbia; S. and E. Gay to AK, Sept. 24, 1847, AAS; Susan Cabot to AK, Jan. 16, [1848], AAS; J. E. Jones to AK, Jan. 23, 1848, AAS.

10. AK to Gay, Nov. 16, 1849, Columbia; AK to MWC, Jan. 21, March 20, 1848, BPL; AK to LS, March 29, 1848, NAWSA, LOC; LIB, May 5, 1848; AK to Lydia Dennett, March 17, [1849], March 30, 1849, Houghton; Lydia Dennett to AK, March 25, 1849, AAS; AK to Helen Garrison, March 30, 1849, Houghton; AK to WP, March 31, 1849, Houghton; WP to Westons, [1849], Houghton.

11. LIB, May 12, June 9, Sept, 1, Sept. 8, Sept. 15, 1848.

12. Morris, ed.; E. Foner, *Free Soil*.

13. J. E. Jones to AK, April 18, 1848, Jan. 23, 1848, AAS; WLG to Helen Garrison, July 18, 1848, WLG to MWC, July 19, 1848; WLG to E. Quincy, Aug. 10, 1848, in Merrill and Ruchames, v. 3; LIB, Sept. 22, 1848; AK to Executive Committee, Nov. 6, 1848, Houghton; AK to WP, April 12 [1849], Houghton; AK to Gay, April 20, 1849, Columbia.

14. *Woman's Journal*, July 4, 1874; AK to SSF, April 3, 1849, AAS; AK to Gay, April 20, 1849, Columbia; AK to WP, April 12, April 24, 1849, Houghton.

15. AK to WP, April 16, [1849], Houghton; LIB, May 18, 1849; AK to Gay, May 24, 1849, May 7, [1849], June 25, [1849], Columbia; AK to Phillipses, Aug. 23, 1849, Houghton.

16. AK to Gay, July 23, 1849, Columbia; account book, WHM; Executive Committee Minutes, June 1, 1849, BPL; AK to Gay, Aug. 17, [1849], July 15, July 23, [1849], Nov. 16, [1849], Columbia.

17. AK to Betsy Cowles, [Oct.] 1, 1849, Kent State; AK to Gay, May 24, May 28, 1849, Columbia; Caroline Foster to AK, March 22, 1849; Alla Foster to AK, July 6, 1849, AAS; AK to Anne Weston, Nov. 27, 1849, BPL.

18. SSF to AK, April 4, April 11, 1850, AAS; SSF to AK, Sept. 11, 1850, AAS; Executive Committee Minutes, Oct. 17, 1849, BPL; AK to SSF, April 16, April 29, 1850, AAS; AK to Gay, April 19, 1850, Columbia; LIB, May 17, May 24, June 14, 1850.

19. AK to Gay, March 19, 1850, Columbia; Ruth Pollard to AK, July 28, 1850, AAS; SSF to AK, Aug. 5, Aug. 15, 1850, AAS; AK to SSF, [June 1850], Aug. 11, 1850, AAS; AK to SSF, Sept. 18, 1850, WHM; SSF to AK, Sept. 27, 1850, AAS.

20. AK to SSF, June 22, [1850], AAS; BUGLE, July 13, 1850; Douglass to Gay, Sept. 1847 in P. Foner, v. 1; BUGLE, Sept. 14, July 20, Sept. 7, 1850, Aug. 24, 1850; SSF to AK, Aug. 5, 1850, AAS; AK to WP, Oct. 6, 1850, Houghton; BUGLE, Sept. 28, 1850, Aug. 24, Aug. 31, Sept. 14, 1850; Chadwick, ed.; AK to SSF, Aug. 6, 1850, AAS; SSF to AK, July 21, 1850, AAS; AK to SSF, Sept. 18, 1850, WHM.

CHAPTER 14: BLOODY FEET, SISTERS!

1. Blackwell; Stanton, Anthony, et al., v. 1; AK to WP, Oct. 6, 1850, Houghton; LIB, Nov. 15, 1850; NASS, Oct. 21, 1850; Hunt; Suhl; Flexner.
2. *New York Tribune*, Oct. 17, 18, 20, 1851; *New York Herald*, Oct. 16, 19, 21, 1851; Stanton, Anthony, et al., v. 1; AK, "Speech," Smith; Suhl; Flexner, *Mary Wollstonecraft*.
3. Chambers-Schiller, *Liberty, a Better Husband* and "The Cab"; WP to Pease, March 9, 1851 in W. P. and F. J. Garrison, v. 3; AK to WP, [Winter 1851], Houghton; LIB, Feb. 21, 1851; George Thompson to AK, Feb. 17, 1851, AAS.
4. NASS, Feb. 27, March 20, March 27, April 3, 1851; LIB, Feb. 28, April 4, 1851; Jacqueline Bernard; George Thompson to Anne Weston, Feb. 28, 1851, in Taylor; AK to ECS, Jan. 11, 1851, Stanton Papers, LOC; ECS to AK, Jan. 12, 1851, AAS; WP to AK, [Spring 1851], AAS.
5. George Thompson to Anne Weston, Feb. 24, Feb. 28, March 12, March 17, 1851, in Taylor; AK to Garrisons, March 16, 1851, BPL; WLG to AK, April 6, 1851, AAS; LIB, May 16, May 23, 1851; P. Foner, v. 2; LIB, June 27, 1851; AK to George Thompson, Aug. 19, 1851, AAS.
6. P. Foner, v. 2; AK to Gay, March 19, 1850, Columbia; AK to WLG, March 30, 1852, BPL; AK to Gay, March 28, 1852, Columbia; Hewitt; LIB, May 7, 1852; NASS, Sept. 24, 1853; LIB, Nov. 18, Dec. 2, 1853; Quarles, *Frederick Douglass*; P. Foner, v. 2; LIB, April 6, 1855.
7. Powell; Harper, v. 1; Chadwick, ed.; Caroline Putnam to Samuel May, Jan. 22, 1887, MHS.
8. WLG to AK, Aug. 12, 1851, AAS; AK to WLG, Aug. 22, 1851, BPL; AK to Gay, Dec. 9, 1851, Columbia; AK to SSF, Dec. 2, 1851, AAS; F. Douglass to Gerrit Smith, May 15, 1851, Feb. 19, 1852, in P. Foner, v. 2.
9. SSF to S. May, Jr., Sept. 24, 1851, BPL; SSF to AK, Sept. 21, Sept, 24, 1851, AAS, Dec. 2, 1851, WHM; Graham; S. May, Jr., to AK, Dec. 1, 1851, AAS; S. May, Jr., to SSF, Dec. 1, 1851, AAS; Wrobel; AK to SSF, April 3, [1849], AAS, Dec. 2, 1851, AAS; John L. Thomas; LIB, May 28, 1852; Stewart, *Giddings*; SSF to AK, Sept. 5, 1851, AAS.
10. AK to Gay, [Jan. 1852], Feb. 9, 1852, Columbia.
11. Buckmaster; Sterling, *Forever Free*; LIB, May 16, 1851; John L. Thomas.
12. LIB, May 21, 1852; Friedman; Siebert; Edelstein; T. W. Higginson, *Cheerful Yesterdays* and "Stephen Foster's Death," *Woman's Journal*, Sept. 17, 1881; LIB, June 22, 1855; LIB, Aug. 5, 1853.
13. NASS, April 15, 1853; Harlow; S. Holley to AK, Feb. 17, 1852, AAS; AK to S. May, Jr. Aug. 18, 1852, BPL; S. Holley to Fosters, Nov. 15, 1852, WHM; Chadwick, ed.; S. Holley to AK, [1854], AAS; S. Holley to AK, May 13, 1857, AAS; SSF to AK, Aug. 17, 1851, WHM; Foster Rem; BUGLE, Aug. 20, 1853.
14. SSF to AK, April 16, 1854; Donald; Chadwick, ed.; AK to Alla Foster, April 17, 1852, WHM; LMC to Osgoods, May 11, 1856, Meltzer and Holland; Foster Rem; SSF to

AK, April 27, 1852, AAS; SSF to AK, Sept. 3, 1851, July 27, 1851, Sept. 21, 1851, AAS.
15. LIB, May 20, May 27, 1853; NASS, May 19, 1853; Blackwell; Harper, v. 1.

CHAPTER 15: GENERAL AGENT

1. NASS, May 19, 1853; LIB, Sept. 9, 1853; WLG to Abolitionists of the U.S., in Merrill and Ruchames, v. 4; Adams Foster to SSF, Feb. 20, 1854, AAS; AK to S. May, Jr., Sept. 15, 1853, BPL; WPA, *Guide to Michigan*; WLG to Helen Garrison, Oct. 10, Oct. 15, 1853, in Merrill and Ruchames, v. 4; Chadwick, ed.; BUGLE, Sept. 24, Oct. 8, 1853; James et al., eds.
2. LIB, Nov. 11, Nov. 18, 1853; AK to S. May, Jr., Nov. 9, 1853, BPL; LIB, Nov. 18, 1853; WLG to Helen Garrison, Oct. 17, 1853, in Merrill and Ruchames, v. 4; BUGLE, Feb. 18, Feb. 25, 1854; LIB, Oct. 14, 1853.
3. BUGLE, March 11, 1853; AK to Alla Foster, [spring 1854], AAS; Jan. 5, 1854, WHM; Sept. 14, [1853], WHM; Alla Foster to AK, [spring 1854], [Jan. 1854], WHM.
4. AK to LIB, May 26, 1854.
5. LIB, May 26, 1854, June 2, June 9, June 16, June 23, June 30, 1854; NASS, June 17, 1854; Buckmaster; Sterling, *Forever Free*; WP to E. Pease, Aug. 7, 1854, in Taylor.
6. Executive Committee Minutes, May 19, July 31, 1854, BPL; LIB, July 14, July 28, 1854; NASS, June 17, 1854; LIB, July 7, July 14, 1854; NASS, Aug. 12, 1854; John L. Thomas.
7. SSF to AK, Oct. 31, 1854, AAS; *Massachusetts Spy*, Nov. 1, Nov. 8, Nov. 22, Nov. 29, 1854; LIB, Nov. 3, Nov. 10, Nov. 24, 1854; NASS, Nov. 11, 1854; Edelstein; Caroline Putnam to S. May, Jan. 22, 1887, MHS.
8. WP to AK, May 31, 1855, WHM; LIB, June 22, 1855; AK to SSF, [1855], AAS; AK to SSF, Oct. 4, 1855, AAS; SSF to AK, Aug. 25, Sept. 12, Sept. 15, Sept. 27, Oct. 12, 1855, AAS; AK to SSF, Sept. 15, [1855], Oct. 4, 1855, AAS.
9. WLG, Jr., to his parents, Aug. 27, 1854, Smith; AK to SSF, Sept. 15, [1855], AAS; LIB, Feb. 2, 1855, Feb. 8, 1856, Dec. 12, 1856; Merrill and Ruchames, v. 4; SSF to AK, Feb. 12, [1855], AAS; AK to "My Dear Friend," Dec. 17, [1855], NAWSA, LOC; SSF, *Revolution the Only Remedy*; Caroline Putnam to AK, Nov. 8, 1857, Aug. 22, 1858, AAS; LIB, Feb. 8, 1856, Feb. 22, 1859, Jan. 25, 1861, ff.
10. Harper, v. 1; LIB, Sept. 28, 1855, Jan. 4, 1856, March 4, 1853; Wheeler; Nathan; Paulina W. Davis to ECS, December 12, [1851], E. C. Stanton Papers, Rutgers, February 9, [1852], Stanton Papers, LOC; Caroline Putnam to AK, Sept. 24, 1855, AAS.
11. LIB, Jan. 4, 1856; J. E. Jones to AK, Nov. 4, 1856, AAS; E. Quincy to AK, Feb. 13, 1855, WHM; Charles Hovey to SSF, Aug. 8, 1855, WHM; Sterling, *Forever Free*; Sherwin; LIB, Jan. 25, 1856; AK to WP, June 24, [1857], Houghton; LIB, May 30, June 6, 1856; NASS, May 31, June 7, 1856; LMC to Osgoods, July 20, 1856, to Sarah Shaw, Aug. 3, 1856, Meltzer and Holland; LIB, Oct. 31, 1856.

12. S. Holley to AK, July 19, 1856, AAS; AK to WP, March 29, [1857], Houghton; Myerson and Sheedy, eds.; *Macbeth*, act V, scene III: "My way of life/Is fall'n into the sear, the yellow leaf"; WP to AK, May 9, 1857, WHM.

13. Wyman and Wyman, v. 1; SBA to Fosters, April 20, 1857, AAS; Executive Committee Minutes, Aug. 3, 1857, BPL; AK to MWC, July 15, [1857], BPL; Lucretia Mott to Martha Wright, July 9, 1857, Smith; AK to WP, July 24, [1857], Houghton; AK to SSF, July 16, [1857], WHM; AK to MWC, Nov. 17, [1857], BPL; SSF to Alla Foster, Jan. 1, 1864, AAS; J. Sargent to AK, Aug. 23, 1857, WHM.

14. LIB, Aug. 7, Aug. 14, 1857.

15. AK to SSF, Aug. 7, [1857] AAS; LIB, Feb. 1, 1850, Jan. 25, 1856; Longfellow; AK to SSF, Dec. 4, [1857], AAS.

16. NASS, Aug. 22, 1857; Morris, ed.; NASS, Sept. 10, 1857; BUGLE, Sept. 12, Sept. 19, Sept. 26, Oct. 3, 1857; Sarah Remond to AK, Dec. 21, 1858, AAS; NASS, Oct. 10, 1857; AK to WP, Oct. 10, [1857], Houghton; NASS, Jan. 2, 1858; NASS, Oct. 24, Oct. 31, 1857; AK to SSF, Dec. 4, [1857], AAS; NASS, Nov. 21, Nov. 7, Nov. 14, 1857.

CHAPTER 16: THE IRREPRESSIBLE CONFLICT

1. AK to MWC, Nov. 17, [1857], BPL; AK to SSF, Dec. 4, [1857], AAS; Executive Committee Minutes, Nov. 27, Dec. 11, 1857, BPL.

2. AK to SSF, Dec. 4, Dec. 14, [1857], AAS; LIB, Nov. 20, Dec. 18, 1857.

3. NASS, Jan. 9, 1858; LIB, Feb. 5, 1858.

4. Alla Foster to AK, July 15, [1857], AAS; "The Two Sisters," by Alla Foster, [1857?], "Jack Frost," by Alla Foster, Dec. 24, 1861, AAS; SSF to Alla Foster, Oct. 5, 1857, WHM; AK to Alla Foster, Aug. 9, [1857], AAS; Francis Jackson to AK, Jan. 14, 1858, AAS; AK to MWC, Feb. 11, [1858], BPL; SSF to AK, Feb. 14, [1858], AAS; AK to SSF, March 12, [1858], AAS; WLG to SBA, April 14, 1858, in Merrill and Ruchames, v. 4.

5. AK to Phillipses, Aug. 20, [1858], Houghton; WLG to Fosters, Sept. 7, 1858, AAS; WP to SSF, Oct. 5, [1858], AAS; AK to Ann Phillips, nd., SSF to Ann Phillips, nd., Houghton.

6. Pease and Pease; AK to WP, June 23, [1859], Houghton; LIB, Feb. 11, 1859.

7. NASS, Feb. 5, 1859; LIB, Feb. 4, 1859; WLG to Pillsbury, June 3, 1859, BPL; AK to SSF, Dec. 12, [1857], AAS.

8. LIB, April 8, April 22, May 6, 1859; Charles Hovey to SSF, Oct. 15, 1858, Feb. 9, 1859, WHM; Charles Hovey to AK, Sept. 17, 1858, WHM; AK to WP, May 17, [1859], Houghton; "Extracts from Will of the Late Charles Hovey, Esq.," BPL.

9. LIB, June 3, 1859; S. May, Jr., to WP, June 10, 1859, Houghton; WP to AK, June 19, June 30, [1859] AAS; AK to WP, June 23, [1859], Houghton; WLG to AK, July 22, July 25, Sept. 8, 1859, AAS; AK to WLG, July 24, 1859, [July 1859], AAS; AK to Board of Managers, Jan. 15, 1860, Houghton; AK to WLG, Jr., Aug. 1861, AAS.

10. WP to AK, June 30, [1859], AAS; LIB, May 18, 1860; Executive Committee Minutes,

Feb. 1859, BPL; NASS, June 25, July 9, 1859; AK to WP, June 23, [1859], AAS; NASS, July 30, 1859; Executive Committee Minutes, June 1, July 19, July 26, Sept. 9, 1859, BPL.
  11. AK to WP, Aug. 1, Sept. 18 [1859], Houghton; S. May, Jr., to WP, June 10, 1859, Houghton; Hovey Fund receipts from S. May, Jr., SBA, Lydia Mott, 1861, Houghton.
  12. John L. Thomas; Villard; LIB, June 8, 1860; LIB, Nov. 4, Dec. 2, 1859; BUGLE, Oct. 6, 1860; *Practical Christian*, Nov. 26, 1859.
  13. Sandburg; LIB, March 30, May 25, June 8, June 15, 1860; NASS, June 23, 1860; LIB, July 13, 1860, Sept. 28, Oct. 5, 1860; Edelstein; SSF to ECS, Aug. 21, 1860, Stanton Papers, LOC.
  14. BUGLE, Oct. 6, 1860; Baker; BUGLE, Oct. 27, 1860; Stewart, *Wendell Phillips*; AK to WP, Dec. 9, 1860, Houghton; *Cleveland Weekly Review*, quoted in NASS, April 6, 1861; BUGLE, March 30, May 4, 1861; NASS, April 6, 1861.

CHAPTER 17: NOTHING IS DONE WHILE ANYTHING REMAINS TO BE DONE

  1. McPherson; NASS, April 27, 1861; LIB, July 12, 1861.
  2. Sterling, *Forever Free*; *Springfield Register*, quoted in LIB, Feb. 28, 1862; McPherson; LIB, Jan. 10, 1862, Dec. 13, 1861, ff.; SSF to WP, Nov. 8, 1861, Houghton; Stewart, *Wendell Phillips*; Bartlett, *New Light*; LIB, June 9, 1865; Edelstein; NASS, July 5, 1862.
  3. LIB, June 6, 1862.
  4. SSF to WP, Nov. 8, 1861, Houghton; SSF to George Thompson, March 16, 1862, AAS; Dunglison; Sterling, *Forever Free*; S. Holley to AK, Sept. 30, 1862, WHM; LIB, Dec. 26, 1862, Feb. 6, 1863.
  5. LIB, Jan. 15, 1864; NASS, May 11, 1863; AK to SBA, April 20, 1863, in Stanton, Anthony, et al., v. 1, Appendix; NASS, May 30, June 6, 1863; Harper, v. 1; SBA to ECS, Oct. 10, 1863, Stanton Papers, LOC; Flexner; NASS, May 13, 1865; McPherson.
  6. LIB, Dec. 11, 1863, June 5, 1863; NASS, July 4, Dec. 12, Dec. 19, 1863; Lutz; Pease and Pease; Stewart, *Wendell Phillips*; LIB, Jan. 15, Jan. 29, 1863; McPherson.
  7. McPherson; Stewart, *Wendell Phillips*; LIB, Feb. 5, 1864; *Hartford Times*, quoted in NASS, Feb. 20, 1864; SSF and AK to WP, Feb. 1, 1864, Houghton; LIB, June 3, June 17, 1864; NASS, June 11, June 18, June 25, July 23, Aug. 6, Aug. 20, 1864; LIB, June 24, 1864; WLG to Oliver Johnson, June 17, June 20, 1864, in Merrill and Ruchames, v. 5; LIB, June 3, Dec. 30, 1864, Jan. 27, 1865.
  8. LIB, Jan. 27, Feb. 3, Feb. 10, 1865; McPherson; LIB, May 19, May 26, June 2, 1865; NASS, May 13, May 27, 1865; Oliver Johnson to MWC, May 4, 1865, BPL; LIB, Dec. 29, 1865.
  9. AK to WP, July 28, [1866], Houghton; NASS, March 16, 1863, ff., Jan. 27, 1866, April 6, 1867, ff.; letter to author from Richard J. Wolfe, curator of rare books and manuscripts, Boston Medical Library, Oct. 18, 1988; Kelly and Burrage; T. G. Thomas; AK to WP, July 28, [1866], Houghton; NASS, June 8, June 15, June 29, 1867.

10. Harper, v. 1; Stanton; NASS, June 15, 1867; LS to AK, Jan. 24, 1867, Blackwell Family Papers, LOC; AK to LS, Feb. 10, 1867, NAWSA, LOC; Flexner; NASS, Dec. 10, 1865; DuBois, *Elizabeth Cady Stanton, Susan B. Anthony*; Stanton, Anthony, et al., v. 2.

11. NASS, Aug. 8, Aug. 15, Aug. 29, 1868; T. G. Thomas; Ann Phillips to AK, Aug. 19, 1868, AAS; S. May, Jr., to Richard Webb, Aug. 15, Aug. 25, Oct. 28, 1868, BPL.

12. Vassar College Alumnae Records; Horowitz; *Woman's Journal*, Jan. 13, 1872; AK to Alla Foster, Sept. 22, 1868, AAS; Family Records, AAS; NASS, Nov. 28, 1868.

13. AK to Olympia Brown, Schlesinger; DuBois, *Feminism and Suffrage*; NASS, Nov. 28, Dec. 5, 1868; Stanton, Anthony, et al., v. 2; AK to Gerrit Smith, Jan. 13, 1869, Syracuse; Executive Committee Minutes, Dec. 26, 1868, Jan. 27, Jan. 29, 1869, BPL; NASS, Feb. 6, Feb. 20, Feb. 27, 1869.

14. NASS, Feb. 6, Feb. 20, 1869; Alla Foster to AK, May 3, 1869, AAS; NASS, May 22, 1869; Stanton, Anthony, et al., v. 2; SSF to G. Thompson, Jan. 15, 1870, AAS; Executive Committee Minutes, Feb. 20, 1870, BPL; Alla Foster to AK, March 5, 1870, WHM; NASS, April 16, 1870; AK to Gerrit Smith, April 25, 1869, Syracuse.

CHAPTER 18: A LONELY ROCKET IN A DARK SKY

1. AK to Alla Foster, Sept. 22, 1868, Dec. 9, 1870, March 5, 1870, AAS; Alla Foster to AK, March 5, 1870, WHM, Feb. 26, 1871, May 3, 1869, Feb. 20, 1871, AAS; Vassar College Alumnae Records; Cornell University Alumni Records; SSF to Dr. Wilson, Dec. 20, 1872, WHM.

2. *Worcester Gazette*, quoted in *Woman's Journal*, April 29, 1876; *Woman's Journal*, May 6, 1876; SSF to Phillipses, Oct. 3, 1864, Houghton; Sallie Holley to AK, Oct. 3, 1857, AAS.

3. AK to Ann Phillips, Jan. 19, 1871, Houghton; AK to Sargents, Jan. 19, 1871, Houghton; National Register of Historic Places Inventory, March 5, 1975, AAS; *Woman's Journal*, Feb. 28, 1874; AK to "My dear Friend," Oct. 22, 1870, Clements; O'Flynn; Chadwick, ed.; Caroline Putnam to S. May, Jan. 22, 1887, MHS; AK to Welds, Jan. 4, 1874, Clements; AK to Hudsons, Nov. 15, 1880, U. Mass; Wyman and Wyman, v. 1; WP to AK, Aug. 17, [1870s], WP to Fosters, July 12, [1870s], WP to AK, Dec. 21, 1874, ff., AAS; Ann Phillips to AK, March 14, [1870s], Ann Phillips to Alla Foster, Aug. 25, [1870s–1880s], AAS.

4. NASS, Aug. 21, 1869; *Woman's Journal*, March 31, 1877; Sargent; Howe; NASS, June 26, Oct. 23, Dec. 18, 1869, Feb. 5, Feb. 19, 1870.

5. AK to [William Lloyd Garrison, Jr.], May 3, 1885, Smith; Wyman; WLG to Helen Garrison, July 23, 1865, BPL; AK to WLG, Nov. 8, 1877, BPL; WLG to AK, Nov. 12, 1877, AAS.

6. AK to "My dear friend," Oct. 22, 1870, Clements; *National Standard*, Feb. 18, 1871; S. May to Richard Webb, March 26, 1871, BPL; *Woman's Journal*, Jan. 22, 1887.

7. Flexner; *Woman's Journal*, Feb. 4, 1871, ff., Dec. 9, 1871; S. May to Richard Webb,

March 26, 1871, BPL; *Woman's Journal*, Feb. 4, 1871, Feb. 1, 1873, June 3, 1876; NASS, Dec. 25, 1869, Jan. 1, 1870; Matthew 23:27, 33.

8. *Woman's Journal*, Sept. 21, 1872, May 31, 1873; James et al. eds.; *Woman's Journal*, June 1, 1872, May 31, 1873.

9. *Woman's Journal*, Feb. 3, 1872; Blackwell; *Woman's Journal*, June 21, 1873; Feb. 28, 1874, Feb. 14, 1874; T. W. Higginson to AK, Feb. 15, 1874, WHM; WLG to AK, Feb. 16, 1874, AAS; *Woman's Journal*, Jan. 3, Jan. 17, 1874, ff.; Speare; *Woman's Journal*, Feb. 14, 1874.

10. WLG to AK, Feb. 16, 1874, AAS; *Woman's Journal*, Feb. 28, March 7, 1874; *Massachusetts Weekly Spy*, Feb. 27, 1874; WP to AK, [Feb. 1874], WHM; J. T. Sargent to AK, Feb. 25, 1874, AAS; *Woman's Journal*, March 14, May 30, July 4, 1874, July 3, 1875; *Worcester Daily Spy*, Sept. 12, 1881; *Woman's Journal*, July 11, 1874, March 31, 1877, Nov. 18, 1876; Blackwell.

11. Pease; WLG to AK, Sept. 13, 1876, AAS; WLG to AK, Nov. 16, 1878, AAS; *Woman's Journal*, Feb. 14, 1880, Sept. 25, 1880, Oct. 30, Nov. 6, 1880; Stanton, Anthony, et al., v. 3; *Woman's Journal*, Oct. 30, 1880.

12. AK to Francis Garrison, March 15, 1875, BPL; AK to Hudsons, Nov. 15, 1880, AAS; *Woman's Journal*, Feb. 10, 1877, Jan. 1, 1878, June 3, June 17, 1882, Sept. 20, 1884; Wyman and Wyman, v. 2; *Woman's Journal*, 1876–1880, for deaths; WP to Fosters, April 24, 1880, WHM; William H. Channing to Fosters, July 4, 1877, WHM; Pillsbury to SSF, May 10, 1876, Feb. 2, 1880, May 22, 1881, June 3, 1881, AAS; AK to Francis Garrison, March 15, 1875, BPL; AK to Wendell Garrison, July 28, 1879, BPL; W. P. and F. J. Garrison.

13. Wyman; WP to AK, [July 26, 1880], AAS; *Worcester Daily Spy*, Sept. 9, 1881; *Woman's Journal*, Sept. 10, Oct. 1, Oct. 8, 1881, Sept. 17, 1881.

14. Frederick Douglass to AK, Oct. 13, 1881, AAS; AK to Frederick Douglass, Nov. 9, 1881, Douglass Papers, LOC; *Woman's Journal*, Jan. 22, 1887; Flint; letter from Richard J. Wolfe to author, May 23, 1989; Family Records, AAS; AK to Francis Garrison, Jan. 12, 1883, Rochester; AK to [Francis Garrison], Jan. 17, 1883, Schomburg; Caroline Putnam to S. May, Jan. 22, 1887, MHS; AK to Alla Foster, Aug. 14, Oct. 2, 1883, AAS.

15. Account book, 1881–84, WHM; AK to Alla Foster, June 20, 1884, WHM, June 21, 1886, AAS; WP to AK, Aug. 10, 1883, AAS; Stewart, *Wendell Phillips*; AK to Alla Foster, Feb. 8, 1884, AAS; AK to Alla Foster, June 7, 1884, WHM, Aug. 14, 1883, AAS, Oct. 7, Nov. 21, 1884, AAS, June 18, 1885, WHM, June 13, June 20, 1884, WHM.

16. *Woman's Journal*, Sept. 20, 1884, April 24, 1886; Alla Foster to AK, Sept. 23, Nov. 11, 1883, Oct. 14, 1883, AAS; James et al., eds.; Alla Foster to AK, Feb. 26, 1884, AAS; AK to Alla Foster, Feb. 8, 1884, June 21, 1886, June 20, 1884, Nov. 2, 1885, June 21, 1886, AAS; AK to Alla Foster, June 7, 1884, WHM; AK to Alla Foster, Feb. 8, 1884, Nov. 2, 1885, AAS; AK to Alla Foster, June 13, 1884, June 18, 1885, WHM.

17. AK to [Alla Foster, Jan. 26, 1885], WHM; AK to *Woman's Journal*, Jan. 30, 1886; AK to Alla Foster, Jan. 29, 1886, AAS; AK to Francis Garrison, Jan. 7, 1886, Schlesinger; Chadwick, "Samuel May"; *Woman's Journal*, Nov. 14, 1885, May 1, 1886; AK to Alla Foster, June 30, July 3, 1885, WHM; John Greenleaf Whittier to Benjamin Jones, July 18, 1840 (in

AK's handwriting), AAS; AK to Lucy Stone, Oct. 16, 1886, NAWSA, LOC; Lucy Stone to AK, Oct. 12, 1886, AAS; Wyman and Wyman, v. 2; Wendell Garrison to Alla Foster, Jan. 15, 1887, AAS; photograph of reunion, Smith; AK to LS, July 16, 1886, NAWSA, LOC; *Woman's Journal*, July 10, 1886.

18. S. May to Lillie Chace, Jan. 18, 1887, in Wyman and Wyman, v. 2; *National Cyclopaedia of American Biography*, v. 2; Oliver Johnson; Alla Foster to LS, Jan. 14, [1887], NAWSA, LOC; LS to Elizabeth B. Chace, in Wyman and Wyman, v. 2; *Woman's Journal*, Jan. 22, 1887.

SELECTED BIBLIOGRAPHY

BOOKS, ARTICLES, DISSERTATIONS

Altschuler, Glenn C., and Jan M. Saltzgaber. *Revivalism, Social Conscience, and Community in the Burned-Over District: The Trial of Rhoda Bement.* Ithaca, 1983.

Austin, George L. *The Life and Times of Wendell Phillips.* Boston, 1884.

Bacon, Margaret. *I Speak for My Slave Sister.* New York, 1974.

——. *Valiant Friend: The Life of Lucretia Mott.* New York, 1980.

Baker, Jean H. *Mary Todd Lincoln.* New York, 1987.

Baldwin, Thomas W., ed. *Vital Records of Uxbridge, Massachusetts to the Year 1850.* Boston, 1916.

Ballou, Adin. *Autobiography of Adin Ballou 1803–1890.* Completed and edited by his son-in-law William S. Heywood, Lowell, 1896.

——. *History of Milford, Worcester County, Mass.* Milford, 1882. 2 vols.

Barker-Benfield, G. J. *The Horrors of the Half-Known Life: Male Attitudes toward Women and Sexuality in Nineteenth-Century America.* New York, 1976.

Barnes, Gilbert H., and Dwight L. Dumond, eds. *Letters of Theodore Dwight Weld, Angelina Grimké Weld and Sarah Grimké. 1822–1844.* New York, 1934. 2 vols.

Bartlett, Irving R., ed. *New Light on Wendell Phillips: The Community of Reform* in *Perspectives in American History,* v. xii. Cambridge, Mass., 1979.

——. *Wendell Phillips: Brahmin Radical.* Boston, 1961.

Beard, Charles and Mary. *The Rise of American Civilization.* New York, 1936.

Bernard, Jacqueline. *Journey toward Freedom: The Story of Sojourner Truth.* New York, 1967.

Bernard, Joel. *Authority, Autonomy, and Radical Commitment: Stephen and Abby Kelley Foster.* Worcester, Mass., 1980.

Bidwell, Percy. *Rural Economy in New England at the Beginning of the Nineteenth Century.* 1916. Reprinted Clifton, N.J., 1972.

Birney, Catherine H. *Sarah and Angelina Grimké: The First American Women Advocates of Abolition and Woman's Rights.* Boston, 1885.

Blackwell, Alice Stone. *Lucy Stone: Pioneer of Woman's Rights.* Boston, 1930.

Bridgwater, William, and Seymour Kurtz. *The Columbia Encyclopedia.* New York, 1963.

Brinton, Howard. *Friends for 300 Years.* New York, 1952.

Brock, Peter. *Pacifism in the United States from the Colonial Era to the First World War.* Princeton, 1968.

Buckmaster, Henrietta. *Let My People Go.* Boston, 1941.

Burkett, Nancy. *Abby Kelley Foster and Stephen S. Foster.* Worcester, Mass., 1976.

Catalogue of the Officers and Students at the Friends Boarding School, Providence, R.I. Providence, 1833.

Chadwick, John White. *A Life for Liberty: Anti-Slavery and Other Letters of Sallie Holley,* ed., New York, 1899.

————. "Samuel May of Leicester." *New England Magazine* (April 1899).

Chambers-Schiller, Lee. "The Cab: A Trans-Atlantic Community, Aspects of Nineteenth Century Reform." Ph.D. dissertation, University Microfilms. Ann Arbor, 1977.

————. *Liberty, a Better Husband: Single Women in America: The Generations of 1780–1840.* New Haven, 1984.

Chapman, Maria W. "Right and Wrong in the Boston Female Anti-Slavery Society." *Liberator* extra. Microfilm, 1840.

————. "Right and Wrong in Massachusetts." Boston, 1839. Reprinted New York, 1969.

————. *Harriet Martineau's Autobiography and Memorials of Harriet Martineau.* Boston, 1877. 2 vols.

Cornell, Thomas C. *Adam and Anne Mott: Their Ancestors and Descendants.* Poughkeepsie, 1890.

Cromwell, Otelia. *Lucretia Mott.* Cambridge, Mass., 1958.

Cross, Whitney R. *The Burned-Over District: The Social and Intellectual History of Enthusiastic Religion in Western New York, 1800–1850.* Ithaca, 1950.

Curti, Merle. "Non-Resistance in New England." *New England Quarterly* (1929).

Davies, John D. *Phrenology Fad and Science: A 19th-Century American Crusade.* New Haven, 1955.

Dawley, Alan. *Class and Community: The Industrial Revolution in Lynn.* Cambridge, Mass., 1976.

Degler, Carl N. *At Odds: Women and the Family in America from the Revolution to the Present.* New York, 1980.

Dickens, Charles. *American Notes.* Boston, 1877.

Donald, David. *Charles Sumner and the Coming of the Civil War.* New York, 1960.

Douglass, Frederick. *Life and Times of Frederick Douglass.* Reprinted New York, 1962.

Drake, Thomas E. *Quakers and Slavery in America.* New Haven, 1950.

DuBois, Ellen C. *Feminism and Suffrage: The Emergence of an Independent Woman's Movement in America, 1848–1869.* Ithaca, 1978.

————. *Elizabeth Cady Stanton, Susan B. Anthony, Correspondence, Writings, Speeches.* New York, 1981.

Dunglison, Robley, M.D. *The Practice of Medicine: A Treatise on Special Pathology and Therapeutics.* Philadelphia, 1844.

Earle, Alice Morse. *Child Life in Colonial Times.* New York, 1915.

Eckhardt, Celia Morris. *Fanny Wright, Rebel in America.* Cambridge, Mass., 1984.

Edelstein, Tilden G. *Strange Enthusiasm: A Life of Thomas Wentworth Higginson*. New Haven, 1968.

Emerson, Sarah Hopper, ed. *Life of Abby Hopper Gibbons*. New York, 1897. 2 vols.

Faler, Paul G. *Mechanics and Manufacturers in the Early Industrial Revolution, Lynn, Mass., 1780–1860*. Albany, 1981.

Filler, Louis. "Parker Pillsbury: An Anti-Slavery Apostle." *New England Quarterly* (1946).

Fletcher, Juanita D. "Against the Consensus: Oberlin College and the Education of American Negroes, 1835–1865." Ph.D. dissertation, University Microfilms, Ann Arbor, 1978.

Flexner, Eleanor. *Century of Struggle: The Woman's Rights Movement in the United States*. Cambridge, Mass., 1959.

————. *Mary Wollstonecraft*. New York, 1972.

Flint, Austin, M.D. *A Treatise on the Principles and Practice of Medicine*. Philadelphia, 1881.

Foner, Eric. *Free Soil, Free Labor, Free Men*. New York, 1970.

————. *Politics and Ideology in the Age of the Civil War*. New York, 1980.

Foner, Philip, ed. *Life and Writings of Frederick Douglass*. New York, 1950. 4 vols.

Foster, Alla W. "Reminiscences of Mrs. Abby Kelley Foster." *Woman's Journal* (February 7, 1891).

Foster, Abby Kelley. Speech at Woman's Rights Convention, Worcester, October 16, 1851.

————. "What Hinders Us?" *Liberty Bell* (1858).

————. "What Is Real Anti-Slavery Work?" *Liberty Bell* (1845).

Foster, Stephen S. *The Brotherhood of Thieves or a True Picture of the American Church and Clergy*. New London, 1843.

————. *Revolution the Only Remedy for Slavery*. New York, 1855.

Fowler, Orson S. *Matrimony or Phrenology and Physiology Applied to the Selection of Congenial Companions for Life*. New York, 1847.

Friedman, Lawrence J. *Gregarious Saints*. New York, 1982.

Fuller, Frank E., ed. *Shadow of the Elms: Reminiscences of Moses Brown School 1784–1984*. Providence, 1983.

Gamble, Douglas A. "The Western Anti-Slavery Society: Garrisonian Abolitionists in Ohio." Masters thesis, Ohio State University, 1970, np.

Garrison, W. P., and F. J. Garrison. *William Lloyd Garrison: The Story of His Life Told by His Children*. New York, 1885. 4 vols.

Gettleman, Marvin E. *The Dorr Rebellion: A Study in American Radicalism, 1833–49*. New York, 1973.

Graham, Sylvester. *Aesculapian Tablets*. 1834.

Green, Martin. *Tolstoi and Gandhi, Men of Peace*. New York, 1983.

Griffith, Elisabeth. *In Her Own Right: The Life of Elizabeth Cady Stanton*. New York, 1984.

Griscom, John H., M.D. *Memoir of John Griscom, LLD*. New York, 1859.

Hacker, Sallie H. "The Society of Friends at Lynn, Mass." *Historical Collections of the Essex Institute* (October 1905).

Hallowell, Anna Davis, ed. *James and Lucretia Mott: Life and Letters*. Boston, 1884.

Harlow, Ralph V. *Gerrit Smith, Philanthropist and Reformer*. New York, 1939.

Harper, Ida Husted. *The Life and Work of Susan B. Anthony.* Indianapolis, 1899. 2 vols.

Hawkes, Nathan Mortimer. *Hearths and Homes of Old Lynn.* Lynn, Mass., 1907.

Heilbrun, Carolyn G. *Writing a Woman's Life.* New York, 1988.

Hersey, Charles. *History of Worcester, Massachusetts from 1836 to 1861.* Worcester, 1862.

Hersh, Blanche. *The Slavery of Sex.* Urbana, Ill., 1978.

Hewitt, Nancy Ann. "Women's Activities and Social Change: The Case of Rochester, New York, 1822–1872." Ph.D. dissertation, University of Pennsylvania, 1981.

Higginson, Thomas Wentworth. *John Greenleaf Whittier.* New York, 1902.

———. *Cheerful Yesterdays.* 1899. Reprinted Salem, N.H., 1968.

———. "Anti-Slavery Days." *Outlook* (1898).

History of Pennsylvania Hall Which Was Burned by a Mob on the 17th of May. Philadelphia, 1838.

Holland, Patricia G., and Milton Meltzer, eds. *The Collected Correspondence of Lydia Maria Child, 1817–80.* Microfiche. Millwood, N.Y., 1980.

Horney, Karen. "Dread of Women," *Feminine Psychology.* New York, 1967.

Horowitz, Helen Lefkowitz. *Alma Mater.* New York, 1984.

Hough, Henry B. *Thoreau of Walden.* New York, 1956.

Howe, Julia Ward. *Reminiscences.* Boston, 1900.

Howland, Henry J. *Worcester in 1850.* Worcester, Mass., 1850.

Hunt, Harriot. *Glances and Glimpses.* Boston, 1856.

James, Edward T., and Janet Wilson James, eds. *Notable American Women.* Cambridge, Mass., 1971. 3 vols.

James, William. *Varieties of Religious Experience.* Reprinted New York, 1982.

Johnson, Oliver. *William Lloyd Garrison and His Times.* Boston, 1879.

Jones, Augustine. "An Historical Sketch of Friends School." *Phoenix Echo,* v. 12 (June 19, 1900). Providence, 1900.

Jones, Rufus. *A Small Town Boy.* New York, 1941.

Kelly, Howard A., and Walter L. Burrage. *American Medical Biographies.* Baltimore, 1920.

Kelsey, Rayner Wickersham. *Centennial History of Moses Brown School, 1819–1919.* Introduction by Rufus M. Jones. Providence, 1919.

Koppelman, Susan, ed. *Old Maids.* Boston, 1984.

Kraditor, Aileen S. *Means and Ends in American Abolitionism.* New York, 1967.

Lemons, J. Stanley, and Michael McKenna. "Re-enfranchisement of Rhode Island Negroes, *Rhode Island History* (February, 1971).

Lerner, Gerda. *The Grimké Sisters from South Carolina.* Boston, 1967.

Lewis, Eleanor, ed. "Letters of Wendell Phillips to Lydia Maria Child." *New England Quarterly* (June 1982).

Lincoln, William. *History of Worcester, Massachusetts from Its Earliest Settlement to September, 1836.* Worcester, 1862.

Litwack, Leon. *North of Slavery.* Chicago, 1961.

Longfellow, Henry Wadsworth. *The Poetical Works of Henry Wadsworth Longfellow.* Boston, 1882.

Lowell, James Russell. *The Biglow Papers.* Boston, 1848.

Lumpkin, Katherine Du Pre. *The Emancipation of Angelina Grimké*. Chapel Hill, 1974.

Lutz, Alma. *Crusade for Freedom: Women of the Antislavery Movement*. Boston, 1968.

Lynd, Staughton, ed. *Nonviolence in America: A Documentary History*. New York, 1966.

McGowan, James A. *Station Master on the Underground Railroad: The Life and Letters of Thomas Garrett*. Moylan, Pa., 1977.

McPherson, James M. *The Struggle for Equality: Abolitionists and the Negro in the Civil War and Reconstruction*. Princeton, 1964.

Madison, James. *Papers*. Charlottesville, Va., 1977–89. 16 vols.

Marshall, Thurgood. "Remarks at the Annual Seminar of the San Francisco Patent and Trademark Law Association." May 6, 1987.

Martineau, Harriet. *The Martyr Age of the United States*. Reprinted New York, 1969.

Massachusetts Anti-Slavery Society Annual Reports. Reprinted Westport, Conn., 1970.

May, Samuel J. *Some Recollections of Our Anti-Slavery Conflict*. Boston, 1869.

Melder, Keith E. *Beginnings of Sisterhood: The American Woman's Rights Movement, 1800–1850*. New York, 1977.

Meltzer, Milton, and Patricia G. Holland, eds. *Lydia Maria Child: Selected Letters, 1817–1880*. Amherst, Mass., 1982.

Merrill, Walter M. *Against Wind and Tide, a Biography of William Lloyd Garrison*. Cambridge, Mass., 1963.

———, ed. *Behold Me Once More: The Confessions of James Holley Garrison Brother of William Lloyd Garrison*. Boston, 1954.

———, and Louis Ruchames, eds. *The Letters of William Lloyd Garrison*. Cambridge, Mass., 1971–79. 5 vols.

Millbury. *Centennial History of the Town of Millbury, Massachusetts*. Published under the direction of a committee appointed by the town. Millbury, 1915.

Mordell, Albert. *Quaker Militant, John Greenleaf Whittier*. New York, 1933.

Morris, Richard B., ed. *Encyclopedia of American History*. New York, 1953.

Munsterberg, Margaret. "The Weston Sisters and the Boston Controversy." *Boston Public Library Quarterly* (April 1938).

Myerson, Joel, Daniel Sheedy; and Madeleine B. Stern, eds. *The Selected Letters of Louisa May Alcott*. Boston, 1987.

Nathan, Amy. "Paulina Wright Davis." Senior honors thesis. Brown University, 1977, np.

The National Cyclopaedia of American Biography, v. II. New York, 1899.

Nevins, Allan. *Ordeal of the Union*. New York, 1947.

Nissenbaum, Stephen. *Sex, Diet and Debility in Jacksonian America*. Westport, Conn., 1980.

Norton, Mary Beth, and Carol Berkin, eds., *Women of America*. Boston, 1976.

O'Flynn, Thomas F. *The Story of Worcester*. Boston, 1910.

O'Connor, Lillian. *Pioneer Women Orators*. New York, 1954.

Parmenter, C. O. *History of Pelham, Mass. from 1738 to 1898*. Amherst, 1898.

Pease, Jane H. "The Freshness of Fanaticism: Abby Kelley Foster." Ph.D. dissertation, University of Rochester, 1969; University Microfilms, Ann Arbor, 1970.

———, and William H. Pease. *Bound with Them in Chains: A Biographical History of the Antislavery Movement*. Westport, Conn., 1972.

Percival, Benjamin. "Abolitionism in Lynn and Essex County." *Register of the Lynn Historical Society*, no. XII. Lynn, Mass., 1908.

Perry, Lewis. *Radical Abolitionism Anarchy and the Government of God in Antislavery Thought.* Ithaca, 1973.

Pickard, John B. "John Greenleaf Whittier and the Abolitionist Schism of 1840." *New England Quarterly* (June 1964).

Pickard, Samuel T. *Life and Letters of John Greenleaf Whittier.* Boston, 1894. 2 vols.

Pillsbury, Parker. *Acts of the Anti-Slavery Apostles.* Concord, N.H., 1883.

————. "Stephen Symonds Foster." *Granite Monthly* (August 1882).

Powell, Aaron M. *Personal Reminiscences of the Anti-Slavery and Other Reforms and Reformers.* New York, 1899.

Proceedings of the Anti-Slavery Convention of American Women. New York, 1837; Philadelphia, 1838 and 1839.

Pugh. *Memorial of Sarah Pugh: A Tribute of Respect from Her Cousins.* Philadelphia, 1888.

Quarles, Benjamin. *Black Abolitionists.* New York, 1969.

————. *Frederick Douglass.* Washington, D.C., 1948.

Rossi, Alice, ed. *The Feminist Papers.* New York, 1973.

Ruchames, Louis. "Race, Marriage, Abolition in Massachusetts." *Journal of Negro History* (July 1955).

Sanborn, F. B. *Memoirs of Pliny Earle.* Boston, 1898.

Sandburg, Carl. *Abraham Lincoln: The Prairie Years.* New York, 1926.

Sargent, Mary E. *Sketches and Reminiscences of the Radical Club.* Boston, 1880.

Schlesinger, Arthur, Jr. *The Age of Jackson.* New York, 1945.

Schwartz, Hillel. *Never Satisfied: A Cultural History of Diets, Fantasies, and Fats.* New York, 1986.

Sherwin, Oscar. *Prophet of Liberty: The Life and Times of Wendell Phillips.* New York, 1958.

Siebert, Wilbur H. "The Underground Railroad in Massachusetts." American Antiquarian Society *Proceedings* (April 1935).

Sklar, Kathryn Kish. *Catharine Beecher.* New York, 1973.

Smith, Daniel Scott, and Michael S. Hindus. "Premarital Pregnancy in America 1640–1971: An Overview and Interpretation." *Journal of Interdisciplinary History* (Spring 1975).

Society of Friends. *Proceedings of the Society of Friends in the Case of William Bassett.* Worcester, Mass., 1840.

Southwick, Sarah H. *Reminiscences of Early Anti-Slavery Days.* Macon, Ga. Reprinted, 1971.

Speare, Elizabeth. "Abby, Julia and the Cows." *American Heritage* (1957).

Stanton, Elizabeth C.; Susan B. Anthony; and Matilda J. Gage. *The History of Women Suffrage*, v. 1–3. New York, 1881–86.

————. *Eighty Years and More: Reminiscences, 1815–1897.* New York. Reprinted 1971.

Stearns, Ezra S. *Genealogy and Family History of the State of New Hampshire.* New York, 1908. 4 vols.

Sterling, Dorothy. *Forever Free.* New York, 1963.

————. *Lucretia Mott, Gentle Warrior.* New York, 1964.

————, ed. *Speak Out in Thunder Tones*. New York, 1973.

————, ed. *Turning the World Upside Down*. New York, 1987.

————, ed. *We Are Your Sisters*. New York, 1984.

Stewart, James Brewer. *Joshua R. Giddings and the Tactics of Radical Politics*. Cleveland, 1970.

————. *Wendell Phillips, Liberty's Hero*. Baton Rouge, 1986.

Strother, Horatio T. *The Underground Railroad in Connecticut*. Middletown, Conn., 1962.

Suhl, Yuri. *Ernestine L. Rose and the Battle for Human Rights*. New York, 1959.

Swerdlow, Amy. "Abolition's Conservative Sisters: The Ladies' New York City Anti-Slavery Societies 1834–40." Presented at Third Berkshire Conference on the History of Women, June 1976, np.

————. "An Examination of the New York City Anti-Slavery Societies 1834–40." M.A. thesis, Sarah Lawrence, 1974, np.

Taylor, Clare. *British and American Abolitionists: An Episode in Transatlantic Understanding*. Edinburgh, 1974.

Thomas, Benjamin P. *Theodore Weld, Crusader for Freedom*. New Brunswick, N.J., 1950.

Thomas, John L. *The Liberator: William Lloyd Garrison*. Boston, 1963.

Thomas, T. Gaillard. *A Practical Treatise on the Diseases of Women*. Philadelphia, 1868.

Thompson, Mack. *Moses Brown, Reluctant Reformer*. Chapel Hill, 1962.

Tolles, Frederick B. *Meeting House and Counting House: The Quaker Merchants of Colonial Philadelphia*. Chapel Hill, 1948.

————, ed. *Slavery and "the Woman Question": Lucretia Mott's Diary, 1840*. Haverford, Pa., 1952.

Trollope, Frances. *Domestic Manners of the Americans*. New York, 1949.

U.S. Congress. *Interference of the Executive in Affairs of Rhode Island*. Report No. 546, 28 Congress, 1st Sess. 1844.

U.S. Department of Commerce. *Historical Statistics of the U.S.* Washington, D.C., 1961.

Uxbridge. *Vital Records of Uxbridge, Massachusetts to the Year 1850*. Boston, 1916.

Villard, Oswald Garrison. *John Brown 1800–1859: A Biography Fifty Years After*. New York, 1943.

Wall, Caleb A. *Reminiscences of Worcester*. Worcester, Mass., 1877.

Welter, Barbara. "The Cult of True Womanhood." *Dimity Convictions*. Athens, Ohio, 1976.

Wheeler, Leslie, ed. *Loving Warriors: Selected Letters of Lucy Stone and Henry B. Blackwell, 1853–1893*. New York, 1981.

Williams, William W. *History of Ashtabula County, Ohio*. 1878.

Works Progress Administration (WPA), Federal Writers Project. *Connecticut: A Guide to Its Roads, Lore and People*. Boston, 1938.

————. *Michigan: A Guide to the Wolverine State*. New York, 1941.

————. *New York City Guide*. New York, 1939.

————. *New York Panorama*. New York, 1938.

————. *New York: A Guide to the Empire State*. New York, 1940.

————. *The Ohio Guide*. New York, 1940.

————. *The WPA Guide to Massachusetts*. New York, 1937.

Wrobel, Arthur. *Pseudo-Science and Society in Nineteenth-Century America*. Lexington, Ky., 1987.

Wyatt-Brown, Bertram. *Lewis Tappan and the Evangelical War against Slavery*. Cleveland, 1969.

Wyman, Lillie B. Chace. "Reminiscences of Two Abolitionists." *New England Magazine* (January 1903).

————, and Arthur Crawford Wyman. *Elizabeth Buffum Chace 1806–1899: Her Life and Its Environment*. Boston, 1914. 2 vols.

INDEX

"Abbey Kelleyites" and "Abby Kelleyism," 3, 11, 106, 230–31, 311
Abington, Mass., 308–09
abolitionists
"come-outers" among, 122, 124, 160, 180
AK feels alienated from, 305
wives of, their status, 176*n.*
See also antislavery movement, "Boston clique"; *and individuals and societies, by name*
abolitionists, black
and election of 1864, 342
on goals of abolitionist movement, 340
role in antislavery movement, 46, 100–101
women, 42, 45, 46, 47 and *n.*, 63, 65
See also individuals by name
abolitionists, female, 39–41
black, 42, 45, 46, 47 and *n*, 63, 65
criticism of and opposition to, 33, 35, 39, 64–66, 68–69, 83–84, 104–05, 107–09, 112–13. *See also* public speakers, women as; violence and abolitionists
lack self-confidence, 38–39, 51, 146–47, 165–68, 189, 276, 299, 310–11; AK, 71, 74–75, 76
national conventions of (1837, 1838), 39, 42, 43–50, 62–66, 80–81
in Ohio, 229–31
role of: in American Society, 37–38, 43, 80–81, 83–84, 275; in New England Society, 68–69
societies of, 33
Woman's Loyal National League, 336–38
Adams, John Quincy, 109, 148
Adrian, Mich., 287–88
African-Americans. *See* black Americans
Agassiz, Louis, 46*n.*

aging, AK's, 276, 305, 318 and *n.*, 382
widowhood (1881–87), 377–86
Alcott, Bronson, 264, 362
Alcott, Louisa May, 358, 362
"amalgamationism," 46, 63, 66
American and Foreign Anti-Slavery Society, 105
American Anti-Slavery Society, 32–33
annual meetings: (1837), 38, 43; (1839), 81, 82–84; (1840), 102–06; (1842), 147–48; (1844), 192; (1845), 211–12; (1846), 226; (1848), 247; (1850), 255–57; (1851), 272–73; (1852), 274, 281; (1854), 292; (1863), 338–40; (1865), 343–44
Band of Seventy lecturers, 37–38, 40
Boston clique, 175–76, 180–81, 192, 195, 311–12, 313, 333
conflicts within, 79–80, 94–106, 194–95
dissolution of, 339, 342, 343–44, 355
final meeting (April 1870), 355–56
financial situation, 105, 147–48, 313–14.
See also financial support for anti-slavery movement
AK's offices in: as general agent, 306; as general financial agent, 293
leadership in transition, 249
Massachusetts Society and, 79–80, 176, 250
"no organization" anarchy in, 194–95
philosophy and principles, 94–95
reduced activity of, 250
and Thirteenth Amendment petition drive, 337
women's role in, 37–38, 43, 80–81, 83–84, 104–05, 275
American Colonization Society, 32, 47
American Equal Rights Association, 346, 347, 348, 354

419

Michigan, 286, 287–90, 311
Michigan Anti-Slavery Society, 288
Millbury, Mass.
  Foster lectures in (1841), 136–37
  AK's parents' home in, 27, 146, 149
  AK visits, 55–56, 67, 93, 111, 119, 122,
    133–37, 144; final visit (1842), 148–49
Millbury Female Anti-Slavery Society, 77
  fair, 134, 135
Miller, Elizabeth Smith, 271 and *n.*
ministers. *See* clergy
Mitchell, Maria, 350 and *n.*
Monroe, James, 231
moral suasion, 33
mother, AK as, 243, 284–85, 357–58
  childbirth, 241–42
  others' advice on, 246
  pregnancy, 232–33, 234, 238, 241
  withdraws from antislavery work to be
    with Alla, 253–54, 273, 282, 284, 297,
    316–17, 319
  See also family *vs.* antislavery activities,
    AK's conflict
Mott, Abigail, 159 and *n.*
Mott, Lucretia, 40, 102, 112, 250, 253, 362
  death (1880), 374
  AK and, 113–14, 243, 253, 266, 307
  leadership in antislavery movement, 44, 63,
    80–81, 105
  and woman's rights movement, 185–86,
    266, 286
Mott, Lydia, 264, 325
music
  in antislavery movement, 158, 169, 218,
    230, 260
  AK and, 158, 163

name, AK's, 11, 14, 19, 221–22
names, married women's, 49, 222 and *n.*,
  301*n.*
Napoléon I, emperor of the French (quoted
  by AK), 339
National Anti-Slavery Standard (newspaper),
  110, 125, 176–77, 244–45, 275*n.*
  becomes *Standard* (1870), 356
  (D.) Child and, 126, 127, 176, 177, 180,
    181, 192
  (M.) Child and, 126–27, 168–69
  financial status, 126, 127, 215

AK and, 125–27, 146, 168, 176–77, 215,
  252
National Woman's Rights Convention,
  Worcester, Mass.
  (1st, 1850), 264–66
  (2nd, 1851), 267–68
  jubilee celebration of, 373
National Woman Suffrage Association, 364,
  365
Native Americans, 78–79, 186
Neall, Elizabeth. *See* Gay, Elizabeth Neall
Nell, Louisa, 101
Nell, William C., 274
New Brighton, Penna., 220–21
New England Anti-Slavery Society
  annual meetings, 67–69, 110, 148, 226–27,
    257, 292, 303–04, 320–21, 335, 341
  dissolution of, as issue, 345–46
  women's role in, 68–69
New England Emigrant Aid Society, 302
New England Friends Boarding School,
  Providence, R.I., 19–25
New England Non-Resistance Society, 72,
  194, 208, 234–35
New England Political Anti-Slavery Society,
  326–27
New England Woman's Rights Convention
  (Boston, 1854), 292–93
New England Woman Suffrage Association,
  351
New Hampshire
  AK's antislavery work in, 129, 132, 193
  See also Concord
New Hampshire Anti-Slavery Society, 128,
  129–30, 194, 195
New Haven, Conn., 107
New Lisbon (*later*, Lisbon), Ohio, 213–14
newspapers. *See* press
newspapers, antislavery
  and disunion, 272–73
  Douglass's, 244–45, 273, 274
  financial status, 126, 127, 215, 218, 273,
    328, 330
  growth and increase of, 83, 214
  AK supports and sells subscriptions to, 2,
    125, 127, 158, 215, 218, 237, 252, 261,
    273, 274, 290, 291, 328, 330
  See also *Anti-Slavery Bugle*; *Emancipator*;
    Frederick Douglass's Paper; *Herald of*

Washington, Conn., 117–18
Waterloo, N.Y., 164, 180
Waters, Asa, 135, 137
Welch, Benjamin, 114
Welch, Sarah, 114, 115
Weld, Angelina Grimké, 40, 41, 45, 48–49,
  361
  death, 374
  health, 84
  AK and, 56, 75–76, 84–85, 307
  lectures, 40–41, 50, 52, 57, 60
  pamphlets and letters, 55
  and woman's rights movement, 267
Weld (Angelina G.) and Theodore Weld,
  60–62, 133, 293
  AK and, 75, 84–85
Weld, Theodore, 40, 44, 55, 361, 385
  American Slavery as It Is, 75, 146n.
  and AK, 64–65, 75, 76
West, Lucy Kelley. See Barton, Lucy (i.e.
  Margaretta Lucy) Kelley West (AK's
  sister)
West, Samuel W., 149, 239
Western Anti-Slavery Society, 227, 242, 248,
  249, 261, 287, 310, 325, 328, 334. See also
  Ohio American Anti-Slavery Society
Western New York Anti-Slavery Society,
  154, 164, 173
Western Peace Society, 227
Weston, Anne Warren, 40, 66–67, 101,
  104–05
  and Dickens, 145–46
  leadership in antislavery movement, 45, 51,
  63, 110, 249, 343
Weston, Caroline, 40, 99, 101
Weston, Deborah, 40, 97
Weston, Maria. See Chapman, Maria Weston
Whig party, 180, 181, 248
Whittier, John Greenleaf, 29, 31 and n., 293,
  353, 384
  critical of women in public roles, 55, 69,
  105–06
  "On Leaving Me and Taking a Wife," 61
Whole World's Temperance Convention
  (New York, 1853), 286
Willimantic, Conn., 111, 124
Willis, Phebe, 288
Wilmington, Del., 198–99
Wilson, Henry, 292, 327, 334, 351, 352

Wollstonecraft, Mary (Godwin), 268
  Vindication of the Rights of Women, 268n.
womanhood. See True Womanhood, cult of
Woman's Christian Temperance Union
  (WCTU), 364 and n.
Woman's Journal (newspaper), 365
Woman's Loyal National League, 336–37,
  338
Woman's Rights Convention
  (1st, Seneca Falls, N.Y., 1848), 185–86,
  264, 271
  (2nd, Rochester, N.Y.), 264
  (3rd, Syracuse, N.Y., 1852), 267n.
  See also National Woman's Rights Convention (Worcester, Mass.)
woman's rights (movement)
  vs. abolition, as competing priorities, 55,
  275. See also women's suffrage: vs. black
  suffrage
  American Anti-Slavery Society and, 256
  equal pay issue, 268, 269
  Fosters' tax protest for, 367–72
  fundamentalist arguments against, 108, 109
  AK's role in, 3, 69, 108, 263–64, 266, 267–
  69, 292, 300–301, 346–48, 364–73, 384,
  387
  press and, 266–67
  Seneca Falls convention (1848), 185–86
  Worcester conventions (1850, 1851), 264–
  66, 267–68
  See also woman's suffrage
woman's suffrage, 266, 269
  vs. black suffrage, 3, 346–48,
  354
  in Britain, 266–67
  AK and, 3–4, 346–48, 351, 364–73
women as abolitionists. See abolitionists,
  female
women as public speakers. See public
  speakers, women as
women in public life
  Grimké (A.) on, 48–49, 55
  AK encourages, 3, 146–47, 160, 165–67,
  229–32, 261–62, 275–77, 299–300,
  310–11
  opposition to, 44, 53, 54–55, 70, 108
  pregnancy as taboo, 234
  See also public speakers, women as
women, single, 31 and n.

Worcester, Mass., 15
  antislavery fair, 246
  Fosters buy Cook place. *See* Fosters' farm, Worcester, Mass.
  fugitive slaves in, 281–82, 296
  growth and economic conditions, 239
  AK's childhood in, 15–20
  National Woman's Rights Conventions (1850, 1851), 264–66, 267–68
  Tatnuck section, 18, 239–40, 361

temperance movement in, 364
World's Anti-Slavery Convention (London, 1840), 112–13
World's Temperance Convention (New York, 1853), 285–86
Wright, Elizur, Jr., 38, 80, 91, 95, 96, 97
Wright, Frances ("Fanny"), 41, 114, 218
Wright, Francis, 159–61, 202
Wright, Henry C., 51, 69, 102, 110, 261
Wright, Paulina. *See* Davis, Paulina Wright